MARY CHESNUT'S DIARY

By MARY BOYKIN CHESNUT

Mary Chesnut's Diary
By Mary Boykin Chesnut

Print ISBN 13: 978-1-4209-6557-5
eBook ISBN 13: 978-1-4209-6558-2

This edition copyright © 2019. Digireads.com Publishing.

Cover Image: a detail of "Confederate flag at Fort Sumter, South Carolina, October 20, 1863", oil on canvas, by Conrad Wise Chapman (1842-1913). American Civil War, United States, 19th century / De Agostini Picture Library / Bridgeman Images.

Please visit *www.digireads.com*

CONTENTS

A DIARY FROM

DIXIE, *as written by*

MARY BOYKIN CHESNUT, *wife of* JAMES

CHESNUT, JR., *United States Senator from South
Carolina, 1859-1861, and afterward an Aide
to Jefferson Davis and a Brigadier-
General in the Confederate Army*

EDITED BY

ISABELLA D. MARTIN AND

MYRTA LOCKETT

AVARY

INTRODUCTION. THE AUTHOR AND HER BOOK

In Mrs. Chesnut's Diary are vivid pictures of the social life that went on uninterruptedly in the midst of war; of the economic conditions that resulted from blockaded ports; of the manner in which the spirits of the people rose and fell with each victory or defeat, and of the momentous events that took place in Charleston, Montgomery, and Richmond. But the Diary has an importance quite apart from the interest that lies in these pictures.

Mrs. Chesnut was close to forty years of age when the war began, and thus had lived through the most stirring scenes in the controversies that led to it. In this Diary, as perhaps nowhere else in the literature of the war, will be found the Southern spirit of that time expressed in words which are not alone charming as literature, but genuinely human in their spontaneousness, their delightfully unconscious frankness. Her words are the farthest possible removed from anything deliberate, academic, or purely intellectual They ring so true that they start echoes. The most uncompromising Northern heart can scarcely fail to be moved by their abounding sincerity, surcharged though it be with that old Southern fire which overwhelmed the army of McDowell at Bull Run.

In making more clear the unyielding tenacity of the South and the stern conditions in which the war was prosecuted, the Diary has further importance. At the beginning there was no Southern leader, in so far as we can gather from Mrs. Chesnut's reports of her talks with them, who had any hope that the South would win in the end, provided the North should be able to enlist her full resources. The result, however, was that the South struck something like terror to many hearts, and raised serious expectations that two great European powers would recognize her independence. The South fought as long as she had any soldiers left who were capable of fighting, and at last "robbed the cradle and the grave." Nothing then remained except to "wait for another generation to grow up." The North, so far as her stock of men of fighting age was concerned, had done scarcely more than make a beginning, while the South was virtually exhausted when the war was half over.

Unlike the South, the North was never reduced to extremities which led the wives of Cabinet officers and commanding generals to gather in Washington hotels and private drawing-rooms, in order to knit heavy socks for soldiers whose feet otherwise would go bare: scenes like these were common in Richmond, and Mrs. Chesnut often made one of the company. Nor were gently nurtured women of the North forced to wear coarse and ill-fitting shoes, such as negro cobblers made, the alternative being to dispense with shoes altogether. Gold might rise in the North to 2.80, but there came a time in the South, when a thousand dollars in paper money were needed to buy a kitchen utensil, which before the war could have been bought for less than one dollar in gold. Long before the conflict ended it was a common remark in the South that, "in going to market, you take your money in your basket, and bring your purchases home in your pocket."

In the North the counterpart to these facts were such items as butter at 50 cents a pound and flour at 12 a barrel. People in the North actually thrived on high prices. Villages and small towns, as well as large cities, had their "bloated bondholders" in plenty, while farmers everywhere were able to clear their lands of mortgages and put money in the bank besides. Planters in the South, meanwhile, were borrowing money to support the negroes in idleness at home, while they themselves were fighting at the front. Old Colonel Chesnut, the author's father-in-law, in April, 1862, estimated that he had already lost half a million in bank stock and railroad bonds. When the war closed, he had borrowed such large sums himself and had such large sums due to him from others, that he saw no likelihood of the obligations on either side ever being discharged.

Mrs. Chesnut wrote her Diary from day to day, as the mood or an occasion prompted her to do so. The fortunes of war changed the place of her abode almost as frequently as the seasons changed, but wherever she might be the Diary was continued. She began to write in Charleston when the Convention was passing the Ordinance of Secession. Thence she went to Montgomery, Ala., where the Confederacy was organized and Jefferson Davis was inaugurated as its President. She went to receptions where, sitting aside on sofas with Davis, Stephens, Toombs, Cobb, or Hunter, she talked of the probable outcome of the war, should war come, setting down in her Diary what she heard from others and all that she thought herself. Returning to Charleston, where her husband, in a small boat, conveyed to Major Anderson the ultimatum of the Governor of South Carolina, she saw from a housetop the first act of war committed in the bombardment of Fort Sumter. During the ensuing four years, Mrs. Chesnut's time was mainly passed between Columbia and Richmond. For shorter periods she was at the Fauquier White Sulphur Springs in Virginia, Flat Rock in North Carolina, Portland in Alabama (the home of her mother), Camden and Chester in South Carolina, and Lincolnton in North Carolina.

In all these places Mrs. Chesnut was in close touch with men and women who were in the forefront of the social, military, and political life of the South. Those who live in her pages make up indeed a catalogue of the heroes of, the Confederacy-President Jefferson Davis, Vice-President Alexander H. Stephens, General Robert E. Lee, General "Stonewall" Jackson, General Joseph E. Johnston, General Pierre G. T. Beauregard, General Wade Hampton, General Joseph B. Kershaw, General John B. Hood, General John S. Preston, General Robert

Toombs, R. M. T. Hunter, Judge Louis T. Wigfall, and so many others that one almost hears the roll-call. That this statement is not exaggerated may be judged from a glance at the index, which has been prepared with a view to the inclusion of all important names mentioned in the text.

As her Diary constantly shows, Mrs. Chesnut was a woman of society in the best sense. She had love of companionship, native wit, an acute mind, knowledge of books, and a searching insight into the motives of men and women. She was also a notable housewife, much given to hospitality; and her heart was of the warmest and tenderest, as those who knew her well bore witness.

Mary Boykin Miller, born March 31, 1823, was the daughter of Stephen Decatur Miller, a man of distinction in the public affairs of South Carolina. Mr. Miller was elected to Congress in 1817, became Governor in 1828, and was chosen United States Senator in 1830. He was a strong supporter of the Nullification movement. In 1833, owing to ill-health, he resigned his seat in the Senate and not long afterward removed to Mississippi, where he engaged in cotton planting until his death, in March, 1838.

His daughter, Mary, was married to James Chesnut, Jr., April 23, 1840, when seventeen years of age. Thenceforth her home was mainly at Mulberry, near Camden, one of several plantations owned by her father-in-law. Of the domestic life at Mulberry a pleasing picture has come down to us, as preserved in a time-worn scrap-book and written some years before the war:

"In our drive of about three miles to Mulberry, we were struck with the wealth of forest trees along our way for which the environs of Camden are noted. Here is a bridge completely canopied with overarching branches; and, for the remainder of our journey, we pass through an aromatic avenue of crab-trees with the Yellow Jessamine and the Cherokee rose, entwining every shrub, post, and pillar within reach and lending an almost tropical luxuriance and sweetness to the way.

"But here is the house—a brick building, capacious and massive, a house that is a home for a large family, one of the homesteads of the olden times, where home comforts and blessings cluster, sacred alike for its joys and its sorrows. Birthdays, wedding-days, 'Merry Christmases,' departures for school and college, and home returnings have enriched this abode with the treasures of life.

"A warm welcome greets us as we enter. The furniture within is in keeping with things without; nothing is tawdry; there is no gingerbread gilding; all is handsome and substantial. In the 'old arm-chair' sits the venerable mother. The father is on his usual ride about the plantation;

but will be back presently. A lovely old age is this mother's, calm and serene, as the soft mellow days of our own gentle autumn. She came from the North to the South many years ago, a fair young bride.

"The Old Colonel enters. He bears himself erect, walks at a brisk gait, and needs no spectacles, yet he is over eighty. He is a typical Southern planter. From the beginning he has been one of the most intelligent patrons of the Wateree Mission to the Negroes, taking a personal interest in them, attending the mission church and worshiping with his own people. May his children see to it that this holy charity is continued to their servants forever!"

James Chesnut, Jr., was the son and heir of Colonel James Chesnut, whose wife was Mary Coxe, of Philadelphia. Mary Coxe's sister married Horace Binney, the eminent Philadelphia lawyer. James Chesnut, Jr., was born in 1815 and graduated from Princeton. For fourteen years he served in the legislature of South Carolina, and in January, 1859, was appointed to fill a vacancy in the United States Senate. In November, 1860, when South Carolina was about to secede, he resigned from the Senate and thenceforth was active in the Southern cause, first as an aide to General Beauregard, then as an aide to President Davis, and finally as a brigadier-general of reserves in command of the coast of South Carolina.

General Chesnut was active in public life in South Carolina after the war, in so far as the circumstances of Reconstruction permitted, and in 1868 was a delegate from that State to the National convention which nominated Horatio Seymour for President. His death occurred at Sarsfield, February 1, 1885. One who knew him well wrote:

"While papers were teeming with tribute to this knightly gentleman, whose services to his State were part of her history in her prime—tribute that did him no more than justice, in recounting his public virtues—I thought there was another phase of his character which the world did not know and the press did not chronicle—that which showed his beautiful kindness and his courtesy to his own household, and especially to his dependents.

"Among all the preachers of the South Carolina Conference, a few remained of those who ever counted it as one of the highest honors conferred upon them by their Lord that it was permitted to them to preach the gospel to the slaves of the Southern plantations. Some of these retained kind recollections of the cordial hospitality shown the plantation missionary at Mulberry and Sandy Hill, and of the care taken at these places that the plantation chapel should be neat and comfortable, and that the slaves should have their spiritual as well as their bodily needs supplied.

"To these it was no matter of surprise to learn that at his death

General Chesnut, statesman and soldier, was surrounded by faithful friends, born in slavery on his own plantation, and that the last prayer he ever heard came from the lips of a negro man, old Scipio, his father's body-servant; and that he was borne to his grave amid the tears and lamentations of those whom no Emancipation Proclamation could sever from him, and who cried aloud: 'O my master! my master! he was so good to me! He was all to us! We have lost our best friend!'

"Mrs. Chesnut's anguish when her husband died, is not to be forgotten; the 'bitter cry' never quite spent itself, though she was brave and bright to the end. Her friends were near in that supreme moment at Sarsfield, when, on November 22, 1886, her own heart ceased to beat. Her servants had been true to her; no blandishments of freedom had drawn Ellen or Molly away from 'Miss Mary.' Mrs. Chesnut lies buried in the family cemetery at Knight's Hill, where also sleep her husband and many other members of the Chesnut family."

The Chesnuts settled in South Carolina at the close of the war with France, but lived originally on the frontier of Virginia. Their Virginia home had been invaded by French and Indians, and in an expedition to Fort Duquesne the father was killed. John Chesnut removed from Virginia to South Carolina soon afterward and served in the Revolution as a captain. His son James, the "Old Colonel," was educated at Princeton, took an active part in public affairs in South Carolina, and prospered greatly as a planter. He survived until after the War, being a nonogenarian when the conflict closed. In a charming sketch of him in one of the closing pages of this Diary, occurs the following passage: "Colonel Chesnut, now ninety-three, blind and deaf, is apparently as strong as ever, and certainly as resolute of will. Partly patriarch, partly grand seigneur, this old man is of a species that we shall see no more; the last of a race of lordly planters who ruled this Southern world, but now a splendid wreck."

Three miles from Camden still stands Mulberry. During one of the raids committed in the neighborhood by Sherman's men early in 1865, the house escaped destruction almost as if by accident. The picture of it in this book is from a recent photograph. A change has indeed come over it, since the days when the household servants and dependents numbered between sixty and seventy, and its owner was lord of a thousand slaves. After the war, Mulberry ceased to be the author's home, she and General Chesnut building for themselves another to which they gave the name of Sarsfield. Sarsfield, of which an illustration is given, still stands in the pine lands not far from Mulberry. Bloomsbury, another of old Colonel Chesnut's plantation dwellings, survived the march of Sherman, and is now the home of David R. Williams, Jr., and Ellen Manning, his wife, whose children roam its halls, as grandchildren of the author's sister Kate. Other Chesnut plantations were Cool Spring, Knight's Hill, The Hermitage, and Sandy Hill.

The Diary, as it now exists in forty-eight thin volumes, of the small quarto size, is entirely in Mrs. Chesnut's handwriting. She originally wrote it on what was known as "Confederate paper," but transcribed it afterward. When Richmond was threatened, or when Sherman was coming, she buried it or in some other way secreted it from the enemy. On occasion it shared its hiding-place with family silver, or with a drinking-cup which had been presented to General Hood by the ladies of Richmond. Mrs. Chesnut was fond of inserting on blank pages of the Diary current newspaper accounts of campaigns and battles, or lists of killed and wounded. One item of this kind, a newspaper "extra," issued in Chester, S. C., and announcing the assassination of Lincoln, is reproduced in this volume.

Mrs. Chesnut, by oral and written bequest, gave the Diary to her friend whose name leads the signatures to this Introduction. In the Diary, here and there, Mrs. Chesnut's expectation that the work would some day be printed is disclosed, but at the time of her death it did not seem wise to undertake publication for a considerable period. Yellow with age as the pages now are, the only harm that has come to them in the passing of many years, is that a few corners have been broken and frayed, as shown in one of the pages here reproduced in facsimile.

In the summer of 1904, the woman whose office it has been to assist in preparing the Diary for the press, went South to collect material for another work to follow her *A Virginia Girl in the Civil War*. Her investigations led her to Columbia, where, while the guest of Miss Martin, she learned of the Diary's existence. Soon afterward an arrangement was made with her publishers under which the Diary's owner and herself agreed to condense and revise the manuscript for publication. The Diary was found to be of too great length for reproduction in full, parts of it being of personal or local interest rather than general. The editing of the book called also for the insertion of a considerable number of foot-notes, in order that persons named, or events referred to, might be the better understood by the present generation.

Mrs. Chesnut was a conspicuous example of the well-born and high-bred woman, who, with active sympathy and unremitting courage, supported the Southern cause. Born and reared when Nullification was in the ascendant, and acquiring an education which developed and refined her natural literary gifts, she found in the throes of a great conflict at arms the impulse which wrought into vital expression in words her steadfast loyalty to the waning fortunes of a political faith, which, in South Carolina, had become a religion.

Many men have produced narratives of the war between the States, and a few women have written notable chronicles of it but none has given to the world a record more radiant than hers, or one more passionately sincere. Every line in this Diary throbs with the tumult of deep spiritual passion, and bespeaks the luminous mind, the unconquered soul, of the woman who wrote it.

ISABELLA D. MARTIN,
MYRTA LOCKETT AVARY.

CHAPTER I. CHARLESTON, S. C.

November 8, 1860—*December* 27, 1860

Charleston, S. C., *November* 8, *1860.*—Yesterday on the train, just before we reached Fernandina, a woman called out: "That settles the hash." Tanny touched me on the shoulder and said: "Lincoln's elected." "How do you know?" "The man over there has a telegram." The excitement was very great. Everybody was talking at the same time. One, a little more moved than the others, stood up and said despondently: "The die is cast; no more vain regrets; sad forebodings are useless; the stake is life or death." "Did you ever!" was the prevailing exclamation, and some one cried out: "Now that the black radical Republicans have the power I suppose they will Brown[1] us all." No doubt of it.

I have always kept a journal after a fashion of my own, with dates and a line of poetry or prose, mere quotations, which I understood and no one else, and I have kept letters and extracts from the papers. From to-day forward I will tell the story in my own way. I now wish I had a chronicle of the two delightful and eventful years that have just passed. Those delights have fled and one's breath is taken away to think what events have since crowded in. Like the woman's record in her journal, we have had "earthquakes, as usual"—daily shocks.

At Fernandina I saw young men running up a Palmetto flag, and shouting a little prematurely, "South Carolina has seceded!" I was overjoyed to find Florida so sympathetic, but Tanny told me the young men were Gadsdens, Porchers, and Gourdins,[2] names as inevitably South Carolinian as Moses and Lazarus are Jewish.

From my window I can hear a grand and mighty flow of eloquence. Bartow and a delegation from Savannah are having a supper given to them in the dining-room below. The noise of the speaking and cheering is pretty hard on a tired traveler. Suddenly I found myself listening with pleasure. Voice, tone, temper, sentiment, language, all were perfect. I sent Tanny to see who it was that spoke. He came back saying, "Mr. Alfred Huger, the old postmaster." He may not have been the wisest or wittiest man there, but he certainly made the best after supper speech.

December 10th.—We have been up to the Mulberry Plantation with Colonel Colcock and Judge Magrath, who were sent to Columbia by their fellow-citizens in the low country, to hasten the slow movement of the wisdom assembled in the State Capital. Their message

---

[1] A reference to John Brown of Harper's Ferry.
[2] This and other French names to be met with in this Diary are of Huguenot origin.

was, they said: "Go ahead, dissolve the Union, and be done with it, or it will be worse for you. The fire in the rear is hottest." And yet people talk of the politicians leading! Everywhere that I have been people have been complaining bitterly of slow and lukewarm public leaders.

Judge Magrath is a local celebrity, who has been stretched across the street in effigy, showing him tearing off his robes of office. The painting is in vivid colors, the canvas huge, and the rope hardly discernible. He is depicted with a countenance flaming with contending emotions—rage, disgust, and disdain. We agreed that the time had now come. We had talked so much heretofore. Let the fire-eaters have it out. Massachusetts and South Carolina are always coming up before the footlights.

As a woman, of course, it is easy for me to be brave under the skins of other people; so I said: "Fight it out. Bluffton[3] I has brought on a fever that only bloodletting will cure." My companions breathed fire and fury, but I dare say they were amusing themselves with my dismay, for, talk as I would, that I could not hide.

At Kingsville we encountered James Chesnut, fresh from Columbia, where he had resigned his seat in the United States Senate the day before. Said some one spitefully, "Mrs. Chesnut does not look at all resigned." For once in her life, Mrs. Chesnut held her tongue: she was dumb. In the high-flown style which of late seems to have gotten into the very air, she was offering up her life to the cause.

We have had a brief pause. The men who are all, like Pickens,[4] "insensible to fear," are very sensible in case of small-pox. There being now an epidemic of small-pox in Columbia, they have adjourned to Charleston. In Camden we were busy and frantic with excitement, drilling, marching, arming, and wearing high blue cockades. Red sashes, guns, and swords were ordinary fireside accompaniments. So wild were we, I saw at a grand parade of the home-guard a woman, the wife of a man who says he is a secessionist *per se*, driving about to see the drilling of this new company, although her father was buried the day before.

Edward J. Pringle writes me from San Francisco on November 30th: "I see that Mr. Chesnut has resigned and that South Carolina is hastening into a Convention, perhaps to secession. Mr. Chesnut is probably to be President of the Convention. I see all of the leaders in the State are in favor of secession. But I confess I hope the black Republicans will take the alarm and submit some treaty of peace that

---

[3] A reference to what was known as "the Bluffton movement" of 1844, in South Carolina. It aimed at secession, but was voted down.

[4] Francis W. Pickens, Governor of South Carolina, 1860-62. He had been elected to Congress in 1834 as a Nullifier, but had voted against the "Bluffton movement." From 1858 to 1860, he was Minister to Russia. He was a wealthy planter and had fame as an orator.

will enable us now and forever to settle the question, and save our generation from the prostration of business and the decay of prosperity that must come both to the North and South from a disruption of the Union. However, I won't speculate. Before this reaches you, South Carolina may be off on her own hook—a separate republic."

December 21st.—Mrs. Charles Lowndes was sitting with us to-day, when Mrs. Kirkland brought in a copy of the Secession Ordinance. I wonder if my face grew as white as hers. She said after a moment: "God help us. As our day, so shall our strength be." How grateful we were for this pious ejaculation of hers! They say I had better take my last look at this beautiful place, Combahee. It is on the coast, open to gunboats.

We mean business this time, because of this convocation of the notables, this convention.[5] In it are all our wisest and best. They really have tried to send the ablest men, the good men and true.) South Carolina was never more splendidly represented. Patriotism aside, it makes society delightful. One need not regret having left Washington.

December 27th.—Mrs. Gidiere came in quietly from her marketing to-day, and in her neat, incisive manner exploded this bombshell: "Major Anderson[6] has moved into Fort Sumter, while Governor Pickens slept serenely." The row is fast and furious now. State after State is taking its forts and fortresses. They say if we had been left out in the cold alone, we might have sulked a while, but back we would have had to go, and would merely have fretted and fumed and quarreled among ourselves. We needed a little wholesome neglect. Anderson has blocked that game, but now our sister States have joined us, and we are strong. I give the condensed essence of the table-talk: "Anderson has united the cotton States. Now for Virginia!" "Anderson has opened the ball." Those who want a row are in high glee. Those who dread it are glum and thoughtful enough.

A letter from Susan Rutledge: "Captain Humphrey folded the United States Army flag just before dinnertime. Ours was run up in its place. You know the Arsenal is in sight. What is the next move? I pray God to guide us. We stand in need of wise counsel; something more than courage. The talk is: 'Fort Sumter must be taken; and it is one of the strongest forts.' How in the name of sense are they to manage? I shudder to think of rash moves."

---

[5] The Convention, which on December 20, 1860, passed the famous Ordinance of Secession, and had first met in Columbia, the State capital.

[6] Robert Anderson, Major of the First Artillery, United States Army, who, on November 20, 1860, was placed in command of the troops in Charleston harbor. On the night of December 26th, fearing an attack, he had moved his command to Fort Sumter. Anderson was a graduate of West Point and a veteran of the Black Hawk, Florida, and Mexican Wars.

CHAPTER II. MONTGOMERY, ALA.

February 19, 1861—*March* 11, 1861

Montgomery, Ala., *February 19, 1861.*—The brand-new Confederacy is making or remodeling its Constitution. Everybody wants Mr. Davis to be General-in-Chief or President. Keitt and Boyce and a party preferred Howell Cobb[7] for President. And the fire-eaters *per se* wanted Barnwell Rhett.

My brother Stephen brought the officers of the "Montgomery Blues" to dinner. "Very soiled Blues," they said, apologizing for their rough condition. Poor fellows! they had been a month before Fort Pickens and not allowed to attack it. They said Colonel Chase built it, and so were sure it was impregnable. Colonel Lomax telegraphed to Governor Moore[8] if he might try to take it, "Chase or no Chase," and got for his answer, "No." "And now," say the Blues, "we have worked like niggers, and when the fun and fighting begin, they send us home and put regulars there." They have an immense amount of powder. The wheel of the car in which it was carried took fire. There was an escape for you! We are packing a hamper of eatables for them.

I am despondent once more. If I thought them in earnest because at first they put their best in front, what now? We have to meet tremendous odds by pluck, activity, zeal, dash, endurance of the toughest, military instinct. We have had to choose born leaders of men who could attract love and secure trust. Everywhere political intrigue is as rife as in Washington.

Cecil's saying of Sir Walter Raleigh that he could "toil terribly" was an electric touch. Above all, let the men who are to save South Carolina be young and vigorous. While I was reflecting on what kind of men we ought to choose, I fell on Clarendon, and it was easy to construct my man out of his portraits. What has been may be again, so the men need not be purely ideal types.

Mr. Toombs[9] told us a story of General Scott and himself. He said

---

[7] A native of Georgia, Howell Cobb had long served in Congress, and in 1849 was elected Speaker. In 1851 he was elected Governor of Georgia, and in 1857 became Secretary of the Treasury in Buchanan's Administration. In 1861 he was a delegate from Georgia to the Provisional Congress which adopted the Constitution of the Confederacy, and presided over each of its four sessions

[8] Andrew Bary Moore, elected Governor of Alabama in 1859. In 1861, before Alabama seceded, he directed the seizure of United States forts and arsenals and was active afterward in the equipment of State troops.

[9] Robert Toombs, a native of Georgia, who early acquired fame as a lawyer, served in the Creek War under General Scott, became known in 1842 as a "State Rights Whig," being elected to Congress, where he was active in the Compromise measures of 1850. He served in the United States Senate from 1853 to 1861, where he was a pronounced

he was dining in Washington with Scott, who seasoned every dish and every glass of wine with the eternal refrain, "Save the Union; the Union must be preserved." Toombs remarked that he knew why the Union was so dear to the General, and illustrated his point by a steamboat anecdote, an explosion, of course. While the passengers were struggling in the water a woman ran up and down the bank crying, "Oh, save the red-headed man!" The red-headed man was saved, and his preserver, after landing him noticed with surprise how little interest in him the woman who had made such moving appeals seemed to feel. He asked her "Why did you make that pathetic outcry?" She answered, "Oh, he owes me ten thousand dollars." "Now General," said Toombs, "the Union owes you seventeen thousand dollars a year!" I can imagine the scorn on old Scott's face.

February 25th—Find every one working very hard here. As I dozed on the sofa last night, could hear the scratch, scratch of my husband's pen as he wrote at the table until midnight.

After church to-day, Captain Ingraham called. He left me so uncomfortable. He dared to express regrets that he had to leave the United States Navy. Ha had been stationed in the Mediterranean, where he liked to be , and expected to be these two years, and to take those lovely daughters of his to Florence. Then came Abraham Lincoln, and rampant black Republicanism, and he must lay down his life for South Carolina. He, however, does not make any moan. He says we lack everything necessary in naval gear to retake Fort Sumter. Of course, he only expects the navy to take it. He is a fish out of water here. He is one of the finest sea-captains; so I suppose they will soon give him a ship and send him back to his own element.

At dinner Judge—was loudly abusive of Congress. He said: "They have trampled the Constitution underfoot. They have provided President Davis with a house." He was disgusted with the folly of parading the President at the inauguration in a coach drawn by four white horses. Then some one said Mrs. Fitzpatrick was the only lady who sat with the Congress. After the inaugural she poked Jeff Davis in the back with her parasol that he might turn and speak to her. "I am sure that was democratic enough," said some one.

Governor Moore came in with the latest news—a telegram from Governor Pickens to the President, "that a war steamer is lying off the Charleston bar laden with reenforcements for Fort Sumter, and what must we do?" Answer: "Use your own discretion!" There is faith for you, after all is said and done. It is believed there is still some discretion left in South Carolina fit for use.

---

advocate of the sovereignty of States, the extension of slavery, and secession. He was a member of the Confederate Congress at its first session and, by a single vote, failed of election as President of the Confederacy. After the war, he was conspicuous for his hostility to the Union.

Everybody who comes here wants an office, and the many who, of course, are disappointed raise a cry of corruption against the few who are successful. I thought we had left all that in Washington. Nobody is willing to be out of sight, and all will take office.

"Constitution" Browne says he is going to Washington for twenty-four hours. I mean to send by him to Mary Garnett for a bonnet ribbon. If they take him up as a traitor, he may cause a civil war. War is now our dread. Mr. Chesnut told him not to make himself a bone of contention.

Everybody means to go into the army. If Sumter is attacked, then Jeff Davis's troubles will begin. The Judge says a military despotism would be best for us—anything to prevent a triumph of the Yankees. All right, but every man objects to any despot but himself.

Mr. Chesnut, in high spirits, dines to-day with the Louisiana delegation. Breakfasted with "Constitution" Browne, who is appointed Assistant Secretary of State, and so does not go to Washington. There was at table the man who advertised for a wife, with the wife so obtained. She was not pretty. We dine at Mr. Pollard's and go to a ball afterward at Judge Bibb's. The New York Herald says Lincoln stood before Washington's picture at his inauguration, which was taken by the country as a good sign. We are always frantic for a good sign. Let us pray that a Cæsar or a Napoleon may be sent us. That would be our best sign of success. But they still say, "No war." Peace let it be, kind Heaven!

Dr. De Leon called, fresh from Washington, and says General Scott is using all his power and influence to prevent officers from the South resigning their commissions, among other things promising that they shall never be sent against us in case of war. Captain Ingraham, in his short, curt way, said: "That will never do. If they take their government's pay they must do its fighting."

A brilliant dinner at the Pollards's. Mr. Barnwell[10] took me down. Came home and found the Judge and Governor Moore waiting to go with me to the Bibbs's. And they say it is dull in Montgomery! Clayton, fresh from Washington, was at the party and told us "there was to be peace."

February 28th.—In the drawing-room a literary lady began a violent attack upon this mischief-making South Carolina. She told me she was a successful writer in the magazines of the day, but when I found she used "incredible" for "incredulous," I said not a word in

---

[10] Robert Woodward Barnwell, of South Carolina, a graduate of Harvard, twice a member of Congress and afterward United States Senator. In 1860, after the passage of the Ordinance of Secession, he was one of the Commissioners who went to Washington to treat with the National Government for its property within the State. He was a member of the Convention at Montgomery and gave the casting vote which made Jefferson Davis President of the Confederacy

defense of my native land. I left her "incredible." Another person came in, while she was pouring upon me her home troubles, and asked if she did not know I was a Carolinian. Then she gracefully reversed her engine, and took the other tack, sounding our praise, but I left her incredible and I remained incredulous, too.

Brewster says the war specks are growing in size. Nobody at the North, or in Virginia, believes we are in earnest. They think we are sulking and that Jeff Davis and Stephens[11] are getting up a very pretty little comedy. The Virginia delegates were insulted at the peace conference; Brewster said, "kicked out."

The Judge thought Jefferson Davis rude to him when the latter was Secretary of War. Mr. Chesnut persuaded the Judge to forego his private wrong for the public good, and so he voted for him, but now his old grudge has come back with an increased venomousness. What a pity to bring the spites of the old Union into this new one! It seems to me already men are willing to risk an injury to our cause, if they may in so doing hurt Jeff Davis.

March 1st.-Dined to-day with Mr. Hill[12] from Georgia, and his wife. After he left us she told me he was the celebrated individual who, for Christian scruples, refused to fight a duel with Stephens.[13] She seemed very proud of him for his conduct in the affair. Ignoramus that I am, I had not heard of it. I am having all kinds of experiences. Drove to-day with a lady who fervently wished her husband would go down to Pensacola and be shot. I was dumb with amazement, of course. Telling my story to one who knew the parties, was informed, "Don't you know he beats her?" So I have seen a man "who lifts his hand against a woman in aught save kindness."

Brewster says Lincoln passed through Baltimore disguised, and at night, and that he did well, for just now Baltimore is dangerous ground. He says that he hears from all quarters that the vulgarity of Lincoln, his wife, and his son is beyond credence, a thing you must see before you can believe it. Senator Stephen A. Douglas told Mr. Chesnut that

---

[11] Alexander H. Stephens, the eminent statesman of Georgia, who before the war had been conspicuous in all the political movements of his time and in 1861 became Vice-President of the Confederacy. After the war he again became conspicuous in Congress and wrote a history entitled "The War between the States."

[12] Benjamin H. Hill, who had already been active in State and National affairs when the Secession movement was carried through. He had been an earnest advocate of the Union until in Georgia the resolution was passed declaring that the State ought to secede. He then became a prominent supporter of secession. He was a member of the Confederate Congress, which met in Montgomery in 1861, and served in the Confederate Senate until the end of the war. After the war, he was elected to Congress and opposed the Reconstruction policy of that body. In 1877 he was elected United States Senator from Georgia.

[13] Governor Herschel V. Johnson also declined, and doubtless for similar reasons, to accept a challenge from Alexander H. Stephens, who, though endowed with the courage of a gladiator, was very small and frail.

"Lincoln is awfully clever, and that he had found him a heavy handful."

Went to pay my respects to Mrs. Jefferson Davis. She met me with open arms. We did not allude to anything by which we are surrounded. We eschewed politics and our changed relations.

March 3d.—Everybody in fine spirits in my world. They have one and all spoken in the Congress[14] to their own perfect satisfaction. To my amazement the Judge took me aside, and, after delivering a panegyric upon himself (but here, later, comes in the amazement), he praised my husband to the skies, and said he was the fittest man of all for a foreign mission. Aye; and the farther away they send us from this Congress the better I will like it.

Saw Jere Clemens and Nick Davis, social curiosities. They are Anti-Secession leaders; then George Sanders and George Deas. The Georges are of opinion that it is folly to try to take back Fort Sumter from Anderson and the United States; that is, before we are ready. They saw in Charleston the devoted band prepared for the sacrifice; I mean, ready to run their heads against a stone wall. Dare devils they are. They have dash and courage enough, but science only could take that fort. They shook their heads.

March 4th.—The Washington Congress has passed peace measures. Glory be to God (as my Irish Margaret used to preface every remark, both great and small).

At last, according to his wish, I was able to introduce Mr. Hill, of Georgia, to Mr. Mallory,[15] and also Governor Moore and Brewster, the latter the only man without a title of some sort that I know in this democratic subdivided republic.

I have seen a negro woman sold on the block at auction. She overtopped the crowd. I was walking and felt faint, seasick. The creature looked so like my good little Nancy, a bright mulatto with a pleasant face. She was magnificently gotten up in silks and satins. She seemed delighted with it all, sometimes ogling the bidders, sometimes looking quiet, coy, and modest, but her mouth never relaxed from its expanded grin of excitement. I dare say the poor thing knew who would buy her. I sat down on a stool in a shop and disciplined my wild thoughts. I tried it Sterne fashion. You know how women sell themselves and are sold in marriage from queens downward, eh? You know what the Bible says about slavery and marriage; poor women! poor slaves! Sterne, with his starling—what did he know? He only thought, he did not feel.

---

[14] It was at this Congress that Jefferson Davis, on February 9, 1861, was elected President, and Alexander H. Stephens Vice-President of the Confederacy. The Congress continued to meet in Montgomery until its removal to Richmond, in July, 1861.

[15] Stephen R. Mallory was the son of a shipmaster of Connecticut, who had settled in Key West in 1820. From 1851 to 1861 Mr. Mallory was United States Senator from Florida, and after the formation of the Confederacy, became its Secretary of the Navy.

In Evan Harrington I read: "Like a true English female, she believed in her own inflexible virtue, but never trusted her husband out of sight."

The New York Herald says: "Lincoln's carriage is not bomb-proof; so he does not drive out." Two flags and a bundle of sticks have been sent him as gentle reminders. The sticks are to break our heads with. The English are gushingly unhappy as to our family quarrel. Magnanimous of them, for it is their opportunity.

March 5th.—We stood on the balcony to see our Confederate flag go up. Roars of cannon, etc., etc. Miss Sanders complained (so said Captain Ingraham) of the deadness of the mob. "It was utterly spiritless," she said; "no cheering, or so little, and no enthusiasm." Captain Ingraham suggested that gentlemen "are apt to be quiet," and this was "a thoughtful crowd, the true mob element with us just -now is hoeing corn." And yet! It is uncomfortable that the idea has gone abroad that we have no joy, no pride, in this thing. The band was playing "Massa in the cold, cold ground." Miss Tyler, daughter of the former President of the United States, ran up the flag.

Captain Ingraham pulled out of his pocket some verses sent to him by a Boston girl. They were well rhymed and amounted to this: she held a rope ready to hang him, though she shed tears when she remembered his heroic rescue of Koszta. Koszta, the rebel! She calls us rebels, too. So it depends upon whom one rebels against—whether to save or not shall be heroic.

I must read Lincoln's inaugural. Oh, "comes he in peace, or comes he in war, or to tread but one measure as Young Lochinvar?" Lincoln's aim is to seduce the border States.

The people, the natives, I mean, are astounded that I calmly affirm, in all truth and candor, that if there were awful things in society in Washington, I did not see or hear of them. One must have been hard to please who did not like the people I knew in Washington.

Mr. Chesnut has gone with a list of names to the President—de Treville, Kershaw, Baker, and Robert Rutledge. They are taking a walk, I see. I hope there will be good places in the army for our list.

March 8th.—Judge Campbell,[16] of the United States Supreme Court, has resigned. Lord! how he must have hated to do it. How other men who are resigning high positions must hate to do it.

Now we may be sure the bridge is broken. And yet in the Alabama Convention they say Reconstructionists abound and are busy.

Met a distinguished gentleman that I knew when he was in more affluent circumstances. I was willing enough to speak to him, but when

---

[16] John Archibald Campbell, who had settled in Montgomery and was appointed Associate Justice of the United States Supreme Court by President Pierce in 1853. Before he resigned, he exerted all his influence to prevent Civil War and opposed secession, although he believed that States had a right to secede.

he saw me advancing for that purpose, to avoid me, he suddenly dodged around a corner—William, Mrs. de Saussure's former coachman. I remember him on his box, driving a handsome pair of bays, dressed sumptuously in blue broadcloth and brass buttons; a stout, respectable, fine-looking, middle-aged mulatto. He was very high and mighty.

Night after night we used to meet him as fiddler-in-chief of all our parties. He sat in solemn dignity, making faces over his bow, and patting his foot with an emphasis that shook the floor. We gave him five dollars a night; that was his price. His mistress never refused to let him play for any party. He had stable-boys in abundance. He was far above any physical fear for his sleek and well-fed person. How majestically he scraped his foot as a sign that he was tuned up and ready to begin!

Now he is a shabby creature indeed. He must have felt his fallen fortunes when he met me—one who knew him in his prosperity. He ran away, this stately yellow gentleman, from wife and children, home and comfort. My Molly asked him "Why? Miss Liza was good to you, I know." I wonder who owns him now; he looked forlorn.

Governor Moore brought in, to be presented to me, the President of the Alabama Convention. It seems I had known him before he had danced with me at a dancing-school ball when I was in short frocks, with sash, flounces, and a wreath of roses. He was one of those clever boys of our neighborhood, in whom my father[17] saw promise of better things, and so helped him in every way to rise, with books, counsel, sympathy. I was enjoying his conversation immensely, for he was praising my father I without stint, when the Judge came in, breathing fire and fury. Congress has incurred his displeasure. We are abusing one another as fiercely as ever we have abased Yankees. It is disheartening.

March 10th.—Mrs. Childs was here to-night (Mary Anderson, from Statesburg), with several children. She is lovely. Her hair is piled up on the top of her head oddly. Fashions from France still creep into Texas across Mexican borders. Mrs. Childs is fresh from Texas. Her husband is an artillery officer, or was. They will be glad to promote him here. Mrs. Childs had the sweetest Southern voice, absolute music. But then, she has all of the high spirit of those sweet-voiced Carolina women, too.

Then Mr. Browne came in with his fine English accent, so pleasant

[17] Mrs. Chesnut's father was Stephen Decatur Miller, who was born in South Carolina in 1787, and died in Mississippi in 1838. He was elected to Congress in 1816, as an Anti-Calhoun Democrat, and from 1828 to 1830 was Governor of South Carolina. He favored Nullification, and in 1830 was elected United States Senator from South Carolina, but resigned three years afterward in consequence of ill health. In 1835 he removed to Mississippi and engaged in cotton growing.

to the ear. He tells us that Washington society is not reconciled to the Yankee *régime*. Mrs. Lincoln means to economize. She at once informed the majordomo that they were poor and hoped to save twelve thousand dollars every year from their salary of twenty thousand. Mr. Browne said Mr. Buchanan's farewell was far more imposing than Lincoln's inauguration.

The people were so amusing, so full of Western stories. Dr. Boykin behaved strangely. All day he had been gaily driving about with us, and never was man in finer spirits. To-night, in this brilliant company, he sat dead still as if in a trance. Once, he waked somewhat—when a high public functionary came in with a present for me, a miniature gondola, "A perfect Venetian specimen," he assured me again and again. In an undertone Dr. Boykin muttered: "That fellow has been drinking." "Why do you think so?" "Because he has told you exactly the same thing four times." Wonderful! Some of these great statesmen always tell me the same thing—and have been telling me the same thing ever since we came here.

A man came in and some one said in an undertone, "The age of chivalry is not past, O ye Americans!" "What do you mean?" "That man was once nominated by President Buchanan for a foreign mission, but some Senator stood up and read a paper printed by this man abusive of a woman, and signed by his name in full. After that the Senate would have none of him; his chance was gone forever."

March 11th.—In full conclave to-night, the drawing-room crowded with Judges, Governors, Senators, Generals, Congressmen. They were exalting John C. Calhoun's hospitality. He allowed everybody to stay all night who chose to stop at his house. An ill-mannered person, on one occasion, refused to attend family prayers. Mr. Calhoun said to the servant, "Saddle that man's horse and let him go." From the traveler Calhoun would take no excuse for the "Deity offended." I believe in Mr. Calhoun's hospitality, but not in his family prayers. Mr. Calhoun's piety was of the most philosophical type, from all accounts.[18]

The latest news is counted good news; that is, the last man who left Washington tells us that Seward is in the ascendancy. He is thought to be the friend of peace. The man did say, however that "that serpent Seward is in the ascendancy just now."

Harriet Lane has eleven suitors. One is described as likely to win, or he would be likely to win, except that he is too heavily weighted. He has been married before and goes about with children and two mothers. There are limits beyond which! Two mothers-in-law!

Mr. Ledyard spoke to Mrs. Lincoln in behalf of a doorkeeper who almost felt he had a vested right, having been there since Jackson's

---

[18] John C. Calhoun had died in March, 1850.

time; but met with the same answer; she had brought her own girl and must economize. Mr. Ledyard thought the twenty thousand (and little enough it is) was given to the President of these United States to enable him to live in proper style, and to maintain an establishment of such dignity as befits the head of a great nation. It is an infamy to economize with the public money and to put it into one's private purse. Mrs. Browne was walking with me when we were airing our indignation against Mrs. Lincoln and her shabby economy. The Herald says three only of the *élite* Washington families attended the Inauguration Ball.

The Judge has just come in and said: "Last night, after Dr. Boykin left on the cars, there came a telegram that his little daughter, Amanda, had died suddenly." In some way he must have known it beforehand. He changed so suddenly yesterday, and seemed so careworn and unhappy. He believes in clairvoyance, magnetism, and all that. Certainly, there was some terrible foreboding of this kind on his part.

Tuesday.—Now this, they say, is positive: "Fort Sumter is to be released and we are to have no war." After all, far too good to be true. Mr. Browne told us that, at one of the peace intervals (I mean intervals in the interest of peace), Lincoln flew through Baltimore, locked up in an express car. He wore a Scotch cap.

We went to the Congress. Governor Cobb, who presides over that august body, put James Chesnut in the chair, and came down to talk to us. He told us why the pay of Congressmen was fixed in secret session, and why the amount of it was never divulged—to prevent the lodginghouse and hotel people from making their bills of a size to cover it all. "The bill would be sure to correspond with the pay," he said.

In the hotel parlor we had a scene. Mrs. Scott was describing Lincoln, who is of the cleverest Yankee type. She said: "Awfully ugly, even grotesque in appearance, the kind who are always at the corner stores, sitting on boxes, whittling sticks, and telling stories as funny as they are vulgar." Here I interposed: "But Stephen A. Douglas said one day to Mr. Chesnut, 'Lincoln is the hardest fellow to handle I have ever encountered yet.'" Mr. Scott is from California, and said Lincoln is "an utter American specimen, coarse, rouge, and strong; a good-natured, kind creature; as pleasant-tempered as he is clever, and if this country can be joked and laughed out of its rights he is the kind-hearted fellow to do it. Now if there is a war and it pinches the Yankee pocket instead of filling it—"

Here a shrill voice came from the next room (which opened upon the one we were in by folding doors thrown wide open) and said: "Yankees are no more mean and stingy than you are. People at the North are just as good as people at the South." The speaker advanced upon us in great wrath.

Mrs. Scott apologized and made some smooth, polite remark,

though evidently much embarrassed. But the vinegar face and curly pate refused to receive any concessions, and replied: "That comes with a very bad grace after what you were saying," and she harangued us loudly for several minutes. Some one in the other room giggled outright, but we were quiet as mice. Nobody wanted to hurt her feelings. She was one against so many. If I were at the North, I should expect them to belabor us, and should hold my tongue. We separated North from South because of incompatibility of temper. We are divorced because we have hated each other so. If we could only separate, a "*separation à l'agréable*," as the French say it, and not have a horrid fight for divorce.

The poor exile had already been insulted, she said. She was playing "Yankee Doodle" on the piano before breakfast to soothe her wounded spirit, and the Judge came in and calmly requested her to "leave out the Yankee while she played the Doodle." The Yankee end of it did not suit our climate, he said; was totally out of place and had got out of its latitude.

A man said aloud: "This war talk is nothing. It will soon blow over. Only a fuss gotten up by that Charleston clique." Mr. Toombs asked him to show his passports, for a man who uses such language is a suspicious character.

CHAPTER III. CHARLESTON, S. C.

March 26, 1861—*April* 15, 1861

Charleston, S. C., *March 26, 1861.*—I have just come from Mulberry, where the snow was a foot deep—winter at last after months of apparently May or June weather. Even the climate, like everything else, is upside down. But after that den of dirt and horror, Montgomery Hall, how white the sheets looked, luxurious bed linen once more, delicious fresh cream with my coffee! I breakfasted in bed.

Dueling was rife in Camden. William M. Shannon challenged Leitner. Rochelle Blair was Shannon's second and Artemus Goodwyn was Leitner's. My husband was riding hard all day to stop the foolish people. Mr. Chesnut finally arranged the difficulty. There was a court of honor and no duel. Mr. Leitner had struck Mr. Shannon at a negro trial. That's the way the row began. Everybody knows of it. We suggested that Judge Withers should arrest the belligerents. Dr. Boykin and Joe Kershaw[19] aided Mr. Chesnut to put an end to the useless risk of life.

---

[19] Joseph B. Kershaw, a native of Camden, S. C., who became famous in connection with "The Kershaw Brigade" and its brilliant record at Bull Run, Fredericksburg, Chickamauga, Spottsylvania, and elsewhere throughout the war.

John Chesnut is a pretty soft-hearted slave-owner. He had two negroes arrested for selling whisky to his people on his plantation, and buying stolen corn from them. The culprits in jail sent for him. He found them (this snowy weather) lying in the cold on a bare floor, and he thought that punishment enough; they having had weeks of it. But they were not satisfied to be allowed to evade justice and slip away. They begged of him (and got) five dollars to buy shoes to run away in. I said: "Why, this is flat compounding a felony." And Johnny put his hands in the armholes of his waistcoat and stalked majestically before me, saying, "Woman, what do you know about law?"

Mrs. Reynolds stopped the carriage one day to tell me Kitty Boykin was to be married to Savage Heyward. He has only ten children already. These people take the old Hebrew pride in the number of children they have. This is the true colonizing spirit. There is no danger of crowding here and inhabitants are wanted. Old Colonel Chesnut[20] said one day: "Wife, you must feel that you have not been useless in your day and generation. You have now twenty-seven great-grandchildren."

Wednesday.—I have been mobbed by my own house servants. Some of them are at the plantation, some hired out at the Camden hotel, some are at Mulberry. They agreed to come in a body and beg me to stay at home to keep my own house once more, "as I ought not to have them scattered and distributed every which way." I had not been a month in Camden since 1858. So a house there would be for their benefit solely, not mine. I asked my cook if she lacked anything on the plantation at the Hermitage. "Lack anything?" she said, "I lack everything. What are corn-meal, bacon, milk, and molasses? Would that be all you wanted? Ain't I been living and eating exactly as you does all these years? When I cook for you, didn't I have some of all? Dere, now!" Then she doubled herself up laughing. They all shouted, "Missis, we is crazy for you to stay home."

Armsted, my butler, said he hated the hotel. Besides, he heard a man there abusing Marster, but Mr. Clyburne took it up and made him stop short. Armsted said he wanted Marster to know Mr. Clyburne was his friend and would let nobody say a word behind his back against him, etc., etc. Stay in Camden? Not if I can help it. "Festers in provincial sloth"—that's Tennyson's way of putting it.

"We" came down here by rail, as the English say. Such a crowd of

---

[20] Colonel Chesnut, the author's father-in-law, was born about 1760. He was a prominent South Carolina planter and a public-spirited man. The family had originally settled in Virginia, where the farm had been overrun by the French and Indians at the time of Braddock's campaign, the head of the family being killed at Fort Duquesne. Colonel Chesnut, of Mulberry, had been educated at Princeton, and his wife was a Philadelphia woman. In the final chapter of this Diary, the author gives a charming sketch of Colonel Chesnut.

Convention men on board. John Manning[21] flew in to beg me to reserve a seat by me for a young lady under his charge. *"Place aux dames,"* said my husband politely, and went off to seek a seat somewhere else. As soon as we were fairly under way, Governor Manning came back and threw himself cheerily down into the vacant place. After arranging his umbrella and overcoat to his satisfaction, he coolly remarked: "I am the young lady." He is always the handsomest man alive (now that poor William Taber has been killed in a duel), and he can be very agreeable that is, when he pleases to be so. He does not always please. He seemed to have made his little maneuver principally to warn me of impending danger to my husband's political career. "Every election now will be a surprise. New cliques are not formed yet. The old ones are principally bent upon displacing one another." "But the Yankees, those dreadful Yankees!" "Oh, never mind, we are going to take care of home folks first! How will you like to rusticate?—go back and mind your own business?" "If I only knew what that was—what was my own business."

Our round table consists of the Judge, Langdon Cheves,[22] Trescott,[23] and ourselves. Here are four of the cleverest men that we have, but such very different people, as opposite in every characteristic as the four points of the compass. Langdon Cheves and my husband have feelings and ideas in common. Mr. Petigru,[24] said of the brilliant Trescott: "He is a man without indignation." Trescott and I laugh at everything.

The Judge, from his life as solicitor, and then on the bench, has learned to look for the darkest motives for every action. His judgment on men and things is always so harsh, it shocks and repels even his best friends. To-day he said: "Your conversation reminds me of a flashy second-rate novel." "How?" "By the quantity of French you sprinkle over it. Do you wish to prevent us from understanding you?" "No,"

---

[21] John Lawrence Manning was a son of Richard I. Manning, a former Governor of South Carolina. He was himself elected Governor of that State in 1852, was a delegate to the convention that nominated Buchanan, and during the War of Secession served on the staff of General Beauregard. In 1865 he was chosen United States Senator from South Carolina, but was not allowed to take his seat.

[22] Son of Langdon Cheves, an eminent lawyer of South Carolina, who served in Congress from 1810 to 1814; he was elected Speaker of the House of Representatives, and from 1819 to 1823 was President of the United States Bank; he favored Secession, but died before it was accomplished—in 1857.

[23] William Henry Trescott, a native of Charleston, was Assistant Secretary of State of the United States in 1860, but resigned after South Carolina seceded. After the war he had a successful career as a lawyer and diplomatist.

[24] James Louis Petigru before the war had reached great distinction as a lawyer and stood almost alone in his State as an opponent of the Nullification movement of 1830-1832. In 1860 he strongly opposed disunion, although he was then an old man of 71. His reputation has survived among lawyers because of the fine work he did in codifying the laws of South Carolina.

said Trescott, "we are using French against Africa. We know the black waiters are all ears now, and we want to keep what we have to say dark. We can't afford to take them into our confidence, you know."

This explanation Trescott gave with great rapidity and many gestures toward the men standing behind us. Still speaking the French language, his apology was exasperating, so the Judge glared at him, and, in unabated rage, turned to talk with Mr. Cheves, who found it hard to keep a calm countenance.

On the Battery with the Rutledges, Captain Hartstein was introduced to me. He has done some heroic things—brought home some ships and is a man of mark. Afterward he sent me a beautiful bouquet, not half so beautiful, however, as Mr. Robert Gourdin's, which already occupied the place of honor on my center table. What a dear, delightful place is Charleston!

A lady (who shall be nameless because of her story) came to see me to-day. Her husband has been on the Island with the troops for months. She has just been down to see him. She meant only to call on him, but he persuaded her to stay two days. She carried him some clothes made from his old measure. Now they are a mile too wide. "So much for a hard life!" I said.

"No, no," said she, "they are all jolly down there. He has trained down; says it is good for him, and he likes the life." Then she became confidential, although it was her first visit to me, a perfect stranger. She had taken no clothes down there—pushed, as she was, in that manner under Achilles's tent. But she managed things; she tied her petticoat around her neck for a nightgown.

April 2d.—Governor Manning came to breakfast at our table. The others had breakfasted hours before. I looked at him in amazement, as he was in full dress, ready for a ball, swallow-tail and all, and at that hour. "What is the matter with you?" "Nothing, I am not mad, most noble madam. I am only going to the photographer. My wife wants me taken thus." He insisted on my going, too, and we captured Mr. Chesnut and Governor Means.[25] The latter presented me with a book, a photo-book, in which I am to pillory all the celebrities.

Doctor Gibbes says the Convention is in a snarl. It was called as a Secession Convention. A secession of places seems to be what it calls for first of all. It has not stretched its eyes out to the Yankees yet; it has them turned inward; introspection is its occupation still.

Last night, as I turned down the gas, I said to myself: "Certainly this has been one of the pleasantest days of my life." I can only give the skeleton of it, so many pleasant people, so much good talk, for, after

---

[25] John Hugh Means was elected Governor of South Carolina in 1850, and had long been an advocate of secession. He was a delegate to the Convention of 1860 and affixed his name to the Ordinance of Secession. He was killed at the second battle of Bull Run in August, 1862.

all, it was talk, talk, talk *à la Caroline du Sud*. And yet the day began rather dismally. Mrs. Capers and Mrs. Tom Middleton came for me and we drove to Magnolia Cemetery. I saw William Taber's broken column. It was hard to shake off the blues after this graveyard business. The others were off at a dinner party. I dined *tête-à-tête* with Langdon Cheves, so quiet, so intelligent, so very sensible withal. There never was a pleasanter person, or a better man than he. While we were at table, Judge Whitner, Tom Frost, and Isaac Hayne came. They broke up our deeply interesting conversation, for I was hearing what an honest and brave man feared for his country, and then the Rutledges dislodged the newcomers and bore me off to drive on the Battery. On the staircase met Mrs. Izard, who came for the same purpose. On the Battery Governor Adams[26] stopped us. He had heard of my saying he looked like Marshal Pelissier, and he came to say that at last I had made a personal remark which pleased him, for once in my life. When we came home Mrs. Isaac Hayne and Chancellor Carroll called to ask us to join their excursion to the Island Forts to-morrow. With them was William Haskell. Last summer at the White Sulphur he was a pale, slim student from the university. To-day he is a soldier, stout and robust. A few months in camp, with soldiering in the open air, has worked this wonder. Camping out proves a wholesome life after all. Then came those nice, sweet, fresh, pure-looking Pringle girls. We had a charming topic in common—their clever brother Edward.

A letter from Eliza B., who is in Montgomery: "Mrs. Mallory got a letter from a lady in Washington a few days ago, who said that there had recently been several attempts to be gay in Washington, but they proved dismal failures. The Black Republicans were invited and came, and stared at their entertainers and their new Republican companions looked unhappy while they said they were enchanted showed no illtemper at the hardly stifled grumbling and growling of our friends, who thus found themselves condemned to meet their despised enemy."

I had a letter from the Gwinns to-day. They say Washington offers a perfect realization of Goldsmith's Deserted Village.

Celebrated my 38th birthday, but I am too old now to dwell in public on that unimportant anniversary. A long, dusty day ahead on those windy islands; never for me, so I was up early to write a note of excuse to Chancellor Carroll. My husband went. I hope Anderson will not pay them the compliment of a salute with shotted guns, as they pass Fort Sumter, as pass they must.

Here I am interrupted by an exquisite bouquet from the Rutledges. Are there such roses anywhere else in the world? Now a loud banging at my door. I get up in a pet and throw it wide open. "Oh!" said John

---

[26] James H. Adams was a graduate of Yale, who in 1832 strongly opposed Nullification, and in 1855 was elected Governor of South Carolina.

Manning, standing there, smiling radiantly; "pray excuse the noise I made. I mistook the number; I thought it was Rice's room; that is my excuse. Now that I am here, come, go with us to Quinby's. Everybody will be there who are not at the Island. To be photographed is the rage just now.

We had a nice open carriage, and we made a number of calls, Mrs. Izard, the Pringles, and the Tradd Street Rutledges, the handsome ex-Governor doing the honors gallantly. He had ordered dinner at six, and we dined tete-a-tete. If he should prove as great a captain in ordering his line of battle as he is in ordering a dinner, it will be as well for the country as it was for me to-day.

Fortunately for the men, the beautiful Mrs. Joe Heyward sits at the next table, so they take her beauty as one of the goods the gods provide. And it helps to make life pleasant with English grouse and venison from the West. Not to speak of the salmon from the lakes which began the feast. They have me to listen, an appreciative audience, while they talk, and Mrs. Joe Heyward to look at.

Beauregard[27] called. He is the hero of the hour. That is, he is believed to be capable of great things. A hero worshiper was struck dumb because I said: "So far, he has only been a captain of artillery, or engineers, or something." I did not see him. Mrs. Wigfall did and reproached my laziness in not coming out.

Last Sunday at church beheld one of the peculiar local sights, old negro maumas going up to the communion, in their white turbans and kneeling devoutly around the chancel rail.

The morning papers say Mr. Chesnut made the best shot on the Island at target practice. No war yet, thank God. Likewise they tell me Mr. Chesnut has made a capital speech in the Convention.

Not one word of what is going on now. "Out of the fulness of the heart the mouth speaketh," says the Psalmist. Not so here. Our hearts are in doleful dumps, but we are as gay, as madly jolly, as sailors who break into the strong-room when the ship is going down. At first in our great agony we were out alone. We longed for some of our big brothers to come out and help us. Well, they are out, too, and now it is Fort Sumter and that ill-advised Anderson. There stands Fort Sumter, *en evidence*, and thereby hangs peace or war.

Wigfall[28] says before he left Washington, Pickens, our Governor,

---

[27] Pierre Gustave Toutant Beauregard was born in New Orleans in 1818, and graduated from West Point in the class of 1838. He served in the war with Mexico; had been superintendent of the Military Academy at West Point a few days only, when in February, 1861, he resigned his commission in the Army of the United States and offered his services to the Confederacy.

[28] Louis Trezevant Wigfall was a native of South Carolina, but removed to Texas after being admitted to the bar, and from that State was elected United States Senator, becoming an uncompromising defender of the South on the slave question. After the war

and Trescott were openly against secession; Trescott does not pretend to like it now. He grumbles all the time, but Governor Pickens is fire-eater down to the ground. "At the White House Mrs. Davis wore a badge. Jeff Davis is no seceder," says Mrs. Wigfall.

Captain Ingraham comments in his rapid way, words tumbling over each other out of his mouth: "Now, Charlotte Wigfall meant that as a fling at those people. I think better of men who stop to think; it is too rash to rush on as some do." "And so," adds Mrs. Wigfall, "the eleventh-hour men are rewarded; the half-hearted are traitors in this row."

April 3d.—Met the lovely Lucy Holcombe, now Mrs. Governor Pickens, last night at Isaac Hayne's. I saw Miles now begging in dumb show for three violets she had in her breastpin. She is a consummate actress and he well up in the part of male flirt. So it was well done.

"And you, who are laughing in your sleeves at the scene, where did you get that huge bunch?" "Oh, there is no sentiment when there is a pile like that of anything!" "Oh, oh!"

To-day at the breakfast table there was a tragic bestowal of heartsease on the well-known inquirer who, once more says in austere tones: "Who is the flirt now?" And so we fool on into the black cloud ahead of us. And after heartsease cometh rue.

April 4th.—Mr. Hayne said his wife moaned over the hardness of the chaperones' seats at St. Andrew's Hall at a Cecilia Ball.[29] She was hopelessly deposited on one for hours. "And the walls are harder, my dear. What are your feelings to those of the poor old fellows leaning there, with, their beautiful young wives waltzing as if they could never tire and in the arms of every man in the room. Watch their haggard, weary faces, the old boys, you know. At church I had to move my pew. The lovely Laura was too much for my boys. They all made eyes at her, and nudged each other and quarreled so, for she gave them glance for glance. Wink, blink, and snicker as they would, she liked it. I say, my dear, the old husbands have not exactly a bed of roses; their wives twirling in the arms of young men, they hugging the wall."

While we were at supper at the Haynes's, Wigfall was sent for to address a crowd before the Mills House piazza. Like James Fitz James when he visits Glen Alpin again, it is to be in the saddle, etc. So let Washington beware. We were sad that we could not hear the speaking. But the supper was a consolation—*pâté de foie gras* salad, biscuit glacé and champagne frappé.

A ship was fired into yesterday, and went back to sea. Is that the

---

he lived in England, but in 1873 settled in Baltimore. He had a wide Southern reputation as a forcible and impassioned speaker.

[29] The annual balls of the St. Cecilia Society in Charleston are still the social events of the season. To become a member of the St. Cecilia Society is a sort of presentation at court in the sense of giving social recognition to one who was without the pale.

first shot? How can one settle down to anything; one's heart is in one's mouth all the time. Any moment the cannon may open on us, the fleet come in.

April 6th.—The plot thickens, the air is red hot with rumors; the mystery is to find out where these utterly groundless tales originate. In spite of all, Tom Huger came for us and we went on the Planter to take a look at Morris Island and its present inhabitants—Mrs. Wigfall and the Cheves girls, Maxcy Gregg and Colonel Whiting, also John Rutledge, of the Navy, Dan Hamilton, and William Haskell. John Rutledge was a figurehead to be proud of. He did not speak to us. But he stood with a Scotch shawl draped about him, as handsome and stately a creature as ever Queen Elizabeth loved to look upon.

There came up such a wind we could not land. I was not too sorry, though it blew so hard (I am never seasick). Colonel Whiting explained everything about the forts, what they lacked, etc., in the most interesting way, and Maxcy Gregg supplemented his report by stating all the deficiencies and shortcomings by land.

Beauregard is a demigod here to most of the natives, but there are always seers who see and say. They give you to understand that Whiting has all the brains now in use for our defense. He does the work and Beauregard reaps the glory. Things seem to draw near a crisis. And one must think. Colonel Whiting is clever enough for anything, so we made up our minds to-day, Maxcy Gregg and I, as judges. Mr. Gregg told me that my husband was in a minority in the Convention; so much for cool sense when the atmosphere is phosphorescent. Mrs. Wigfall says we are mismatched. She should pair with my cool, quiet, self-poised Colonel. And her stormy petrel is but a male reflection of me.

April 8th.—Yesterday Mrs. Wigfall and I made a few visits. At the first house they wanted Mrs. Wigfall to settle a dispute. "Was she, indeed, fifty-five?" Fancy her face, more than ten years bestowed upon her so freely. Then Mrs. Gibbes asked me if I had ever been in Charleston before. Says Charlotte Wigfall (to pay me for my snigger when that false fifty was flung in her teeth), "and she thinks this is her native heath and her name is McGregor." She said it all came upon us for breaking the Sabbath, for indeed it was Sunday.

Allen Green came up to speak to me at dinner in all his soldier's toggery. It sent a shiver through me. Tried to read Margaret Fuller Ossoli, but could not. The air is too full of war news, and we are all so restless.

Went to see Miss Pinckney, one of the last of the old-world Pinckneys. She inquired particularly about a portrait of her father, Charles Cotesworth Pinckney,[30] which she said had been sent by him to

---

[30] Charles Cotesworth Pinckney was a brigadier-general in the Revolution and a member of the Convention that framed the Constitution of the United States. He was an

my husband's grandfather. I gave a good account of it. It hangs in the place of honor in the drawing-room at Mulberry. She wanted to see my husband, for "his grandfather, my father's friend, was one of the handsomest men of his day." We came home, and soon Mr. Robert Gourdin and Mr. Miles called. Governor Manning walked in, bowed gravely, and seated himself by me. Again he bowed low in mock heroic style, and with a grand wave of his hand, said: "Madame, your country is invaded." When I had breath to speak, I asked, "What does he mean?" He meant this: there are six men-of-war outside the bar. Talbot and Chew have come to say that hostilities are to begin. Governor Pickens and Beauregard are holding a council of war. Mr. Chesnut then came in and confirmed the story. Wigfall next entered in boisterous spirits, and said: "There was a sound of revelry by night." In any stir or confusion my heart is apt to beat so painfully. Now the agony was so stifling I could hardly see or hear. The men went off almost immediately. And I crept silently to my room, where I sat down to a good cry.

Mrs. Wigfall came in and we had it out on the subject of civil war. We solaced ourselves with dwelling on all its known horrors, and then we added what we had a right to expect with Yankees in front and negroes in the rear. "The slave-owners must expect a servile insurrection, of course," said Mrs. Wigfall, to make sure that we were unhappy enough.

Suddenly loud shooting was heard. We ran out. Cannon after cannon roared. We met Mrs. Allen Green in the passageway with blanched cheeks and streaming eyes. Governor Means rushed out of his room in his dressing-gown and begged us to be calm. "Governor Pickens," said he, "has ordered in the plenitude of his wisdom, seven cannon to be fired as a signal to the Seventh Regiment. Anderson will hear as well as the Seventh Regiment. Now you go back and be quiet; fighting in the streets has not begun yet."

So we retired. Dr. Gibbes calls Mrs. Allen Green Dame Placid. There was no placidity to-day, with cannon bursting and Allen on the Island. No sleep for anybody last night. The streets were alive with soldiers, men shouting, marching, singing. Wigfall, the "stormy petrel," is in his glory, the only thoroughly happy person I see. To-day things seem to have settled down a little. One can but hope still. Lincoln, or Seward, has made such silly advances and then far sillier drawings back. There may be a chance for peace after all. Things are happening so fast. My husband has been made an aide-de-camp to General

Beauregard.

Three hours ago we were quickly packing to go home. The Convention has adjourned. Now he tells me the attack on Fort Sumter may begin to-night; depends upon Anderson and the fleet outside. The Herald says that this show of war outside of the bar is intended for Texas. John Manning came in with his sword and red sash, pleased as a boy to be on Beauregard's staff, while the row goes on. He has gone with Wigfall to Captain Hartstein with instructions. Mr. Chesnut is finishing a report he had to make to the Convention.

Mrs. Hayne called. She had, she said, but one feeling; pity for those who are not here. Jack Preston, Willie Alston, "the take-life-easys," as they are called, with John Green, "the big brave," have gone down to the islands—volunteered as privates. Seven hundred men were sent over. Ammunition wagons were rumbling along the streets all night. Anderson is burning blue lights, signs, and signals for the fleet outside, I suppose.

To-day at dinner there was no allusion to things as they stand in Charleston Harbor. There was an undercurrent of intense excitement. There could not have been a more brilliant circle. In addition to our usual quartette (Judge Withers, Langdon Cheves, and Trescott), our two ex-Governors dined with us, Means and Manning. These men all talked so delightfully. For once in my life I listened. That over, business began in earnest. Governor Means had rummaged a sword and red sash from somewhere and brought it for Colonel Chesnut, who had gone to demand the surrender of Fort Sumter. And now patience—we must wait.

Why did that green goose Anderson go into Fort Sumter? Then everything began to go wrong. Now they have intercepted a letter from him urging them to let him surrender.

He paints the horrors likely to ensue if they will not. He ought to have thought of all that before he put his head in the hole.

April 12th.—Anderson will not capitulate. Yesterday's was the merriest, maddest dinner we have had yet. Men were audaciously wise and witty. We had an unspoken foreboding that it was to be our last pleasant meeting. Mr. Miles dined with us to-day. Mrs. Henry King rushed in saying, "The news, I come for the latest news. All the men of the King family are on the Island," of which fact she seemed proud.

While she was here our peace negotiator, or envoy, came in—that is, Mr. Chesnut returned. His interview with Colonel Anderson had been deeply interesting, but Mr. Chesnut was not inclined to be communicative. He wanted his dinner. He felt for Anderson and had telegraphed to President Davis for instructions—what answer to give Anderson, etc. He has now gone back to Fort Sumter with additional instructions. When they were about to leave the wharf A. H. Boykin sprang into the boat in great excitement. He thought himself ill-used, with a likelihood of fighting and he to be left behind!

I do not pretend to go to sleep. How can I? If Anderson does not accept terms at four, the orders are, he shall be fired upon. I count four, St. Michael's bells chime out and I begin to hope. At half-past four the heavy booming of a cannon. I sprang out of bed, and on my knees prostrate I prayed as I never prayed before.

There was a sound of stir all over the house, pattering of feet in the corridors. All seemed hurrying one way. I put on my double-gown and a shawl and went, too. It was to the housetop. The shells were bursting. In the dark I heard a man say, "Waste of ammunition." I knew my husband was rowing about in a boat somewhere in that dark bay, and that the shells were roofing it over, bursting toward the fort. If Anderson was obstinate, Colonel Chesnut was to order the fort on one side to open fire. Certainly fire had begun. The regular roar of the cannon, there it was. And who could tell what each volley accomplished of death and destruction?

The women were wild there on the housetop. Prayers came from the women and imprecations from the men. And then a shell would light up the scene. To-night they say the forces are to attempt to land. We watched up there, and everybody wondered that Fort Sumter did not fire a shot.

To-day Miles and Manning, colonels now, aides to Beauregard, dined with us. The latter hoped I would keep the peace. I gave him only good words, for he was to be under fire all day and night, down in the bay carrying orders, etc.

Last night, or this morning truly, up on the housetop I was so weak and weary I sat down on something that looked like a black stool. "Get up, you foolish woman. Your dress is on fire," cried a man. And he put me out. I was on a chimney and the sparks had caught my clothes. Susan Preston and Mr. Venable then came up. But my fire had been extinguished before it burst out into a regular blaze.

Do you know, after all that noise and our tears and prayers, nobody has been hurt; sound and fury signifying nothing—a delusion and a snare.

Louisa Hamilton came here now. This is a sort of news center. Jack Hamilton, her handsome young husband, has all the credit of a famous battery, which is made of railroad iron. Mr. Petigru calls it the boomerang, because it throws the balls back the way they came; so Lou Hamilton tells us. During her first marriage, she had no children; hence the value of this lately achieved baby. To divert Louisa from the glories of "the Battery," of which she raves, we asked if the baby could talk yet. "No, not exactly, but he imitates the big gun when he hears that. He claps his hands and cries 'Boom, boom.'" Her mind is distinctly occupied by three things: Lieutenant Hamilton, whom she calls "Randolph," the baby, and the big gun, and it refuses to hold more.

Pryor, of Virginia, spoke from the piazza of the Charleston hotel. I asked what he said. An irreverent woman replied: "Oh, they all say the same thing, but he made great play with that long hair of his, which he is always tossing aside!"

Somebody came in just now and reported Colonel Chesnut asleep on the sofa in General Beauregard's room. After two such nights he must be so tired as to be able to sleep anywhere.

Just bade farewell to Langdon Cheves. He is forced to go home and leave this interesting place. Says he feels like the man that was not killed at Thermopylae. I think he said that unfortunate had to hang himself when he got home for very shame. Maybe he fell on his sword, which was the strictly classic way of ending matters.

I do not wonder at Louisa Hamilton's baby; we hear nothing, can listen to nothing; boom, boom goes the cannon all the time. The nervous strain is awful, alone in this darkened room. "Richmond and Washington ablaze," say the papers—blazing with excitement. Why not? To us these last days' events seem frightfully great. We were all women on that iron balcony. Men are only seen at a distance now. Stark Means, marching under the piazza at the head of his regiment, held his cap in his hand all the time he was in sight. Mrs. Means was leaning over and looking with tearful eyes, when an unknown creature asked, "Why did he take his hat off?" Mrs. Means stood straight up and said: "He did that in honor of his mother; he saw me." She is a proud mother, and at the same time most unhappy. Her lovely daughter Emma is dying in there, before her eyes, of consumption. At that moment I am sure Mrs. Means had a spasm of the heart; at least, she looked as I feel sometimes. She took my arm and we came in.

April 13th.—Nobody has been hurt after all. How gay we were last night. Reaction after the dread of all the slaughter we thought those dreadful cannon were making. Not even a battery the worse for wear. Fort Sumter has been on fire. Anderson has not yet silenced any of our guns. So the aides, still with swords and red sashes by way of uniform, tell us. But the sound of those guns makes regular meals impossible. None of us go to table. Tea-trays pervade the corridors going everywhere. Some of the anxious hearts lie on their beds and moan in solitary misery. Mrs. Wigfall and I solace ourselves with tea in my room. These women have all a satisfying faith. "God is on our side," they say. When we are shut in Mrs. Wigfall and I ask "Why?" "Of course, He hates the Yankees, we are told. You'll think that well of Him."

Not by one word or look can we detect any change in the demeanor of these negro servants. Lawrence sits at our door, sleepy and respectful, and profoundly indifferent. So are they all, but they carry it too far. You could not tell that they even heard the awful roar going on in the bay, though it has been dinning in their ears night and day.

People talk before them as if they were chairs and tables. They make no sign. ~~Are they stolidly stupid? or wiser than we are; silent and strong, biding their time?~~

~~So tea and toast~~ came; also came Colonel Manning, red sash and sword, to announce that he had been under fire, and didn't mind it. He said gaily: "It is one of those things a fellow never knows how he will come out until he has been tried. Now I know I am a worthy descendant of my old Irish hero of an ancestor, who held the British officer before him as a shield in the Revolution, and backed out of danger gracefully." We talked of St. Valentine's eve, or the maid of Perth, and the drop of the white doe's blood that sometimes spoiled all.

The war-steamers are still there, outside the bar. And there are people who thought the Charleston bar "no good" to Charleston. The bar is the silent partner, or sleeping partner, and in this fray it is doing us yeoman service.

April 15th.—I did not know that one could live such days of excitement. Some one called: "Come out! There is a crowd coming." A mob it was, indeed, but it was headed by Colonels Chesnut and Manning. The crowd was shouting and showing these two as messengers of good news. They were escorted to Beauregard's headquarters. Fort Sumter had surrendered! Those upon the housetops shouted to us "The fort is on fire." That had been the story once or twice before.

When we had calmed down, Colonel Chesnut, who had taken it all quietly enough, if anything more unruffled than usual in his serenity, told us how the surrender came about. Wigfall was with them on Morris Island when they saw the fire in the fort; he jumped in a little boat, and with his handkerchief as a white flag, rowed over. Wigfall went in through a porthole. When Colonel Chesnut arrived shortly after, and was received at the regular entrance, Colonel Anderson told him he had need to pick his way warily, for the place was all mined. As far as I can make out the fort surrendered to Wigfall. But it is all confusion. Our flag is flying there. Fire-engines have been sent for to put out the fire. Everybody tells you half of something and then rushes off to tell something else or to hear the last news.

In the afternoon, Mrs. Preston,[31] Mrs. Joe Heyward, and I drove around the Battery. We were in an open carriage.

What a changed scene—the very liveliest crowd I think I ever saw, everybody talking at once. All glasses were still turned on the grim old fort.

---

[31] Caroline Hampton, a daughter of General Wade Hampton, of the Revolution. was the wife of John S. Preston, an ardent advocate of secession, who served on the staff of Beauregard at Bull Run and subsequently reached the rank of brigadier-general.

Russell,[32] the correspondent of the London Times, was there. They took him everywhere. One man got out Thackeray to converse with him on equal terms. Poor Russell was awfully bored, they say. He only wanted to see the fort and to get news suitable to make up into an interesting article. Thackeray had become stale over the water.

Mrs. Frank Hampton[33] and I went to see the camp of the Richland troops. South Carolina College had volunteered to a boy. Professor Venable (the mathematical), intends to raise a company from among them for the war, a permanent company. This is a grand frolic no more for the students, at least. Even the staid and severe of aspect, Clingman, is here. He says Virginia and North Carolina are arming to come to our rescue, for now the North will swoop down on us. Of that we may be sure. We have burned our ships. We are obliged to go on now. He calls us a poor, little, hot-blooded, headlong, rash, and troublesome sister State. General McQueen is in a rage because we are to send troops to Virginia.

Preston Hampton is in all the flush of his youth and beauty, six feet in stature; and after all only in his teens; he appeared in fine clothes and lemon-colored kid gloves to grace the scene. The camp in a fit of horse-play seized him and rubbed him in the mud. He fought manfully, but took it all naturally as a good joke.

Mrs. Frank Hampton knows already what civil war means. Her brother was in the New York Seventh Regiment, so roughly received in Baltimore. Frank will be in the opposite camp.

Good stories there may be and to spare for Russell, the man of the London Times, who has come over here to find out our weakness and our strength and to tell all the rest of the world about us.

CHAPTER IV. CAMDEN, S. C.

April 20, 1861—*April* 23, 1861

Camden, S. C., *April 20, 1861.*—Home again at Mulberry. In those last days of my stay in Charleston I did not find time to write a word.

And so we took Fort Sumter, *nous autres*; we—Mrs. Frank Hampton, and others—in the passageway of the Mills House between the reception-room and the drawing-room, for there we held a sofa against all comers. All the agreeable people South seemed to have flocked to Charleston at the first gun. That was after we had found out

---

[32] William Howard Russell, a native of Dublin, who served as a correspondent of the London Times during the Crimean War, the Indian Mutiny, the War of Secession and the Franco-German War. He has been familiarly known as "Bull Run Russell." In 1875 he was honorary Secretary to the Prince of Wales during the Prince's visit to India.

[33] The "Sally Baxter" of the recently published "Thackeray Letters to an American Family."

that bombarding did not kill anybody. Before that, we wept and prayed and took our tea in groups in our rooms, away from the haunts of men.

Captain Ingraham and his kind also took Fort Sumter—from the Battery with field-glasses and figures made with their sticks in the sand to show what ought to be done.

Wigfall, Chesnut, Miles, Manning, took it rowing about the harbor in small boats from fort to fort under the enemy's guns, with bombs bursting in air.

And then the boys and men who worked those guns so faithfully at the forts—they took it, too, in their own way.

Old Colonel Beaufort Watts told me this story and many more of the *jeunesse dorée* under fire. They took the fire easily, as they do most things. They had cotton bag bomb-proofs at Fort Moultrie, and when Anderson's shot knocked them about some one called out "Cotton is falling." Then down went the kitchen chimney, loaves of bread flew out, and they cheered gaily, shouting, "Breadstuffs are rising."

Willie Preston fired the shot which broke Anderson's flag-staff. Mrs. Hampton from Columbia telegraphed him, "Well done, Willie!" She is his grandmother, the wife, or widow, of General Hampton, of the Revolution, and the mildest, sweetest, gentlest of old ladies. This shows how the war spirit is waking us all up.

Colonel Miles (who won his spurs in a boat, so William Gilmore Simms[34] said) gave us this characteristic anecdote. They met a negro out in the bay rowing toward the city with some plantation supplies, etc. "Are you not afraid of Colonel Anderson's cannon?" he was asked. "No, sar, Mars Anderson ain't daresn't hit me; he know Marster wouldn't 'low it."

I have been sitting idly to-day looking out upon this beautiful lawn, wondering if this can be the same world I was in a few days ago. After the smoke and the din of the battle, a calm.

April 22d.—Arranging my photograph book. On the first page, Colonel Watts. Here goes a sketch of his life; romantic enough, surely: Beaufort Watts; bluest blood; gentleman to the tips of his fingers; chivalry incarnate. He was placed in charge of a large amount of money, in bank bills. The money belonged to the State and he was to deposit it in the bank. On the way he was obliged to stay over one night. He put the roll on a table at his bedside, locked himself in, and slept the sleep of the righteous. Lo, next day when he awaked, the money was gone. Well! all who knew him believed him innocent, of course. He searched and they searched, high and low, but to no purpose. The money had vanished. It was a damaging story, in spite of

---

[34] William Gilmore Simms, the Southern novelist, was born in Charleston in 1806. He was the author of a great many volumes dealing with Southern life, and at one time they were widely read.

his previous character, and a cloud rested on him.

Years afterward the house in which he had taken that disastrous sleep was pulled down. In the wall, behind the wainscot, was found his pile of money. How the rats got it through so narrow a crack it seemed hard to realize. Like the hole mentioned by Mercutio, it was not as deep as a well nor as wide as a church door, but it did for Beaufort Watts until the money was found. Suppose that house had been burned or the rats had gnawed up the bills past recognition?

People in power understood how this proud man suffered those many years in silence. Many men looked askance at him. The country tried to repair the work of blasting the man's character. He was made Secretary of Legation to Russia, and was afterward our Consul at Santa Fe de Bogota. When he was too old to wander far afield, they made him Secretary to all the Governors of South Carolina in regular succession.

I knew him more than twenty years ago as Secretary to the Governor. He was a made-up old battered dandy, the soul of honor. His eccentricities were all humored. Misfortune had made him sacred. He stood hat in hand before ladies and bowed as I suppose Sir Charles Grandison might have done. It was hard not to laugh at the purple and green shades of his overblack hair. He came at one time to show me the sword presented to Colonel Shelton for killing the only Indian who was killed in the Seminole war. We bagged Osceola and Micanopy under a flag of truce—that is, they were snared, not shot on the wing.

To go back to my knight-errant: he knelt, handed me the sword, and then kissed my hand. I was barely sixteen and did not know how to behave under the circumstances. He said, leaning on the sword, "My dear child, learn that it is a much greater liberty to shake hands with a lady than to kiss her hand. I have kissed the Empress of Russia's hand and she did not make faces at me." He looks now just as he did then. He is in uniform, covered with epaulettes, aigulettes, etc., shining in the sun, and with his plumed hat reins up his war-steed and bows low as ever.

Now I will bid farewell for a while as Othello did to all the "pomp, pride, and circumstance of glorious war," and come down to my domestic strifes and troubles. I have a sort of volunteer maid, the daughter of my husband's nurse, dear old Betsy. She waits on me because she so pleases. Besides, I pay her. She belongs to my father-in-law, who has too many slaves to care very much about their way of life. So Maria Whitaker came, all in tears. She brushes hair delightfully, and as she stood at my back I could see her face in the glass. "Maria, are you crying because all this war talk scares you?" said I. "No, ma'am." "What is the matter with you?" "Nothing more than common." "Now listen. Let the war end either way and you will be free. We will have to free you before we get out of this thing. Won't you be glad?"

"Everybody knows Mars Jeems wants us free, and it is only old Marster holds hard. He ain't going to free anybody any way, you see."

And then came the story of her troubles. "Now, Miss Mary, you see me married to Jeems Whitaker yourself. I was a good and faithful wife to him, and we were comfortable every way—good house, everything. He had no cause of complaint, but he has left me." "For heaven's sake! Why?" "Because I had twins. He says they are not his because nobody named Whitaker ever had twins."

Maria is proud in her way, and the behavior of this bad husband has nearly mortified her to death. She has had three children in two years. No wonder the man was frightened. But then Maria does not depend on him for anything. She was inconsolable, and I could find nothing better to say than, "Come, now, Maria! Never mind, your old Missis and Marster are so good to you. Now let us look up something for the twins." The twins are named "John and Jeems," the latter for her false loon of a husband. Maria is one of the good colored women. She deserved a better fate in her honest matrimonial attempt. But they do say she has a trying temper. Jeems was tried, and he failed to stand the trial.

April 23d.—Note the glaring inconsistencies of life. Our chatelaine locked up Eugene Sue, and returned even Washington Allston's novel with thanks and a decided hint that it should be burned; at least it should not remain in her house. Bad books are not allowed house room, except in the library under lock and key, the key in the Master's pocket; but bad women, if they are not white, or serve in a menial capacity, may swarm the house unmolested; the ostrich game is thought a Christian act. Such women are no more regarded as a dangerous contingent than canary birds would be.

If you show by a chance remark that you see some particular creature, more shameless than the rest, has no end of children, and no beginning of a husband, you are frowned down; you are talking on improper subjects. There are certain subjects pure-minded ladies never touch upon, even in their thoughts. It does not do to be so hard and cruel. It is best to let the sinners alone, poor things. If they are good servants otherwise, do not dismiss them; all that will come straight as they grow older, and it does! They are frantic, one and all, to be members of the church. The Methodist Church is not so pure-minded as to shut its eyes; it takes them up and turns them out with a high hand if they are found going astray as to any of the ten commandments.

CHAPTER V. MONTGOMERY, ALA.

April 27, 1861—*May* 20, 1861

Montgomery, Ala., *April* 27, 1861.—Here we are once more. Hon. Robert Barnwell came with us. His benevolent spectacles give him a most Pickwickian expression. We Carolinians revere his goodness above all things. Everywhere, when the car stopped, the people wanted a speech, and we had one stream of fervid oratory. We came along with a man whose wife lived in Washington. He was bringing her to Georgia as the safest place.

The Alabama crowd are not as confident of taking Fort Pickens as we were of taking Fort Sumter.

Baltimore is in a blaze. They say Colonel Ben Huger is in command there—son of the "Olmutz" Huger. General Robert E. Lee, son of Light Horse Harry Lee, has been made General-in-Chief of Virginia. With such men to the fore, we have hope. The New York Herald says, "Slavery must be extinguished, if in blood." It thinks we are shaking in our shoes at their great mass meetings. We are jolly as larks, all the same.

Mr. Chesnut has gone with Wade Hampton[35] to see President Davis about the legion Wade wants to get up.

The President came across the aisle to speak to me at church to-day. He was very cordial, and I appreciated the honor.

Wigfall is black with rage at Colonel Anderson's account of the fall of Sumter. Wigfall did behave magnanimously, but Anderson does not seem to see it in that light. "Catch me risking my life to save him again," says Wigfall. "He might have been man enough to tell the truth to those New Yorkers, however unpalatable to them a good word for us might have been. We did behave well to him. The only men of his killed, he killed himself, or they killed themselves firing a salute to their old striped rag."

Mr. Chesnut was delighted with the way Anderson spoke to him when he went to demand the surrender. They parted quite tenderly. Anderson said: "If we do not meet again on earth, I hope we may meet in Heaven." How Wigfall laughed at Anderson "giving Chesnut a howdy in the other world!"

---

[35] Wade Hampton was a son of another Wade Hampton, who was an aide to General Jackson at the battle of New Orleans, and a grandson of still another Wade Hampton, who was a general in the Revolution. He was not in favor of secession, but when the war began he enlisted as a private and then raised a command of infantry, cavalry, and artillery, which as "Hampton's Legion" won distinction in the war. After the war, he was elected Governor of South Carolina and was then elected to the United States Senate.

What a kind welcome the old gentlemen gave me! One, more affectionate and homely than the others, slapped me on the back. Several bouquets were brought me, and I put them in water around my plate. Then General Owens gave me some violets, which I put in my breastpin.

"Oh," said my "Gutta Percha" Hemphill,[36] "if I had known how those bouquets were to be honored I would have been up by daylight seeking the sweetest flowers!" Governor Moore came in, and of course seats were offered him. "This is a most comfortable chair," cried an overly polite person. "The most comfortable chair is beside Mrs. Chesnut," said the Governor, facing the music gallantly, as he sank into it gracefully. Well done, old fogies!

Browne said: "These Southern men have an awfully flattering Way with women." "Oh, so many are descendants of Irishmen, and so the blarney remains yet, even and in spite of their gray hairs!" For it was a group of silver-gray flatterers. Yes, blarney as well as bravery came in with the Irish.

At Mrs. Davis's reception dismal news, for civil war seems certain. At Mrs. Toombs's reception Mr. Stephens came by me. Twice before we have had it out on the subject of this Confederacy, once on the cars, coming from Georgia here, once at a supper, where he sat next to me. To-day he was not cheerful in his views. I called him half-hearted, and accused him of looking back. Man after man came and interrupted the conversation with some frivle-fravle, but we held on. He was deeply interesting, and he gave me some new ideas as to our dangerous situation. Fears for the future and not exultation at our successes pervade his discourse.

Dined at the President's and never had a pleasanter day. He is as witty as he is wise. He was very agreeable; he took me in to dinner. The talk was of Washington; nothing of our present difficulties.

A General Anderson from Alexandria, D. C., was in doleful dumps. He says the North are so much better prepared than we are. They are organized, or will be, by General Scott. We are in wild confusion. Their army is the best in the world. We are wretchedly armed, etc., etc. They have ships and arms that were ours and theirs.

Mrs. Walker, resplendently dressed, one of those gorgeously arrayed persons who fairly shine in the sun, tells me she mistook the inevitable Morrow for Mr. Chesnut, and added, "Pass over the affront to my powers of selection." I told her it was "an insult to the Palmetto flag." Think of a South Carolina Senator like that!

Men come rushing in from Washington with white lips, crying,

---

[36] John Hemphill was a native of South Carolina, who had removed to Texas, where he became Chief Justice of the Supreme Court of the State, and in 1858 was elected United States Senator.

"Danger, danger!" It is very tiresome to have these people always harping on this: "The enemy's troops are the finest body of men we ever saw." "Why did you not make friends of them," I feel disposed to say. We would have war, and now we seem to be letting our golden opportunity pass; we are not preparing for war. There is talk, talk, talk in that Congress—lazy legislators, and rash, reckless, headlong, devil-may-care, proud, passionate, unruly, raw material for soldiers. They say we have among us a regiment of spies, men and women, sent here by the wily Seward. Why? Our newspapers tell every word there is to be told, by friend or foe.

A two-hours' call from Hon. Robert Barnwell. His theory is, all would have been right if we had taken Fort Sumter six months ago. He made this very plain to me. He is clever, if erratic. I forget why it ought to have been attacked before. At another reception, Mrs. Davis was in fine spirits. Captain Dacier was here. Came over in his own yacht. Russell, of The London Times, wondered how we had the heart to enjoy life so thoroughly when all the Northern papers said we were to be exterminated in such a short time.

May 9th.—Virginia Commissioners here. Mr. Staples and Mr. Edmonston came to see me. They say Virginia "has no grievance; she comes out on a point of honor; could she stand by and see her sovereign sister States invaded?"

Sumter Anderson has been offered a Kentucky regiment. Can they raise a regiment in Kentucky against us? In Kentucky, our sister State?

Suddenly General Beauregard and his aide (the last left him of the galaxy who surrounded him in Charleston), John Manning, have gone—Heaven knows where, but out on a war-path certainly. Governor Manning called himself "the last rose of summer left blooming alone" of that fancy staff. A new fight will gather them again.

Ben McCulloch, the Texas Ranger, is here, and Mr. Ward,[37] my "Gutta Percha" friend's colleague from Texas. Senator Ward in appearance is the exact opposite of Senator Hemphill. The latter, with the face of an old man, has the hair of a boy of twenty. Mr. Ward is fresh and fair, with blue eyes and a boyish face, but his head is white as snow. Whether he turned it white in a single night or by slower process I do not know, but it is strangely out of keeping with his clear young eye. He is thin, and has a queer stooping figure.

This story he told me of his own experience. On a Western steamer there was a great crowd and no unoccupied berth, or sleeping place of any sort whatsoever in the gentlemen's cabin—saloon, I think they called it. He had taken a stateroom, 110, but he could not eject the

----

[37] Matthias Ward was a native of Georgia, but had removed to Texas in 1836, He vice a delegate to National Democratic Conventions, and in 1858 was appointed to acancy from Texas in the United States Senate, holding that office until 1860.

people who had already seized it and were asleep in it. Neither could the Captain. It would have been a case of revolver or "'leven inch Bowie-knife."

Near the ladies' Saloon the steward took pity on him. "This man," said he, "is 110, and I can find no place for him, poor fellow." There was a peep out of bright eyes: "I say, steward, have you a man 110 years old out there? Let us see him. He must be a natural curiosity." "We are overcrowded," was the answer, "and we can't find a place for him to sleep." "Poor old soul; bring him in here. We will take care of him."

"Stoop and totter," sniggered the steward to No. 110, "and go in."

"Ah," said Mr. Ward, "how those houris patted and pitied me and hustled me about and gave me the best berth! I tried not to look; I knew it was wrong, but I looked. I saw them undoing their back hair and was lost in amazement at the collapse when the huge hoop-skirts fell off, unheeded on the cabin floor."

. One beauty who was disporting herself near his curtain suddenly caught his eye. She stooped and gathered up her belongings as she said: "I say, stewardess, your old hundred and ten is a humbug. His eyes are too blue for anything," and she fled as he shut himself in, nearly frightened to death. I forget how it ended. There was so much laughing at his story I did not hear it all. So much for hoary locks and their reverence-inspiring power!

Russell, the wandering English newspaper correspondent, was telling how very odd some of our plantation habits were. He was staying at the house of an ex-Cabinet Minister, and Madame would stand on the back piazza and send her voice three fields off, calling a servant. Now that is not a Southern peculiarity. Our women are soft, and sweet, low-toned, indolent, graceful, quiescent. I dare say there are bawling, squalling, vulgar people everywhere.

May 13th.—We have been down from Montgomery on the boat to that God-forsaken landing, Portland, Ala. Found everybody drunk—that is, the three men who were there. At last secured a carriage to carry us to my brother-in-law's house. Mr. Chesnut had to drive seven miles, pitch dark, over an unknown road. My heart was in my mouth, which last I did not open.

Next day a patriotic person informed us that, so great was the war fever only six men could be found in Dallas County. I whispered to Mr. Chesnut: "We found three of the lone ones *hors de combat* at Portland." So much for the corps of reserves—alcoholized patriots.

Saw for the first time the demoralization produced by hopes of freedom. My mother's butler (whom I taught to read, sitting on his knife-board) contrived to keep from speaking to us. He was as efficient as ever in his proper place, but he did not come behind the scenes as usual and have a friendly chat. Held himself aloof so grand and stately we had to send him a "tip" through his wife Hetty, mother's maid, who, however, showed no signs of disaffection. She came to my bedside next morning with everything that was nice for breakfast. She had let me sleep till midday, and embraced me over and over again. I remarked: "What a capital cook they have here!" She curtsied to the ground. "I cooked every mouthful on that tray—as if I did not know what you liked to eat since you was a baby."

May 19th.—Mrs. Fitzpatrick says Mr. Davis is too gloomy for her. He says we must prepare for a long war and unmerciful reverses at first, because they are readier for war and so much stronger numerically. Men and money count so in war. "As they do everywhere else," said I, doubting her accurate account of Mr. Davis's spoken words, though she tried to give them faithfully. We need patience and persistence. There is enough and to spare of pluck and dash among us, the do-and-dare style.

I drove out with Mrs. Davis. She finds playing Mrs. President of this small confederacy slow work, after leaving friends such as Mrs. Emory and Mrs. Joe Johnston[38] in Washington. I do not blame her. The wrench has been awful with us all, but we don't mean to be turned into pillars of salt.

Mr. Mallory came for us to go to Mrs. Toombs's reception. Mr. Chesnut would not go, and I decided to remain with him. This proved a wise decision. First Mr. Hunter[39] came. In college they called him from his initials, R. M. T., "Run Mad Tom" Hunter. Just now I think he is the sanest, if not the wisest, man in our new-born Confederacy. I remember when I first met him. He sat next to me at some state dinner in Washington. Mr. Clay had taken me in to dinner, but seemed quite satisfied that my "other side" should take me off his hands.

Mr. Hunter did not know me, nor I him. I suppose he inquired, or looked at my card, lying on the table, as I looked at his. At any rate, we began a conversation which lasted steadily through the whole thing from soup to dessert. Mr. Hunter, though in evening dress, presented a rather tumbled-up appearance. His waistcoat wanted pulling down, and his hair wanted brushing. He delivered unconsciously that day a lecture on English literature which, if printed, I still think would be a valuable

---

[38] Mrs. Johnston was Lydia McLane, a daughter of Louis McLane, United States Senator from Delaware from 1827 to 1829, and afterward Minister to England. In 1831 he became Secretary of the Treasury and in 1833 Secretary of State. General Joseph E. Johnston was graduated from West Point in 1829 and had served in the Black Hawk, Seminole, and Mexican Wars. He resigned his commission in the United States Army on April 22, 1861.

[39] Mr. Hunter was a Virginian. He had long served in Congress, was twice speaker of the House, and in 1844 was elected a United States Senator, serving until 1861. He supported slavery and became active in the secession movement. At the Charleston Convention in 1860, he received the next highest vote to Stephen A. Douglas for President.

addition to that literature. Since then, I have always looked forward to a talk with the Senator from Virginia with undisguised pleasure. Next came Mr. Miles and Mr. Jameson, of South Carolina. The latter was President of our Secession Convention; also has written a life of Du Guesclin that is not so bad. So my unexpected reception was of the most charming. Judge Frost came a little later. They all remained until the return of the crowd from Mrs. Toombs's.

These men are not sanguine—I can't say, without hope, exactly. They are agreed in one thing: it is worth while to try a while, if only to get away from New England. Captain Ingraham was here, too. He is South Carolina to the tips of his fingers; yet he has it dyed in the wool—it is part of his nature—to believe the United States Navy can whip anything in the world. All of these little inconsistencies and contrarieties make the times very exciting. One never knows what tack any one of them will take at the next word.

May 20th.—Lunched at Mrs. Davis's; everything nice to eat, and I was ravenous. For a fortnight I have not even gone to the dinner table. Yesterday I was forced to dine on cold asparagus and blackberries, so repulsive in aspect was the other food they sent me. Mrs. Davis was as nice as the luncheon. When she is in the mood, I do not know so pleasant a person. She is awfully clever, always.

We talked of this move from Montgomery. Mr. Chesnut opposes it violently, because this is so central a position for our government. He wants our troops sent into Maryland in order to make our fight on the border, and so to encompass Washington. I see that the uncomfortable hotels here will at last move the Congress. Our statesmen love their ease, and it will be hot here in summer. "I do hope they will go," Mrs. Davis said. "The Yankees will make it hot for us, go where we will, and truly so if war comes." "And it, has come," said I. "Yes, I fancy these dainty folks may live to regret losing even the fare of the Montgomery hotels." "Never."

Mr. Chesnut has three distinct manias. The Maryland scheme is one, and he rushes off to Jeff Davis, who, I dare say, has fifty men every day come to him with infallible plans to save the country. If only he can keep his temper. Mrs. Davis says he answers all advisers in softly modulated, dulcet accents.

What a rough menagerie we have here. And if nice people come to see you, up walks an irate Judge, who engrosses the conversation and abuses the friends of the company generally; that is, abuses everybody and prophesies every possible evil to the country, provided he finds that denouncing your friends does not sufficiently depress you. Everybody has manias—up North, too, by the papers.

But of Mr. Chesnut's three crazes: Maryland is to be made the seat of war, old Morrow's idea of buying up steamers abroad for our coast defenses should be adopted, and, last of all, but far from the least, we must make much cotton and send it to England as a bank to draw on. The very cotton we have now, if sent across the water, would be a gold mine to us.

CHAPTER VI. CHARLESTON, S. C.

May 25, 1861—June 24, 1861

Charleston, S. C., *May 25, 1861.*—We have come back to South Carolina from the Montgomery Congress, stopping over at Mulberry. We came with R. M. T. Hunter and Mr. Barnwell. Mr. Barnwell has excellent reasons for keeping cotton at home, but I forget what they are. Generally, people take what he says, also Mr. Hunter's wisdom, as unanswerable. Not so Mr. Chesnut, who growls at both, much as he likes them. We also had Tom Lang and his wife, and Doctor Boykin. Surely there never was a more congenial party. The younger men had been in the South Carolina College while Mr. Barnwell was President. Their love and respect for him were immeasurable and he benignly received it, smiling behind those spectacles.

Met John Darby at Atlanta and told him he was Surgeon of the Hampton Legion, which delighted him. He had had adventures. With only a few moments on the platform to interchange confidences, he said he had remained a little too long in the Medical College in Philadelphia, where he was some kind of a professor, and they had been within an ace of hanging him as a Southern spy. "Rope was ready," he sniggered. At Atlanta when he unguardedly said he was fresh from Philadelphia, he barely escaped lynching, being taken for a Northern spy. "Lively life I am having among you, on both sides," he said, hurrying away. And I moaned, "Here was John Darby like to have been killed by both sides, and no time to tell me the curious coincidences." What marvelous experiences a little war begins to produce.

May 27th.—They look for a fight at Norfolk. Beauregard is there. I think if I were a man I'd be there, too. Also Harper's Ferry is to be attacked. The Confederate flag has been cut down at Alexandria by a man named Ellsworth,[40] who was in command of Zouaves. Jackson was the name of the person who shot Ellsworth in the act. Sixty of our cavalry have been taken by Sherman's brigade. Deeper and deeper we go in.

---

[40] Ephraim Elmer Ellsworth was a native of Saratoga County, New York. In 1860 he organized a regiment of Zouaves and became its Colonel. He accompanied Lincoln to Washington in 1861 and was soon sent with his regiment to Alexandria, where, on seeing a Confederate flag floating from a hotel, he personally rushed to the roof and tore it down. The owner of the hotel, a man named Jackson, met him as he was descending and shot him dead. Frank E. Brownell, one of Ellsworth's men, then killed Jackson.

Mary Boykin Chesnut

Thirty of Tom Boykin's company have come home from Richmond. They went as a rifle company, armed with muskets. They were sandhill tackeys—those fastidious ones, not very anxious to fight with anything, or in any way, I fancy. Richmond ladies had come for them in carriages, feted them, waved handkerchiefs to them, brought them dainties with their own hands, in the faith that every Carolinian was a gentleman, and every man south of Mason and Dixon's line a hero. But these are not exactly descendants of the Scotch Hay, who fought the Danes with his plowshare, or the oxen's yoke, or something that could hit hard and that came handy.

Johnny has gone as a private in Gregg's regiment. He could not stand it at home any longer. Mr. Chesnut was willing for him to go, because those sandhill men said "this was a rich man's war," and the rich men would be the officers and have an easy time and the poor ones would be privates. So he said: "Let the gentlemen set the example; let them go in the ranks." So John Chesnut is a gentleman private. He took his servant with him all the same.

Johnny reproved me for saying, "If I were a man, I would not sit here and dole and drink and drivel and forget the fight going on in Virginia." He said it was my duty not to talk so rashly and make enemies. He "had the money in his pocket to raise a company last fall, but it has slipped through his fingers, and now he is a common soldier." "You wasted it or spent it foolishly," said I. "I do not know where it has gone," said he. "There was too much consulting over me, too much good counsel was given to me, and everybody gave me different advice." "Don't you ever know your own mind?" "We will do very well in the ranks; men and officers all alike; we know everybody."

So I repeated Mrs. Lowndes's solemn words when she heard that South Carolina had seceded alone: "As thy days so shall thy strength be." Don't know exactly what I meant, but thought I must be impressive as he was going away. Saw him off at the train. Forgot to say anything there, but cried my eyes out.

Sent Mrs. Wigfall a telegram—"Where shrieks the wild sea-mew?" She answered: "Sea-mew at the Spotswood Hotel. Will shriek soon. I will remain here."

June 6th.—Davin! Have had a talk concerning him to-day with two opposite extremes of people.

Mrs. Chesnut, my mother-in-law, praises everybody, good and bad. "Judge not," she says. She is a philosopher; she would not give herself the pain to find fault. The Judge abuses everybody, and he does it so well—short, sharp, and incisive are his sentences, and he revels in condemning the world *en bloc*, as the French say. So nobody is the better for her good word, or the, worse for his bad one.

In Camden I found myself in a flurry of women. "Traitors," they cried. "Spies; they ought to be hanged; Davin is taken up, Dean and

Davis are his accomplices." "What has Davin done?" "He'll be hanged, never you mind." "For what?" "They caught him walking on the trestle work in the swamp, after no good, you may be sure." "They won't hang him for that!" "Hanging is too good for him!" "You wait till Colonel Chesnut comes." "He is a lawyer," I said, gravely. "Ladies, he will disappoint you. There will be no lynching if he goes to that meeting to-day. He will not move a step except by habeas corpus and trial by jury, and a quantity of bench and bar to speak long speeches."

Mr. Chesnut did come, and gave a more definite account of poor Davin's precarious situation. They had intercepted treasonable letters of his at the Post Office. I believe it was not a very black treason after all. At any rate, Mr. Chesnut spoke for him with might and main at the meeting. It was composed (the meeting) of intelligent men with cool heads. And they banished Davin to Fort Sumter. The poor Music Master can't do much harm in the casemates there. He may thank his stars that Mr. Chesnut gave him a helping hand. In the red hot state our public mind now is in there will be a short shrift for spies. Judge Withers said that Mr. Chesnut never made a more telling speech in his life than he did to save this poor Frenchman for whom Judge Lynch was ready. I had never heard of Davin in my life until I heard he was to be hanged.

Judge Stephen A. Douglas, the "little giant," is dead; one of those killed by the war, no doubt; trouble of mind.

Charleston people are thin-skinned. They shrink from Russell's touches. I find his criticisms mild. He has a light touch. I expected so much worse. Those Englishmen come, somebody says, with three P's—pen, paper, prejudices. I dread some of those after-dinner stories. As to that day in the harbor, he let us off easily. He says our men are so fine looking. Who denies it? Not one of us. Also that it is a silly impression which has gone abroad that men can not work in this climate. We live in the open air, and work like Trojans at all manly sports, riding hard, hunting, playing at being soldiers. These fine, manly specimens have been in the habit of leaving the coast when it became too hot there, and also of fighting a duel or two, if kept long sweltering under a Charleston sun. Handsome youths, whose size and muscle he admired so much as they prowled around the Mills House, would not relish hard work in the fields between May and December. Negroes stand a tropical or semitropical sun at noon-day better than white men. In fighting it is different. Men will not then mind sun, or rain, or wind.

Major Emory,[41] when he was ordered West, placed his resignation

---

[41] William H. Emory had served in Charleston harbor during the Nullification troubles of 1831-1836. In 1846 he went to California, afterward served in the Mexican War, and later assisted in running the boundary line between Mexico and the United States under the Gadsden Treaty of 1853. In 1854 he was in Kansas and in 1858 in Utah.

in the hands of his Maryland brothers. After the Baltimore row the brothers sent it in, but Maryland declined to secede. Mrs. Emory, who at least is two-thirds of that copartnership, being old Franklin's granddaughter, and true to her blood, tried to get it back. The President refused point blank, though she went on her knees. That I do not believe. The Franklin race are stiff-necked and stiff-kneed; not much given to kneeling to God or man from all accounts.

If Major Emory comes to us won't he have a good time? Mrs. Davis adores Mrs. Emory. No wonder I fell in love with her myself. I heard of her before I saw her in this wise. Little Banks told me the story. She was dancing at a ball when some bad accident maker for the Evening News rushed up and informed her that Major Emory had been massacred by ten Indians somewhere out West. She coolly answered him that she had later intelligence; it was not so. Turning a deaf ear then, she went on dancing. Next night the same officious fool met her with this congratulation: "Oh, Mrs. Emory, it was all a hoax! The Major is alive." She cried: "You are always running about with your bad news," and turned her back on him; or, I think it was, "You delight in spiteful stories," or, "You are a harbinger of evil." Banks is a newspaper man and knows how to arrange an anecdote for effect.

June 12th.—Have been looking at Mrs. O'Dowd as she burnished the "Meejor's arrms" before Waterloo. And I have been busy, too. My husband has gone to join Beauregard, somewhere beyond Richmond. I feel blue-black with melancholy. But I hope to be in Richmond before long myself. That is some comfort.

The war is making us all tenderly sentimental. No casualties yet, no real mourning, nobody hurt. So it is all parade, fife, and fine feathers. Posing we are *en grande tenue*. There is no imagination here to forestall woe, and only the excitement and wild awakening from every-day stagnant life are felt. That is, when one gets away from the two or three sensible men who are still left in the world.

When Beauregard's report of the capture of Fort Sumter was printed, Willie Ancrum said: "How is this? Tom Ancrum and Ham Boykin's names are not here. We thought from what they told us that they did most of the fighting."

Colonel Magruder[42] has done something splendid on the peninsula.

After resigning his commission, as related by the author, he was reappointed a Lieutenant-Colonel in the United States Army and took an active part in the war on the side of the North.

[42] John Bankhead Magruder was a graduate of West Point, who had served in the Mexican War, and afterward while stationed at Newport, R. I., had become famous for his entertainments. When Virginia seceded, he resigned his commission in the United States Army. After the war he settled in Houston, Texas. The battle of Big Bethel was fought on June 10, 1861. The Federals lost in killed and wounded about 100, among them Theodore Winthrop, of New York, author of Cecil Dreeme. The Confederate losses were very slight.

Bethel is the name of the battle. Three hundred of the enemy killed, they say.

Our people, Southerners, I mean, continue to drop in from the outside world. And what a contempt those who seceded a few days sooner feel for those who have just come out! A Camden notable, called Jim Velipigue, said in the street to-day: "At heart Robert E. Lee is against us; that I know." What will not people say in war times! Also, he said that Colonel Kershaw wanted General Beauregard to change the name of the stream near Manassas Station. Bull's Run is so unrefined. Beauregard answered: "Let us try and make it as great a name as your South Carolina Cowpens."[43]

Mrs. Chesnut, born in Philadelphia, can not see what right we have to take Mt. Vernon from our Northern sisters. She thinks that ought to be common to both parties. We think they will, get their share of this world's goods, do what we may, and we will keep Mt. Vernon if we can. No comfort in Mr. Chesnut's letter from Richmond. Unutterable confusion prevails, and discord already.

In Charleston a butcher has been clandestinely supplying the Yankee fleet outside the bar with beef. They say he gave the information which led to the capture of the Savannah. They will hang him.

Mr. Petigru alone in South Carolina has not seceded. When they pray for our President, he gets up from his knees. He might risk a prayer for Mr. Davis. I doubt if it would seriously do Mr. Davis any good. Mr. Petigru is too clever to think himself one of the righteous whose prayers avail so overly much. Mr. Petigru's disciple, Mr. Bryan, followed his example. Mr. Petigru has such a keen sense of the ridiculous he must be laughing in his sleeve at the hubbub this untimely trait of independence has raised.

Looking out for a battle at Manassas Station. I am always ill. The name of my disease is a longing to get away from here and to go to Richmond.

June 19th.—In England Mr. Gregory and Mr. Lyndsey rise to say a good word for us. Heaven reward them; shower down its choicest blessings on their devoted heads, as the fiction folks say.

Barnwell Heyward telegraphed me to meet him at Kingsville, but I was at Cool Spring, Johnny's plantation, and all my clothes were at Sandy Hill, our home in the Sand Hills; so I lost that good opportunity of the very nicest escort to Richmond. Tried to rise above the agonies of every-day life. Read Emerson; too restless—Manassas on the brain.

Russell's letters are filled with rubbish about our wanting an

---

[43] The battle of the Cowpens in South Carolina was fought on January 17, 1781; the British, under Colonel Tarleton, being defeated by General Morgan, with a loss to the British of 300 killed and wounded and 500 prisoners.

English prince to reign over us. He actually intimates that the noisy arming, drumming, marching, proclaiming at the North, scares us. Yes, as the making of faces and turning of somersaults by the Chinese scared the English.

Mr. Binney[44] has written a letter. It is in the Intelligencer of Philadelphia. He offers Lincoln his life and fortune; all that he has put at Lincoln's disposal to conquer us. Queer; we only want to separate from them, and they put such an inordinate value on us. They are willing to risk all, life and limb, and all their money to keep us, they love us so.

Mr. Chesnut is accused of firing the first shot, and his cousin, an ex-West Pointer, writes in a martial fury. They confounded the best shot made on the Island the day of the picnic with the first shot at Fort Sumter. This last is claimed by Captain James. Others say it was one of the Gibbeses who first fired. But it was Anderson who fired the train which blew up the Union. He slipped into Fort Sumter that night, when we expected to talk it all over. A letter from my husband dated, "Headquarters, Manassas Junction, June 16, 1861":

MY DEAR MARY: I wrote you a short letter from Richmond last Wednesday, and came here next day. Found the camp all busy and preparing for a vigorous defense. We have here at this camp seven regiments, and in the same command, at posts in the neighborhood, six others—say, ten thousand good men. The General and the men feel confident that they can whip twice that number of the enemy, at least.

I have been in the saddle for two days, all day, with the General, to become familiar with the topography of the country, and the posts he intends to assume, and the communications between them.

We learned General Johnston has evacuated Harper's Ferry, and taken up his position at Winchester, to meet the advancing column of McClellan, and to avoid being cut off by the three columns which were advancing upon him. Neither Johnston nor Beauregard considers Harper's Ferry as very important in a strategic point of view.

I think it most probable that the next battle you will hear of will be between the forces of Johnston and McClellan.

I think what we particularly need is a head in the field—a Major-General to combine and conduct all the forces as well as plan a general and energetic campaign. Still, we have all confidence that we will defeat the enemy whenever and wherever we meet in general engagement. Although the majority of the people just around here are with us, still there are many who are against us.

[44] Horace Binney, one of the foremost lawyers of Philadelphia, who was closely associated with the literary, scientific, and philanthropic interests of his time. His wife was a sister of Mrs. Chesnut, the author's mother-in-law.

God bless you.

Yours,

JAMES CHESNUT, JR.

Mary Hammy and myself are off for Richmond. Rev. Mr. Meynardie, of the Methodist persuasion, goes with us. We are to be under his care. War-cloud lowering.

Isaac Hayne, the man who fought a duel with Ben Alston across the dinner-table and yet lives, is the bravest of the brave. He attacks Russell in the Mercury—in the public prints—for saying we wanted an English prince to the fore. Not we, indeed! Every man wants to be at the head of affairs himself. If he can not be king himself, then a republic, of course. It was hardly necessary to do more than laugh at Russell's absurd idea. There was a great deal of the wildest kind of talk at the Mills House. Russell writes candidly enough of the British in India. We can hardly expect him to suppress what is to our detriment.

June 24th.—Last night I was awakened by loud talking and candles flashing, tramping of feet, growls dying away in the distance, loud calls from point to point in the yard. Up I started, my heart in my mouth. Some dreadful thing had happened, a battle, a death, a horrible accident. Some one was screaming aloft—that is, from the top of the stairway, hoarsely like a boatswain in a storm. Old Colonel Chesnut was storming at the sleepy negroes looking for fire, with lighted candles, in closets and everywhere else. I dressed and came upon the scene of action.

"What is it? Any news?" "No, no, only mamma smells a smell; she thinks something is burning somewhere." The whole yard was alive, literally swarming. There are sixty or seventy people kept here to wait upon this household, two-thirds of them too old or too young to be of any use, but families remain intact. The old Colonel has a magnificent voice. I am sure it can be heard for miles. Literally, he was roaring from the piazza, giving orders to the busy crowd who were hunting the smell of fire.

Old Mrs. Chesnut is deaf; so she did not know what a commotion she was creating. She is very sensitive to bad odors. Candles have to be taken out of the room to be snuffed. Lamps are extinguished only in the porticoes, or farther afield. She finds violets oppressive; can only tolerate a single kind of sweet rose. A tea-rose she will not have in her room. She was totally innocent of the storm she had raised, and in a mild, sweet voice was suggesting places to be searched. I was weak enough to laugh hysterically. The bombardment of Fort Sumter was nothing to this.

After this alarm, enough to wake the dead, the smell was found. A family had been boiling soap. Around the soap-pot they had swept up some woolen rags. Raking up the fire to make all safe before going to

bed, this was heaped up with the ashes, and its faint smoldering taintᴜ_
the air, at least to Mrs. Chesnut's nose, two hundred yards or more
away.

Yesterday some of the negro men on the plantation were found
with pistols. I have never before seen aught about any negro to show
that they knew we had a war on hand in which they have any interest.

Mrs. John de Saussure bade me good-by and God bless you. I was
touched. Camden people never show any more feeling or sympathy
than red Indians, except at a funeral. It is expected of all to howl then,
and if you don't "show feeling," indignation awaits the delinquent.

CHAPTER VII. RICHMOND, VA.

June 27, 1861—*July* 4, 1861

Richmond, Va., *June 27, 1861.*—Mr. Meynardie was perfect in the
part of traveling companion. He had his pleasures, too. The most pious
and eloquent of parsons is human, and he enjoyed the converse of the
"eminent persons" who turned up on every hand and gave their views
freely on all matters of state.

Mr. Lawrence Keitt joined us *en route*. With him came his wife
and baby. We don't think alike, but Mr. Keitt is always original and
entertaining. Already he pronounces Jeff Davis a failure and his
Cabinet a farce. "Prophetic," I suggested, as he gave his opinion before
the administration had fairly got under way. He was fierce in his fault-
finding as to Mr. Chesnut's vote for Jeff Davis. He says Mr. Chesnut
overpersuaded the Judge, and those two turned the tide, at least with the
South Carolina delegation. We wrangled, as we always do. He says
Howell Cobb's common sense might have saved us.

Two quiet, unobtrusive Yankee school-teachers were on the train. I
had spoken to them, and they had told me all about themselves. So I
wrote on a scrap of paper, "Do not abuse our home and house so before
these Yankee strangers, going North. Those girls are schoolmistresses
returning from whence they came."

Soldiers everywhere. They seem to be in the air, and certainly to
fill all space. Keitt quoted a funny Georgia man who says we try our
soldiers to see if they are hot enough before we enlist them. If , when
water is thrown on them they do not sizz, they won't do; their
patriotism is too cool.

To show they were wide awake and sympathizing enthusiastically,
every woman from every window of every house we passed waved a
handkerchief, if she had one. This fluttering of white flags from every
side never ceased from Camden to Richmond. Another new
symptom—Parties of girls came to every station simply to look at the
troops passing. They always stood (the girls , I mean) in solid phalanx,

and as the sun was generally in their eyes, they made faces. Mary
Hammy never tired of laughing at this peculiarity of her sister patriots.

At the depot in Richmond, Mr. Mallory, with Wigfall and Garnett,
met us. We had no cause to complain of the warmth of our reception.
They had a carriage for us, and our rooms were taken at the Spotswood.
But then the people who were in the rooms engaged for us had not
departed at the time they said they were going. They lingered among
the delights of Richmond, and we knew of no law to make them keep
their words and go. Mrs. Preston had gone for a few days to Manassas.
So we took her room. Mrs. Davis is as kind as ever. She met us in one
of the corridors accidentally, and asked us to join her party and to take
our meals at her table. Mr. Preston came, and we moved into a room so
small there was only space for a bed, wash-stand, and glass over it. My
things were hung up out of the way on nails behind the door.

As soon as my husband heard we had arrived, he came, too. After
dinner he sat smoking, the solitary chair of the apartment tilted against
the door as he smoked, and my poor dresses were fumigated. I
remonstrated feebly. "War times," said he; "nobody is fussy now.
When I go back to Manassas to-morrow you will be awfully sorry you
snubbed me about those trumpery things up there." So he smoked the
pipe of peace, for I knew that his remarks were painfully true. As soon
as he was once more under the enemy's guns, I would repent in
sackcloth and ashes.

Captain Ingraham came with Colonel Lamar.[45] The latter said he
could only stay five minutes; he was obliged to go back at once to his
camp. That was a little before eight. However, at twelve he was still
talking to us on that sofa. We taunted him with his fine words to the the
F. F. V. crowd before the Spotswood: "Virginia has no grievance. She
raises her strong arm to catch the blow aimed at her weaker sisters." He
liked it well, however, that we knew his speech by heart.

This Spotswood is a miniature world. The war topic is not so much
avoided, as that everybody has some personal dignity to take care of
and everybody else is indifferent to it. I mean the "personal dignity of"
autrui. In this wild confusion everything likely and unlikely is told you,
and then everything is as flatly contradicted. At any rate, it is safest not
to talk of the war.

Trescott was telling us how they laughed at little South Carolina in

---

[45] Lucius Quintus Cincinnatus Lamar, a native of Georgia and of Huguenot descent,
who got his classical names from his father: his father got them from an uncle who
claimed the privilege of bestowing upon his nephew the full name of his favorite hero.
When the war began, Mr. Lamar had lived for some years in Mississippi, where he had
become successful. as a lawyer and had been elected to Congress. He entered the
Confederate Army as the Colonel of a Mississippi regiment. He served in Congress after
the war and was elected to the United States Senate in 1877. In 1885 he became Secretary
of the Interior, and in 1888, a justice of the United States Supreme Court.

Washington. People said it was almost as large as Long Island, which is hardly more than a tailfeather of New York. Always there is a child who sulks and won't play; that was our role. And we were posing as San Marino and all model-spirited, though small, republics, pose.

He tells us that Lincoln is a humorist. Lincoln sees the fun of things; he thinks if they had left us in a corner or out in the cold a while pouting, with our fingers in our mouth, by hook or by crook he could have got us back, but Anderson spoiled all.

In Mrs. Davis's drawing-room last night, the President took a seat by me on the sofa where I sat. He talked for nearly an hour. He laughed at our faith in our own powers. We are like the British. We think every Southerner equal to three Yankees at least. We will have to be equivalent to a dozen now. After his experience of the fighting qualities of Southerners in Mexico, he believes that we will do all that can be done by pluck and muscle, endurance, and dogged courage, dash, and red-hot patriotism. And yet his tone was not sanguine. There was a sad refrain running through it all. For one thing, either way, he thinks it will be a long war. That floored me at once. It has been too long for me already. Then he said, before the end came we would have many a bitter experience. He said only fools doubted the courage of the Yankees, or their willingness to fight when they saw fit. And now that we have stung their pride, we have roused them till they will fight like devils.

Mrs. Bradley Johnson is here, a regular heroine. She outgeneraled the Governor of North Carolina in some way and has got arms and clothes and ammunition for her husband's regiment.[46] There was some joke. The regimental breeches were all wrong, but a tailor righted that—hind part before, or something odd.

Captain Hartstein came to-day with Mrs. Bartow. Colonel Bartow is Colonel of a Georgia regiment now in Virginia. He was the Mayor of Savannah who helped to wake the patriotic echoes the livelong night under my sleepless head into the small hours in Charleston in November last. His wife is a charming person, witty and wise, daughter of Judge Berrien. She had on a white muslin apron with pink bows on the pockets. It gave her a gay and girlish air, and yet she must be as old as I am.

Mr. Lamar, who does not love slavery more than Sumner does, nor than I do, laughs at the compliment New England pays us. We want to separate from them; to be rid of the Yankees forever at any price. And they hate us so, and would clasp us, or grapple us, as Polonius has it, to their bosoms "with hooks of steel." We are an unwilling bride. I think

---

[46] Bradley Tyler Johnson, a native of Maryland, and graduate of Princeton, who had studied law at Harvard. At the beginning of the war he organized a company at his own expense in defense of the South. He was the author of a *Life of General Joseph E. Johnston.*

incompatibility of temper began when it was made plain to us that we got all the opprobrium of slavery and they all the money there was in it with their tariff.

Mr. Lamar says, the young men are light-hearted because there is a fight on hand, but those few who look ahead, the clear heads, they see all the risk, the loss of land, limb, and life, home, wife, and children. As in "the brave days of old," they take to it for their country's sake. They are ready and willing, come what may. But not so light-hearted as the *jeunesse dorée.*

June 29th.—Mrs. Preston, Mrs. Wigfall, Mary Hammy and I drove in a fine open carriage to see the *Champ de Mars.* It was a grand tableau out there. Mr. Davis rode a beautiful gray horse, the Arab Edwin de Leon brought him from Egypt. His worst enemy will allow that he is a consummate rider, graceful and easy in the saddle, and Mr. Chesnut, who has talked horse with his father ever since he was born, owns that Mr. Davis knows more about horses than any man he has met yet. General Lee was there with him; also Joe Davis and Wigfall acting as his aides.

Poor Mr. Lamar has been brought from his camp—paralysis or some sort of shock. Every woman in the house is ready to rush into the Florence Nightingale business. I think I will wait for a wounded man, to make my first effort as Sister of Charity. Mr. Lamar sent for me. As everybody went, Mr. Davis setting the example, so did I. Lamar will not die this time. Will men flatter and make eyes, until their eyes close in death, at the ministering angels? He was the same old Lamar of the drawing-room.

It is pleasant at the President's table. My seat is next to Joe Davis, with Mr. Browne on the other side, and Mr. Mallory opposite. There is great constraint, however. As soon as I came I repeated what the North Carolina man said on the cars, that North Carolina had 20,000 men ready and they were kept back by Mr. Walker, etc. The President caught something of what I was saying, and asked me to repeat it, which I did, although I was scared to death. "Madame, when you see that person tell him his statement is false. We are too anxious here for troops to refuse a man who offers himself, not to speak of 20,000 men." Silence ensued—of the most profound.

Uncle H. gave me three hundred dollars for his daughter Mary's expenses, making four in all that I have of hers. He would pay me one hundred, which he said he owed my husband for a horse. I thought it an excuse to lend me money. I told him I had enough and to spare for all my needs until my Colonel came home from the wars.

Ben Allston, the Governor's son, is here—came to see me; does not show much of the wit of the Petigrus; pleasant person, however. Mr. Brewster and Wigfall came at the same time. The former, chafing at Wigfall's anomalous position here, gave him fiery advice. Mr.

Wigfall was calm and full of common sense. A brave man, and without a thought of any necessity for displaying his temper, he said: "Brewster, at this time, before the country is strong and settled in her new career, it would be disastrous for us, the head men, to engage in a row among ourselves."

As I was brushing flies away and fanning the prostrate Lamar, I reported Mr. Davis's conversation of the night before. "He is all right," said Mr. Lamar, "the fight had to come. We are men, not women. The quarrel had lasted long enough. We hate each other so, the fight had to come. Even Homer's heroes, after they had stormed and scolded enough, fought like brave men, long and well. If the athlete, Sumner, had stood on his manhood and training and struck back when Preston Brooks assailed him, Preston Brooks's blow need not have been the opening skirmish of the war. Sumner's country took up the fight because he did not. Sumner chose his own battle-field, and it was the worse for us. What an awful blunder that Preston Brooks business was!" Lamar said Yankees did not fight for the fun of it; they always made it pay or let it alone.

Met Mr. Lyon with news, indeed—a man here in the midst of us, taken with Lincoln's passports, etc., in his pocket—a palpable spy. Mr. Lyon said he would be hanged—in all human probability, that is.

A letter from my husband written at Camp Pickens, and saying: "If you and Mrs. Preston can make up your minds to leave Richmond, and can come up to a nice little country house near Orange Court House, we could come to see you frequently while the army is stationed here. It would be a safe place for the present, near the scene of action, and directly in the line of news from all sides." So we go to Orange Court House.

Read the story of Soulouque,[47] the Haytian man: he has wonderful interest just now. Slavery has to go, of course, and joy go with it. These Yankees may kill us and lay waste our land for a while, but conquer us—never!

July 4th.—Russell abuses us in his letters. People here care a great deal for what Russell says, because he represents the London Times, and the Times reflects the sentiment of the English people. How we do cling to the idea of an alliance with England or France! Without France even Washington could not have done it.

We drove to the camp to see the President present a flag to a Maryland regiment. Having lived on the battlefield (Kirkwood), near

---

[47] Faustin Elie Soulouque, a negro slave of Hayti, who, having been freed, took part in the insurrection against the French in 1803, and rose by successive steps until in August, 1849, by the unanimous action of the parliament, he was proclaimed emperor.

Camden,[48] we have an immense respect for the Maryland line. When our militia in that fight ran away, Colonel Howard and the Marylanders held their own against Rawdon, Cornwallis, and the rest, and everywhere around are places named for a doughty captain killed in our defense—Kirkwood, De Kalb, etc. The last, however, was a Prussian count. A letter from my husband, written June 22d, has just reached me. He says:

"We are very strongly posted, entrenched, and have now at our command about 15,000 of the best troops in the world. We have besides, two batteries of artillery, a regiment of cavalry, and daily expect a battalion of flying artillery from Richmond. We have sent forward seven regiments of infantry and rifles toward Alexandria. Our outposts have felt the enemy several times, and in every instance the enemy recoils. General Johnston has had several encounters—the advancing columns of the two armies—and with him, too, the enemy, although always superior in numbers, are invariably driven back.

"There is great deficiency in the matter of ammunition. General Johnston's command, in the very face of overwhelming numbers, have only thirty rounds each. If they had been well provided in this respect, they could and would have defeated Cadwallader and Paterson with great ease. I find the opinion prevails throughout the army that there is great imbecility and shameful neglect in the War Department.

"Unless the Republicans fall back, we must soon come together on both lines, and have a decided engagement. But the opinion prevails here that Lincoln's army will not meet us if they can avoid it. They have already fallen back before a slight check from 400 of Johnston's men. They had 700 and were badly beaten. You have no idea how dirty and irksome the camp life is. You would hardly know your best friend in camp guise."

Noise of drums, tramp of marching regiments all day long; rattling of artillery wagons, bands of music, friends from every quarter coming in. We ought to be miserable and anxious, and yet these are pleasant days. Perhaps we are unnaturally exhilarated and excited.

Heard some people in the drawing-room say: "Mrs. Davis's ladies are not young, are not pretty," and I am one of them. The truthfulness of the remark did not tend to alleviate its bitterness. We must put Maggie Howell and Mary Hammy in the foreground, as youth and beauty are in request. At least they are young things—bright spots in a somber-tinted picture. The President does not forbid our going, but he is very much averse to it. We are consequently frightened by our own audacity, but we are wilful women, and so we go.

---

[48] At Camden in August, 1780, was fought a battle between General Gates and Lord Cornwallis, in which Gates was defeated. In April of the following year near Camden, Lord Rawdon defeated General Greene.

CHAPTER VIII. FAUQUIER WHITE SULPHUR SPRINGS, VA.

July 6, 1861—*July* 11, 1861

Fauquier White Sulphur Springs, Va., *July 6, 1861.*—Mr. Brewster came here with us. The cars were jammed with soldiers to the muzzle. They were very polite and considerate, and we had an agreeable journey, in spite of heat, dust, and crowd. Rev. Robert Barnwell was with us. He means to organize a hospital for sick and wounded. There was not an inch of standing-room even; so dusty, so close, but everybody in tip-top spirits.

Mr. Preston and Mr. Chesnut met us at Warrenton. Saw across the lawn, but did not speak to them, some of Judge Campbell's family. There they wander disconsolate, just outside the gates of their Paradise: a resigned Judge of the Supreme Court of the United States; resigned, and for a cause that he is hardly more than half in sympathy with, Judge Campbell's is one of the hardest cases.

July 7th.—This water is making us young again. How these men enjoy the baths. They say Beauregard can stop the way with sixty thousand; that many are coming.

An antique female, with every hair curled and frizzed, said to be a Yankee spy, sits opposite us. Brewster solemnly wondered "with eternity and the judgment to come so near at hand, how she could waste her few remaining minutes curling her hair." He bade me be very polite, for she would ask me questions. When we were walking away from table, I demanded his approval of my self-control under such trying circumstances. It seems I was not as calm and forbearing as I thought myself. Brewster answered with emphasis: "Do you always carry brickbats like that in your pocket ready for the first word that offends you? You must not do so, when you are with spies from the other side." I do not feel at all afraid of spies hearing anything through me, for I do not know anything.

But our men could not tarry with us in these cool shades and comfortable quarters, with water unlimited, excellent table, etc. They have gone back to Manassas, and the faithful Brewster with them to bring us the latest news. They left us in excellent spirits, which we shared until they were out of sight. We went with them to Warrenton, and then heard that General Johnston was in full retreat, and that a column was advancing upon Beauregard. So we came back, all forlorn. If our husbands are taken prisoners, what will they do with them? Are they soldiers or traitors?

Mrs. Ould read us a letter from Richmond. How horrified they are there at Joe Johnston's retreating. And the enemies of the War Department accuse Walker of not sending General Johnston ammunition in sufficient quantities; say that is the real cause of his retreat. Now will they not make the ears of that slow-coach, the Secretary of War, buzz?

Mrs. Preston's maid Maria has a way of rushing in—"Don't you hear the cannon?" We fly to the windows, lean out to our waists, pull all the hair away from our ears, but can not hear it. Lincoln wants four hundred millions of money and men in proportion. Can he get them? He will find us a heavy handful. Midnight. I hear Maria's guns.

We are always picking up some good thing of the rough Illinoisan's saying. Lincoln objects to some man—"Oh, he is too *interruptious*"; that is a horrid style of man or woman, the interruptious. I know the thing, but had no name for it before.

July 9th.—Our battle summer. May it be our first and our last, so called. After all we have not had any of the horrors of war. Could there have been a gayer, or pleasanter, life than we led in Charleston. And Montgomery, how exciting it all was there! So many clever men and women congregated from every part of the South. Mosquitoes, and a want of neatness, and a want of good things to eat, drove us away. In Richmond the girls say it is perfectly delightful. We found it so, too, but the bickering and quarreling have begun there.

At table to-day we heard Mrs. Davis's ladies described. They were said to wear red frocks and flats on their heads. We sat mute as mice. One woman said she found the drawing-room of the Spotswood was warm, stuffy, and stifling. "Poor soul," murmured the inevitable Brewster, "and no man came to air her in the moonlight stroll, you know. Why didn't somebody ask her out on the piazza to see the comet?" Heavens above, what philandering was done in the name of the comet! When you stumbled on a couple on the piazza they lifted their eyes, and "comet" was the only word you heard. Brewster came back with a paper from Washington with terrific threats of what they will do to us. Threatened men live long.

There was a soft, sweet, low, and slow young lady opposite to us. She seemed so gentle and refined, and so uncertain of everything. Mr. Brewster called her Miss Albina McClush, who always asked her maid when a new book was mentioned, "Seraphina, have I perused that volume?"

Mary Hammy, having a *fiancé* in the wars, is inclined at times to be sad and tearful. Mrs. Preston quoted her negro nurse to her: "Never take any more trouble in your heart than you can kick off at the end of your toes."

July 11th.—We did hear cannon to-day. The woman who slandered Mrs. Davis's republican court, of which we are honorable members, by saying they—well, were not young; that they wore gaudy colors, and dressed badly—I took an inventory to-day as to her charms. She is darkly, deeply, beautifully freckled; she wears a wig which is kept in place by a tiara of mock jewels; she has the fattest of arms and wears black bead bracelets.

The one who is under a cloud, shadowed as a Yankee spy, has confirmed our worst suspicions. She exhibited unholy joy, as she reported seven hundred sick soldiers in the hospital at Culpeper, and that Beauregard had sent a flag of truce to Washington.

What a night we had! Maria had seen suspicious persons hovering about all day, and Mrs. Preston a ladder which could easily be placed so as to reach our rooms. Mary Hammy saw lights glancing about among the trees, and we all heard guns. So we sat up. Consequently, I am writing in bed to-day. A letter from my husband saying, in particular: "Our orders are to move on," the date, July 10th. "Here we are still and no more prospect of movement now than when I last wrote to you. It is true, however, that the enemy is advancing slowly in our front, and we are preparing to receive him. He comes in great force, being more than three times our number."

The spy, so-called, gave us a parting shot: said Beauregard had arrested her brother in order that he might take a fine horse which the aforesaid brother was riding. Why? Beauregard, at a moment's notice, could have any horse in South Carolina, or Louisiana, for that matter. This man was arrested and sent to Richmond, and "will be acquitted as they always are," said Brewster. "They send them first to Richmond to see and hear everything there; then they acquit them, and send them out of the country by way of Norfolk to see everything there. But, after all, what does it matter? They have no need for spies: our newspapers keep no secrets hid. The thoughts of our hearts are all revealed. Everything with us is open and aboveboard.

"At Bethel the Yankees fired too high. Every daily paper is jeering them about it yet. They'll fire low enough next time, but no newspaper man will be there to get the benefit of their improved practise, alas!"

CHAPTER IX. RICHMOND, VA.

July 13, 1861—*September* 2, 1861

Richmond, Va., *July 13, 1861.*—Now we feel safe and comfortable. We can not be flanked. Mr. Preston met us at Warrenton. Mr. Chesnut doubtless had too many spies to receive from Washington, galloping in with the exact numbers of the enemy done up in their back hair.

Wade Hampton is here; Doctor Nott also—Nott and Glyddon known to fame. Everybody is here, en route for the army, or staying for the meeting of Congress.

Lamar is out on crutches. His father-in-law, once known only as the humorist Longstreet,[49] author of Georgia Scenes, now a staid Methodist, who has outgrown the follies of his youth, bore him off to-day. They say Judge Longstreet has lost the keen sense of fun that illuminated his life in days of yore. Mrs. Lamar and her daughter were here.

The President met us cordially, but he laughed at our sudden retreat, with baggage lost, etc. He tried to keep us from going; said it was a dangerous experiment. Dare say he knows more about the situation of things than he chooses to tell us.

To-day in the drawing-room, saw a *vivandière* in the flesh. She was in the uniform of her regiment, but wore Turkish pantaloons. She frisked about in her hat and feathers; did not uncover her head as a man would have done; played the piano; and sang war-songs. She had no drum, but she gave us rataplan. She was followed at every step by a mob of admiring soldiers and boys.

Yesterday, as we left the cars, we had a glimpse of war. It was the saddest sight: the memory of it is hard to shake off—sick soldiers, not wounded ones. There were quite two hundred (they said) lying about as best they might on the platform. Robert Barnwell[50] was there doing all he could. Their pale, ghastly faces! So here is one of the horrors of war we had not reckoned on. There were many good men and women with Robert Barnwell, rendering all the service possible in the circumstances.

Just now I happened to look up and saw Mr. Chesnut with a smile on his face watching me from the passageway. I flew across the room, and as I got half-way saw Mrs. Davis touch him on the shoulder. She said he was to go at once into Mr. Davis's room, where General Lee and General Cooper were. After he left us, Mrs. Davis told me General Beauregard had sent Mr. Chesnut here on , some army business.

July 14th.—Mr. Chesnut remained closeted with the President and General Lee all the afternoon. The news does not seem pleasant. At least, he is not inclined to tell me any of it. He satisfied himself with telling me how sensible and soldierly this handsome General Lee is. General Lee's military sagacity was also his theme. of course the President dominated the party, as well by his weight of brain as by his position. I did not care a fig for a description of the war council. I wanted to know what is in the wind now?

July 16th.—Dined to-day at the President's table. Joe Davis, the nephew, asked me if I liked white port wine. I said I did not know; "all

---

[49] Augustus Baldwin Longstreet had great distinction in the South as a lawyer, clergyman, teacher, journalist, and author, and was successively president of five different colleges. His Georgia Scenes, a series of humorous papers, enjoyed great popularity for many years.

[50] Rev. Robert Barnwell, nephew of Hon. Robert Barnwell, established in Richmond a hospital for South Carolinians.

that I had ever known had been dark red." So he poured me out a glass. I drank it, and it nearly burned up my mouth and throat. It was horrid, but I did not let him see how it annoyed me. I pretended to be glad that any one found me still young enough to play off a practical joke upon me. It was thirty years since I had thought of such a thing.

Met Colonel Baldwin in the drawing-room. He pointed significantly to his Confederate colonel's buttons and gray coat. At the White Sulphur last summer he was a "Union man" to the last point. "How much have you changed besides your coat?" "I was always true to our country," he said. "She leaves me no choice now."

As far as I can make out, Beauregard sent Mr. Chesnut to the President to gain permission for the forces of Joe Johnston and Beauregard to join, and, united, to push the enemy, if possible, over the Potomac. Now every day we grow weaker and they stronger; so we had better give a telling blow at once. Already, we begin to cry out for more ammunition, and already the blockade is beginning to shut it all out.

A young Emory is here. His mother writes him to go back. Her Franklin blood certainly calls him with no uncertain sound to the Northern side, while his fatherland is wavering and undecided, split in half by factions. Mrs. Wigfall says he is half inclined to go. She wondered that he did not. With a father in the enemy's army, he will always be "suspect" here, let the President and Mrs. Davis do for him what they will.

I did not know there was such a "bitter cry" left in me, but I wept my heart away to-day when my husband went off. Things do look so black. When he comes up here he rarely brings his body-servant, a negro man. Lawrence has charge of all Mr. Chesnut's things—watch, clothes, and two or three hundred gold pieces that lie in the tray of his trunk. All these, papers, etc., he tells Lawrence to bring to me if anything happens to him. But I said: "Maybe he will pack off to the Yankees and freedom with all that." "Fiddlesticks! He is not going to leave me for anybody else. After all, what can he ever be, better than he is now—a gentleman's gentleman?" "He is within sound of the enemy's guns, and when he gets to the other army he is free." Maria said of Mr. Preston's man: "What he want with anything more, ef he was free? Don't he live just as well as Mars John do now?"

Mrs. McLane, Mrs. Joe Johnston, Mrs. Wigfall, all came. I am sure so many clever women could divert a soul *in extremis.* The Hampton Legion all in a snarl—about, I forget what; standing on their dignity, I suppose. I have come to detest a man who says, "My own personal dignity and self-respect require." I long to cry, "No need to respect yourself until you can make other people do it."

July 19th.—Beauregard telegraphed yesterday (they say, to General Johnston), "Come down and help us, or we shall be crushed by numbers." The President telegraphed General Johnston to move down to Beauregard's aid. At Bull Run, Bonham's Brigade, Ewell's, and Longstreet's encountered the foe and repulsed him. Six hundred prisoners have been sent here.

I arose, as the Scriptures say, and washed my face and anointed my head and went down-stairs. At the foot of them stood General Cooper, radiant, one finger nervously arranging his shirt collar, or adjusting his neck to it after his fashion. He called out: "Your South Carolina man, Bonham, has done a capital thing at Bull Run—driven back the enemy, if not defeated him; with killed and prisoners," etc. , etc. Clingman came to tell the particulars, and Colonel Smith (one of the trio with Garnett, McClellan, who were sent to Europe to inspect and report on military matters). Poor Garnett is killed. There was cowardice or treachery on the part of natives up there, or some of Governor Letcher's appointments to military posts. I hear all these things said. I do not understand, but it was a fatal business.

Mrs. McLane says she finds we do not believe a word of any news unless it comes in this guise: "A great battle fought. Not one Confederate killed. Enemy's loss in killed, wounded, and prisoners taken by us, immense." I was in hopes there would be no battle until Mr. Chesnut was forced to give up his amateur aideship to come and attend to his regular duties in the Congress.

Keitt has come in. He says Bonham's battle was a skirmish of outposts. Joe Davis, Jr., said: "Would Heaven only send us a Napoleon!" Not one bit of use. If Heaven did, Walker would not give him a commission. Mrs. Davis and Mrs. Joe Johnston, "her dear Lydia," were in fine spirits. The effect upon *nous autres* was evident; we rallied visibly. South Carolina troops pass every day. They go by with a gay step. Tom Taylor and John Rhett bowed to us from their horses as we leaned out of the windows. Such shaking of handkerchiefs. We are forever at the windows.

It was not such a mere skirmish. We took three rifled cannon and six hundred stands of arms. Mr. Davis has gone to Manassas. He did not let Wigfall know he was going. That ends the delusion of Wigfall's aideship. No mistake to-day. I was too ill to move out of my bed. So they all sat in my room.

July 22d.—Mrs. Davis came in so softly that I did not know she was here until she leaned over me and said: "A great battle has been fought.[51] Joe Johnston led the right wing, and Beauregard the left wing of the army. Your husband is all right. Wade Hampton is wounded. Colonel Johnston of the Legion killed; so are Colonel Bee and Colonel

---

[51] The first battle of Bull Run, or Manassas, fought on July 21, 1861, the Confederates being commanded by General Beauregard, and the Federals by General McDowell. Bull Run is a small stream tributary to the Potomac.

Bartow. Kirby Smith[52] is wounded or killed."

I had no breath to speak; she went on in that desperate, calm way, to which people betake themselves under the greatest excitement: "Bartow, rallying his men, leading them into the hottest of the light, died gallantly at the head of his regiment. The President telegraphs me only that 'it is a great victory.' General Cooper has all the other telegrams."

Still I said nothing; I was stunned; then I was so grateful. Those nearest and dearest to me were safe still. She then began, in the same concentrated voice, to read from a paper she held in her hand: "Dead and dying cover the field. Sherman's battery taken. Lynchburg regiment cut to pieces. Three hundred of the Legion wounded."

That got me up. Times were too wild with excitement to stay in bed. We went into Mrs. Preston's room, and she made me lie down on her bed. Men, women, and children streamed in. Every living soul had a story to tell. "Complete victory," you heard everywhere. We had been such anxious wretches. The revulsion of feeling was almost too much to bear.

To-day I met my friend, Mr. Hunter. I was on my way to Mrs. Bartow's room and begged him to call at some other time. I was too tearful just then for a morning visit from even the most sympathetic person.

A woman from Mrs. Bartow's country was in a fury because they had stopped her as she rushed to be the first to tell Mrs. Bartow her husband was killed, it having been decided that Mrs. Davis should tell her. Poor thing! She was found lying on her bed when Mrs. Davis knocked. "Come in," she said. When she saw it was Mrs. Davis, she sat up, ready to spring to her feet, but then there was something in Mrs. Davis's pale face that took the life out of her. She stared at Mrs. Davis, then sank back, and covered her face as she asked: "Is it bad news for me?" Mrs. Davis did not speak. "Is he killed?" Afterward Mrs. Bartow said to me: "As soon as I saw Mrs. Davis's face I could not say one word. I knew it all in an instant. I knew it before I wrapped the shawl about my head."

Maria, Mrs. Preston's maid, furiously patriotic, came into my room. "These colored people say it is printed in the papers here that the Virginia people done it all. Now Mars Wade had so many of his men killed and he wounded, it stands to reason that South Carolina was no ways backward. If there was ever anything plain, that's plain."

Tuesday.—Witnessed for the first time a military funeral. As that march came wailing up, they say Mrs. Bartow fainted. The empty

---

[52] Edmund Kirby Smith, a native of Florida, who had graduated from West Point, served in the Mexican War, and been Professor of Mathematics at West Point. He resigned his commission in the United States Army after the secession of Florida.

saddle and the led war-horse—we saw and heard it all, and now it seems we are never out of the sound of the Dead March in Saul. It comes and it comes, until I feel inclined to close my ears and scream.

Yesterday, Mrs. Singleton and ourselves sat on a bedside and mingled our tears for those noble spirits—John Darby, Theodore Barker, and James Lowndes. To-day we find we wasted our grief; they are not so much as wounded. I dare say all the rest is true about them—in the face of the enemy, with flags in their hands, leading their men. "But Dr. Darby is a surgeon." He is as likely to forget that as I am. He is grandson of Colonel Thomson of the Revolution, called, by way of pet name, by his soldiers, "Old Danger." Thank Heaven they are all quite alive. And we will not cry next time until officially notified.

July 24th.—Here Mr. Chesnut opened my door and walked in. Out of the fulness of the heart the mouth speaketh. I had to ask no questions. He gave me an account of the battle as he saw it (walking up and down my room, occasionally seating himself on a window sill, but too restless to remain still many moments); and told what regiments he was sent to bring up. He took the orders to Colonel Jackson, whose regiment stood so stock still under file that they were called a "stone wall." Also, they call Beauregard, Eugene, and Johnston, Marlboro. Mr. Chesnut rode with Lay's cavalry after the retreating enemy in the pursuit, they following them until midnight. Then there came such a fall of rain—rain such as is only known in semitropical lands.

In the drawing-room, Colonel Chesnut was the "belle of the ball"; they crowded him so for news. He was the first arrival that they could get at from the field of battle. But the women had to give way to the dignitaries of the land, who were as filled with curiosity as themselves—Mr. Barnwell, Mr. Hunter, Mr. Cobb, Captain Ingraham, etc.

Wilmot de Saussure says Wilson of Massachusetts, a Senator of the United States,[53] came to Manassas, *en route* to Richmond, with his dancing shoes ready for a festive scene which was to celebrate a triumph. The New York Tribune said: "In a few days we shall have Richmond, Memphis, and New Orleans. They must be taken and at once." For "a few days" maybe now they will modestly substitute "in a few years."

They brought me a Yankee soldier's portfolio from the battle-field. The letters had been franked by Senator Harlan.[54] One might shed tears

---

[53] Henry Wilson, son of a farm laborer and self-educated, who rose to much prominence in the Anti-Slavery contests before the war. He was elected United States Senator from Massachusetts in 1855, holding the office until 1873, when he resigned, having been elected Vice-President of the United States on the ticket with Ulysses S. Grant.

[54] James Harlan, United States Senator from Iowa from 1855 to 1865. In 1865 he was appointed Secretary of the Interior.

over some of the letters. Women, wives and mothers, are the same everywhere. What a comfort the spelling was! We had been willing to admit that their universal free-school education had put them, rank and file, ahead of us *literarily*, but these letters do not attest that fact. The spelling is comically bad.

July 27th.—Mrs. Davis's drawing-room last night was brilliant, and she was in great force. Outside a mob called for the President. He did speak—an old war-horse, who scents the battle-fields from afar. His enthusiasm was contagious. They called for Colonel Chesnut, and he gave them a capital speech, too. As public speakers say sometimes, "It was the proudest moment of my life." I did not hear a great deal of it, for always, when anything happens of any moment, my heart beats up in my ears, but the distinguished Carolinians who crowded round told me how good a speech he made. I was dazed. There goes the Dead March for some poor soul.

To-day, the President told us at dinner that Mr. Chesnut's eulogy of Bartow in the Congress was highly praised. Men liked it. Two eminently satisfactory speeches in twenty-four hours is doing pretty well. And now I could be happy, but this Cabinet of ours are in such bitter quarrels among themselves—everybody abusing everybody.

Last night, while those splendid descriptions of the battle were being given to the crowd below from our windows, I said: "Then, why do we not go on to Washington?" "You mean why did they not; the opportunity is lost." Mr. Barnwell said to me: "Silence, we want to listen to the speaker," and Mr. Hunter smiled compassionately, "Don't ask awkward questions."

Kirby Smith came down on the turnpike in the very nick of time. Still, the heroes who fought all day and held the Yankees in check deserve credit beyond words, or it would all have been over before the Joe Johnston contingent came. It is another case of the eleventh-hour scrape; the eleventh-hour men claim all the credit, and they who bore the heat and brunt and burden of the day do not like that.

Everybody said at first, "Pshaw! There will be no war." Those who foresaw evil were called ravens, ill-foreboders. Now the same sanguine people all cry, "The war is over"—the very same who were packing to leave Richmond a few days ago. Many were ready to move on at a moment's warning, when the good news came. There are such owls everywhere.

But, to revert to the other kind, the sage and circumspect, those who say very little, but that little shows they think the war barely begun. Mr. Rives and Mr. Seddon have just called. Arnoldus Van der Horst came to see me at the same time. He said there was no great show of victory on our side until two o'clock, but when we began to win, we did it in double-quick time. I mean, of course, the battle last Sunday.

Arnold Harris told Mr. Wigfall the news from Washington last Sunday. For hours the telegrams reported at rapid intervals, "Great victory," "Defeating them at all points." The couriers began to come in on horseback, and at last, after two or three o'clock, there was a sudden cessation of all news, About nine messengers with bulletins came on foot or on horseback—wounded, weary, draggled, footsore, panic-stricken—spreading in their path on every hand terror and dismay. That was our opportunity. Wigfall can see nothing that could have stopped us, and when they explain why we did not go to Washington I understand it all less than ever. Yet here we will dilly-dally, and Congress orate, and generals parade, until they in the North, get up an army three times as large as McDowell's, which we have just defeated.

Trescott says this victory will be our ruin. It lulls us into a fool's paradise of conceit at our superior valor, and the shameful farce of their flight will wake every inch of their manhood. It was the very fillip they needed. There are a quieter sort here who know their Yankees well. They say if the thing begins to pay—government contracts, and all that—we will never hear the end of it, at least, until they get their pay in some way out of us. They will not lose money by us. Of that we may be sure. Trust Yankee shrewdness and vim for that.

There seems to be a battle raging at Bethel, but no mortal here can be got to think of anything but Manassas. Mrs. McLean says she does not see that it was such a great victory, and if it be so great, how can one defeat hurt a nation like the North.

John Waties fought the whole battle over for me. Now I understand it. Before this nobody would take the time to tell the thing consecutively, rationally, and in order. Mr. Venable said he did not see a braver thing done than the cool performance of a Columbia negro. He carried his master a bucket of ham and rice, which he had cooked for him, and he cried: "You must be so tired and hungry, marster; make haste and eat." This was in the thickest of the fight, under the heaviest of the enemy's guns.

The Federal Congressmen had been making a picnic of it: their luggage was all ticketed to Richmond. Cameron has issued a proclamation. They are making ready to come after us on a magnificent scale. They acknowledge us at last foemen worthy of their steel. The Lord help us, since England and France won't, or don't. If we could only get a friend outside and open a port.

One of these men told me he had seen a Yankee prisoner, who asked him "what sort of a diggins Richmond was for trade." He was tired of the old concern, and would like to take the oath and settle here. They brought us handcuffs found in the *débacle* of the Yankee army. For whom were they? Jeff Davis, no doubt, and the ringleaders. "Tell that to the marines." We have outgrown the handcuff business on this side of the water.

Dr. Gibbes says he was at a country house near Manassas, when a Federal soldier, who had lost his way, came in exhausted. He asked for brandy, which the lady of the house gave him. Upon second thought, he declined it. She brought it to him so promptly he said he thought it might be poisoned; his mind was; she was enraged, and said: "Sir, I am a Virginia woman. Do you think I could be as base as that? Here, Bill, Tom, disarm this man. He is our prisoner." The negroes came running, and the man surrendered without more ado.

Another Federal was drinking at the well. A negro girl said: "You go in and see Missis." The man went in and she followed, crying triumphantly: "Look here, Missis, I got a prisoner, too!" This lady sent in her two prisoners, and Beauregard complimented her on her pluck and patriotism, and her presence of mind. These negroes were rewarded by their owners.

Now if slavery is as disagreeable to negroes as we think it, why don't they all march over the border where they would be received with open arms? It all amazes me. I am always studying these creatures. They are to me inscrutable in their way and past finding out. Our negroes were not ripe for John Brown.

This is how I saw Robert E. Lee for the first time: though his family, then living at Arlington, called to see me while I was in Washington (I thought because of old Colonel Chesnut's intimacy with Nellie Custis in the old Philadelphia days, Mrs. Lee being Nelly Custis's niece), I had not known the head of the Lee family. He was somewhere with the army then.

Last summer at the White Sulphur were Roony Lee and his wife, that sweet little Charlotte Wickam, and I spoke of Roony with great praise. Mrs. Izard said: "Don't waste your admiration on him; wait till you see his father. He is the nearest to a perfect man I ever saw." "How?" "In every way—handsome, clever, agreeable, high-bred."

Now, Mrs. Stanard came for Mrs. Preston and me to drive to the camp in an open carriage. A man riding a beautiful horse joined us. He wore a hat with something of a military look to it, sat his horse gracefully, and was so distinguished at all points that I very much regretted not catching his name as Mrs. Stanard gave it to us. He, however, heard ours, and bowed as gracefully as he rode, and the few remarks he made to each of us showed he knew all about us.

But Mrs. Stanard was in ecstasies of pleasurable excitement. I felt that she had bagged a big fish, for just then they abounded in Richmond. Mrs. Stanard accused him of being ambitious, etc. He remonstrated and said his tastes were "of the simplest." He only wanted "a Virginia farm, no end of cream and fresh butter and fried chicken— not one fried chicken, or two, but unlimited fried chicken."

To all this light chat did we seriously incline, because the man and horse and everything about him were so fine-looking; perfection, in fact; no fault to be found if you hunted for it. As he left us, I said eagerly, "Who is he?" "You did not know! Why, it was Robert E. Lee, son of Light Horse Harry Lee, the first man in Virginia," raising her voice as she enumerated his glories. All the same, I like Smith Lee better, and I like his looks, too. I know Smith Lee well. Can anybody say they know his brother? I doubt it. He looks so cold, quiet, and grand.

Kirby Smith is our Blücher; he came on the field in the nick of time, as Blücher at Waterloo, and now we are as the British, who do not remember Blücher. It is all Wellington. So every individual man I see fought and won the battle. From Kershaw up and down, all the eleventh-hour men won the battle; turned the tide. The Marylanders— Elzey & Co.—one never hears of—as little as one hears of Blücher in the English stories of Waterloo.

Mr. Venable was praising Hugh Garden and Kershaw's regiment generally. This was delightful. They are my friends and neighbors at home. I showed him Mary Stark's letter, and we agreed with her. At the bottom of our hearts we believe every Confederate soldier to be a hero, *sans peur et sans reproche.*

Hope for the best to-day. Things must be on a pleasanter footing all over the world. Met the President in the corridor. He took me by both hands. "Have you breakfasted?" said he. "Come in and breakfast with me?" Alas! I had had my breakfast.

At the public dining-room, where I had taken my breakfast with Mr. Chesnut, Mrs. Davis came to him, while we were at table. She said she had been to our rooms. She wanted Wigfall hunted up. Mr. Davis thought Chesnut would be apt to know his whereabouts. I ran to Mrs. Wigfall's room, who told me she was sure he could be found with his regiment in camp, but Mr. Chesnut had not to go to the camp, for Wigfall came to his wife's room while I was there. Mr. Davis and Wigfall would be friends, if—if -

The Northern papers say we hung and quartered a Zouave; cut him into four pieces; and that we tie prisoners to a tree and bayonet them. In other words, we are savages. It ought to teach us not to credit what our papers say of them. It is so absurd an imagination of evil. We are absolutely treating their prisoners as well as our own men: we are complained of for it here. I am going to the hospitals for the enemy's sick and wounded in order to see for myself.

Why did we not follow the flying foe across the Potomac? That is the question of the hour in the drawing-room with those of us who are not contending as to "who took Rickett's Battery?" Allen Green, for one, took it. Allen told us that, finding a portmanteau with nice clean shirts, he was so hot and dusty he stepped behind a tree and put on a clean Yankee shirt, and was more comfortable.

The New York Tribune soothes the Yankee self-conceit, which has received a shock, by saying we had 100,000 men on the field at Manassas; we had about 15,000 effective men in all. And then, the Tribune tries to inflame and envenom them against us by telling lies as to our treatment of prisoners. They say when they come against us next it will be in overwhelming force. I long to see Russell's letter to the London Times about Bull Run and Manassas. It will be rich and rare. In Washington, it is crimination and recrimination. Well, let them abuse one another to their hearts' content.

August 1st.—Mrs. Wigfall, with the "Lone Star" flag in her carriage, called for me. We drove to the fair grounds. Mrs. Davis's landau, with her spanking bays, rolled along in front of us. The fair grounds are as covered with tents, soldiers, etc., as ever. As one regiment moves off to the army, a fresh one from home comes to be mustered in and take its place.

The President, with his aides, dashed by. My husband was riding with him. The President presented the flag to the Texans. Mr. Chesnut came to us for the flag, and bore it aloft to the President. We seemed to come in for part of the glory. We were too far off to hear the speech, but Jeff Davis is very good at that sort of thing, and we were satisfied that it was well done.

Heavens! how that redoubtable Wigfall did rush those poor Texans about! He maneuvered and marched them until I was weary for their sakes. Poor fellows; it was a hot afternoon in August and the thermometer in the nineties. Mr. Davis uncovered to speak. Wigfall replied with his hat on. Is that military?

At the fair grounds to-day, such music, mustering, and marching, such cheering and flying of flags, such firing of guns and all that sort of thing. A gala day it was, with double-distilled Fourth-of-July feeling. In the midst of it all, a messenger came to tell Mrs. Wigfall that a telegram had been received, saying her children were safe across the lines in Gordonsville. That was something to thank God for, without any doubt.

These two little girls came from somewhere in Connecticut, with Mrs. Wigfall's sister—the one who gave me my Bogotsky, the only person in the world, except Susan Rutledge who ever seemed to think I had a soul to save. Now suppose Seward had held Louisa and Fanny as hostages for Louis Wigfall's good behavior; eh?

Excitement number two: that bold brigadier, the Georgia General Toombs, charging about too recklessly, got thrown. His horse dragged him up to the wheels of our carriage. For a moment it was frightful. Down there among the horses' hoofs was a face turned up toward us, purple with rage. His foot was still in the stirrup, and he had not let go the bridle. The horse was prancing over him, tearing and plunging; everybody was hemming him in, and they seemed so slow and awkward about it. We felt it an eternity, looking down at him, and expecting him to be killed before our very faces. However, he soon got it all straight, and, though awfully tousled and tumbled, dusty, rumpled, and flushed, with redder face and wilder hair than ever, he rode off gallantly, having to our admiration bravely remounted the recalcitrant charger.

Now if I were to pick out the best abused one, where all catch it so bountifully, I should say Mr. Commissary-General Northrop was the most "cussed" and villified man in the Confederacy. He is held accountable for everything that goes wrong in the army. He may not be efficient, but having been a classmate and crony of Jeff Davis at West Point, points the moral and adorns the tale. I hear that alluded to oftenest of his many crimes. They say Beauregard writes that his army is upon the verge of starvation. Here every man, woman, and child is ready to hang to the first lamp-post anybody of whom that army complains. Every Manassas soldier is a hero dear to our patriotic hearts. Put up with any neglect of the heroes of the 21st July—never!

And now they say we did not move on right after the flying foe because we had no provisions, no wagons, no ammunition, etc. Rain, mud, and Northrop. Where were the enemy's supplies that we bragged so of bagging? Echo answers where? Where there is a will there is a way. We stopped to plunder that rich convoy, and somehow, for a day or so, everybody thought the war was over and stopped to rejoice: so it appeared here. All this was our dinner-table talk to-day. Mr. Mason dined with us and Mr. Barnwell sits by me always. The latter reproved me sharply, but Mr. Mason laughed at "this headlong, unreasonable woman's harangue and female tactics and their war-ways." A freshet in the autumn does not compensate for a drought in the spring. Time and tide wait for no man, and there was a tide in our affairs which might have led to Washington, and we did not take it and lost our fortune this round. Things which nobody could deny.

McClellan virtually supersedes the Titan Scott. Physically General Scott is the largest man I ever saw. Mrs. Scott said, "nobody but his wife could ever know how little he was." And yet they say, old Winfield Scott could have organized an army for them if they had had patience. They would not give him time.

August 2d.—Prince Jerome[55] has gone to Washington. Now the Yankees so far are as little trained as we are; raw troops are they as yet. Suppose France takes the other side and we have to meet disciplined and armed men, soldiers who understand war, Frenchmen, with all the elan we boast of .

Ransom Calhoun, Willie Preston, and Doctor Nott's boys are here.

---

[55] Jerome Napoleon Bonaparte, a grandson of Napoleon Bonaparte's brother Jerome and of Elizabeth Patterson of Baltimore. He was a graduate of West Point, but had entered the French Army, where he saw service in the Crimea, Algiers, and Italy, taking part in the battle of Balaklava, the siege of Sebastopol, and the battle of Solferino. He died in Massachusetts in 1893.

These foolish, rash, hare-brained Southern lads have been within an ace of a fight with a Maryland company for their camping grounds. It is much too Irish to be so ready to fight anybody, friend or foe. Men are thrilling with fiery ardor. The red-hot Southern martial spirit is in the air. These young men, however, were all educated abroad. And it is French or German ideas that they are filled with. The Marylanders were as rash and reckless as the others, and had their coat-tails ready for anybody to tread on, Donnybrook Fair fashion. One would think there were Yankees enough and to spare for any killing to be done. It began about picketing their horses. But these quarrelsome young soldiers have lovely manners. They are so sweet-tempered when seen here among us at the Arlington.

August 5th.—A heavy, heavy heart. Another missive from Jordan, querulous and fault-finding; things are all wrong—Beauregard's Jordan had been crossed, not the stream "in Canaan's fair and happy land, where our possessions lie." They seem to feel that the war is over here, except the President and Mr. Barnwell; above all that foreboding friend of mine, Captain Ingraham. He thinks it hardly begun.

Another outburst from Jordan. Beauregard is not seconded properly. *Hélas!* To think that any mortal general (even though he had sprung up in a month or so from captain of artillery to general) could be so puffed up with vanity, so blinded by any false idea of his own consequence as to write, to intimate that man, or men, would sacrifice their country, injure themselves, ruin their families, to spite the aforesaid general! Conceit and self-assertion can never reach a higher point than that. And yet they give you to understand Mr. Davis does not like Beauregard. In point of fact they fancy he is jealous of him, and rather than Beauregard shall have a showing the President (who would be hanged at least if things go wrong) will cripple the army to spite Beauregard. Mr. Mallory says, "How we could laugh, but you see it is no laughing matter to have our fate in the hands of such self-sufficient, vain, army idiots." So the amenities of life are spreading.

In the meantime we seem to be resting on our oars, debating in Congress, while the enterprising Yankees are quadrupling their army at their leisure. Every day some of our regiments march away from here. The town is crowded with soldiers. These new ones are fairly running in; fearing the war will be over before they get a sight of the fun. Every man from every little precinct wants a place in the picture.

Tuesday.—The North requires 600,000 men to invade us. Truly we are a formidable power! The Herald says it is useless to move with a man less than that. England has made it all up with them, or rather, she will not break with them. Jerome Napoleon is in Washington and not our friend.

Doctor Gibbes is a bird of ill omen. To-day he tells me eight of our men have died at the Charlottesville Hospital. It seems sickness is more

redoubtable in an army than the enemy's guns. There are 1,100 there
hors de combat, and typhoid fever is with them. They want money,
clothes, and nurses. So, as I am writing, right and left the letters fly,
calling for help from the sister societies at home. Good and patriotic
women at home are easily stirred to their work.

Mary Hammy has many strings to her bow—a *fiancé* in the army,
and Doctor Berrien in town. To-day she drove out with Major Smith
and Colonel Hood. Yesterday, Custis Lee was here. She is a prudent
little puss and needs no good advice, if I were one to give it.

Lawrence does all our shopping. All his master's money has been
in his hands until now. I thought it injudicious when gold is at such a
premium to leave it lying loose in the tray of a trunk. So I have sewed it
up in a belt, which I can wear upon an emergency. The cloth is wadded
and my diamonds are there, too. It has strong strings, and can be tied
under my hoops about my waist if the worst comes to the worst, as the
saying is. Lawrence wears the same bronze mask. No sign of anything
he may feel or think of my latest fancy. Only, I know he asks for twice
as much money now when he goes to buy things.

August 8th.—To-day I saw a sword captured at Manassas. The
man who brought the sword, in the early part of the fray, was taken
prisoner by the Yankees. They stripped him, possessed themselves of
his sleeve-buttons, and were in the act of depriving him of his boots
when the rout began and the play was reversed; proceedings then took
the opposite tack.

From a small rill in the mountain has flowed the mighty stream
which has made at last Louis Wigfall the worst enemy the President has
in the Congress, a fact which complicates our affairs no little. Mr.
Davis's hands ought to be strengthened; he ought to be upheld. A
divided house must fall, we all say.

Mrs. Sam Jones, who is called Becky by her friends and cronies,
male and female, said that Mrs. Pickens had confided to the aforesaid
Jones (*née* Taylor, and so of the President Taylor family and cousin of
Mr. Davis's first wife), that Mrs. Wigfall "described Mrs. Davis to Mrs.
Pickens as a coarse Western woman." Now the fair Lucy Holcombe
and Mrs. Wigfall had a quarrel of their own out in Texas, and, though
reconciled, there was bitterness underneath. At first, Mrs. Joe Johnston
called Mrs. Davis "a Western belle,"[56] but when the quarrel between
General Johnston and the President broke out, Mrs. Johnston took back
the "belle" and substituted "woman" in the narrative derived from Mrs.
Jones.

---

[56] Mrs. Davis was born in Natchez, Mississippi, and educated in Philadelphia. She
was married to Mr. Davis in 1845. In recent years her home has been in New York City,
where she still resides (Dec. 1904).

Commodore Barron[57] came with glad tidings. We had taken three prizes at sea, and brought them in safely, one laden with molasses. General Toombs told us the President complimented Mr. Chesnut when he described the battle scene to his Cabinet, etc. General Toombs is certain Colonel Chesnut will be made one of the new batch of brigadiers. Next came Mr. Clayton, who calmly informed us Jeff Davis would not get the vote of this Congress for President, so we might count him out.

Mr. Meynardie first told us how pious a Christian Soldier was Kershaw, how he prayed, got up, dusted his knees and led his men on to victory with a dash and courage equal to any Old Testament mighty man of war.

Governor Manning's account of Prince Jerome Napoleon: "He is stout and he is not handsome. Neither is he young, and as he reviewed our troops he was terribly overheated." He heard him say "*en avant*," of that he could testify of his own knowledge, and he was told he had been heard to say with unction "*Allons*" more than once. The sight of the battle-field had made the Prince seasick, and he received gratefully a draft of fiery whisky.

Arrago seemed deeply interested in Confederate statistics, and praised our doughty deeds to the skies. It was but soldier fare our guests received, though we did our best. It was hard sleeping and worse eating in camp. Beauregard is half Frenchman and speaks French like a native. So one awkward mess was done away with, and it was a comfort to see Beauregard speak without the agony of finding words in the foreign language and forming them, with damp brow, into sentences. A different fate befell others who spoke "a little French."

General and Mrs. Cooper came to see us. She is Mrs. Smith Lee's sister. They were talking of old George Mason—in Virginia a name to conjure with. George Mason violently opposed the extension of slavery. He was a thorough aristocrat, and gave as his reason for refusing the blessing of slaves to the new States, Southwest and Northwest, that vulgar new people were unworthy of so sacred a right as that of holding slaves. It was not an institution intended for such people as they were. Mrs. Lee said: "After all, what good does it do my sons that they are Light Horse Harry Lee's grandsons and George Mason's? I do not see that it helps them at all."

A friend in Washington writes me that we might have walked into Washington any day for a week after Manassas, such were the consternation and confusion there. But the god Pan was still blowing his horn in the woods. Now she says Northern troops are literally

---

[57] Samuel Barron was a native of Virginia, who had risen to be a captain in the United States Navy. At the time of Secession he received a commission as Commodore in the Confederate Navy.

pouring in from all quarters. The horses cover acres of ground. And she thinks we have lost our chance forever.

A man named Grey (the same gentleman whom Secretary of War Walker so astonished by greeting him with, "Well, sir, and what is your business?") described the battle of the 21st as one succession of blunders, redeemed by the indomitable courage of the two-thirds who did not run away on our side. Doctor Mason said a fugitive on the other side informed him that "a million of men with the devil at their back could not have whipped the rebels at Bull Run." That's nice.

There must be opposition in a free country. But it is very uncomfortable. "United we stand, divided we fall." Mrs. Davis showed us in The New York Tribune an extract from an Augusta (Georgia) paper saying, "Cobb is our man. Davis is at heart a reconstructionist." We may be flies on the wheel, we know our insignificance; but Mrs. Preston and myself have entered into an agreement; our oath is recorded on high. We mean to stand by our President and to stop all fault-finding with the powers that be, if we can and where we can, be the fault-finders generals or Cabinet Ministers.

August 13th.—Hon. Robert Barnwell says, "The Mercury's influence began this opposition to Jeff Davis before he had time to do wrong. They were offended, not with him so much as with the man who was put into what they considered Barnwell Rhett's rightful place. The latter had howled nullification and secession so long that when he found his ideas taken up by all the Confederate world, he felt he had a vested right to leadership."

Jordan, Beauregard's aide, still writes to Mr. Chesnut that the mortality among the raw troops in that camp is fearful. Everybody seems to be doing all they can. Think of the British sick and wounded away off in the Crimea. Our people are only a half-day's journey by rail from Richmond. With a grateful heart I record the fact of reconciliation with the Wigfalls. They dined at the President's yesterday and the little Wigfall girls stayed all night.

Seward is fêting the outsiders, the cousin of the Emperor, Napoleon III., and Russell, of the omnipotent London Times.

August 14th.—Last night there was a crowd of men to see us and they were so markedly critical. I made a futile effort to record their sayings, but sleep and heat overcame me. To-day I can not remember a word. One of Mr. Mason's stories relates to our sources of trustworthy information. A man of very respectable appearance standing on the platform at the depot, announced, "I am just from the seat of war." Out came pencil and paper from the newspaper men on the *qui vive*. "Is Fairfax Court House burned?" they asked. "Yes, burned yesterday." "But I am just from there," said another; "left it standing there all right an hour or so ago." "Oh! But I must do them justice to say they burned only the tavern, for they did not want to tear up and burn anything else after the railroad." "There is no railroad at Fairfax Court House," objected the man just from Fairfax. "Oh! Indeed!" said the seat-of-war man, "I did not know that; is that so?" And he coolly seated himself and began talking of something else.

Our people are lashing themselves into a fury against the prisoners. Only the mob in any country would do that. But I am told to be quiet. Decency and propriety will not be forgotten, and the prisoners will be treated as prisoners of war ought to be in a civilized country.

August 15th.—Mrs. Randolph came. With her were the Freelands, Rose and Maria. The men rave over Mrs. Randolph's beauty; called her a magnificent specimen of the finest type of dark-eyed, rich, and glowing Southern woman-kind. Clear brunette she is, with the reddest lips, the whitest teeth, and glorious eyes; there is no other word for them. Having given Mrs. Randolph the prize among Southern beauties, Mr. Clayton said Prentiss was the finest Southern orator. Mr. Marshall and Mr. Barnwell dissented; they preferred William C. Preston. Mr. Chesnut had found Colquitt the best or most effective stump orator.

Saw Henry Deas Nott. He is just from Paris, via New York. Says New York is ablaze with martial fire. At no time during the Crimean war was there ever in Paris the show of soldiers preparing for the war such as he saw at New York. The face of the earth seemed covered with marching regiments.

Not more than 500 effective men are in Hampton's Legion, but they kept the whole Yankee army at bay until half-past two. Then just as Hampton was wounded and half his colonels shot, Cash and Kershaw (from Mrs. Smith Lee audibly, "How about Kirby Smith?") dashed in and not only turned the tide, but would have driven the fugitives into Washington, but Beauregard recalled them. Mr. Chesnut finds all this very amusing, as he posted many of the regiments and all the time was carrying orders over the filed. The discrepancies in all these private memories amuse him, but he smiles pleasantly and lets every man tell the tale in his own way.

August 16th.—Mr. Barnwell says, Fame is an article usually home made; you must create your own puffs or superintend their manufacture. And you must see that the newspapers print your own military reports. No one else will give you half the credit you take to yourself. No one will look after your fine name before the world with the loving interest and faith you have yourself.

August 17th.—Captain Shannon, of the Kirkwood Rangers, called and stayed three hours. Has not been under fire yet, but is keen to see or to hear the flashing of the guns; proud of himself, proud of his company, but proudest of all that he has no end of the bluest blood of the low country in his troop. He seemed to find my knitting a pair of socks a day for the soldiers droll in some way. The yarn is coarse. He has been so short a time from home he does not know how the poor soldiers need them. He was so overpoweringly flattering to my husband that I found him very pleasant company.

August 18th.—Found it quite exciting to have a spy drinking his tea with us—perhaps because I knew his profession. I did not like his face. He is said to have a scheme by which Washington will fall into our hands like an overripe peach.

Mr. Barnwell urges Mr. Chesnut to remain in the Senate. There are so many generals, or men anxious to be. He says Mr. Chesnut can do his country most good by wise counsels where they are most needed. I do not say to the contrary; I dare not throw my influence on the army side, for if anything happened!

Mr. Miles told us last night that he had another letter from General Beauregard. The General wants to know if Mr. Miles has delivered his message to Colonel Kershaw. Mr. Miles says he has not done so; neither does he mean to do it. They must settle these matters of veracity according to their own military etiquette. He is a civilian once more. It is a foolish wrangle. Colonel Kershaw ought to have reported to his commander-in-chief, and not made an independent report and published it. He meant no harm. He is not yet used to the fine ways of war.

The New York Tribune is so unfair. It began by howling to get rid of us: we were so wicked. Now that we are so willing to leave them to their overrighteous self-consciousness, they cry: "Crush our enemy, or they will subjugate us." The idea that we want to invade or subjugate anybody; we would be only too grateful to be left alone. We ask no more of gods or men.

Went to the hospital with a carriage load of peaches and grapes. Made glad the hearts of some men thereby. When my supplies gave out, those who had none looked so wistfully as I passed out that I made a second raid on the market. Those eyes sunk in cavernous depths and following me from bed to bed haunt me.

Wilmot de Saussure, harrowed my soul by an account of a recent death by drowning on the beach at Sullivan's Island. Mr. Porcher, who was trying to save his sister's life, lost his own and his child's. People seem to die out of the army quite as much as in it.

Mrs. Randolph presided in all her beautiful majesty at an aid association. The ladies were old, and all wanted their own way. They were cross-grained and contradictory, and the blood mounted rebelliously into Mrs. Randolph's clear-cut cheeks, but she held her own with dignity and grace. One of the causes of disturbance was that Mrs. Randolph proposed to divide everything sent on equally with the Yankee wounded and sick prisoners. Some were enthusiastic from a Christian point of view; some shrieked in wrath at the bare idea of putting our noble soldiers on a par with Yankees, living, dying, or dead. Fierce dames were some of them, august, severe matrons, who evidently had not been accustomed to hear the other side of any question from anybody, and just old enough to find the last pleasure in life to reside in power—the power to make their claws felt.

August 23d.—A brother of Doctor Garnett has come fresh and straight from Cambridge, Mass., and says (or is said to have said, with all the difference there is between the two), that "recruiting up there is dead." He came by Cincinnati and Pittsburg and says all the way through it was so sad, mournful, and quiet it looked like Sunday.

I asked Mr. Brewster if it were true Senator Toombs had turned brigadier. "Yes, soldiering is in the air. Every one will have a touch of it. Toombs could not stay in the Cabinet." "Why?" "Incompatibility of temper. He rides too high a horse; that is, for so despotic a person as Jeff Davis. I have tried to find out the sore, but I can't. Mr. Toombs has been out with them all for months." Dissension will break out. Everything does, but it takes a little time. There is a perfect magazine of discord and discontent in that Cabinet; only wants a hand to apply the torch, and up they go. Toombs says old Memminger has his back up as high as any.

Oh, such a day! Since I wrote this morning, I have been with Mrs. Randolph to all the hospitals. I can never again shut out of view the sights I saw there of human misery. I sit thinking, shut my eyes, and see it all; thinking, yes, and there is enough to think about now, God knows. Gilland's was the worst, with long rows of ill men on cots, ill of typhoid fever, of every human ailment; on dinner-tables for eating and drinking, wounds being dressed; all the horrors to be taken in at one glance.

Then we went to the St. Charles. Horrors upon horrors again; want of organization, long rows of dead and dying; awful sights. A boy from home had sent for me. He was dying in a cot, ill of fever. Next him a man died in convulsions as we stood there. I was making arrangements with a nurse, hiring him to take care of this lad; but I do not remember any more, for I fainted. Next that I knew of, the doctor and Mrs. Randolph were having me, a limp rag, put into a carriage at the door of the hospital. Fresh air, I dare say, brought me to. As we drove home the doctor came along with us, I was so upset. He said: "Look at that Georgia regiment marching there; look at their servants on the sidewalk. I have been counting them, making an estimate. There is $16,000—sixteen thousand dollars' worth of negro property which can go off on its own legs to the Yankees whenever it pleases."

August 24th.—Daniel, of The Examiner, was at the President's. Wilmot de Saussure wondered if a fellow did not feel a little queer, paying his respects in person at the house of a man whom he abused daily in his newspaper.

A fiasco: an aide engaged to two young ladies in the same house. The ladies had been quarreling, but became friends unexpectedly when his treachery, among many other secrets, was revealed under that august roof. Fancy the row when it all came out.

Mr. Lowndes said we have already reaped one good result from the war. The orators, the spouters, the furious patriots, that could hardly be held down, and who were so wordily anxious to do or die for their country—they had been the pest of our lives. Now they either have not tried the battle-field at all, or have precipitately left it at their earliest convenience: for very shame we are rid of them for a while. I doubt it. Bright's speech[58] is dead against us. Reading this does not brighten one.

August 25th.—Mr. Barnwell says democracies lead to untruthfulness. To be always electioneering is to be always false; so both we and the Yankees are unreliable as regards our own exploits. "How about empires? Were there ever more stupendous lies than the Emperor Napoleon's?" Mr. Barnwell went on: "People dare not tell the truth in a canvass; they must conciliate their constituents. Now everybody in a democracy always wants an office; at least, everybody in Richmond just now seems to want one." Never heeding interruptions, he went on: "As a nation, the English are the most truthful in the world." "And so are our country gentlemen: they own their constituents—at least, in some of the parishes, where there are few whites; only immense estates peopled by negroes." Thackeray speaks of the lies that were told on both sides in the British wars with France; England kept quite alongside of her rival in that fine art. England lied then as fluently as Russell lies about us now.

Went to see Agnes De Leon, my Columbia school friend. She is fresh from Egypt, and I wished to hear of the Nile, the crocodiles, the mummies, the Sphinx, and the Pyramids. But her head ran upon Washington life, such as we knew it, and her soul was here. No theme was possible but a discussion of the latest war news.

Mr. Clayton, Assistant Secretary of State, says we spend two millions a week. Where is all that money to come from? They don't want us to plant cotton, but to make provisions. Now, cotton always means money, or did when there was an outlet for it and anybody to buy it. Where is money to come from now?

Mr. Barnwell's new joke, I dare say, is a Joe Miller, but Mr. Barnwell laughed in telling it till he cried. A man was fined for contempt of court and then, his case coming on, the Judge talked such arrant nonsense and was so warped in his mind against the poor man, that the "fined one" walked up and handed the august Judge a five-dollar bill. "Why? What is that for?" said the Judge. "Oh, I feel such a contempt of this court coming on again!"

---

[58] The reference is to John Bright, whose advocacy of the cause of the Union in the British Parliament attracted a great deal of attention at the time.

I came up tired to death; took down my hair; had it hanging over me in a Crazy Jane fashion; and sat still, hands over my head (half undressed, but too lazy and sleepy to move). I was sitting in a rocking-chair by an open window taking my ease and the cool night air, when suddenly the door opened and Captain——walked in. He was in the middle of the room before he saw his mistake; he stared and was transfixed, as the novels say. I dare say I looked an ancient Gorgon. Then, with a more frantic glare, he turned and fled without a word. I got up and bolted the door after him, and then looked in the glass and laughed myself into hysterics. I shall never forget to lock the door again. But it does not matter in this case. I looked totally unlike the person bearing my name, who, covered with lace cap, etc., frequents the drawing-room. I doubt if he would know me again.

August 26th.—The Terror has full swing at the North now. All the papers favorable to us have been suppressed. How long would our mob stand a Yankee paper here? But newspapers against our government, such as the Examiner and the Mercury flourish like green bay-trees. A man up to the elbows in finance said to-day: "Clayton's story is all nonsense. They do sometimes pay out two millions a week; they paid the soldiers this week, but they don't pay the soldiers every week." "Not by a long shot," cried a soldier laddie with a grin.

"Why do you write in your diary at all," some one said to me, "if, as you say, you have to contradict every day what you wrote yesterday?" "Because I tell the tale as it is told to me. I write current rumor. I do not vouch for anything."

We went to Pizzini's, that very best of Italian confectioners. From there we went to Miss Sally Tompkins's hospital, loaded with good things for the wounded. The men under Miss Sally's kind care looked so clean and comfortable—cheerful, one might say. They were pleasant and nice to see. One, however, was dismal in tone and aspect, and he repeated at intervals with no change of words, in a forlorn monotone: "What a hard time we have had since we left home." But nobody seemed to heed his wailing, and it did not impair his appetite.

At Mrs. Toombs's, who was raging; so anti-Davis she will not even admit that the President is ill. "All humbug." "But what good could pretending to be ill do him?" "That reception now, was not that a humbug? Such a failure. Mrs. Reagan could have done better than that."

Mrs. Walker is a Montgomery beauty, with such magnificent dresses. She was an heiress, and is so dissatisfied with Richmond, accustomed as she is to being a belle under different conditions. As she is as handsome and well dressed as ever, it must be the men who are all wrong.

"Did you give Lawrence that fifty-dollar bill to go out and change it?" I was asked. "Suppose he takes himself off to the Yankees. He would leave us with not too many fifty-dollar bills." He is not going anywhere, however. I think his situation suits him. That wadded belt of mine, with the gold pieces quilted in, has made me ashamed more than once. I leave it under my pillow and my maid finds it there and hangs it over the back of a chair, in evidence as I reenter the room after breakfast. When I forget and leave my trunk open, Lawrence brings me the keys and tells me, "You oughten to do so, Miss Mary." Mr. Chesnut leaves all his little money in his pockets, and Lawrence says that's why he can't let any one but himself brush Mars Jeems's clothes.

August 27th.—Theodore Barker and James Lowndes came; the latter has been wretchedly treated. A man said, "All that I wish on earth is to be at peace and on my own plantation," to which Mr. Lowndes replied quietly, "I wish I had a plantation to be on, but just now I can't see how any one would feel justified in leaving the army." Mr. Barker was bitter against the spirit of braggadocio so rampant among us. The gentleman who had been answered so completely by James Lowndes said, with spitefulness: "Those women who are so frantic for their husbands to join the army would like them killed, no doubt."

Things were growing rather uncomfortable, but an interruption came in the shape of a card. An old classmate of Mr. Chesnut's— Captain Archer, just now fresh from California—followed his card so quickly that Mr. Chesnut had hardly time to tell us that in Princeton College they called him "Sally." Archer he was so pretty—when he entered. He is good-looking still, but the service and consequent rough life have destroyed all softness and girlishness. He will never be so pretty again.

The North is consolidated; they move as one man, with no States, but an army organized by the central power. Russell in the Northern camp is cursed of Yankees for that Bull Run letter. Russell, in his capacity of Englishman, despises both sides. He divides us equally into North and South. He prefers to attribute our victory at Bull Run to Yankee cowardice rather than to Southern courage. He gives no credit to either side; for good qualities, we are after all mere Americans! Everything not "national" is arrested. It looks like the business of Seward.

I do not know when I have seen a woman without knitting in her hand. Socks for the soldiers is the cry. One poor man said he had dozens of socks and but one shirt. He preferred more shirts and fewer stockings. We make a quaint appearance with this twinkling of needles and the everlasting sock dangling below.

They have arrested Wm. B. Reed and Miss Winder, she boldly proclaiming herself a secessionist. Why should she seek a martyr's crown? Writing people love notoriety. It is so delightful to be of enough consequence to be arrested.

I have often wondered if such incense was ever offered as

Napoleon's so-called persecution and alleged jealousy of Madame de Staël.

*   *   *   *   *

Russell once more, to whom London, Paris, and India have been an every-day sight, and every-night, too, streets and all. How absurd for him to go on in indignation because there have been women on negro plantations who were not vestal virgins. Negro women get married, and after marriage behave as well as other people. Marrying is the amusement of their lives. They take life easily; so do their class everywhere. Bad men are hated here as elsewhere.

"I hate slavery. I hate a man who—You say there are no more fallen women on a plantation than in London in proportion to numbers. But what do you say to this—to a magnate who runs a hideous black harem, with its consequences, under the same roof with his lovely white wife and his beautiful and accomplished daughters? He holds his head high and poses as the model of all human virtues to these poor women whom God and the laws have given him. From the height of his awful majesty he scolds and thunders at them as if he never did wrong in his life. Fancy such a man finding his daughter reading Don Juan. 'You with that immoral book!' he would say, and then he would order her out of his sight. You see Mrs. Stowe did not hit the sorest spot. She makes Legree a bachelor." "Remember George II. and his likes."

"Oh, I know half a Legree—a man said to be as cruel as Legree, but the other half of him did not correspond. He was a man of polished manners, and the best husband and father and member of the church in the world." "Can that be so?"

"Yes, I know it. Exceptional case, that sort of thing, always. And I knew the dissolute half of Legree well. He was high and mighty, but the kindest creature to his slaves. And the unfortunate results of his bad ways were not sold, had not to jump over ice-blocks. They were kept in full view, and provided for handsomely in his will."

"The wife and daughters in the might of their purity and innocence are supposed never to dream of what is as plain before their eyes as the sunlight, and they play their parts of unsuspecting angels to the letter. They profess to adore the father as the model of all saintly goodness." "Well, yes; if he is rich he is the fountain from whence all blessings flow."

"The one I have in my eye—my half of Legree, the dissolute half—was so furious in temper and thundered his wrath so at the poor women, they were glad to let him do as he pleased in peace if they could only escape his everlasting fault-finding, and noisy bluster, making everybody so uncomfortable." "Now—now, do you know any woman of this generation who would stand that sort of thing? No,

never, not for one moment. The make-believe angels were of the last
century. We know, and we won't have it."

"The condition of women is improving, it seems." "Women are
brought up not to judge their fathers or their husbands. They take them
as the Lord provides and are thankful."

"If they should not go to heaven after all; think what lives most
women lead." "No heaven, no purgatory, no—the other thing? Never. I
believe in future rewards and punishments."

"How about the wives of drunkards? I heard a woman say once to
a friend of her husband, tell it as a cruel matter of fact, without
bitterness, without comment, 'Oh, you have not seen him! He has
changed. He has not gone to bed sober in thirty years.' She has had her
purgatory, if not 'the other thing,' here in this world. We all know what
a drunken man is. To think, *for no crime*, a person may be condemned
to live with one thirty years." "You wander from the question I asked.
Are Southern men worse because of the slave system and the facile
black women? Not a bit. They see too much of them. The barroom
people don't drink, the confectionery people loathe candy. They are
sick of the black sight of them."

"You think a nice man from the South is the nicest thing in the
world? I know it. Put him by any other man and see!"

*   *   *   *   *

Have seen Yankee letters taken at Manassas. The spelling is often
atrocious, and we thought they had all gone through a course of blue-
covered Noah Webster spelling-books. Our soldiers do spell
astonishingly. There is Horace Greeley: they say he can't read his own
handwriting. But, he is candid enough and disregards all time-serving.
He says in his paper that in our army the North has a hard nut to crack,
and that the rank and file of our army is superior in education and
general intelligence to theirs.

My wildest imagination will not picture Mr. Mason[59] as a
diplomat. He will say chaw for chew, and he will call himself Jeems,
and he will wear a dress coat to breakfast. Over here, whatever a Mason
does is right in his own eyes. He is above law. Somebody asked him
how he pronounced his wife's maiden name: she was a Miss Chew

---

[59] James Murray Mason was a grandson of George Mason, and had been elected
United States Senator from Virginia in 1847. In 1851 he drafted the Fugitive Slave Law.
His mission to England in 1861 was shared by John Slidell. On November 8, 1861, while
on board the British steamer Trent, in the Bahamas, they were captured by an American
med Wilkes, and imprisoned in Boston until January 2, 1862. A famous diplomatic
fficulty arose with England over this affair. John Slidell was a native of New York,
o had settled in Louisiana and became a Member of Congress from that State in 1843.
1853 he was elected to the United States Senate.

from Philadelphia.

They say the English will like Mr. Mason; he is so manly, so straightforward, so truthful and bold. "A fine old English gentleman," so said Russell to me, "but for tobacco." "I like Mr. Mason and Mr. Hunter better than anybody else." "And yet they are wonderfully unlike." "Now you just listen to me," said I. "Is Mrs. Davis in hearing—no? Well, this sending Mr. Mason to London is the maddest thing yet. Worse in some points of view than Yancey, and that was a catastrophe."

August 29th.—No more feminine gossip, but the licensed slanderer, the mighty Russell, of the Times. He says the battle of the 21st was fought at long range: 500 yards apart were the combatants. The Confederates were steadily retreating when some commotion in the wagon train frightened the "Yanks," and they made tracks. In good English, they fled amain. And on our side we were too frightened to follow them—in high-flown English, to pursue the flying foe.

In spite of all this, there are glimpses of the truth sometimes, and the story leads to our credit with all the sneers and jeers. When he speaks of the Yankees' cowardice, falsehood, dishonesty, and braggadocio, the best words are in his mouth. He repeats the thrice-told tale, so often refuted and denied, that we were harsh to wounded prisoners. Dr. Gibson told me that their surgeon-general has written to thank our surgeons: Yankee officers write very differently from Russell. I know that in that hospital with the Sisters of Charity they were better off than our men were at the other hospitals: that I saw with my own eyes. These poor souls are jealously guarded night and day. It is a hideous tale—what they tell of their sufferings.

Women who come before the public are in a bad box now. False hair is taken off and searched for papers. Bustles are "suspect." All manner of things, they say, come over the border under the huge hoops now worn; so they are ruthlessly torn off. Not legs but arms are looked for under hoops, and, sad to say, found. Then women are used as detectives and searchers, to see that no men slip over in petticoats. So the poor creatures coming this way are humiliated to the deepest degree. To men, glory, honor, praise, and power, if they are patriots. To women, daughters of Eve, punishment comes still in some shape, do what they will.

Mary Hammy's eyes were starting from her head with amazement, while a very large and handsome South Carolinian talked rapidly. "What is it?" asked I after he had gone. "Oh, what a year can bring forth—one year! Last summer you remember how he swore he was in love with me? He told you, he told me, he told everybody, and if I did refuse to marry him I believed him. Now he says he has seen, fallen in love with, courted, and married another person, and he raves of his little daughter's beauty. And they say time goes slowly" thus spoke Mary

Hammy, with a sigh of wonder at his wonderful cure.

"Time works wonders," said the explainer-general. "What conclusion did you come to as to Southern men at the grand pow-wow, you know?" "They are nicer than the nicest—the gentlemen, you know. There are not too many of that kind anywhere. Ours are generous, truthful, brave, and—and—devoted to us, you know. A Southern husband is not a bad thing to have about the house."

Mrs. Frank Hampton said: "For one thing, you could not flirt with these South Carolinians. They would not stay at the tepid degree of flirtation. They grow so horridly in earnest before you know where you are." "Do you think two married people ever lived together without finding each other out? I mean, knowing exactly how good or how shabby, how weak or how strong, above all, how selfish each was?" "Yes; unless they are dolts, they know to a tittle; but you see if they have common sense they make believe and get on, so so." Like the Marchioness's orange-peel wine in Old Curiosity Shop.

A violent attack upon the North to-day in the Albion. They mean to let freedom slide a while until they subjugate us. The Albion says they use *lettres de cachet*, passports, and all the despotic apparatus of regal governments. Russell hears the tramp of the coming man—the king and kaiser tyrant that is to rule them. Is it McClellan?—"Little Mac"? We may tremble when he comes. We down here have only "the many-headed monster thing," armed democracy. Our chiefs quarrel among themselves.

McClellan is of a forgiving spirit. He does not resent Russell's slurs upon Yankees, but with good policy has Russell with him as a guest.

The Adonis of an aide avers, as one who knows, that "Sumter" Anderson's heart is with us; that he will not fight the South. After all is said and done that sounds like nonsense. "Sumter" Anderson's wife was a daughter of Governor Clinch, of Georgia. Does that explain it? He also told me something of Garnett (who was killed at Rich Mountain).[60] He had been an unlucky man clear through. In the army before the war, the aide had found him proud, reserved, and morose, cold as an icicle to all. But for his wife and child he was a different creature. He adored them and cared for nothing else.

One day he went off on an expedition and was gone six weeks. He was out in the Northwest, and the Indians were troublesome. When he came back, his wife and child were underground. He said not one word, but they found him more frozen, stern, and isolated than ever; that was all. The night before he left Richmond he said in his quiet way: "They

---

[60] The battle of Rich Mountain, in Western Virginia, was fought July 11, 1861, and General Garnett, Commander of the Confederate forces, pursued by General McClellan, was killed at Carrick's Ford, July 13th, while trying to rally his rear-guard.

have not given me an adequate force. I can do nothing. They have sent me to my death." It is acknowledged that he threw away his life—"a dreary-hearted man," said the aide, "and the unluckiest."

* * * * *

On the front steps every evening we take our seats and discourse at our pleasure. A nicer or more agreeable set of people were never assembled than our present Arlington crowd. To-night it was Yancey[61] who occupied our tongues. Send a man to England who had killed his father-in-law in a street brawl! That was not knowing England or Englishmen, surely. Who wants eloquence? We want somebody who can hold his tongue. People avoid great talkers, men who orate, men given to monologue, as they would avoid fire, famine, or pestilence. Yancey will have no mobs to harangue. No stump speeches will be possible, superb as are his of their kind, but little quiet conversation is best with slow, solid, common-sense people, who begin to suspect as soon as any flourish of trumpets meets their ear. If Yancey should use his fine words, who would care for them over there?

Commodore Barron, when he was a middy, accompanied Phil Augustus Stockton to claim his bride. He, the said Stockton, had secretly wedded a fair heiress (Sally Cantey). She was married by a magistrate and returned to Mrs. Grillaud's boarding-school until it was time to go home—that is, to Camden.

Lieutenant Stockton (a descendant of the Signer) was the handsomest man in the navy, and irresistible. The bride was barely sixteen. When he was to go down South among those fire-eaters and claim her, Commodore Barron, then his intimate friend, went as his backer. They were to announce the marriage and defy the guardians. Commodore Barron said he anticipated a rough job of it all, but they were prepared for all risks. "You expected to find us a horde of savages, no doubt," said I. "We did not expect to get off under a half-dozen duels." They looked for insults from every quarter and they found a polished and refined people who lived *en prince*, to say the least of it. They were received with a cold, stately, and faultless politeness, which made them feel as if they had been sheep-stealing.

The young lady had confessed to her guardians and they were for making the best of it; above all, for saving her name from all gossip or publicity. Colonel John Boykin, one of them, took Young Lochinvar to stay with him. His friend, Barron, was also a guest. Colonel Deas sent for a parson, and made assurance doubly sure by marrying them over

---

[61] William Lowndes Yancey was a native of Virginia, who settled in Alabama, and in 1844 was elected to Congress, where he became a leader among the supporters of slavery and an advocate of secession. He was famous in his day as an effective public speaker.

again. Their wish was to keep things quiet and not to make a nine-days'
wonder of the young lady.

Then came balls, parties, and festivities without end. He was
enchanted with the easy-going life of these people, with dinners the
finest in the world, deer-hunting, and fox-hunting, dancing, and pretty
girls, in fact everything that heart could wish. But then, said
Commodore Barron, "the better it was, and the kinder the treatment, the
more ashamed I grew of my business down there. After all, it was
stealing an heiress, you know."

I told him how the same fate still haunted that estate in Camden.
Mr. Stockton sold it to a gentleman, who later sold it to an old man
who had married when near eighty, and who left it to the daughter born
of that marriage. This pretty child of his old age was left an orphan
quite young. At the age of fifteen, she ran away and married a boy of
seventeen, a canny Scotchman. The young couple lived to grow up, and
it proved after all a happy marriage. This last heiress left six children;
so the estate will now be divided, and no longer tempt the fortune-
hunters.

The Commodore said: "To think how we two youngsters in our
blue uniforms went down there to bully those people." He was much at
Colonel Chesnut's. Mrs. Chesnut being a Philadelphian, he was
somewhat at ease with them. It was the most thoroughly appointed
establishment he had then ever visited.

*   *   *   *   *

Went with our leviathan of loveliness to a ladies' meeting. No
scandal to-day, no wrangling, all harmonious, everybody knitting. Dare
say that soothing occupation helped our perturbed spirits to be calm.
Mrs. C—- is lovely, a perfect beauty. Said Brewster: "In Circassia,
think what a price would be set upon her, for there beauty sells by the
pound!"

Coming home the following conversation: "So Mrs. Blank thinks
purgatory will hold its own—never be abolished while women and
children have to live with drunken fathers and brothers." "She knows."
"She is too bitter. She says worse than that. She says we have an
institution worse than the Spanish Inquisition, worse than Torquemada,
and all that sort of thing." "What does she mean?" "You ask her. Her
words are sharp arrows. I am a dull creature, and I should spoil all by
repeating what she says."

"It is your own family that she calls the familiars of the Inquisition.
She declares that they set upon you, fall foul of you, watch and harass
you from morn till dewy eve. They have a perfect right to your life,
night and day, unto the fourth and fifth generation. They drop in at
breakfast and say, 'Are you not imprudent to eat that?' 'Take care now,

don't overdo it.' 'I think you eat too much so early in the day.' And they help themselves to the only thing you care for on the table. They abuse your friends and tell you it is your duty to praise your enemies. They tell you of all your faults candidly, because they love you so; that gives them a right to speak. What family interest they take in you. You ought to do this; you ought to do that, and then the everlasting 'you ought to have done,' which comes near making you a murderer, at least in heart. 'Blood's thicker than water,' they say, and there is where the longing to spill it comes in. No locks or bolts or bars can keep them out. Are they not your nearest family? They dine with you, dropping in after you are at soup. They come after you have gone to bed, when all the servants have gone away, and the man of the house, in his nightshirt, standing sternly at the door with the huge wooden bar in his hand, nearly scares them to death, and you are glad of it."

"Private life, indeed!" She says her husband entered public life and they went off to live in a far-away city. Then for the first time in her life she knew privacy. She never will forget how she jumped for joy as she told her servant not to admit a soul until after two o'clock in the day. Afterward, she took a fixed day at home. Then she was free indeed. She could read and write, stay at home, go out at her own sweet will, no longer sitting for hours with her fingers between the leaves of a frantically interesting book, while her kin slowly driveled nonsense by the yard—waiting, waiting, yawning. Would they never go? Then for hurting you, who is like a relative? They do it from a sense of duty. For stinging you, for cutting you to the quick, who like one of your own household? In point of fact, they alone can do it. They know the sore, and how to hit it every time. You are in their power. She says, did you ever see a really respectable, responsible, revered and beloved head of a family who ever opened his mouth at home except to find fault? He really thinks that is his business in life and that all enjoyment is sinful. He is there to prevent the women from such frivolous things as pleasure, etc., etc.

I sat placidly rocking in my chair by the window, trying to hope all was for the best. Mary Hammy rushed in literally drowned in tears. I never saw so drenched a face in my life. My heart stopped still. "Commodore Barron is taken prisoner," said she. "The Yankees have captured him and all his lieutenants. Poor Imogen—and there is my father scouting about, the Lord knows where. I only know he is in the advance guard. The Barron's time has come. Mine may come any minute. Oh, Cousin Mary, when Mrs. Lee told Imogen, she fainted! Those poor girls; they are nearly dead with trouble and fright."

"Go straight back to those children," I said. "Nobody will touch a hair of their father's head. Tell them I say so. They dare not. They are not savages quite. This is a civilized war, you know."

Mrs. Lee said to Mrs. Eustis (Mr. Corcoran's daughter) yesterday:

"Have you seen those accounts of arrests in Washington?" Mrs. Eustis answered calmly: "Yes, I know all about it. I suppose you allude to the fact that my father has been imprisoned." "No, no," interrupted the explainer, "she means the incarceration of those mature Washington belles suspected as spies." But Mrs. Eustis continued, "I have no fears for my father's safety."

August 31st.—Congress adjourns to-day. Jeff Davis ill. We go home on Monday if I am able to travel. Already I feel the dread stillness and torpor of our Sahara of a Sand Hill creeping into my veins. It chills the marrow of my bones. I am reveling in the noise of city life. I know what is before me. Nothing more cheering than the cry of the lone whippoorwill will break the silence at Sandy Hill, except as night draws near, when the screech-owl will add his mournful note.

September 1st.—North Carolina writes for arms for her soldiers. Have we any to send? No. Brewster, the plainspoken, says, "The President is ill, and our affairs are in the hands of noodles. All the generals away with the army; nobody here; General Lee in Western Virginia. Reading the third Psalm. The devil is sick, the devil a saint would be. Lord, how are they increased that trouble me? Many are they that rise up against me!"

September 2d.—Mr. Miles says he is not going anywhere at all, not even home. He is to sit here permanently—chairman of a committee to overhaul camps, commissariats, etc., etc.

We exchanged our ideas of Mr. Mason, in which we agreed perfectly. In the first place, he has a noble presence—really a handsome man; is a manly old Virginian, straightforward, brave, truthful, clever, the very beau-ideal of an independent, high-spirited F. F. V. If the English value a genuine man they will have one here. In every particular he is the exact opposite of Talleyrand. He has some peculiarities. He had never an ache or a pain himself; his physique is perfect, and he loudly declares that he hates to see persons ill; seems to him an unpardonable weakness.

It began to grow late. Many people had come to say good-by to me. I had fever as usual to-day, but in the excitement of this crowd of friends the invalid forgot fever. Mr. Chesnut held up his watch to me warningly and intimated "it was late, indeed, for one who has to travel tomorrow." So, as the Yankees say after every defeat, I "retired in good order."

Not quite, for I forgot handkerchief and fan. Gonzales rushed after and met me at the foot of the stairs. In his foreign, pathetic, polite, high-bred way, he bowed low and said he had made an excuse for the fan, for he had a present to make me, and then, though "startled and amazed, I paused and on the stranger gazed." Alas! I am a woman approaching forty, and the offering proved to be a bottle of cherry bounce. Nothing could have been more opportune, and with a little ice, etc., will help, I am sure, to save my life on that dreadful journey home. No discouragement now felt at the North. They take our forts and are satisfied for a while. Then the English are strictly neutral. Like the woman who saw her husband fight the bear, "It was the first fight she ever saw when she did not care who whipped."

Mr. Davis was very kind about it all. He told Mr. Chesnut to go home and have an eye to all the State defenses, etc., and that he would give him any position he asked for if he still wished to continue in the army. Now, this would be all that heart could wish, but Mr. Chesnut will never ask for anything. What will he ask for? That's the rub. I am certain of very few things in life now, but this is one I am certain of : Mr. Chesnut will never ask mortal man for any promotion for himself or for one of his own family.

CHAPTER X. CAMDEN, S. C.

September 9, 1861—*September* 19, 1861

Camden, S. C., *September 9, 1861.*—Home again at Mulberry, the fever in full possession of me. My sister, Kate, is my ideal woman, the most agreeable person I know in the world, with her soft, low, and sweet voice, her graceful, gracious ways, and her glorious gray eyes, that I looked into so often as we confided our very souls to each other.

God bless old Betsey's yellow face! She is a nurse in a thousand, and would do anything for "Mars Jeems' wife." My small ailments in all this comfort set me mourning over the dead and dying soldiers I saw in Virginia. How feeble my compassion proves, after all.

I handed the old Colonel a letter from his son in the army. He said, as he folded up the missive from the seat of war, "With this war we may die out. Your husband is the last—of my family." He means that my husband is his only living son; his grandsons are in the army, and they, too, may be killed—even Johnny, the gallant and gay, may not be bullet-proof. No child have I.

Now this old man of ninety years was born when it was not the fashion for a gentleman to be a saint, and being lord of all he surveyed for so many years, irresponsible, in the center of his huge domain, it is wonderful he was not a greater tyrant—the softening influence of that angel wife, no doubt. Saint or sinner, he understands the world about him—*au fond.*

Have had a violent attack of something wrong about my heart. It stopped beating, then it took to trembling, creaking and thumping like a Mississippi high-pressure steamboat, and the noise in my ears was more like an ammunition wagon rattling over the stones in Richmond. That was yesterday, and yet I am alive. That kind of thing makes one feel very mortal.

Russell writes how disappointed Prince Jerome Napoleon was with the appearance of our troops, and "he did not like Beauregard at all." Well! I give Bogar up to him. But how a man can find fault with our soldiers, as I have seen them individually and collectively in Charleston, Richmond, and everywhere—that beats me.

The British are the most conceited nation in the world, the most self-sufficient, self-satisfied, and arrogant. But each individual man does not blow his own penny whistle; they brag wholesale. Wellington—he certainly left it for others to sound his praises—though Mr. Binney thought the statue of Napoleon at the entrance of Apsley House was a little like "'Who killed Cock Robin?' 'I, said the sparrow, with my bow and arrow.'" But then it is so pleasant to hear them when it is a lump sum of praise, with no private crowing—praise of Trafalgar, Waterloo, the Scots Greys.

Fighting this and fighting that, with their crack corps stirs the blood and every heart responds—three times three! Hurrah!

But our people feel that they must send forth their own reported prowess: with an, "I did this and I did that." I know they did it; but I hang my head.

In those Tarleton Memoirs, in Lee's Memoirs, in Moultrie's, and in Lord Rawdon's letters, self is never brought to the front. I have been reading them over and admire their modesty and good taste as much as their courage and cleverness. That kind of British eloquence takes me. It is not, "*Soldats! marchons, gloire!*" Not a bit of it; but, "Now, my lads, stand firm!" and, "Now up, and let them have it!"

Our name has not gone out of print. To-day, the Examiner, as usual, pitches into the President. It thinks Toombs, Cobb, Slidell, Lamar, or Chesnut would have been far better in the office. There is considerable choice in that lot. Five men more utterly dissimilar were never named in the same paragraph.

September 19th.—A painful piece of news came to us yesterday—our cousin, Mrs. Witherspoon, of Society Hill, was found dead in her bed. She was quite well the night before. Killed, people say, by family sorrows. She was a proud and high-strung woman. Nothing shabby in word, thought, or deed ever came nigh her. She was of a warm and tender heart, too; truth and uprightness itself. Few persons have ever been more loved and looked up to. She was a very handsome old lady, of fine presence, dignified and commanding.

"Killed by family sorrows," so they said when Mrs. John N. Williams died. So Uncle John said yesterday of his brother, Burwell. "Death deserts the army," said that quaint old soul, "and takes fancy shots of the most eccentric kind nearer home."

The high and disinterested conduct our enemies seem to expect of us is involuntary and unconscious praise. They pay us the compliment to look for from us (and execrate us for the want of it) a degree of virtue they were never able to practise themselves. It is a crowning misdemeanor for us to hold still in slavery those Africans whom they brought here from Africa, or sold to us when they found it did not pay to own them themselves. Gradually, they slid or sold them off down here; or freed them prospectively, giving themselves years in which to get rid of them in a remunerative way. We want to spread them over other lands, too—West and South, or Northwest, where the climate would free them or kill them, or improve them out of the world, as our friends up North do the Indians. If they had been forced to keep the negroes in New England, I dare say the negroes might have shared the Indians' fate, for they are wise in their generation, these Yankee children of light. Those pernicious Africans! So have just spoken Mr. Chesnut and Uncle John, both *ci-devant* Union men, now utterly for State rights.

It is queer how different the same man may appear viewed from different standpoints. "What a perfect gentleman," said one person of another; "so fine-looking, high-bred, distinguished, easy, free, and above all graceful in his bearing; so high-toned! He is always indignant at any symptom of wrong-doing. He is charming—the man of all others I like to have strangers see—a noble representative of our country." "Yes, every word of that is true," was the reply. "He is all that. And then the other side of the picture is true, too. You can always find him. You know *where* to find him! Wherever there is a looking-glass, a bottle, or a woman, there will he be also." "My God! and you call yourself his friend." "Yes, I know him down to the ground."

This conversation I overheard from an upper window when looking down on the piazza below—a complicated character truly beyond La Bruyère—with what Mrs. Preston calls refinement spread thin until it is skin-deep only.

An iron steamer has run the blockade at Savannah. We now raise our wilted heads like flowers after a shower. This drop of good news revives us.[62]

---

[62] By reason of illness, preoccupation in other affairs, and various deterrent causes besides, Mrs. Chesnut allowed a considerable period to elapse before making another entry in her diary.

CHAPTER XI. COLUMBIA, S. C.

February 20, 1862—*July* 21, 1862

Columbia, S. C., *February 20, 1862.*—Had an appetite for my dainty breakfast. Always breakfast in bed now. But then, my Mercury contained such bad news. That is an appetizing style of matutinal newspaper. Fort Donelson[63] has fallen, but no men fell with it. It is prisoners for them that we can not spare, or prisoners for us that we may not be able to feed: that is so much to be "forefended," as Keitt says. They lost six thousand, we two thousand; I grudge that proportion. In vain, alas! ye gallant few—few, but undismayed. Again, they make a stand. We have Buckner, Beauregard, and Albert Sidney Johnston. With such leaders and God's help we may be saved from the hated Yankees; who knows?

February 21st.—A crowd collected here last night and there was a serenade. I am like Mrs. Nickleby, who never saw a horse coming full speed but she thought the Cheerybles had sent post-haste to take Nicholas into co-partnership. So I got up and dressed, late as it was. I felt sure England had sought our alliance at last, and we would make a Yorktown of it before long. Who was it? Will you ever guess?—Artemus Goodwyn and General Owens, of Florida.

Just then, Mr. Chesnut rushed in, put out the light, locked the door and sat still as a mouse. Rap, rap, came at the door. "I say, Chesnut, they are calling for you." At last we heard Janney (hotel-keeper) loudly proclaiming from the piazza that "Colonel Chesnut was not here at all, at all." After a while, when they had all gone from the street, and the very house itself had subsided into perfect quiet, the door again was roughly shaken. "I say, Chesnut, old fellow, come out—I know you are there. Nobody here now wants to hear you make a speech. That crowd has all gone. We want a little quiet talk with you. I am just from Richmond." That was the open sesame, and to-day I hear none of the Richmond news is encouraging. Colonel Shaw is blamed for the shameful Roanoke surrender.[64]

Toombs is out on a rampage and swears he will not accept a seat in the Confederate Senate given in the insulting way his was by the

---

[63] Fort Donelson stood on the Cumberland River about 60 miles northwest of Nashville. The Confederate garrison numbered about 18,000 men. General Grant invested the Fort on February 13, 1862, and General Buckner, who commanded it, surrendered on February 16th. The Federal force at the time of the surrender numbered 27,000 men; their loss in killed and wounded being 2,660 men and the Confederate loss about 2,000.

[64] General Burnside captured the Confederate garrison at Roanoke Island on February 8, 1862.

Georgia Legislature: calls it shabby treatment, and adds that Georgia is not the only place where good men have been so ill used.

The Governor and Council have fluttered the dove-cotes, or, at least, the tea-tables. They talk of making a call for all silver, etc. I doubt if we have enough to make the sacrifice worth while, but we propose to set the example.

February 22d.—What a beautiful day for our Confederate President to be inaugurated! God speed him; God keep him; God save him!

John Chesnut's letter was quite what we needed. In spirit it is all that one could ask. He says, "Our late reverses are acting finely with the army of the Potomac. A few more thrashings and every man will enlist for the war. Victories made us too sanguine and easy, not to say vainglorious. Now for the rub, and let them have it!"

A lady wrote to Mrs. Bunch: "Dear Emma: When shall I call for you to go and see Madame de St. André?" She was answered: "Dear Lou: I can not go with you to see Madame de St. Andre, but will always retain the kindest feeling toward you on account of our past relations," etc. The astounded friend wrote to ask what all this meant. No answer came, and then she sent her husband to ask and demand an explanation. He was answered thus: "My dear fellow, there can be no explanation possible. Hereafter there will be no intercourse between my wife and yours; simply that, nothing more." So the men meet at the club as before, and there is no further trouble between them. The lady upon whom the slur is cast says, "and I am a woman and can't fight!"

February 23d.—While Mr. Chesnut was in town I was at the Prestons. John Cochran and some other prisoners had asked to walk over the grounds, visit the Hampton Gardens, and some friends in Columbia. After the dreadful state of the public mind at the escape of one of the prisoners, General Preston was obliged to refuse his request. Mrs. Preston and the rest of us wanted him to say "Yes," and so find out who in Columbia were his treacherous friends. Pretty bold people they must be, to receive Yankee invaders in the midst of the row over one enemy already turned loose amid us.

General Preston said: "We are about to sacrifice life and fortune for a fickle multitude who will not stand up to us at last." The harsh comments made as to his lenient conduct to prisoners have embittered him. I told him what I had heard Captain Trenholm say in his speech. He said he would listen to no criticism except from a man with a musket on his shoulder, and who had beside enlisted for the war, had given up all, and had no choice but to succeed or die.

February 24th.—Congress and the newspapers render one desperate, ready to cut one's own throat. They represent everything in our country as deplorable. Then comes some one back from our gay and gallant army at the front. The spirit of our army keeps us up after all. Letters from the army revive one. They come as welcome as the flowers in May. Hopeful and bright, utterly unconscious of our weak despondency.

February 25th.—They have taken at Nashville[65] more men than we had at Manassas; there was bad handling of troops, we poor women think, or this would not be. Mr. Venable added bitterly, "Giving up our soldiers to the enemy means giving up the cause. We can not replace them." The up-country men were Union men generally, and the low-country seceders. The former growl; they never liked those aristocratic boroughs and parishes, they had themselves a good and prosperous country, a good constitution, and were satisfied. But they had to go—to leave all and fight for the others who brought on all the trouble, and who do not show too much disposition to fight for themselves.

That is the extreme up-country view. The extreme low-country says Jeff Davis is not enough out of the Union yet. His inaugural address reads as one of his speeches did four years ago in the United States Senate.

A letter in a morning paper accused Mr. Chesnut of staying too long in Charleston. The editor was asked for the writer's name. He gave it as Little Moses, the Governor's secretary. When Little Moses was spoken to, in a great trepidation he said that Mrs. Pickens wrote it, and got him to publish it; so it was dropped, for Little Moses is such an arrant liar no one can believe him. Besides, if that sort of thing amuses Mrs. Pickens, let her amuse herself.

March 5th.—Mary Preston went back to Mulberry with me from Columbia. She found a man there tall enough to take her in to dinner— Tom Boykin, who is six feet four, the same height as her father. Tom was very handsome in his uniform, and Mary prepared for a nice time, but he looked as if he would so much rather she did not talk to him, and he set her such a good example, saying never a word.

Old Colonel Chesnut came for us. When the train stopped, Quashie, shiny black, was seen on his box, as glossy and perfect in his way as his blooded bays, but the old Colonel would stop and pick up the dirtiest little negro I ever saw who was crying by the roadside. This ragged little black urchin was made to climb up and sit beside Quash. It spoilt the symmetry of the turn-out, but it was a character touch, and the old gentleman knows no law but his own will. He had a biscuit in his pocket which he gave this sniffling little negro, who proved to be his man Scip's son.

I was ill at Mulberry and never left my room. Doctor Boykin came, more military than medical. Colonel Chesnut brought him up, also Teams, who said he was down in the mouth. Our men were not fighting

---

[65] Nashville was evacuated by the Confederates under Albert Sidney Johnston, in February, 1862.

as they should. We had only pluck and luck and a dogged spirit of fighting, to offset their weight in men and munitions of war, I wish I could remember Team's words; this is only his idea. His language was quaint and striking—no grammar, but no end of sense and good feeling. Old Colonel Chesnut, catching a word, began his litany, saying, "Numbers will tell," "Napoleon, you know," etc., etc.

At Mulberry the war has been ever afar off, but threats to take the silver came very near indeed—silver that we had before the Revolution, silver that Mrs. Chesnut brought from Philadelphia. Jack Cantey and Doctor Boykin came back on the train with us. Wade Hampton is the hero.

Sweet May Dacre. Lord Byron and Disraeli make their rosebuds Catholic; May Dacre is another Aurora Raby. I like Disraeli because I find so many clever things in him. I like the sparkle and the glitter. Carlyle does not hold up his hands in holy horror of us because of African slavery. Lord Lyons[66] has gone against us. Lord Derby and Louis Napoleon are silent in our hour of direst need. People call me Cassandra, for I cry that outside hope is quenched. From the outside no help indeed cometh to this beleaguered land.

March 7th.—Mrs. Middleton was dolorous indeed. General Lee had warned the planters about Combahee, etc., that they must take care of themselves now; he could not do it. Confederate soldiers had committed some outrages on the plantations and officers had punished them promptly. She poured contempt Upon Yancey's letter to Lord Russell.[67] It was the letter of a shopkeeper, not in the style of a statesman at all.

We called to see Mary McDuffie.[68] She asked Mary Preston what Doctor Boykin had said of her husband as we came along in the train. She heard it was something very complimentary. Mary P. tried to remember, and to repeat it all, to the joy of the other Mary, who liked to hear nice things about her husband.

Mary was amazed to hear of the list of applicants for promotion. One delicate-minded person accompanied his demand for advancement by a request for a written description of the Manassas battle; he had heard Colonel Chesnut give such a brilliant account of it in Governor Cobb's room.

The Merrimac[69] business has come like a gleam of lightning

---

[66] Richard, Lord Lyons, British minister to the United States from 1858 to 1865.

[67] Lord Russell was Foreign Secretary under the Palmerston administration of 1859 to 1865.

[68] Mary McDuffie was the second wife of Wade Hampton.

[69] The Merrimac was formerly a 40-gun screw frigate of the United States Navy. In April, 1861, when the Norfolk Navy-yard was abandoned by the United States she was sunk. Her hull was afterward raised by the Confederates and she was reconstructed on new plans, and renamed the Virginia. On March 2, 1862, she destroyed the Congress, a sailing-ship of 50 guns, and the Cumberland, a sailing-ship of 30 guns, at Newport News.

illumining a dark scene. Our sky is black and lowering.

The Judge saw his little daughter at my window and he came up. He was very smooth and kind. It was really a delightful visit; not a disagreeable word was spoken. He abused no one whatever, for he never once spoke of any one but himself, and himself he praised without stint. He did not look at me once, though he spoke very kindly to me.

March 10th.—Second year of Confederate independence. I write daily for my own diversion. These *mémoires pour servir* may at some future day afford facts about these times and prove useful to more important people than I am. I do not wish to do any harm or to hurt any one. If any scandalous stories creep in they can easily be burned. It is hard, in such a hurry as things are now, to separate the wheat from the chaff. Now that I have made my protest and written down my wishes, I can scribble on with a free will and free conscience.

Congress at the North is down on us. They talk largely of hanging slave-owners. They say they hold Port Royal, as we did when we took it originally from the aborigines, who fled before us; so we are to be exterminated and improved, *à l'Indienne*, from the face of the earth.

Medea, when asked: "Country, wealth, husband, children, all are gone; and now what remains?" answered: "Medea remains." "There is a time in most men's lives when they resemble Job, sitting among the ashes and drinking in the full bitterness of complicated misfortune."

March 11th.—A freshman came quite eager to be instructed in all the wiles of society. He wanted to try his hand at a flirtation, and requested minute instructions, as he knew nothing whatever: he was so very fresh. "Dance with her," he was told, "and talk with her; walk with her and flatter her; dance until she is warm and tired; then propose to walk in a cool, shady piazza. It must be a somewhat dark piazza. Begin your promenade slowly; warm up to your work; draw her arm closer and closer; then, break her wing."

"Heavens, what is that—break her wing?" "Why, you do not know even that? Put your arm round her waist and kiss her. After that, it is all plain sailing. She comes down when you call like the coon to Captain Scott: 'You need not fire, Captain,' etc."

The aspirant for fame as a flirt followed these lucid directions literally, but when he seized the poor girl and kissed her, she uplifted her voice in terror, and screamed as if the house was on fire. So quick, sharp, and shrill were her yells for help that the bold flirt sprang over the banister, upon which grew a strong climbing rose. This he struggled through, and ran toward the college, taking a bee line. He was so

---

On March 7th she attacked the Minnesota, but was met by the Monitor and defeated in a memorable engagement. Many features of modern battle-ships have been derived from the Merrimac and Monitor.

mangled by the thorns that he had to go home and have them picked out by his family. The girl's brother challenged him. There was no mortal combat, however, for the gay young fellow who had led the freshman's ignorance astray stepped forward and put things straight. An explanation and an apology at every turn hushed it all up.

Now, we all laughed at this foolish story most heartily. But Mr. Venable remained grave and preoccupied, and was asked: "Why are you so unmoved? It is funny." "I like more probable fun; I have been in college and I have kissed many a girl, but never a one scrome yet."

Last Saturday was the bloodiest we have had in proportion to numbers.[70] The enemy lost 1,500. The handful left at home are rushing to arms at last. Bragg has gone to join Beauregard at Columbus, Miss. Old Abe truly took the field in that Scotch cap of his.

Mrs. McCord,[71] the eldest daughter of Langdon Cheves, got up a company for her son, raising it at her own expense. She has the brains and energy of a man. To-day she repeated a remark of a low-country gentleman, who is dissatisfied: "This Government (Confederate) protects neither person nor property." Fancy the scornful turn of her lip! Some one asked for Langdon Cheves, her brother. "Oh, Langdon!" she replied coolly, "he is a pure patriot; he has no ambition. While I was there, he was letting Confederate soldiers ditch through his garden and ruin him at their leisure."

Cotton is five cents a pound and labor of no value at all; it commands no price whatever. People gladly hire out their negroes to have them fed and clothed, which latter can not be done. Cotton osnaburg at 37 1/2 cents a yard, leaves no chance to clothe them. Langdon was for martial law and making the bloodsuckers disgorge their ill-gotten gains. We, poor fools, who are patriotically ruining ourselves will see our children in the gutter while treacherous dogs of millionaires go rolling by in their coaches—coaches that were acquired by taking advantage of our necessities.

This terrible battle of the ships—Monitor, Merrimac, etc. All hands on board the Cumberland went down. She fought gallantly and fired a round as she sank. The Congress ran up a white flag. She fired on our boats as they went up to take off her wounded. She was burned. The worst of it is that all this will arouse them to more furious exertions to destroy us. They hated us so before, but how now?

In Columbia I do not know a half-dozen men who would not gaily

---

[70] On March 7 and 8, 1862, occurred the battle of Pea Ridge in Western Arkansas, where the Confederates were defeated, and on March 8th and 9th, occurred the conflict in Hampton Roads between the warships Merrimac, Cumberland, Congress, and Monitor.

[71] Louisa Susanna McCord, whose husband was David J. McCord, a lawyer of Columbia, who died in 1855. She was educated in Philadelphia, and was the author of several books of verse, including Caius Gracchus, a tragedy; she was also a brilliant pamphleteer.

step into Jeff Davis's shoes with a firm conviction that they would do better in every respect than he does. The monstrous conceit, the fatuous ignorance of these critics! It is pleasant to hear Mrs. McCord on this subject, when they begin to shake their heads and tell us what Jeff Davis ought to do.

March 12th.—In the naval battle the other day we had twenty-five guns in all. The enemy had fifty-four in the Cumberland, forty-four in the St. Lawrence, besides a fleet of gunboats, filled with rifled cannon. Why not? They can have as many as they please. "No pent-up Utica contracts their powers"; the whole boundless world being theirs to recruit in. Ours is only this one little spot of ground—the blockade, or stockade, which hems us in with only the sky open to us, and for all that, how tender-footed and cautious they are as they draw near.

An anonymous letter purports to answer Colonel Chesnut's address to South Carolinians now in the army of the Potomac. The man says, "All that bosh is no good." He knows lots of people whose fathers were notorious Tories in our war for independence and made fortunes by selling their country. Their sons have the best places, and they are cowards and traitors still. Names are given, of course.

Floyd and Pillow[72] are suspended from their commands because of Fort Donelson. The people of Tennessee demand a like fate for Albert Sidney Johnston. They say he is stupid. Can human folly go further than this Tennessee madness?

I did Mrs. Blank a kindness. I told the women when her name came up that she was childless now, but that she had lost three children. I hated to leave her all alone. Women have such a contempt for a childless wife. Now, they will be all sympathy and goodness. I took away her "reproach among women."

March 13th.—Mr. Chesnut fretting and fuming. From the poor old blind bishop downward everybody is besetting him to let off students, theological and other, from going into the army. One comfort is that the boys will go. Mr. Chesnut answers: "Wait until you have saved your country before you make preachers and scholars. When you have a country, there will be no lack of divines, students, scholars to adorn and purify it." He says he is a one-idea man. That idea is to get every possible man into the ranks.

Professor Le Conte[73] is an able auxiliary. He has undertaken to

---

[72] John D. Floyd, who had been Governor of Virginia from 1850 to 1853, became Secretary of War in 1857 He was first in command at Fort Donelson. Gideon J. Pillow had been a Major-General of volunteers in the Mexican War and was second in command at Fort Donelson. He and Floyd escaped from the Fort when it was invested by Grant, leaving General Buckner to make the surrender.

[73] Joseph Le Conte, who afterward arose to much distinction as a geologist and writer of text-books on geology. He died in 1901, while he was connected with the University of California. His work at Columbia was to manufacture, on a large scale, medicines for the Confederate Army, his laboratory being the main source of supply. In

supervise and carry on the powder-making enterprise—the very first attempted in the Confederacy, and Mr. Chesnut is proud of it. It is a brilliant success, thanks to Le Conte.

Mr. Chesnut receives anonymous letters urging him to arrest the Judge as seditious. They say he is a dangerous and disaffected person. His abuse of Jeff Davis and the Council is rabid. Mr. Chesnut laughs and throws the letters into the fire. "Disaffected to Jeff Davis," says he; "disaffected to the Council, that don't count. He knows what he is about; he would not injure his country for the world."

Read Uncle Tom's Cabin again. These negro women have a chance here that women have nowhere else. They can redeem themselves—the "impropers" can. They can marry decently, and nothing is remembered against these colored ladies. It is not a nice topic, but Mrs. Stowe revels in it. How delightfully Pharisaic a feeling it must be to rise superior and fancy we are so degraded as to defend and like to live with such degraded creatures around us—such men as Legree and his women.

The best way to take negroes to your heart is to get as far away from them as possible. As far as I can see, Southern women do all that missionaries could do to prevent and alleviate evils. The social evil has not been suppressed in old England or in New England, in London or in Boston. People in those places expect more virtue from a plantation African than they can insure in practise among themselves with all their own high moral surroundings—light, education, training, and support. Lady Mary Montagu says, "Only men and women at last." "Male and female, created he them," says the Bible. There are cruel, graceful, beautiful mothers of angelic Evas North as well as South, I dare say. The Northern men and women who came here were always hardest, for they expected an African to work and behave as a white man. We do not.

I have often thought from observation truly that perfect beauty hardens the heart, and as to grace, what so graceful as a cat, a tigress, or a panther. Much love, admiration, worship hardens an idol's heart. It becomes utterly callous and selfish. It expects to receive all and to give nothing. It even likes the excitement of seeing people suffer. I speak now of what I have watched with horror and amazement.

Topsys I have known, but none that were beaten or ill-used. Evas are mostly in the heaven of Mrs. Stowe's imagination. People can't love things dirty, ugly, and repulsive, simply because they ought to do so, but they can be good to them at a distance; that's easy. You see, I can not rise very high; I can only judge by what I see.

March 14th.—Thank God for a ship! It has run the blockade with

Professor Le Conte's autobiography published in 1903, are several chapters devoted to his life in the South.

arms and ammunition.

There are no negro sexual relations half so shocking as Mormonism. And yet the United States Government makes no bones of receiving Mormons into its sacred heart. Mr. Venable said England held her hand over "the malignant and the turbaned Turk" to save and protect him, slaves, seraglio, and all. But she rolls up the whites of her eyes at us when slavery, bad as it is, is stepping out into freedom every moment through Christian civilization. They do not grudge the Turk even his bag and Bosphorus privileges. To a recalcitrant wife it is, "Here yawns the sack ; there rolls the sea," etc. And France, the bold, the brave, the ever free, she has not been so tender-footed in Algiers. But then the "you are another" argument is a shabby one. "You see," says Mary Preston sagaciously, "we are white Christian descendants of Huguenots and Cavaliers, and they expect of us different conduct."

Went in Mrs. Preston's landau to bring my boarding-school girls here to dine. At my door met J. F., who wanted me then and there to promise to help him with his commission or put him in the way of one. At the carriage steps I was handed in by Gus Smith, who wants his brother made commissary. The beauty of it all is they think I have some influence, and I have not a particle. The subject of Mr. Chesnut's military affairs, promotions, etc., is never mentioned by me.

March 15th.—When we came home from Richmond, there stood Warren Nelson, propped up against my door, lazily waiting for me, the handsome creature. He said he meant to be heard, so I walked back with him to the drawing-room.

They are wasting their time dancing attendance on me. I can not help them. Let them shoulder their musket and go to the wars like men.

After tea came "Mars Kit"—he said for a talk, but that Mr. Preston would not let him have, for Mr. Preston had arrived some time before him. Mr. Preston said "Mars Kit" thought it "bad form" to laugh. After that you may be sure a laugh from "Mars Kit" was secured. Again and again, he was forced to laugh with a will. I reversed Oliver Wendell Holmes's good resolution—never to be as funny as he could. I did my very utmost.

Mr. Venable interrupted the fun, which was fast and furious, with the very best of bad news! Newbern shelled and burned , cotton, turpentine—everything—There were 5,000 North Carolinians in the fray, 12,000 Yankees. Now there stands Goldsboro. One more step and we are cut in two. The railroad is our backbone, like the Blue Ridge and the Alleghanies, with which it runs parallel. So many discomforts, no wonder we are down-hearted.

Mr. Venable thinks as we do—Garnett is our most thorough scholar; Lamar the most original, and the cleverest of our men—L. Q. C. Lamar—time fails me to write all his name. Then, there is R. M. T. Hunter. Muscoe Russell Garnett and his Northern wife: that match was made at my house in Washington when Garnett was a member of the United States Congress.

March 17th.—Back to the Congaree House to await my husband, who has made a rapid visit to the Wateree region. As we drove up Mr. Chesnut said: "Did you see the stare of respectful admiration E. R. bestowed upon you, so curiously prolonged? I could hardly keep my countenance." "Yes, my dear child, I feel the honor of it, though my individual self goes for nothing in it. I am the wife of the man who has the appointing power just now, with so many commissions to be filled. I am nearly forty, and they do my understanding the credit to suppose I can be made to believe they admire my mature charms. They think they fool me into thinking that they believe me charming. There is hardly any farce in the world more laughable."

Last night a house was set on fire; last week two houses. "The red cock crows in the barn!" Our troubles thicken, indeed, when treachery comes from that dark quarter.

When the President first offered Johnston Pettigrew a brigadier-generalship, his answer was: "Not yet. Too many men are ahead of me who have earned their promotion in the field. I will come after them, not before. So far I have done nothing to merit reward," etc. He would not take rank when he could get it. I fancy he may cool his heels now waiting for it. He was too high and mighty. There was another conscientious man—Burnet, of Kentucky. He gave up his regiment to his lieutenant-colonel when he found the lieutenant-colonel could command the regiment and Burnet could not maneuver it in the field. He went into the fight simply as an aide to Floyd. Modest merit just now is at a premium.

William Gilmore Simms is here; read us his last poetry; have forgotten already what it was about. It was not tiresome, however, and that is a great thing when people will persist in reading their own rhymes.

I did not hear what Mr. Preston was saying. "The last piece of Richmond news," Mr. Chesnut said as he went away, and he looked so fagged out I asked no questions. I knew it was bad.

At daylight there was a loud knocking at my door. I hurried on a dressing-gown and flew to open the door. "Mrs. Chesnut, Mrs. M. says please don't forget her son. Mr. Chesnut, she hears, has come back. Please get her son a commission. He must have an office." I shut the door in the servant's face. If I had the influence these foolish people attribute to me why should I not help my own? I have a brother, two brothers-in-law, and no end of kin, all gentlemen privates, and privates they would stay to the end of time before they said a word to me about commissions. After a long talk we were finally disgusted and the men went off to the bulletin-board. Whatever else it shows, good or bad, there is always woe for some house in the killed and wounded. We have need of stout hearts. I feel a sinking of mine as we drive near the board.

March 18th.—My war archon is beset for commissions, and somebody says for every one given, you make one ingrate and a thousand enemies.

As I entered Miss Mary Stark's I whispered: "He has promised to vote for Louis." What radiant faces. To my friend, Miss Mary said, "Your son-in-law, what is he doing for his country?" "He is a tax collector." Then spoke up the stout old girl: "Look at my cheek; it is red with blushing for you. A great, hale, hearty young man! Fie on him! fie on him! for shame! Tell his wife; run him out of the house with a broomstick; send him down to the coast at least." Fancy my cheeks. I could not raise my eyes to the poor lady, so mercilessly assaulted. My face was as hot with compassion as the outspoken Miss Mary pretended hers to be with vicarious mortification.

Went to see sweet and saintly Mrs. Bartow. She read us a letter from Mississippi—not so bad: "More men there than the enemy suspected, and torpedoes to blow up the wretches when they came." Next to see Mrs. Izard. She had with her a relative just from the North. This lady had asked Seward for passports, and he told her to "hold on a while; the road to South Carolina will soon be open to all, open and safe." To-day Mrs. Arthur Hayne heard from her daughter that Richmond is to be given up. Mrs. Buell is her daughter.

Met Mr. Chesnut, who said: "New Madrid[74] has been given up. I do not know any more than the dead where New Madrid is. It is bad, all the same, this giving up. I can't stand it. The hemming-in process is nearly complete. The ring of fire is almost unbroken."

Mr. Chesnut's negroes offered to fight for him if he would arm them. He pretended to believe them. He says one man can not do it. The whole country must agree to it. He would trust such as he would select, and he would give so many acres of land and his freedom to each one as he enlisted.

Mrs. Albert Rhett came for an office for her son John. I told her Mr. Chesnut would never propose a kinsman for office, but if any one else would bring him forward he would vote for him certainly, as he is so eminently fit for position. Now he is a private.

March 19th.—He who runs may read. Conscription means that we are in a tight place. This war was a volunteer business. To-morrow conscription begins—the *dernier ressort*. The President has remodeled his Cabinet, leaving Bragg for North Carolina. His War Minister is Randolph, of Virginia. A Union man *par excellence*, Watts, of Alabama, is Attorney-General. And now, too late by one year, when all the mechanics are in the army, Mallory begins to telegraph Captain

---

[74] New Madrid, Missouri, had been under siege since March 3, 1862.

Ingraham to build ships at any expense. We are locked in and can not get "the requisites for naval architecture," says a magniloquent person. Henry Frost says all hands wink at cotton going out. Why not send it out and buy ships? "Every now and then there is a holocaust of cotton burning," says the magniloquent. Conscription has waked the Rip Van Winkles. The streets of Columbia were never so crowded with men. To fight and to be made to fight are different things.

To my small wits, whenever people were persistent, united, and rose in their might, no general, however great, succeeded in subjugating them. Have we not swamps, forests, rivers, mountains—every natural barrier? The Carthaginians begged for peace because they were a luxurious people and could not endure the hardship of war, though the enemy suffered as sharply as they did! "Factions among themselves" is the rock on which we split. Now for the great soul who is to rise up and lead us. Why tarry his footsteps?

March 20th.—The Merrimac is now called the Virginia. I think these changes of names so confusing and so senseless. Like the French "Royal Bengal Tiger," "National Tiger," etc. *Rue* this, and next day *Rue* that, the very days and months a symbol, and nothing signified.

I was lying on the sofa in my room, and two men slowly walking up and down the corridor talked aloud as if necessarily all rooms were unoccupied at this midday hour. I asked Maum Mary who they were. "Yeadon and Barnwell Rhett, Jr." They abused the Council roundly, and my husband's name arrested my attention. Afterward, when Yeadon attacked Mr. Chesnut, Mr. Chesnut surprised him by knowing beforehand all he had to say. Naturally I had repeated the loud interchange of views I had overheard in the corridor.

First, Nathan Davis called. Then Gonzales, who presented a fine, soldierly appearance in his soldier clothes, and the likeness to Beauregard was greater than ever. Nathan, all the world knows, is by profession a handsome man.

General Gonzales told us what in the bitterness of his soul he had written to Jeff Davis. He regretted that he had not been his classmate; then he might have been as well treated as Northrop. In any case he would not have been refused a brigadiership, citing General Trapier and Tom Drayton. He had worked for it, had earned it; they had not. To his surprise, Mr. Davis answered him, and in a sharp note of four pages. Mr. Davis demanded from whom he quoted, "not his classmate." General Gonzales responded, "from the public voice only." Now he will fight for us all the same, but go on demanding justice from Jeff Davis until he get his dues—at least, until one of them gets his dues, for he means to go on hitting Jeff Davis over the head whenever he has a chance.

"I am afraid," said I, "you will find it a hard head to crack." He replied in his flowery Spanish way: "Jeff Davis will be the sun, radiating all light, heat, and patronage; he will not be a moon reflecting public opinion, for he has the soul of a despot; he delights to spite public opinion. See, people abused him for making Crittenden brigadier. Straightway he made him major-general, and just after a blundering, besotted defeat, too." Also, he told the President in that letter: "Napoleon made his generals after great deeds on their part, and not for having been educated at St. Cyr, or Brie, or the Polytechnique," etc., etc. Nathan Davis sat as still as a Sioux warrior, not an eyelash moved. And yet he said afterward that he was amused while the Spaniard railed at his great namesake.

Gonzales said: "Mrs. Slidell would proudly say that she was a Creole. They were such fools, they thought Creole meant—" Here Nathan interrupted pleasantly: "At the St. Charles, in New Orleans, on the bill of fare were 'Creole eggs.' When they were brought to a man who had ordered them, with perfect simplicity, he held them up, 'Why, they are only hens' eggs, after all.' What in Heaven's name he expected them to be, who can say?" smiled Nathan the elegant.

One lady says (as I sit reading in the drawing-room window while Maum Mary puts my room to rights): "I clothe my negroes well. I could not bear to see them in dirt and rags; it would be unpleasant to me." Another lady: "Yes. Well, so do I. But not fine clothes, you know. I feel—now—it was one of our sins as a nation, the way we indulged them in sinful finery. We will be punished for it."

Last night, Mrs. Pickens met General Cooper. Madam knew General Cooper only as our adjutant-general, and Mr. Mason's brother-in-law. In her slow, graceful, impressive way, her beautiful eyes eloquent with feeling, she inveighed against Mr. Davis's wickedness in always sending men born at the North to command at Charleston. General Cooper is on his way to make a tour of inspection there now. The dear general settled his head on his cravat with the aid of his forefinger; he tugged rather more nervously with the something that is always wrong inside of his collar, and looked straight up through his spectacles. Some one crossed the room, stood back of Mrs. Pickens, and murmured in her ear, "General Cooper was born in New York." Sudden silence.

Dined with General Cooper at the Prestons. General Hampton and Blanton Duncan were there also; the latter a thoroughly free-and-easy Western man, handsome and clever; more audacious than either, perhaps. He pointed to Buck—Sally Buchanan Campbell Preston. "What's that girl laughing at?" Poor child, how amazed she looked. He bade them "not despair; all the nice young men would not be killed in the war; there would be a few left. For himself, he could give them no hope Mrs. Duncan was uncommonly healthy." Mrs. Duncan is also lovely. We have seen her.

March 24th.—I was asked to the Tognos' tea, so refused a drive with Mary Preston. As I sat at my solitary casemate, waiting for the time to come for the Tognos, saw Mrs. Preston's landau pass, and Mr. Venable making Mary laugh at some of his army stories, as only Mr. Venable can. Already I felt that I had paid too much for my whistle— that is, the Togno tea. The Gibbeses, Trenholms, Edmund Rhett, there. Edmund Rhett has very fine eyes and makes fearful play with them. He sits silent and motionless, with his hands on his knees, his head bent forward, and his eyes fixed upon you. I could think of nothing like it but a setter and a covey of partridges.

As to President Davis, he sank to profounder deeps of abuse of him than even Gonzales. I quoted Yancey: "A crew may not like their captain, but if they are mad enough to mutiny while a storm is raging, all hands are bound to go to the bottom." After that I contented myself with a mild shake of the head when I disagreed with him, and at last I began to shake so persistently it amounted to incipient palsy. "Jeff Davis," he said, "is conceited, wrong-headed, wranglesome, obstinate—a traitor." "Now I have borne much in silence," said I at last, "but that is pernicious nonsense. Do not let us waste any more time listening to your quotations from the Mercury."

He very good-naturedly changed the subject, which was easy just then, for a delicious supper was on the table ready for us. But Doctor Gibbes began anew the fighting. He helped me to some *pâté*—"Not *foie gras*," said Madame Togno, "*pâté perdreaux*." Doctor Gibbes, however, gave it a flavor of his own. "Eat it," said he, "it is good for you; rich and wholesome; healthy as cod-liver oil."

A queer thing happened. At the post-office a man saw a small boy open with a key the box of the Governor and the Council, take the contents of the box and run for his life. Of course, this man called to the urchin to stop. The urchin did not heed, but seeing himself pursued, began tearing up the letters and papers. He was caught and the fragments were picked up. Finding himself a prisoner, he pointed out the negro who gave him the key. The negro was arrested.

Governor Pickens called to see me to-day. We began with Fort Sumter. For an hour did we hammer at that fortress. We took it, gun by gun. He was very pleasant and friendly in his manner.

James Chesnut has been so nice this winter; so reasonable and considerate—that is, for a man. The night I came from Madame Togno's, instead of making a row about the lateness of the hour, he said he was "so wide awake and so hungry." I put on my dressing-gown and scrambled some eggs, etc., there on our own fire. And with our feet on the fender and the small supper-table between us, we enjoyed the supper and glorious gossip. Rather a pleasant state of things when one's own husband is in good humor and cleverer than all the men outside.

This afternoon, the *entente cordiale* still subsisting, Maum Mary beckoned me out mysteriously, but Mr. Chesnut said: "Speak out, old

woman; nobody here but myself." "Mars Nathum Davis wants to speak
to her," said she. So I hurried off to the drawing-room, Maum Mary
flapping her down-at-the-heels shoes in my wake. "He's gwine bekase
somebody done stole his boots. How could he stay bedout boots?" So
Nathan said good-by. Then we met General Gist, Maum Mary still
hovering near, and I congratulated him on being promoted. He is now a
brigadier. This he received with modest complaisance. "I knowed he
was a general," said Maum Mary as he passed on, "he told me as soon
as he got in his room befo' his boy put down his trunks."

As Nathan, the unlucky, said good-by, he informed me that a Mr.
Reed from Montgomery was in the drawingroom and wanted to see me.
Mr. Reed had traveled with our foreign envoy, Yancey. I was keen for
news from abroad. Mr. Reed settled that summarily. "Mr. Yancey says
we need not have one jot of hope. He could bowstring Mallory for not
buying arms in time. The very best citizens wanted to depose the State
government and take things into their own hands, the powers that be
being inefficient. Western men are hurrying to the front, bestirring
themselves. In two more months we shall be ready." What could I do
but laugh? I do hope the enemy will be considerate and charitable
enough to wait for us.

Mr. Reed's calm faith in the power of Mr. Yancey's eloquence was
beautiful to see. He asked for Mr. Chesnut. I went back to our rooms,
swelling with news like a pouter pigeon. Mr. Chesnut said: "Well! four
hours—a call from Nathan Davis of four hours!" Men are too absurd!
So I bear the honors of my forty years gallantly. I can but laugh. "Mr.
Nathan Davis went by the five-o'clock train," I said; "it is now about
six or seven, maybe eight. I have had so many visitors. Mr. Reed, of
Alabama, is asking for you out there." He went without a word, but I
doubt if he went to see Mr. Reed, my laughing had made him so angry.

At last Lincoln threatens us with a proclamation abolishing
slavery[75]—here in the free Southern Confederacy; and they say
McClellan is deposed. They want more fighting -I mean the
government, whose skins are safe, they want more fighting, and trust to
luck for the skill of the new generals.

March 28th.—I did leave with regret Maum Mary. She was such a
good, well-informed old thing. My Molly, though perfection otherwise,
does not receive the confidential communications of new-made
generals at the earliest moment. She is of very limited military
information. Maum Mary was the comfort of my life. She saved me

---

[75] The Emancipation proclamation was not actually issued until September 22,
1862, when it was a notice to the Confederates to return to the Union, emancipation being
proclaimed as a result of their failure to do so. The real proclamation, freeing the slaves,
was delayed until January 1,1863, when it was put forth as a war measure. Mrs.
Chesnut's reference is doubtless to President Lincoln's Message to Congress, March 6,
1862, in which he made recommendations regarding the abolition of slavery.

from all trouble as far as she could. Seventy, if she is a day, she is spry and active as a cat, of a curiosity that knows no bounds, black and clean; also, she knows a joke at first sight, and she is honest. I fancy the negroes are ashamed to rob people as careless as James Chesnut and myself.

One night, just before we left the Congaree House, Mr. Chesnut had forgotten to tell some all-important thing to Governor Gist, who was to leave on a public mission next day. So at the dawn of day he put on his dressing-gown and went to the Governor's room. He found the door unlocked and the Governor fast asleep. He shook him. Half-asleep, the Governor sprang up and threw his arms around Mr. Chesnut's neck and said: "Honey, is it you?" The mistake was rapidly set right, and the bewildered plenipotentiary was given his instructions. Mr. Chesnut came into my room, threw himself on the sofa, and nearly laughed himself to extinction, imitating again and again the pathetic tone of the Governor's greeting.

Mr. Chesnut calls Lawrence "Adolphe," but says he is simply perfect as a servant. Mary Stevens said: "I thought Cousin James the laziest man alive until I knew his man, Lawrence." Lawrence will not move an inch or lift a finger for any one but his master. Mrs. Middleton politely sent him on an errand; Lawrence too, was very polite; hours after, she saw him sitting on the fence of the front yard. "Didn't you go?" she asked. "No, ma'am. I am waiting for Mars Jeems." Mrs. Middleton calls him now, "Mr. Take-it-Easy."

My very last day's experience at the Congaree. I was waiting for Mars Jeems in the drawing-room when a lady there declared herself to be the wife of an officer in Clingman's regiment. A gentleman who seemed quite friendly with her, told her all Mr. Chesnut said, thought, intended to do, wrote, and *felt*. I asked: "Are you certain of all these things you say of Colonel Chesnut?" The man hardly deigned to notice this impertinent interruption from a stranger presuming to speak but who had not been introduced! After he went out, the wife of Clingman's officer was seized with an intuitive curiosity. "Madam, will you tell me your name?" I gave it, adding, "I dare say I showed myself an intelligent listener when my husband's affairs were under discussion." At first, I refused to give my name because it would have embarrassed her friend if she had told him who I was. The man was Mr. Chesnut's secretary, but I had never seen him before.

A letter from Kate says she had been up all night preparing David's things. Little Serena sat up and helped her mother. They did not know that they would ever see him again. Upon reading it, I wept and James Chesnut cursed the Yankees.

Gave the girls a quantity of flannel for soldiers' shirts; also a string of pearls to be raffled for at the Gunboat Fair. Mary Witherspoon has sent a silver tea-pot. We do not spare our precious things now. Our silver and gold, what are they?-when we give up to war our beloved.

April 2d.—Dr. Trezevant, attending Mr. Chesnut, who was ill, came and found his patient gone; he could not stand the news of that last battle. He got up and dressed, weak as he was, and went forth to hear what he could for himself. The doctor was angry with me for permitting this, and more angry with him for such folly. I made him listen to the distinction between feminine folly and virulent vagaries and nonsense. He said: "He will certainly be salivated after all that calomel out in this damp weather."

To-day, the ladies in their landaus were bitterly attacked by the morning paper for lolling back in their silks and satins, with tall footmen in livery, driving up and down the streets while the poor soldiers' wives were on the sidewalks. It is the old story of rich and poor! My little barouche is not here, nor has James Chesnut any of his horses here, but then I drive every day with Mrs. McCord and Mrs. Preston, either of whose turnouts fills the bill. The Governor's carriage, horses, servants, etc., are splendid- just what they should be. Why not?

April 14th.—Our Fair is in full blast. We keep a restaurant. Our waitresses are Mary and Buck Preston, Isabella Martin, and Grace Elmore.

April 15th.—Trescott is too clever ever to be a bore; that was proved to-day, for he stayed two hours; as usual, Mr. Chesnut said "four." Trescott was very surly; calls himself ex-Secretary of State of the United States; now, nothing in particular of South Carolina or the Confederate States. Then he yawned, "What a bore this war is. I wish it was ended, one way or another." He speaks of going across the border and taking service in Mexico. "Rubbish, not much Mexico for you," I answered. Another patriot came then and averred, "I will take my family back to town, that we may all surrender together. I gave it up early in the spring." Trescott made a face behind backs, and said: "*Lache!*"

The enemy have flanked Beauregard at Nashville. There is grief enough for Albert Sidney Johnston now; we begin to see what we have lost. We were pushing them into the river when General Johnston was wounded. Beauregard was lying in his tent, at the rear, in a green sickness- melancholy—but no matter what the name of the malady. He was too slow to move, and lost all the advantage gained by our dead hero.[76] Without him there is no head to our Western army. Pulaski has fallen. What more is there to fall?

April 15th.—Mrs. Middleton: "How did you settle Molly's little

---

[76] The battle of Shiloh, or Pittsburg Landing, in Tennessee, eighty -eight miles east of Memphis, had been fought on April 6 and 7, 1862. The Federals were commanded by General Grant who, on the second day, was reenforced by General Buell. The Confederates were commanded by Albert Sidney Johnston on the first day, when Johnston was killed, and on the second day by General Beauregard.

difficulty with Mrs. McMahan, that 'piece of her mind' that Molly gave our landlady?" "Oh, paid our way out of it, of course, and I apologized for Molly!"

Gladden, the hero of the Palmettos in Mexico, is killed. Shiloh has been a dreadful blow to us. Last winter Stephen, my brother, had it in his power to do such a nice thing for Colonel Gladden. In the dark he heard his name, also that he had to walk twenty-five miles in Alabama mud or go on an ammunition wagon. So he introduced himself as a South Carolinian to Colonel Gladden, whom he knew only by reputation as colonel of the Palmetto regiment in the Mexican war. And they drove him in his carriage comfortably to where he wanted to go— a night drive of fifty miles for Stephen, for he had the return trip, too. I would rather live in Siberia, worse still, in Sahara, than live in a country surrendered to Yankees.

The Carolinian says the conscription bill passed by Congress is fatal to our liberties as a people. Let us be a people "certain and sure," as poor Tom B. said, and then talk of rebelling against our home government.

Sat up all night. Read Eothen straight through, our old Wiley and Putnam edition that we bought in London in 1845. How could I sleep? The power they are bringing to bear against our country is tremendous. Its weight may be irresistible—dare not think of that, however.

April 21st.—Have been ill. One day I dined at Mrs. Preston's, *pâté de foie gras* and partridge prepared for me as I like them. I had been awfully depressed for days and could not sleep at night for anxiety, but I did not know that I was bodily ill. Mrs. Preston came home with me. She said emphatically: "Molly, if your mistress is worse in the night send for me instantly." I thought it very odd. I could not breathe if I attempted to lie down, and very soon I lost my voice. Molly raced out and sent Lawrence for Doctor Trezevant. She said I had the croup. The doctor said, "congestion of the lungs."

So here I am, stranded, laid by the heels. Battle after battle has occurred, disaster after disaster. Every, morning's paper is enough to kill a well woman and age a strong and hearty one.

To-day, the waters of this stagnant pool were wildly stirred. The President telegraphed for my husband to come on to Richmond, and offered him a place on his staff. I was a joyful woman. It was a way opened by Providence from this Slough of Despond, this Council whose counsel no one takes. I wrote to Mr. Davis, "With thanks, and begging your pardon, how I would like to go." Mrs. Preston agrees with me, Mr. Chesnut ought to go. Through Mr. Chesnut the President might hear many things to the advantage of our State, etc.

Letter from Quinton Washington. That was the best tonic yet. He writes so cheerfully. We have fifty thousand men on the Peninsula and McClellan eighty thousand. We expect that much disparity of numbers.

We can stand that.

April 23d.—On April 23, 1840, I was married, aged seventeen; consequently on the 31st of March, 1862, I was thirty-nine. I saw a wedding to-day from my window, which opens on Trinity Church. Nanna Shand married a Doctor Wilson. Then, a beautiful bevy of girls rushed into my room. Such a flutter and a chatter. Well, thank Heaven for a wedding. It is a charming relief from the dismal litany of our daily song.

A letter to-day from our octogenarian at Mulberry. His nephew, Jack Deas, had two horses shot under him; the old Colonel has his growl, "That's enough for glory, and no hurt after all." He ends, however, with his never-failing refrain: We can't fight all the world; two and two only make four; it can't make a thousand; numbers will not lie. He says he has lost half a million already in railroad bonds, bank stock, Western notes of hand, not to speak of negroes to be freed, and lands to be confiscated, for he takes the gloomiest views of all things.

April 26th.—Doleful dumps, alarm-bells ringing. Telegrams say the mortar fleet has passed the forts at New Orleans. Down into the very depths of despair are we.

April 27th.—New Orleans gone[77] and with it the Confederacy. That Mississippi ruins us if lost. The Confederacy has been done to death by the politicians. What wonder we are lost.

The soldiers have done their duty. All honor to the army. Statesmen as busy as bees about their own places, or their personal honor, too busy to see the enemy at a distance. With a microscope they were examining their own interests, or their own wrongs, forgetting the interests of the people they represented. They were concocting newspaper paragraphs to injure the government. No matter how vital it may be, nothing can be kept from the enemy. They must publish themselves, night and day, what they are doing, or the omniscient Buncombe will forget them.

This fall of New Orleans means utter ruin to the private fortunes of the Prestons. Mr. Preston came from New Orleans so satisfied with Mansfield Lovell and the tremendous steam-rams he saw there. While in New Orleans Burnside offered Mr. Preston five hundred thousand dollars, a debt due to him from Burnside, and he refused to take it. He said the money was safer in Burnside's hands than his. And so it may prove, so ugly is the outlook now. Burnside is wide awake; he is not a man to be caught napping.

---

[77] New Orleans had been seized by the Confederates at the outbreak of the war. Steps to capture it were soon taken by the Federals and on April 18, 1862, the mortar flotilla, under Farragut, opened fire on its protecting forts. Making little impression on them, Farragut ran boldly past the forts and destroyed the Confederate fleet, comprising 13 gunboats and two ironclads. On April 27th he took formal possession of the city.

Mary Preston was saying she had asked the Hamptons how they relished the idea of being paupers. If the country is saved none of us will care for that sort of thing. Philosophical and patriotic, Mr. Chesnut came in, saying: "Conrad has been telegraphed from New Orleans that the great iron-clad Louisiana went down at the first shot." Mr. Chesnut and Mary Preston walked off, first to the bulletin-board and then to the Prestons'.

April 29th.—A grand smash, the news from New Orleans fatal to us. Met Mr. Weston. He wanted to know where he could find a place of safety for two hundred negroes. I looked into his face to see if he were in earnest; then to see if he were sane. There was a certain set of two hundred negroes that had grown to be a nuisance. Apparently all the white men of the family had felt bound to stay at home to take care of them. There are people who still believe negroes property—like Noah's neighbors, who insisted that the Deluge would only be a little shower after all.

These negroes, however, were Plowden Weston's, a totally different part of speech. He gave field-rifles to one company and forty thousand dollars to another. He is away with our army at Corinth. So I said: "You may rely upon Mr. Chesnut, who will assist you to his uttermost in finding a home for these people. Nothing belonging to that patriotic gentleman shall come to grief if we have to take charge of them on our own place." Mr. Chesnut did get a place for them, as I said he would.

Had to go to the Governor's or they would think we had hoisted the black flag. Heard there we are going to be beaten as Cortez beat the Mexicans—by superior arms. Mexican bows and arrows made a poor showing in the face of Spanish accoutrements. Our enemies have such superior weapons of war, we hardly any but what we capture from them in the fray. The Saxons and the Normans were in the same plight.

War seems a game of chess, but we have an unequal number of pawns to begin with. We have knights, kings, queens, bishops, and castles enough. But our skilful generals, whenever they can not arrange the board to suit them exactly, burn up everything and march away. We want them to save the country. They seem to think their whole duty is to destroy ships and save the army.

Mr. Robert Barnwell wrote that he had to hang his head for South Carolina. We had not furnished our quota of the new levy, five thousand men. To-day Colonel Chesnut published his statement to show that we have sent thirteen thousand, instead of the mere number required of us; so Mr. Barnwell can hold up his head again.

April 30th.—The last day of this month of calamities. Lovell left the women and children to be shelled, and took the army to a safe place. I do not understand why we do not send the women and children to the safe place and let the army stay where the fighting is to be.

Armies are to save, not to be saved. At least, to be saved is not their *raison d'être* exactly. If this goes on the spirit of our people will be broken. One ray of comfort comes from Henry Marshall. "Our Army of the Peninsula is fine; so good I do not think McClellan will venture to attack it." So mote it be.

May 6th.—Mine is a painful, self-imposed task: but why write when I have nothing to chronicle but disaster?[78] So I read instead: First, Consuelo, then Columba, two ends of the pole certainly, and then a translated edition of Elective Affinities. Food enough for thought in every one of this odd assortment of books.

At the Prestons', where I am staying (because Mr. Chesnut has gone to see his crabbed old father, whom he loves, and who is reported ill), I met Christopher Hampton. He tells us Wigfall is out on a warpath; wants them to strike for Maryland. The President's opinion of the move is not given. Also Mr. Hampton met the first lieutenant of the Kirkwoods, E. M. Boykin. Says he is just the same man he was in the South Carolina College. In whatever company you may meet him, he is the pleasantest man there.

A telegram reads: "We have repulsed the enemy at Williamsburg."[79] Oh, if we could drive them back "to their ain countree!" Richmond was hard pressed this day. The Mercury of to-day says, "Jeff Davis now treats all men as if they were idiotic insects."

Mary Preston said all sisters quarreled. No, we never quarrel, I and mine. We keep all our bitter words for our enemies. We are frank heathens; we hate our enemies and love our friends. Some people (our kind) can never make up after a quarrel; hard words once only and all is over. To us forgiveness is impossible. Forgiveness means calm indifference; philosophy, while love lasts. Forgiveness of love's wrongs is impossible. Those dutiful wives who piously overlook—well, everything—do not care one fig for their husbands. I settled that in my own mind years ago. Some people think it magnanimous to praise their enemies and to show their impartiality and justice by acknowledging the faults of their friends. I am for the simple rule, the good old plan. I praise whom I love and abuse whom I hate.

Mary Preston has been translating Schiller aloud. We are provided with Bulwer's translation, Mrs. Austin's, Coleridge's, and Carlyle's, and we show how each renders the passage Mary is to convert into English. In Wallenstein at one point of the Max and Thekla scene, I like Carlyle better than Coleridge, though they say Coleridge's Wallenstein is the only translation in the world half so good as the original. Mrs.

---

[78] The Siege of Yorktown was begun on April 5, 1862, the place being evacuated by the Confederates on May 4th.

[79] The battle of Williamsburg was fought on May 5, 1862, by a part of McClellan's army, under General Hooker and others, the Confederates being commanded by General Johnston.

Barstow repeated some beautiful scraps by Uhland, which I had never heard before. She is to write them for us. Peace, and a literary leisure for my old age, unbroken by care and anxiety!

General Preston accused me of degenerating into a boarding-house gossip, and is answered triumphantly by his daughters: "But, papa, one you love to gossip with full well."

Hampton estate has fifteen hundred negroes on Lake Washington, Mississippi. Hampton girls talking in the language of James's novels: "Neither Wade nor Preston—that splendid boy!-would lay a lance in rest—or couch it, which is the right phrase for fighting, to preserve slavery. They hate it as we do." "What are they fighting for?" "Southern rights—whatever that is. And they do not want to be understrappers forever to the Yankees. They talk well enough about it, but I forget what they say." Johnny Chesnut says: "No use to give a reason- a fellow could not stay away from the fight—not well." It takes four negroes to wait on Johnny satisfactorily.

*   *   *   *   *

It is this giving up that kills me. Norfolk they talk of now; why not Charleston next? I read in a Western letter, "Not Beauregard, but the soldiers who stopped to drink the whisky they had captured from the enemy, lost us Shiloh." Cock Robin is as dead as he ever will be now; what matters it who killed him?

May 12th.—Mr. Chesnut says he is very glad he went to town. Everything in Charleston is so much more satisfactory than it is reported. Troops are in good spirits. It will take a lot of iron-clads to take that city.

Isaac Hayne said at dinner yesterday that both Beauregard and the President had a great opinion of Mr. Chesnut's natural ability for strategy and military evolution. Hon. Mr. Barnwell concurred; that is, Mr. Barnwell had been told so by the President. "Then why did not the President offer me something better than an aideship?" "I heard he offered to make you a general last year, and you said you could not go over other men's shoulders until you had earned promotion. You are too hard to please." "No, not exactly that, I was only offered a colonelcy, and Mr. Barnwell persuaded me to stick to the Senate; then he wanted my place, and between the two stools I fell to the ground."

My Molly will forget Lige and her babies, too. I asked her who sent me that beautiful bouquet I found on my center-table. "I give it to you. 'Twas give to me." And Molly was all wriggle, giggle, blush.

May 18th.—Norfolk has been burned and the Merrimac sunk without striking a blow since her *coup d'état* in Hampton Roads. Read Milton. See the speech of Adam to Eve in a new light. Women will not stay at home; will go out to see and be seen, even if it be by the devil himself.

Very encouraging letters from Hon. Mr. Memminger and from L. Q. Washington. They tell the same story in very different words. It amounts to this: "Not one foot of Virginia soil is to be given up without a bitter fight for it. We have one hundred and five thousand men in all, McClellan one hundred and ninety thousand. We can stand that disparity."

What things I have been said to have said! Mr.——heard me make scoffing remarks about the Governor and the Council—or he thinks he heard me. James Chesnut wrote him a note that my name was to be kept out of it—indeed, that he was never to mention my name again under any possible circumstances. It was all preposterous nonsense, but it annoyed my husband amazingly. He said it was a scheme to use my chatter to his injury. He was very kind about it. He knows my real style so well that he can always tell my real impudence from what is fabricated for me.

There is said to be an order from Butler[80] turning over the women of New Orleans to his soldiers. Thus is the measure of his iniquities filled. We thought that generals always restrained, by shot or sword if need be, the brutality of soldiers. This hideous, cross-eyed beast orders his men to treat the ladies of New Orleans as women of the town—to punish them, he says, for their insolence.

Footprints on the boundaries of another world once more. Willie Taylor, before he left home for the army, fancied one day—*day*, remember—that he saw Albert Rhett standing by his side. He recoiled from the ghostly presence. "You need not do that, Willie. You will soon be as I am." Willie rushed into the next room to tell them what had happened, and fainted. It had a very depressing effect upon him. And now the other day he died in Virginia.

May 24th.—The enemy are landing at Georgetown. With a little more audacity where could they not land? But we have given them such a scare, they are cautious. If it be true, I hope some cool-headed white men will make the negroes save the rice for us. It is so much needed. They say it might have been done at Port Royal with a little more energy. South Carolinians have pluck enough, but they only work

---

[80] General Benjamin F. Butler took command of New Orleans on May 2, 1862. The author's reference is to his famous "Order No. 28," which reads: "As the officers and soldiers of the United States have been subject to repeated insults from the women (calling themselves ladies) of New Orleans, in return for the most scrupulous non-interference and courtesy on our part, it is ordered that hereafter when any female shall by word, gesture, or movement insult or show contempt for any officer or soldier of the United States she shall be regarded and held liable to be treated as a woman of the town plying her vocation." This and other acts of Butler in New Orleans led Jefferson Davis to issue a proclamation, declaring Butler to be a felon and an outlaw, and if captured that he should be instantly hanged. In December Butler was superseded at New Orleans by General Banks.

by fits and starts; there is no continuous effort; they can't be counted on for steady work. They will stop to play—or enjoy life in some shape.

Without let or hindrance Halleck is being reenforced. Beauregard, unmolested, was making some fine speeches- and issuing proclamations, while we were fatuously looking for him to make a tiger's spring on Huntsville. Why not? Hope springs eternal in the Southern breast.

My Hebrew friend, Mem Cohen, has a son in the war. He is in John Chesnut's company. Cohen is a high name among the Jews: it means Aaron. She has long fits of silence, and is absent-minded. If she is suddenly roused, she is apt to say, with overflowing eyes and clasped hands, "If it please God to spare his life." Her daughter is the sweetest little thing. The son is the mother's idol. Mrs. Cohen was Miriam de Leon. I have known her intimately all my life.

Mrs. Bartow, the widow of Colonel Bartow, who was killed at Manassas, was Miss Berrien, daughter of Judge Berrien, of Georgia. She is now in one of the departments here, cutting bonds—Confederate bonds—for five hundred Confederate dollars a year, a penniless woman. Judge Carroll, her brother-in-law, has been urgent with her to come and live in his home. He has a large family and she will not be an added burden to him. In spite of all he can say, she will not forego her resolution. She will be independent. She is a resolute little woman, with the softest, silkiest voice and ways, and clever to the last point.

Columbia is the place for good living, pleasant people, pleasant dinners, pleasant drives. I feel that I have put the dinners in the wrong place. They are the climax of the good things here. This is the most hospitable place in the world, and the dinners are worthy of it.

In Washington, there was an endless succession of state dinners. I was kindly used. I do not remember ever being condemned to two dull neighbors: on one side or the other was a clever man; so I liked Washington dinners.

In Montgomery, there were a few dinners—Mrs. Pollard's, for instance, but the society was not smoothed down or in shape. Such as it was it was given over to balls and suppers. In Charleston, Mr. Chesnut went to gentlemen's dinners all the time; no ladies present. Flowers were sent to me, and I was taken to drive and asked to tea. There could not have been nicer suppers, more perfect of their kind than were to be found at the winding up of those festivities.

In Richmond, there were balls, which I did not attend- very few to which I was asked: the MacFarlands' and Lyons's, all I can remember. James Chesnut dined out nearly every day. But then the breakfasts—the Virginia breakfasts—where were always pleasant people. Indeed, I have had a good time everywhere—always clever people, and people I liked, and everybody so good to me.

Here in Columbia, family dinners are the specialty. You call, or they pick you up and drive home with you. "Oh, stay to dinner!" and you stay gladly. They send for your husband, and he comes willingly. Then comes a perfect dinner. You do not see how it could be improved; and yet they have not had time to alter things or add because of the unexpected guests. They have everything of the best—silver, glass, china, table linen, and damask, etc. And then the planters live "within themselves," as they call it. From the plantations come mutton, beef, poultry, cream, butter, eggs, fruits, and vegetables.

It is easy to live here, with a cook who has been sent for training to the best eating-house in Charleston. Old Mrs. Chesnut's Romeo was apprenticed at Jones's. I do not know where Mrs. Preston's got his degree, but he deserves a medal.

At the Prestons', James Chesnut induced Buck to declaim something about Joan of Arc, which she does in a manner to touch all hearts. While she was speaking, my husband turned to a young gentleman who was listening to the chatter of several girls, and said: "Écoutez!" The youth stared at him a moment in bewilderment; then, gravely rose and began turning down the gas. Isabella said: "Écoutez, then, means put out the lights."

I recall a scene which took place during a ball given by Mrs. Preston while her husband was in Louisiana. Mrs. Preston was resplendent in diamonds, point lace, and velvet.

There is a gentle dignity about her which is very attractive; her voice is low and sweet, and her will is iron. She is exceedingly well informed, but very quiet, retiring, and reserved. Indeed, her apparent gentleness almost amounts to timidity. She has chiseled regularity of features, a majestic figure, perfectly molded.

Governor Manning said to me: "Look at Sister Caroline. Does she look as if she had the pluck of a heroine?" Then he related how a little while ago William, the butler, came to tell her that John, the footman, was drunk in the cellar—mad with drink; that he had a carving-knife which he was brandishing in drunken fury, and he was keeping everybody from their business, threatening to kill any one who dared to go into the basement. They were like a flock of frightened sheep down there. She did not speak to one of us, but followed William down to the basement, holding up her skirts. She found the servants scurrying everywhere, screaming and shouting that John was crazy and going to kill them. John was bellowing like a bull of Bashan, knife in hand, chasing them at his pleasure.

Mrs. Preston walked up to him. "Give me that knife," she demanded. He handed it to her. She laid it on the table. "Now come with me," she said, putting her hand on his collar. She led him away to the empty smoke-house, and there she locked him in and put the key in her pocket. Then she returned to her guests, without a ripple on her placid face. "She told me of it, smiling and serene as you see her now," the Governor concluded.

Before the war shut him in, General Preston sent to the lakes for his salmon, to Mississippi for his venison, to the mountains for his mutton and grouse. It is good enough, the best dish at all these houses, what the Spanish call "the hearty welcome." Thackeray says at every American table he was first served with "grilled hostess." At the head of the table sat a person, fiery-faced, anxious, nervous, inwardly murmuring, like Falstaff, "Would it were night, Hal, and all were well."

At Mulberry the house is always filled to overflowing, and one day is curiously like another. People are coming and going, carriages driving up or driving off. It has the air of a watering-place, where one does not pay, and where there are no strangers. At Christmas the china closet gives up its treasures. The glass, china, silver, fine linen reserved for grand occasions come forth. As for the dinner itself, it is only a matter of greater quantity—more turkey, more mutton, more partridges, more fish, etc., and more solemn stiffness. Usually a half-dozen persons unexpectedly dropping in make no difference. The family let the housekeeper know; that is all.

People are beginning to come here from Richmond. One swallow does not make a summer, but it shows how the wind blows, these straws do—Mrs. "Constitution" Browne and Mrs. Wise. The Gibsons are at Doctor Gibbes's It does look squally. We are drifting on the breakers.

May 29th.—Betsey, recalcitrant maid of the W.'s, has been sold to a telegraph man. She is as handsome as a mulatto ever gets to be, and clever in every kind of work. My Molly thinks her mistress "very lucky in getting rid of her." She was "a dangerous inmate," but she will be a good cook, a good chambermaid, a good dairymaid, a beautiful clear-starcher, and the most thoroughly good-for-nothing woman I know to her new owners, if she chooses. Molly evidently hates her, but thinks it her duty "to stand by her color."

Mrs. Gibson is a Philadelphia woman. She is true to her husband and children, but she does not believe in us- the Confederacy, I mean. She is despondent and hopeless; as wanting in faith of our ultimate success as is Sally Baxter Hampton. I make allowances for those people. If I had married North, they would have a heavy handful in me just now up there.

Mrs. Chesnut, my mother-in-law, has been sixty years in the South, and she has not changed in feeling or in taste one iota. She can not like hominy for breakfast, or rice for dinner, without a relish to give it some flavor. She can not eat watermelons and sweet potatoes *sans discrétion*, as we do. She will not eat hot corn bread *à discrétion*, and hot buttered biscuit without any.

"Richmond is obliged to fall," sighed Mrs. Gibson. "You would say so, too, if you had seen our poor soldiers." "Poor soldiers?" said I.

"Are you talking of Stonewall Jackson's men? Poor soldiers, indeed!" She said her mind was fixed on one point, and had ever been, though she married and came South: she never would own slaves. "Who would that was not born to it?" I cried, more excited than ever. She is very handsome, very clever, and has very agreeable manners.

"Dear madam," she says, with tears in her beautiful eyes, "they have three armies." "But Stonewall has routed one of them already. Heath another." She only answered by an unbelieving moan. "Nothing seemed to suit her," I said, as we went away. "You did not certainly," said some one to me; "you contradicted every word she said, with a sort of indignant protest."

We met Mrs. Hampton Gibbes at the door—another Virginia woman as good as gold. They told us Mrs. Davis was delightfully situated at Raleigh; North Carolinians so loyal, so hospitable; she had not been allowed to eat a meal at the hotel. "How different from Columbia," said Doctor Gibbes, looking at Mrs. Gibson, who has no doubt been left to take all of her meals at his house. "Oh, no!" cried Mary, "you do Columbia injustice. Mrs. Chesnut used to tell us that she was never once turned over to the tender mercies of the Congaree cuisine, and at McMahan's it is fruit, flowers, invitations to dinner every day."

After we came away, "Why did you not back me up?" I was asked. "Why did you let them slander Columbia?"

"It was awfully awkward," I said, "but you see it would have been worse to let Doctor Gibbes and Mrs. Gibson see how different it was with other people."

Took a moonlight walk after tea at the Halcott Greens'. All the company did honor to the beautiful night by walking home with me.

Uncle Hamilton Boykin is here, staying at the de Saussures'. He says, "Manassas was play to Williamsburg," and he was at both battles. He lead a part of Stuart's cavalry in the charge at Williamsburg, riding a hundred yards ahead of his company.

Toombs is ready for another revolution, and curses freely everything Confederate from the President down to a horse boy. He thinks there is a conspiracy against him in the army. Why? Heavens and earth—why?

June 2d.—A battle[81] is said to be raging round Richmond. I am at the Prestons'. James Chesnut has gone to Richmond suddenly on business of the Military Department. It is always his luck to arrive in the nick of time and be present at a great battle.

Wade Hampton shot in the foot, and Johnston Pettigrew killed. A

---

[81] The Battle of Fair Oaks or Seven Pines, took place a few miles east of Richmond, on May 31 and June 1, 1862, the Federals being commanded by McClellan and the Confederates by General Joseph E. Johnston.

telegram says Lee and Davis were both on the field: the enemy being repulsed. Telegraph operator said: "Madam, our men are fighting." "Of course they are. What else is there for them to do now but fight?" "But, madam, the news is encouraging." Each army is burying its dead: that looks like a drawn battle. We haunt the bulletin-board.

Back to McMahan's. Mem Cohen is ill. Her daughter, Isabel, warns me not to mention the battle raging around Richmond. Young Cohen is in it. Mrs. Preston, anxious and unhappy about her sons. John is with General Huger at Richmond; Willie in the swamps on the coast with his company. Mem tells me her cousin, Edwin de Leon, is sent by Mr. Davis on a mission to England.

Rev. Robert Barnwell has returned to the hospital. Oh, that we had given our thousand dollars to the hospital and not to the gunboat! "Stonewall Jackson's movements," the Herald says, "do us no harm; it is bringing out volunteers in great numbers." And a Philadelphia paper abused us so fervently I felt all the blood in me rush to my head with rage.

June 3d.—Doctor John Cheves is making infernal machines in Charleston to blow the Yankees up; pretty name they have, those machines. My horses, the overseer says, are too poor to send over. There was corn enough on the place for two years, they said, in January; now, in June, they write that it will not last until the new crop comes in. Somebody is having a good time on the plantation, if it be not my poor horses.

Molly will tell me all when she comes back, and more. Mr. Venable has been made an aide to General Robert E. Lee. He is at Vicksburg, and writes, "When the fight is over here, I shall be glad to go to Virginia." He is in capital spirits. I notice army men all are when they write.

Apropos of calling Major Venable "Mr." Let it be noted that in social intercourse we are not prone to give handles to the names of those we know well and of our nearest and dearest. A general's wife thinks it bad form to call her husband anything but "Mr." When she gives him his title, she simply "drops" into it by accident. If I am "mixed" on titles in this diary, let no one blame me.

Telegrams come from Richmond ordering troops from Charleston. Can not be sent, for the Yankees are attacking Charleston, doubtless with the purpose to prevent Lee's receiving reenforcements from there.

Sat down at my window in the beautiful moonlight, and tried hard for pleasant thoughts. A man began to play on the flute, with piano accompaniment, first, "Ever of thee I am fondly dreaming," and then, "The long, long, weary day." At first, I found this but a complement to the beautiful scene, and it was soothing to my wrought-up nerves. But Von Weber's "Last Waltz" was too much; I broke down. Heavens, what a bitter cry came forth, with such floods of tears! the wonder is there was any of me left.

I learn that Richmond women go in their carriages for the wounded, carry them home and nurse them. One saw a man too weak to hold his musket. She took it from him, put it on her shoulder, and helped the poor fellow along.

If ever there was a man who could control every expression of emotion, who could play stoic, or an Indian chief, it is James Chesnut. But one day when he came in from the Council he had to own to a break-down. He was awfully ashamed of his weakness. There was a letter from Mrs. Gaillard asking him to help her, and he tried to read it to the Council. She wanted a permit to go on to her son, who lies wounded in Virginia. Colonel Chesnut could not control his voice. There was not a dry eye there, when suddenly one man called out, "God bless the woman."

Johnston Pettigrew's aide says he left his chief mortally wounded on the battle-field. Just before Johnston Pettigrew went to Italy to take a hand in the war there for freedom, I met him one day at Mrs. Frank Hampton's. A number of people were present. Some one spoke of the engagement of the beautiful Miss—to Hugh Rose. Some one else asked: "How do you know they are engaged?" "Well, I never heard it, but I saw it. In London, a month or so ago, I entered Mrs.—'s drawing-room, and I saw these two young people seated on a sofa opposite the door." "Well, that amounted to nothing." "No, not in itself. But they looked so foolish and so happy. I have noticed newly engaged people always look that way." And so on. Johnston Pettigrew was white and red in quick succession during this turn of the conversation; he was in a rage of indignation and disgust. "I think this kind of talk is taking a liberty with the young lady's name," he exclaimed finally, "and that it is an impertinence in us." I fancy him left dying alone! I wonder what they feel—those who are left to die of their wounds—alone—on the battle-field.

Free schools are not everything, as witness this spelling. Yankee epistles found in camp show how illiterate they can be, with all their boasted schools. Fredericksburg is spelled "Fredrexbirg," medicine, "metison," and we read, "To my sweat brother," etc. For the first time in my life no books can interest me. Life is so real, so utterly earnest, that fiction is flat. Nothing but what is going on in this distracted world of ours can arrest my attention for ten minutes at a time.

June 4th.—Battles occur near Richmond, with bombardment of Charleston. Beauregard is said to be fighting his way out or in.

Mrs. Gibson is here, at Doctor Gibbes's. Tears are always in her eyes. Her eldest son is Willie Preston's lieutenant. They are down on the coast. She owns that she has no hope at all. She was a Miss Ayer, of Philadelphia, and says, "We may look for Burnside now, our troops which held him down to his iron flotilla have been withdrawn. They are three to one against us now, and they have hardly begun to put out their strength—in numbers, I mean. We have come to the end of our tether, except we wait for the yearly crop of boys as they grow up to the requisite age." She would make despondent the most sanguine person alive. "As a general rule," says Mrs. Gibson, "government people are sanguine, but the son of one high functionary whispered to Mary G., as he handed her into the car, 'Richmond is bound to go.'" The idea now is that we are to be starved out. If they shut us in, prolong the agony, it can then have but one end.

Mrs. Preston and I speak in whispers, but Mrs. McCord scorns whispers, and speaks out. She says: "There are our soldiers. Since the world began there never were better but God does not deign to send us a general worthy of them. I do not mean drill-sergeants or military old maids, who will not fight until everything is just so. The real ammunition of our war is faith in ourselves and enthusiasm in our cause. West Point sits down on enthusiasm, laughs it to scorn. It wants discipline. And now comes a new danger, these blockade-runners. They are filling their pockets and they gibe and sneer at the fools who fight. Don't you see this Stonewall, how he fires the soldiers' hearts; he will be our leader, maybe after all. They say he does not care how many are killed. His business is to save the country, not the army. He fights to win, God bless him, and he wins. If they do not want to be killed, they can stay at home. They say he leaves the sick and wounded to be cared for by those whose business it is to do so. His business is war. They say he wants to hoist the black flag, have a short, sharp, decisive war and end it. He is a Christian soldier."

June 5th.—Beauregard retreating and his rear-guard cut off. If Beauregard's veterans will not stand, why should we expect our newly levied reserves to do it? The Yankee general who is besieging Savannah announces his orders are "to take Savannah in two weeks' time, and then proceed to erase Charleston from the face of the earth."

Albert Luryea was killed in the battle of June 1st. Last summer when a bomb fell in the very thick of his company he picked it up and threw it into the water. Think of that, those of ye who love life! The company sent the bomb to his father. Inscribed on it were the words, "Albert Luryea, bravest where all are brave." Isaac Hayne did the same thing at Fort Moultrie. This race has brains enough, but they are not active-minded like those old Revolutionary characters, the Middletons, Lowndeses, Rutledges, Marions, Summers. They have come direct from active-minded forefathers, or they would not have been ̅ ͞ ͞ ͞ but. with two or three generations of gentlemen planters, how cha the blood become! Of late, all the active-minded men who ha to the front in our government were immediate descendants or Scotch-Irish-Calhoun, McDuffie, Cheves, and Peti Huguenotted his name, but could not tie up his Irish. Our ꝑ nice fellows, but slow to move; impulsive but hard to keep moving. They are wonderful for a spurt, but with all their strength, they like to rest.

June 6th.—Paul Hayne, the poet, has taken rooms here. My husband came and offered to buy me a pair of horses. He says I need more exercise in the open air. "Come, now, are you providing me with the means of a rapid retreat?" said I. "I am pretty badly equipped for marching."

Mrs. Rose Greenhow is in Richmond. One-half of the ungrateful Confederates say Seward sent her. My husband says the Confederacy owes her a debt it can never pay. She warned them at Manassas, and so they got Joe Johnston and his Paladins to appear upon the stage in the very nick of time. In Washington they said Lord Napier left her a legacy to the British Legation, which accepted the gift, unlike the British nation, who would not accept Emma Hamilton and her daughter, Horatia, though they were willed to the nation by Lord Nelson.

Mem Cohen, fresh from the hospital where she went with a beautiful Jewish friend. Rachel, as we will call her (be it her name or no), was put to feed a very weak patient. Mem noticed what a handsome fellow he was and how quiet and clean. She fancied by those tokens that he was a gentleman. In performance of her duties, the lovely young nurse leaned kindly over him and held the cup to his lips. When that ceremony was over and she had wiped his mouth, to her horror she felt a pair of by no means weak arms around her neck and a kiss upon her lips, which she thought strong, indeed. She did not say a word; she made no complaint. She slipped away from the hospital, and hereafter in her hospital work will minister at long range, no matter how weak and weary, sick and sore, the patient may be. "And," said Mem, "I thought he was a gentleman." "Well, a gentleman is a man, after all, and she ought not to have put those red lips of hers so near."

June 7th.—Cheves McCord's battery on the coast has three guns and one hundred men. If this battery should be captured John's Island and James Island would be open to the enemy, and so Charleston exposed utterly.

Wade Hampton writes to his wife that Chickahominy was not as decided a victory as he could have wished. Fort Pillow and Memphis[82] have been given up. Next! and next!

June 9th.—When we read of the battles in India, in Italy, in the Crimea, what did we care? Only an interesting topic, like any other, to

---

[82] Fort Pillow was on the Mississippi above Memphis. It had been erected by the Confederates, but was occupied by the Federals on June 5, 1862, the Confederates having evacuated and partially destroyed it the day before. On June 6, 1862, the Federal fleet defeated the Confederates near Memphis. The city soon afterward was occupied by the ᵗerals.

look for in the paper. Now you hear of a battle with a thrill and a shudder. It has come home to us; half the people that we know in the world are under the enemy's guns. A telegram reaches you, and you leave it on your lap. You are pale with fright. You handle it, or you dread to touch it, as you would a rattlesnake; worse, worse, a snake could only strike you. How many, many will this scrap of paper tell you have gone to their death?

When you meet people, sad and sorrowful is the greeting; they press your hand; tears stand in their eyes or roll down their cheeks, as they happen to possess more or less self-control. They have brother, father, or sons as the case may be, in battle. And now this thing seems never to stop. We have no breathing time given us. It can not be so at the North, for the papers say gentlemen do not go into the ranks there, but are officers, or clerks of departments. Then we see so many members of foreign regiments among our prisoners—Germans, Irish, Scotch. The proportion of trouble is awfully against us. Every company on the field, rank and file, is filled with our nearest and dearest, who are common soldiers.

Mem Cohen's story to-day. A woman she knew heard her son was killed, and had hardly taken in the horror of it when they came to say it was all a mistake in the name. She fell on her knees with a shout of joy. "Praise the Lord, O my soul!" she cried, in her wild delight. The household was totally upset, the swing-back of the pendulum from the scene of weeping and wailing of a few moments before was very exciting. In the midst of this hubbub the hearse drove up with the poor boy in his metallic coffin. Does anybody wonder so many women die? Grief and constant anxiety kill nearly as many women at home as men are killed on the battle-field. Mem's friend is at the point of death with brain fever; the sudden changes from grief to joy and joy to grief were more than she could bear.

A story from New Orleans. As some Yankees passed two boys playing in the street, one of the boys threw a handful of burned cotton at them, saying, "I keep this for you." The other, not to be outdone, spit at the Yankees, and said, "I keep this for you." The Yankees marked the house. Afterward, a corporal's guard came. Madam was affably conversing with a friend, and in vain, the friend, who was a mere morning caller, protested he was not the master of the house; he was marched off to prison.

Mr. Moise got his money out of New Orleans. He went to a station with his two sons, who were quite small boys. When he got there, the carriage that he expected was not to be seen. He had brought no money with him, knowing he might be searched. Some friend called out, "I will lend you my horse, but then you will be obliged to leave the children." This offer was accepted, and, as he rode off, one of the boys called out, "Papa, here is your tobacco, which you have forgotten." Mr.

Moise turned back and the boy handed up a roll of tobacco, which he had held openly in his hand all the time. Mr. Moise took it, and galloped off, waving his hat to them. In that roll of tobacco was encased twenty-five thousand dollars.

Now, the Mississippi is virtually open to the Yankees. Beauregard has evacuated Corinth.[83]

Henry Nott was killed at Shiloh; Mrs. Auzé wrote to tell us. She had no hope. To be conquered and ruined had always been her fate, strive as she might, and now she knew it would be through her country that she would be made to feel. She had had more than most women to endure, and the battle of life she had tried to fight with courage, patience, faith. Long years ago, when she was young, her lover died. Afterward, she married another. Then her husband died, and next her only son. When New Orleans fell, her only daughter was there and Mrs. Auzé went to her. Well may she say that she has bravely borne her burden till now.[84]

Stonewall said, in his quaint way: "I like strong drink, so I never touch it." May heaven, who sent him to help us, save him from all harm!

My husband traced Stonewall's triumphal career on the map. He has defeated Frémont and taken all his cannon; now he is after Shields. The language of the telegram is vague: "Stonewall has taken plenty of prisoners"—plenty, no doubt, and enough and to spare. We can't feed our own soldiers, and how are we to feed prisoners?

They denounce Toombs in some Georgia paper, which I saw to-day, for planting a full crop of cotton. They say he ought to plant provisions for soldiers.

And now every man in Virginia, and the eastern part of South Carolina is in revolt, because old men and boys are ordered out as a reserve corps, and worst of all, sacred property, that is, negroes, have been seized and sent out to work on the fortifications along the coast line. We are in a fine condition to fortify Columbia!

June 10th.—General Gregg writes that Chickahominy[85] was a victory *manqué*, because Joe Johnston received a disabling wound and G. W. Smith was ill. The subordinates in command had not been made acquainted with the plan of battle.

A letter from John Chesnut, who says it must be all a mistake about Wade Hampton's wound, for he saw him in the field to the very last; that is, until late that night. Hampton writes to Mary McDuffie that the ball was extracted from his foot on the field, and that he was in the

---

[83] Corinth was besieged by the Federals, under General Halleck, in May, 1862, and was evacuated by the Confederates under Beauregard on May 29th.

[84] She lost her life in the Windsor Hotel fire in New York.

[85] This must be a reference to the Battle of Seven Pines or to the Campaign of the Chickahominy, up to and inclusive of that battle.

saddle all day, but that, when he tried to take his boot off at night his foot was so inflamed and swollen, the boot had to be cut away, and the wound became more troublesome than he had expected.

Mrs. Preston sent her carriage to take us to see Mrs. Herbemont, whom Mary Gibson calls her "Mrs. Burgamot." Miss Bay came down, ever-blooming, in a cap so formidable, I could but laugh. It was covered with a bristling row of white satin spikes. She coyly refused to enter Mrs. Preston's carriage—"to put foot into it," to use her own words; but she allowed herself to be overpersuaded.

I am so ill. Mrs. Ben Taylor said to Doctor Trezevant, "Surely, she is too ill to be going about; she ought to be in bed." "She is very feeble, very nervous, as you say, but then she is living on nervous excitement. If you shut her up she would die at once." A queer weakness of the heart, I have. Sometimes it beats so feebly I am sure it has stopped altogether. Then they say I have fainted, but I never lose consciousness.

Mrs. Preston and I were talking of negroes and cows. A negro, no matter how sensible he is on any other subject, can never be convinced that there is any necessity to feed a cow. "Turn 'em out, and let 'em grass. Grass good nuff for cow."

Famous news comes from Richmond, but not so good from the coast. Mrs. Izard said, quoting I forget whom: "If West Point could give brains as well as training!" Smith is under arrest for disobedience of orders—Pemberton's orders. This is the third general whom Pemberton has displaced within a few weeks—Ripley, Mercer, and now Smith.

When I told my husband that Molly was full of airs since her late trip home, he made answer: "Tell her to go to the devil—she or anybody else on the plantation who is dissatisfied; let them go. It is bother enough to feed and clothe them now." When he went over to the plantation he returned charmed with their loyalty to him, their affection and their faithfulness.

Sixteen more Yankee regiments have landed on James Island. Eason writes, "They have twice the energy and enterprise of our people." I answered, "Wait a while. Let them alone until climate and mosquitoes and sand-flies and dealing with negroes takes it all out of them." Stonewall is a regular brick, going all the time, winning his way wherever he goes. Governor Pickens called to see me. His wife is in great trouble, anxiety, uncertainty. Her brother and her brother-in-law are either killed or taken prisoners.

Tom Taylor says Wade Hampton did not leave the field on account of his wound. "What heroism!" said some one. No, what luck! He is the luckiest man alive. He'll never be killed. He was shot in the temple, but that did not kill him. His soldiers believe in his luck.

General Scott, on Southern soldiers, says, we have *élan*, courage, woodcraft, consummate horsemanship, endurance of pain equal to the

Indians, but that we will not submit to discipline. We will not take care of things, or husband our resources. Where we are there is waste and destruction. If it could all be done by one wild, desperate dash, we would do it. But he does not think we can stand the long, blank months between the acts—the waiting! We can bear pain without a murmur, but we will not submit to be bored, etc.

Now, for the other side. Men of the North can wait; they can bear discipline; they can endure forever. Losses in battle are nothing to them. Their resources in men and materials of war are inexhaustible, and if they see fit they will fight to the bitter end. Here is a nice prospect for us- as comfortable as the old man's croak at Mulberry, "Bad times, worse coming."

Mrs. McCord says, "In the hospital the better born, that is, those born in the purple, the gentry, those who are accustomed to a life of luxury, are the better patients. They endure in silence. They are hardier, stronger, tougher, less liable to break down than the sons of the soil." "Why is that?" I asked, and she answered, "Something in man that is more than the body."

I know how it feels to die. I have felt it again and again. For instance, some one calls out, "Albert Sidney Johnston is killed." My heart stands still. I feel no more. I am, for so many seconds, so many minutes, I know not how long, utterly without sensation of any kind— dead; and then, there is that great throb, that keen agony of physical pain, and the works are wound up again. The ticking of the clock begins, and I take up the burden of life once more. Some day it will stop too long, or my feeble heart will be too worn out to make that awakening jar, and all will be over. I do not think when the end comes that there will be any difference, except the miracle of the new wind-up throb. And now good news is just as exciting as bad. "Hurrah, Stonewall has saved us!" The pleasure is almost pain because of my way of feeling it.

Miriam's Luryea and the coincidences of his life. He was born Moses, and is the hero of the bombshell. His mother was at a hotel in Charleston when kind-hearted Anna De Leon Moses went for her sister-in-law, and gave up her own chamber, that the child might be born in the comfort and privacy of a home. Only our people are given to such excessive hospitality. So little Luryea was born in Anna De Leon's chamber. After Chickahominy when he, now a man, lay mortally wounded, Anna Moses, who was living in Richmond, found him, and she brought him home, though her house was crowded to the door-steps. She gave up her chamber to him, and so, as he had been born in her room, in her room he died.

June 12th.—New England's Butler, best known to us as "Beast" Butler, is famous or infamous now. His amazing order to his soldiers at New Orleans and comments on it are in everybody's mouth. We hardly expected from Massachusetts behavior to shame a Comanche.

One happy moment has come into Mrs. Preston's life. I watched her face to-day as she read the morning papers. Willie's battery is lauded to the skies. Every paper gave him a paragraph of praise.

South Carolina was at Beauregard's feet after Fort Sumter. Since Shiloh, she has gotten up, and looks askance rather when his name is mentioned. And without Price or Beauregard who takes charge of the Western forces? "Can we hold out if England and France hold off?" cries Mem. "No, our time has come."

"For shame, faint heart! Our people are brave, our cause is just; our spirit and our patient endurance beyond reproach." Here came in Mary Cantey's voice: "I may not have any logic, any sense. I give it up. My woman's instinct tells me, all the same, that slavery's time has come. If we don't end it, they will."

After all this, tried to read Uncle Tom, but could not; too sickening; think of a man sending his little son to beat a human being tied to a tree. It is as bad as Squeers beating Smike. Flesh and blood revolt; you must skip that; it is too bad.

Mr. Preston told a story of Joe Johnston as a boy. A party of boys at Abingdon were out on a spree, more boys than horses; so Joe Johnston rode behind John Preston, who is his cousin. While going over the mountains they tried to change horses and got behind a servant who was in charge of them all. The servant's horse kicked up, threw Joe Johnston, and broke his leg; a bone showed itself. "Hello, boys! come here and look: the confounded bone has come clear through," called out Joe, coolly.

They had to carry him on their shoulders, relieving guard. As one party grew tired, another took him up. They knew he must suffer fearfully, but he never said so. He was as cool and quiet after his hurt as before. He was pretty roughly handled, but they could not help it. His father was in a towering rage because his son's leg was to be set by a country doctor, and it might be crooked in the process. At Chickahominy, brave but unlucky Joe had already eleven wounds.

June 13th.—Decca's wedding. It took place last year. We were all lying on the bed or sofas taking it coolly as to undress. Mrs. Singleton had the floor. They were engaged before they went up to Charlottesville; Alexander was on Gregg's staff, and Gregg was not hard on him; Decca was the worst in love girl she ever saw. "Letters came while we were at the hospital, from Alex, urging her to let him marry her at once. In war times human events, life especially, are very uncertain.

"For several days consecutively she cried without ceasing, and then she consented. The rooms at the hospital were all crowded. Decca and I slept together in the same room. It was arranged by letter that the marriage should take place; a luncheon at her grandfather Minor's, and then she was to depart with Alex for a few days at Richmond. That was to be their brief slice of honeymoon.

"The day came. The wedding-breakfast was ready, so was the bride in all her bridal array; but no Alex, no bridegroom. Alas! such is the uncertainty of a soldier's life. The bride said nothing, but she wept like a water-nymph. At dinner she plucked up heart, and at my earnest request was about to join us. And then the cry, 'The bridegroom cometh' He brought his best man and other friends. We had a jolly dinner. 'Circumstances over which he had no control' had kept him away.

"His father sat next to Decca and talked to her all the time as if she had been already married. It was a piece of absent-mindedness on his part, pure and simple, but it was very trying, and the girl had had much to stand that morning, you can well understand. Immediately after dinner the belated bridegroom proposed a walk; so they went for a brief stroll up the mountain. Decca, upon her return, said to me: 'Send for Robert Barnwell. I mean to be married to-day.'

"'Impossible. No spare room in the house. No getting away from here; the trains all gone. Don't you know this hospital place is crammed to the ceiling?' 'Alex says I promised to marry him to-day. It is not his fault; he could not come before.' I shook my head. 'I don't care,' said the positive little thing, 'I promised Alex to marry him to-day and I will. Send for the Rev. Robert Barnwell.' We found Robert after a world of trouble, and the bride, lovely in Swiss muslin, was married.

"Then I proposed they should take another walk, and I went to one of my sister nurses and begged her to take me in for the night, as I wished to resign my room to the young couple. At daylight next day they took the train for Richmond." Such is the small allowance of honeymoon permitted in war time.

Beauregard's telegram: he can not leave the army of the West. His health is bad. No doubt the sea breezes would restore him, but—he can not come now. Such a lovely name——Gustave Tautant Beauregard. But Jackson and Johnston and Smith and Jones will do—and Lee, how short and sweet.

"Every day," says Mem, "they come here in shoals—men to say we can not hold Richmond, and we can not hold Charleston much longer. Wretches, beasts! Why do you come here? Why don't you stay there and fight? Don't you see that you own yourselves cowards by coming away in the very face of a battle? If you are not liars as to the danger, you are cowards to run away from it." Thus roars the practical Mem, growing more furious at each word. These Jeremiahs laugh. They think she means others, not the present company.

Tom Huger resigned his place in the United States Navy and came to us. The Iroquois was his ship in the old navy. They say, as he stood in the rigging, after he was shot in the leg, when his ship was leading the attack upon the Iroquois, his old crew in the Iroquois cheered him, and when his body was borne in, the Federals took off their caps in respect for his gallant conduct. When he was dying, Meta Huger said to him: "An of officer wants to see you: he is one of the enemy." "Let him come in; I have no enemies now." But when he heard the man's name:

"No, no. I do not want to see a Southern man who is now in Lincoln's navy." The officers of the United States Navy attended his funeral.

June 14th.—All things are against us. Memphis gone. Mississippi fleet annihilated, and we hear it all as stolidly apathetic as if it were a story of the English war against China which happened a year or so ago.

The sons of Mrs. John Julius Pringle have come. They were left at school in the North. A young Huger is with them. They seem to have had adventures enough. Walked, waded, rowed in boats, if boats they could find; swam rivers when boats there were none; brave lads are they. One can but admire their pluck and energy. Mrs. Fisher, of Philadelphia, *née* Middleton, gave them money to make the attempt to get home.

Stuart's cavalry have rushed through McClellan's lines and burned five of his transports. Jackson has been reenforced by 16,000 men, and they hope the enemy will be drawn from around Richmond, and the valley be the seat of war.

John Chesnut is in Whiting's brigade, which has been sent to Stonewall. Mem's son is with the Boykin Rangers; Company A, No. 1, we call it. And she has persistently wept ever since she heard the news. It is no child's play, she says, when you are with Stonewall. He doesn't play at soldiering. He doesn't take care of his men at all. He only goes to kill the Yankees.

Wade Hampton is here, shot in the foot, but he knows no more about France than he does of the man in the moon. Wet blanket he is just now. Johnston badly wounded. Lee is King of Spades. They are all once more digging for dear life. Unless we can reenforce Stonewall, the game is up. Our chiefs contrive to dampen and destroy the enthusiasm of all who go near them. So much entrenching and falling back destroys the *morale* of any army. This everlasting retreating, it kills the hearts of the men. Then we are scant of powder.

James Chesnut is awfully proud of Le Conte's powder manufactory here. Le Conte knows how to do it. James Chesnut provides him the means to carry out his plans.

Colonel Venable doesn't mince matters: "If we do not deal a blow, a blow that will be felt, it will be soon all up with us. I he Southwest will be lost to us. We can not afford to shilly-shally much longer."

Thousands are enlisting on the other side in New Orleans. Butler holds out inducements. To be sure, they are principally foreigners who want to escape starvation. Tennessee we may count on as gone, since we abandoned her at Corinth, Fort Pillow, and Memphis. A man must be sent there, or it is all gone now.

"You call a spade by that name, it seems, and not an agricultural implement?" "They call Mars Robert 'Old Spade Lee.' He keeps them digging so." "General Lee is a noble Virginian. Respect something in this world. Cæsar—call him Old Spade Cæsar? As a soldier, he was as much above suspicion, as he required his wife to be, as Cæsar's wife, you know. If I remember Cæsar's Commentaries, he owns up to a lot of entrenching. You let Mars Robert alone. He knows what he is about."

"Tell us of the women folk at New Orleans; how did they take the fall of the city?" "They are an excitable race," the man from that city said. As my informant was standing on the levee a daintily dressed lady picked her way, parasol in hand, toward him. She accosted him with great politeness, and her face was as placid and unmoved as in antebellum days. Her first question was: "Will you be so kind as to tell me what is the last general order?" "No order that I know of, madam; General Disorder prevails now." "Ah! I see; and why are those persons flying and yelling so noisily and racing in the streets in that unseemly way?" "They are looking for a shell to burst over their heads at any moment." "Ah!" Then, with a courtesy of dignity and grace, she waved her parasol and departed, but stopped to arrange that parasol at a proper angle to protect her face from the sun. There was no vulgar haste in her movements. She tripped away as gracefully as she came. My informant had failed to discompose her by his fearful rations. That was the one self-possessed soul then in New Orleans.

Another woman drew near, so overheated and out of breath, she had barely time to say she had run miles of squares in her crazy terror and bewilderment, when a sudden shower came up. In a second she was cool and calm. She forgot all the questions she came to ask. "My bonnet, I must save it at any sacrifice," she said, and so turned her dress over her head, and went off, forgetting her country's trouble and screaming for a cab.

Went to see Mrs. Burroughs at the old de Saussure house. She has such a sweet face, such soft, kind, beautiful, dark-gray eyes. Such eyes are a poem. No wonder she had a long love-story. We sat in the piazza at twelve o'clock of a June day, the glorious Southern sun shining its very hottest. But we were in a dense shade—magnolias in full bloom, ivy, vines of I know not what, and roses in profusion closed us in. It was a living wall of everything beautiful and sweet. In all this flower-garden of a Columbia, that is the most delicious corner I have been in yet.

Got from the Prestons' French library, Fanny, with a brilliant preface by Jules Janier. Now, then, I have come to the worst. There can be no worse book than Fanny. The lover is jealous of the husband. The woman is for the polyandry rule of life. She cheats both and refuses to break with either. But to criticize it one must be as shameless as the book itself. Of course, it is clever to the last degree, or it would be kicked into the gutter. It is not nastier or coarser than Mrs. Stowe, but then it is not written in the interests of philanthropy.

We had an unexpected dinner-party to-day. First, Wade Hampton came and his wife. Then Mr. and Mrs. Rose. I remember that the late Colonel Hampton once said to me, a thing I thought odd at the time, "Mrs. James Rose" (and I forget now who was the other) "are the only two people on this side of the water who know how to give a state dinner." Mr. and Mrs. James Rose: if anybody body wishes to describe old Carolina at its best, let them try their hands at painting these two people.

Wade Hampton still limps a little, but he is rapidly recovering. Here is what he said, and he has fought so well that he is listened to: "If we mean to play at war, as we play a game of chess, West Point tactics prevailing, we are sure to lose the game. They have every advantage. They can lose pawns *ad infinitum*, to the end of time and never feel it. We will be throwing away all that we had hoped so much from— Southern hot-headed dash, reckless gallantry, spirit of adventure, readiness to lead forlorn hopes."

Mrs. Rose is Miss Sarah Parker's aunt. Somehow it came out when I was not in the room, but those girls tell me everything. It seems Miss Sarah said: "The reason I can not bear Mrs. Chesnut is that she laughs at everything and at everybody." If she saw me now she would give me credit for some pretty hearty crying as well as laughing. It was a mortifying thing to hear about one's self, all the same.

General Preston came in and announced that Mr. Chesnut was in town. He had just seen Mr. Alfred Huger, who came up on the Charleston train with him. Then Mrs. McCord came and offered to take me back to Mrs. McMahan's to look him up. I found my room locked up. Lawrence said his master had gone to look for me at the Prestons'.

Mrs. McCord proposed we should further seek for my errant husband. At the door, we met Governor Pickens, who showed us telegrams from the President of the most important nature. The Governor added, "And I have one from Jeems Chesnut, but I hear he has followed it so closely, coming on its heels, as it were, that I need not show you that one."

"You don't look interested at the sound of your husband's name?" said he. "Is that his name?" asked I. "I supposed it was James." "My advice to you is to find him, for Mrs. Pickens says he was last seen in the company of two very handsome women, and now you may call him any name you please."

We soon met. The two beautiful dames Governor Pickens threw in my teeth were some ladies from Rafton Creek, almost neighbors, who live near Camden.

By way of pleasant remark to Wade Hampton: "Oh, General! The next battle will give you a chance to be major-general." "I was very foolish to give up my Legion," he answered gloomily. "Promotion don't really annoy many people." Mary Gibson says her father writes to them, that they may go back. He thinks now that the Confederates can hold Richmond. *Gloria in excelsis!*

Another personal defeat. Little Kate said: "Oh, Cousin Mary, why don't you cultivate heart? They say at Kirkwood that you had better let your brains alone a while and cultivate heart." She had evidently caught up a phrase and repeated it again and again for my benefit. So that is the way they talk of me! The only good of loving any one with your whole heart is to give that person the power to hurt you.

June 24th.—Mr. Chesnut, having missed the Secessionville[86] fight by half a day, was determined to see the one around Richmond. He went off with General Cooper and Wade Hampton. Blanton Duncan sent them for a luncheon on board the cars,—ice, wine, and every manner of good thing.

In all this death and destruction, the women are the same—chatter, patter, clatter. "Oh, the Charleston refugees are so full of airs; there is no sympathy for them here!" "Oh, indeed! That is queer. They are not half as exclusive as these Hamptons and Prestons. The airs these people do give themselves." "Airs, airs," laughed Mrs. Bartow, parodying Tennyson's Charge of the Light Brigade. "Airs to the right of them, Airs to the left of them, some one had blundered." "Volleyed and thundered rhymes but is out of place."

The worst of all airs came from a democratic landlady, who was asked by Mrs. President Davis to have a carpet shaken, and shook herself with rage as she answered, "You know, madam, you need not stay here if my carpet or anything else does not suit you."

John Chesnut gives us a spirited account of their ride around McClellan. I sent the letter to his grandfather. The women ran out screaming with joyful welcome as soon as they caught sight of our soldiers' gray uniforms; ran to them bringing handfuls and armfuls of, food. One gray-headed man, after preparing a hasty meal for them, knelt and prayed as they snatched it, as you may say. They were in the saddle from Friday until Sunday. They were used up; so were their horses. Johnny writes for clothes and more horses. Miss S. C. says: "No need to send any more of his fine horses to be killed or captured by the Yankees; wait and see how the siege of Richmond ends." The horses will go all the same, as Johnny wants them.

June 25th.—I forgot to tell of Mrs. Pickens's reception for General

---

[86] The battle of Secessionville occurred on James Island, in the harbor of Charleston, June 16, 1862.

Hampton. My Mem dear, described it all. "The Governess" ("Tut, Mem! that is not the right name for her—she is not a teacher." "Never mind, it is the easier to say than the Governor's wife." "*Madame la Gouvernante*" was suggested. "Why? That is worse than the other!") "met him at the door, took his crutch away, putting his hand upon her shoulder instead. "That is the way to greet heroes," she said. Her blue eyes were aflame, and in response poor Wade smiled, and smiled until his face hardened into a fixed grin of embarrassment and annoyance. He is a simple-mannered man, you know, and does not want to be made much of by women.

The butler was not in plain clothes, but wore, as the other servants did, magnificent livery brought from the Court of St. Petersburg, one mass of gold embroidery, etc. They had champagne and Russian tea, the latter from a samovar made in Russia. Little Moses was there. Now for us they have never put their servants into Russian livery, nor paraded Little Moses under our noses, but I must confess the Russian tea and champagne set before us left nothing to be desired. "How did General Hampton bear his honors?" "Well, to the last he looked as if he wished they would let him alone."

Met Mr. Ashmore fresh from Richmond. He says Stonewall is coming up behind McClellan. And here comes the tug of war. He thinks we have so many spies in Richmond, they may have found out our strategic movements and so may circumvent them.

Mrs. Bartow's story of a clever Miss Toombs. So many men were in love with her, and the courtship, while it lasted, of each one was as exciting and bewildering as a fox-chase. She liked the fun of the run, but she wanted something more than to know a man was in mad pursuit of her; that he should love her, she agreed, but she must love him, too. How was she to tell? Yet she must be certain of it before she said "Yes." So, as they sat by the lamp she would look at him and inwardly ask herself, "Would I be willing to spend the long winter evenings forever after sitting here darning your old stockings?" Never, echo answered. No, no, a thousand times no. So, each had to make way for another.

June 27th.—We went in a body (half a dozen ladies, with no man on escort duty, for they are all in the army) to a concert. Mrs. Pickens came in. She was joined soon by Secretary Moses and Mr. Follen. Doctor Berrien came to our relief. Nothing could be more execrable than the singing. Financially the thing was a great success, for though the audience was altogether feminine, it was a very large one.

Telegram from Mr. Chesnut, "Safe in Richmond"; that is, if Richmond be safe, with all the power of the United States of America battering at her gates. Strange not a word from Stonewall Jackson, after all! Doctor Gibson telegraphs his wife, "Stay where you are; terrible battle[87] looked for here."

Decca is dead. That poor little darling! Immediately after her baby was born, she took it into her head that Alex was killed. He was wounded, but those around had not told her of it. She surprised them by asking, "Does any one know how the battle has gone since Alex was killed?" She could not read for a day or so before she died. Her head was bewildered, but she would not let any one else touch her letters; so she died with several unopened ones in her bosom. Mrs. Singleton, Decca's mother, fainted dead away, but she shed no tears. We went to the house and saw Alex's mother, a daughter of Langdon Cheves. Annie was with us. She said: "This is the saddest thing for Alex." "No," said his mother, "death is never the saddest thing. If he were not a good man, that would be a far worse thing." Annie, in utter amazement, whimpered, "But Alex is so good already." "Yes, seven years ago the death of one of his sisters that he dearly loved made him a Christian. That death in our family was worth a thousand lives."

One needs a hard heart now. Even old Mr. Shand shed tears. Mary Barnwell sat as still as a statue, as white and stony. "Grief which can relieve itself by tears is a thing to pray for," said the Rev. Mr. Shand. Then came a telegram from Hampton, "All well; so far we are successful." Robert Barnwell had been telegraphed for. His answer came, "Can't leave here; Gregg is fighting across the Chickahominy." Said Alex's mother: "My son, Alex, may never hear this sad news," and her lip settled rigidly. "Go on; what else does Hampton say?" asked she. "Lee has one wing of the army, Stonewall the other."

Annie Hampton came to tell us the latest news—that we have abandoned James Island and are fortifying Morris Island. "And now," she says, "if the enemy will be so kind as to wait, we will be ready for them in two months."

Rev. Mr. Shand and that pious Christian woman, Alex's mother (who looks into your very soul with those large and lustrous blue eyes of hers) agreed that the Yankees, even if they took Charleston, would not destroy it. I think they will, sinner that I am. Mr. Shand remarked to her, "Madam, you have two sons in the army." Alex's mother replied, "I have had six sons in the army; I now have five."

There are people here too small to conceive of any larger business than quarreling in the newspapers. One laughs at squibs in the papers now, in such times as these, with the wolf at our doors. Men safe in their closets writing fiery articles, denouncing those who are at work, are beneath contempt. Only critics with muskets on their shoulders have the right to speak now, as Trenholm said the other night.

---

[87] Malvern Hill, the last of the Seven Days' Battles, was fought near Richmond on the James River, July 1, 1862. The Federals were commanded by McClellan and the Confederates by Lee.

In a pouring rain we went to that poor child's funeral -to Decca's. They buried her in the little white frock she wore when she engaged herself to Alex, and which she again put on for her bridal about a year ago. She lies now in the churchyard, in sight of my window. Is she to be pitied? She said she had had "months of perfect happiness." How many people can say that? So many of us live their long, dreary lives and then happiness never comes to meet them at all. It seems so near, and yet it eludes them forever.

June 28th.—Victory!! Victory heads every telegram now;[88] one reads it on the bulletin-board. It is the anniversary of the battle of Fort Moultrie. The enemy went off so quickly, I wonder if it was not a trap laid for us, to lead us away from Richmond, to some place where they can manage to do us more harm. And now comes the list of killed and wounded. Victory does not seem to soothe sore hearts. Mrs. Haskell has five sons before the enemy's illimitable cannon. Mrs. Preston two. McClellan is routed and we have twelve thousand prisoners. Prisoners! My God! and what are we to do with them? We can't feed our own people.

For the first time since Joe Johnston was wounded at Seven Pines, we may breathe freely; we were so afraid of another general, or a new one. Stonewall can not be everywhere, though he comes near it.

Magruder did splendidly at Big Bethel. It was a wonderful thing how he played his ten thousand before McClellan like fireflies and utterly deluded him. It was partly due to the Manassas scare that we gave them; they will never be foolhardy again. Now we are throwing up our caps for R. E. Lee. We hope from the Lees what the first sprightly running (at Manassas) could not give. We do hope there will be no "ifs." "Ifs" have ruined us. Shiloh was a victory if Albert Sidney Johnston had not been killed; Seven Pines if Joe Johnston had not been wounded. The "ifs" bristle like porcupines. That victory at Manassas did nothing but send us off in a fool's paradise of conceit, and it roused the manhood of the Northern people. For very shame they had to move up.

A French man-of-war lies at the wharf at Charleston to take off French subjects when the bombardment begins. William Mazyck writes that the enemy's gunboats are shelling and burning property up and down the Santee River. They raise the white flag and the negroes rush down on them. Planters might as well have let these negroes be taken by the Council to work on the fortifications. A letter from my husband:

RICHMOND, *June* 29, 1862.

---

[88] The first battle of the Chickahominy, fought on June 27, 1862. It is better known as the battle of Gaines's Mill, or Cold Harbor. It was participated in by a part of Lee's army and a part of McClellan's, and its scene was about eight miles from Richmond.

MY DEAR MARY:

For the last three days I have been a witness of the most stirring events of modern times. On my arrival here, I found the government so absorbed in the great battle pending, that I found it useless to talk of the special business that brought me to this place. As soon as it is over, which will probably be to-morrow, I think that I can easily accomplish all that I was sent for. I have no doubt that we can procure another general and more forces, etc.

The President and General Lee are inclined to listen to me, and to do all they can for us. General Lee is vindicating the high opinion I have ever expressed of him, and his plans and executions of the last great fight will place him high in the roll of really great commanders.

The fight on Friday was the largest and fiercest of the whole war. Some 60,000 or 70,000, with great preponderance on the side of the enemy. Ground, numbers, armament, etc., were all in favor of the enemy. But our men and generals were superior. The higher officers and men behaved with a resolution and dashing heroism that have never been surpassed in any country or in any age.

Our line was three times repulsed by superior numbers and superior artillery impregnably posted. Then Lee, assembling all his generals to the front, told them that victory depended on carrying the batteries and defeating the army before them, ere night should fall. Should night come without victory all was lost, and the work must be done by the bayonet. Our men then made a rapid and irresistible charge, without powder, and carried everything. The enemy melted before them, and ran with the utmost speed, though of the regulars of the Federal army. The fight between the artillery of the opposing forces was terrific and sublime. The field became one dense cloud of smoke, so that nothing could be seen, but the incessant flash of fire. They were within sixteen hundred yards of each other and it rained storms of grape and canister. We took twenty-three pieces of their artillery, many small arms, and small ammunition. They burned most of their stores, wagons, etc.

The victory of the second day was full and complete. Yesterday there was little or no fighting, but some splendid maneuvering, which has placed us completely around them. I think the end must be decisive in our favor. We have lost many men and many officers; I hear Alex Haskell and young McMahan are among them, as well as a son of Dr. Trezevant. Very sad, indeed. We are fighting again today; will let you know the result as soon as possible. Will be at home some time next week. No letter from you yet.

With devotion, yours,

JAMES CHESNUT.

A telegram from my husband of June 29th from Richmond: "Was on the field, saw it all. Things satisfying so far. Can hear nothing of John Chesnut. He is in Stuart's command. Saw Jack Preston; safe so far. No reason why we should not bag McClellan's army or cut it to pieces. From four to six thousand prisoners already." Doctor Gibbes rushed in like a whirlwind to say we were driving McClellan into the river.

June 30th.—First came Dr. Trezevant, who announced Burnet Rhett's death. "No, no; I have just seen the bulletin-board. It was Grimke Rhett's." When the doctor went out it was added: "Howell Trezevant's death is there, too. The doctor will see it as soon as he goes down to the board." The girls went to see Lucy Trezevant. The doctor was lying still as death on a sofa with his face covered.

July 1st.—No more news. It has settled down into this. The general battle, the decisive battle, has to be fought yet. Edward Cheves, only son of John Cheves, killed. His sister kept crying, "Oh, mother, what shall we do; Edward is killed," but the mother sat dead still, white as a sheet, never uttering a word or shedding a tear. Are our women losing the capacity to weep? The father came to-day, Mr. John Cheves. He has been making infernal machines in Charleston to blow up Yankee ships.

While Mrs. McCord was telling me of this terrible trouble in her brother's family, some one said: "Decca's husband died of grief." Stuff and nonsense; silly sentiment, folly! If he is not wounded, he is alive. His brother, John, may die of that shattered arm in this hot weather. Alex will never die of a broken heart. Take my word for it.

July 3d.—Mem says she feels like sitting down, as an Irishwoman does at a wake, and howling night and day. Why did Huger let McClellan slip through his fingers? Arrived at Mrs. McMahan's at the wrong moment. Mrs. Bartow was reading to the stricken mother an account of the death of her son. The letter was written by a man who was standing by him when he was shot through the head. "My God!" he said; that was all, and he fell dead. James Taylor was color-bearer. He was shot three times before he gave in. Then he said, as he handed the colors to the man next him, "You see I can't stand it any longer," and dropped stone dead. He was only seventeen years old.

If anything can reconcile me to the idea of a horrid failure after all efforts to make good our independence of Yankees, it is Lincoln's proclamation freeing the negroes. Especially yours, Messieurs, who write insults to your Governor and Council, dated from Clarendon. Three hundred of Mr. Walter Blake's negroes have gone to the Yankees. Remember, that recalcitrant patriot's property on two legs may walk off without an order from the Council to work on fortifications.

Have been reading The Potiphar Papers by Curtis. Can this be a picture of New York socially? If it were not for this horrid war, how nice it would be here. We might lead such a pleasant life. This is the most perfectly appointed establishment—such beautiful grounds, lowers, and fruits; indeed, all that heart could wish; such delightful dinners, such pleasant drives, such jolly talks, such charming people; but this horrid war poisons everything.

July 5th.—Drove out with Mrs. "Constitution" Browne, who told us the story of Ben McCulloch's devotion to Lucy Gwynn. Poor Ben McCulloch—another dead hero. Called at the Tognos' and saw no one; no wonder. They say Ascelie Togno was to have been married to Grimke Rhett in August, and he is dead on the battle-field. I had not heard of the engagement before I went there.

July 8th.—Gunboat captured on the Santee. So much the worse for us. We do not want any more prisoners, and next time they will send a fleet of boats, if one will not do. The Governor sent me Mr. Chesnut's telegram with a note saying, "I regret the telegram does not come up to what we had hoped might be as to the entire destruction of McClellan's army. I think, however, the strength of the war with its ferocity may now be considered as broken."

Table-talk to-day: This war was undertaken by us to shake off the yoke of foreign invaders. So we consider our cause righteous. The Yankees, since the war has begun, have discovered it is to free the slaves that they are fighting. So their cause is noble. They also expect to make the war pay. Yankees do not undertake anything that does not pay. They think we belong to them. We have been good milk cows— milked by the tariff, or skimmed. We let them have all of our hard earnings. We bear the ban of slavery; they get the money. Cotton pays everybody who handles it, sells it, manufactures it, but rarely pays the man who grows it. Second hand the Yankees received the wages of slavery. They grew rich. We grew poor. The receiver is as bad as the thief. That applies to us, too, for we received the savages they stole from Africa and brought to us in their slave-ships. As with the Egyptians, so it shall be with us: if they let us go, it must be across a Red Sea—but one made red by blood.

July 10th.—My husband has come. He believes from what he heard in Richmond that we are to be recognized as a nation by the crowned heads across the water, at last. Mr. Davis was very kind; he asked him to stay at his house, which he did, and went every day with General Lee and Mr. Davis to the battle-field as a sort of amateur aide to the President. Likewise they admitted him to the informal Cabinet meetings at the President's house. He is so hopeful now that it is pleasant to hear him, and I had not the heart to stick the small pins of Yeadon and Pickens in him yet a while.

Public opinion is hot against Huger and Magruder for McClellan's escape. Doctor Gibbes gave me some letters picked up on the battle-field. One signed "Laura," tells her lover to fight in such a manner that no Southerner can ever taunt Yankees again with cowardice. She speaks of a man at home whom she knows, "who is still talking of his intention to seek the bubble reputation at the cannon's mouth." "Miserable coward!" she writes, "I will never speak to him again." It was a relief to find one silly young person filling three pages with a description of her new bonnet and the bonnet still worn by her rival. Those fiery Joan of Arc damsels who goad on their sweethearts bode us no good.

Rachel Lyons was in Richmond, hand in glove with Mrs. Greenhow. Why not? "So handsome, so clever, so angelically kind," says Rachel of the Greenhow, "and she offers to matronize me."

Mrs. Philips, another beautiful and clever Jewess, has been put into prison again by "Beast" Butler because she happened to be laughing as a Yankee funeral procession went by.

Captain B. told of John Chesnut's pranks. Johnny was riding a powerful horse, captured from the Yankees. The horse dashed with him right into the Yankee ranks. A dozen Confederates galloped after him, shouting, "Stuart! Stuart!" The Yankees, mistaking this mad charge for Stuart's cavalry, broke ranks and fled. Daredevil Camden boys ride like Arabs!

Mr. Chesnut says he was riding with the President when Colonel Browne, his aide, was along. The General commanding rode up and, bowing politely, said: "Mr. President, am I in command here?" "Yes." "Then I forbid you to stand here under the enemy's guns. Any exposure of a life like yours is wrong, and this is useless exposure. You must go back." Mr. Davis answered: "Certainly, I will set an example of obedience to orders. Discipline must be maintained." But he did not go back.

Mr. Chesnut met the Haynes, who had gone on to nurse their wounded son and found him dead. They were standing in the corridor of the Spotswood. Although Mr. Chesnut was staying at the President's, he retained his room at the hotel. So he gave his room to them. Next day, when he went back to his room he found that Mrs. Hayne had thrown herself across the foot of the bed and never moved. No other part of the bed had been touched. She got up and went back to the cars, or was led back. He says these heartbroken mothers are hard to face.

July 12th.—At McMahan's our small colonel, Paul Hayne's son, came into my room. To amuse the child I gave him a photograph album to look over. "You have Lincoln in your book!" said he. "I am astonished at you. I hate him!" And he placed the book on the floor and struck Old Abe in the face with his fist.

An Englishman told me Lincoln has said that had he known such a war would follow his election he never would have set foot in Washington, nor have been inaugurated. He had never dreamed of this awful fratricidal bloodshed. That does not seem like the true John Brown spirit. I was very glad to hear it—to hear something from the President of the United States which was not merely a vulgar joke, and usually a joke so vulgar that you were ashamed to laugh, funny though it was. They say Seward has gone to England and his wily tongue will turn all hearts against us.

Browne told us there was a son of the Duke of Somerset in Richmond. He laughed his fill at our ragged, dirty soldiers, but he stopped his laughing when he saw them under fire. Our men strip the Yankee dead of their shoes, but will not touch the shoes of a comrade. Poor fellows, they are nearly barefoot.

Alex has come. I saw him ride up about dusk and go into the graveyard. I shut up my windows on that side. Poor fellow!

July 13th.—Halcott Green came to see us. Bragg is a stern disciplinarian, according to Halcott. He did not in the least understand citizen soldiers. In the retreat from Shiloh he ordered that not a gun should be fired. A soldier shot a chicken, and then the soldier was shot. "For a chicken!" said Halcott. "A Confederate soldier for a chicken!"

Mrs. McCord says a nurse, who is also a beauty, had better leave her beauty with her cloak and hat at the door. One lovely lady nurse said to a rough old soldier, whose wound could not have been dangerous, "Well, my good soul, what can I do for you?" "Kiss me!" said he. Mrs. McCord's fury was "at the woman's telling it," for it brought her hospital into disrepute, and very properly. She knew there were women who would boast of an insult if it ministered to their vanity. She wanted nurses to come dressed as nurses, as Sisters of Charity, and not as fine ladies. Then there would be no trouble. When she saw them coming in angel sleeves, displaying all their white arms and in their muslin, showing all their beautiful white shoulders and throats, she felt disposed to order them off the premises. That was no proper costume for a nurse. Mrs. Bartow goes in her widow's weeds, which is after Mrs. McCord's own heart. But Mrs. Bartow has her stories, too. A surgeon said to her, "I give you no detailed instructions: a mother necessarily is a nurse." She then passed on quietly, "as smilingly acquiescent, my dear, as if I had ever been a mother."

Mrs. Greenhow has enlightened Rachel Lyons as to Mr. Chesnut's character in Washington. He was "one of the very few men of whom there was not a word of scandal spoken. I do not believe, my dear, that he ever spoke to a woman there." He did know Mrs. John R. Thompson, however.

Walked up and down the college campus with Mrs. McCord. The buildings all lit up with gas, the soldiers seated under the elms in every direction, and in every stage of convalescence. Through the open windows, could see the nurses flitting about. It was a strange, weird scene. Walked home with Mrs. Bartow. We stopped at Judge Carroll's.

Mrs. Carroll gave us a cup of tea. When we got home, found the Prestons had called for me to dine at their house to meet General Magruder.

Last night the Edgefield Band serenaded Governor Pickens. Mrs. Harris stepped on the porch and sang the Marseillaise for them. It has been more than twenty years since I first heard her voice; it was a very fine one then, but there is nothing which the tooth of time lacerates more cruelly than the singing voice of women. There is an incongruous metaphor for you.

The negroes on the coast received the Rutledge's Mounted Rifles apparently with great rejoicings. The troops were gratified-to find the negroes in such a friendly state of mind. One servant whispered to his master, "Don't you mind 'em, don't trust 'em"—meaning the negroes. The master then dressed himself as a Federal officer and went down to a negro quarter. The very first greeting was, "Ki! massa, you come fuh ketch rebels? We kin show you way you kin ketch thirty to-night." They took him to the Confederate camp, or pointed it out, and then added for his edification, "We kin ketch officer fuh you whenever you want 'em."

Bad news. Gunboats have passed Vicksburg. The Yankees are spreading themselves over our fair Southern land like red ants.

July 21st.—Jackson has gone into the enemy's country. Joe Johnston and Wade Hampton are to follow.

Think of Rice, Mr. Senator Rice,[89] who sent us the buffalo-robes. I see from his place in the Senate that he speaks of us as savages, who put powder and whisky into soldiers' canteens to make them mad with ferocity in the fight. No, never. We admire coolness here, because we lack it; we do not need to be fired by drink to be brave. My classical lore is small, indeed, but I faintly remember something of the Spartans who marched to the music of lutes. No drum and fife were needed to revive their fainting spirits. In that one thing we are Spartans.

The Wayside Hospital[90] is duly established at the Columbia Station, where all the railroads meet. All honor to Mrs. Fisher and the other women who work there so faithfully! The young girls of

---

[89] Henry M. Rice, United States Senator from Minnesota, who had emigrated to that State from Vermont in 1835.

[90] Of ameliorations in modern warfare, Dr. John T. Darby said in addressing the South Carolina Medical Association, Charleston, in 1873: "On the route from the army to the general hospital, wounds are dressed and soldiers refreshed at wayside homes; and here be it said with justice and pride that the credit of originating this system is due to the women of South Carolina. In a small room in the capital of this State, the first Wayside Home was founded; and during the war, some seventy-five thousand soldiers were relieved by having their wounds dressed, their ailments attended, and very frequently by being clothed through the patriotic services and good offices of a few untiring ladies in Columbia. From this little nucleus, spread that grand system of wayside hospitals which was established during our own and the late European wars."

Columbia started this hospital. In the first winter of the war, moneyless soldiers, sick and wounded, suffered greatly when they had to lie over here because of faulty connections between trains. Rev. Mr. Martin, whose habit it was to meet trains and offer his aid to these unfortunates, suggested to the Young Ladies' Hospital Association their opportunity; straightway the blessed maidens provided a room where our poor fellows might have their wounds bound up and be refreshed. And now, the "Soldiers' Rest" has grown into the Wayside Hospital, and older heads and hands relieve younger ones of the grimmer work and graver responsibilities. I am ready to help in every way, by subscription and otherwise, but too feeble in health to go there much.

Mrs. Browne heard a man say at the Congaree House, "We are breaking our heads against a stone wall. We are bound to be conquered. We can not keep it up much longer against so powerful a nation as the United States. Crowds of Irish, Dutch, and Scotch are pouring in to swell their armies. They are promised our lands, and they believe they will get them. Even if we are successful we can not live without Yankees." "Now," says Mrs. Browne, "I call that man a Yankee spy." To which I reply, "If he were a spy, he would not dare show his hand so plainly."

"To think," says Mrs. Browne, "that he is not taken up. Seward's little bell would tinkle, a guard would come, and the Grand Inquisition of America would order that man put under arrest in the twinkling of an eye, if he had ventured to speak against Yankees in Yankee land."

General Preston said he had "the right to take up any one who was not in his right place and send him where he belonged." "Then do take up my husband instantly. He is sadly out of his right place in this little Governor's Council." The general stared at me and slowly uttered in his most tragic tones, "If I could put him where I think he ought to be!" This I immediately hailed as a high compliment and was duly ready with my thanks. Upon reflection, it is borne in upon me, that he might have been more explicit. He left too much to the imagination.

Then Mrs. Browne described the Prince of Wales, whose manners, it seems, differ from those of Mrs.—, who arraigned us from morn to dewy eve, and upbraided us with our ill-bred manners and customs. The Prince, when he was here, conformed at once to whatever he saw was the way of those who entertained him. He closely imitated President Buchanan's way of doing things. He took off his gloves at once when he saw that the President wore none. He began by bowing to the people who were presented to him, but when he saw Mr. Buchanan shaking hands, he shook hands, too. When smoking affably with Browne on the White House piazza, he expressed his content with the fine cigars Browne had given him. The President said: "I was keeping some excellent ones for you, but Browne has got ahead of me." Long after Mr. Buchanan had gone to bed, the Prince ran into his room in a jolly, boyish way, and said: "Mr. Buchanan, I have come for the fine cigars you have for me."

As I walked up to the Prestons', along a beautiful shaded back street, a carriage passed with Governor Means in it. As soon as he saw me he threw himself half out and kissed both hands to me again and again. It was a whole-souled greeting, as the saying is, and I returned it with my whole heart, too. "Good-by," he cried, and I responded "Good-by." I may never see him again. I am not sure that I did not shed a few tears.

General Preston and Mr. Chesnut were seated on the piazza of the Hampton house as I walked in. I opened my batteries upon them in this scornful style: "You cold, formal, solemn, overly-polite creatures, weighed down by your own dignity. You will never know the rapture of such a sad farewell as John Means and I have just interchanged. He was in a hack," I proceeded to relate, "and I was on the sidewalk. He was on his way to the war, poor fellow. The hackman drove steadily along in the middle of the street; but for our gray hairs I do not know what he might have thought of us. John Means did not suppress his feelings at an unexpected meeting with an old friend, and a good cry did me good. It is a life of terror and foreboding we lead. My heart is in my mouth half the time. But you two, under no possible circumstances could you forget your manners."

Read Russell's India all day. Saintly folks those English when their blood is up. Sepoys and blacks we do not expect anything better from, but what an example of Christian patience and humanity the white "angels" from the West set them.

The beautiful Jewess, Rachel Lyons, was here to-day. She flattered Paul Hayne audaciously, and he threw back the ball.

To-day I saw the Rowena to this Rebecca, when Mrs. Edward Barnwell called. She is the purest type of Anglo-Saxon—exquisitely beautiful, cold, quiet, calm, lady-like, fair as a lily, with the blackest and longest eyelashes, and her eyes so light in color some one said "they were the hue of cologne and water." At any rate, she has a patent right to them; there are no more like them to be had. The effect is startling, but lovely beyond words.

Blanton Duncan told us a story of Morgan in Kentucky. Morgan walked into a court where they were trying some Secessionists. The Judge was about to pronounce sentence, but Morgan rose, and begged that he might be allowed to call some witnesses. The Judge asked who were his witnesses. "My name is John Morgan, and my witnesses are 1,400 Confederate soldiers."

Mrs. Izard witnessed two instances of patriotism in the caste called "Sandhill lackeys." One forlorn, chill, and fever-freckled crea yellow, dirty, and dry as a nut, was selling peaches at ten cents a de Soldiers collected around her cart. She took the cover off and c

"Eat away. Eat your fill. I never charge our soldiers anything." They tried to make her take pay, but when she steadily refused it, they cheered her madly and said: "Sleep in peace. Now we will fight for you and keep off the Yankees." Another poor Sandhill man refused to sell his cows, and gave them to the hospital.

CHAPTER XII. FLAT ROCK, N. C.

August 1, 1862—*August* 8, 1862

Flat Rock, N. C., *August 1, 1862.*—Being ill I left Mrs. McMahan's for Flat Rock.[91] It was very hot and disagreeable for an invalid in a boarding-house in that climate. The La Bordes and the McCord girls came part of the way with me.

The cars were crowded and a lame soldier had to stand, leaning on his crutches in the thoroughfare that runs between the seats. One of us gave him our seat. You may depend upon it there was no trouble in finding a seat for our party after that. Dr. La Borde quoted a classic anecdote. In some Greek assembly an old man was left standing. A Spartan gave him his seat. The Athenians cheered madly, though they had kept their seats. The comment was, "Lacedemonians practice virtue; Athenians know how to admire it."

Nathan Davis happened accidentally to be at the station at Greenville. He took immediate charge of Molly and myself, for my party had dwindled to us two. He went with us to the hotel, sent for the landlord, told him who I was, secured good rooms for us and saw that we were made comfortable in every way. At dinner I entered that immense dining-room alone, but I saw friends and acquaintances on every side. My first exploit was to repeat to Mrs. Ives Mrs. Pickens's blunder in taking a suspicious attitude toward men born at the North, and calling upon General Cooper to agree with her. Martha Levy explained the grave faces of my auditors by saying that Colonel Ives was a New Yorker. My distress was dire.

Louisa Hamilton was there. She told me that Captain George Cuthbert, with his arm in a sling from a wound by no means healed, was going to risk the shaking of a stagecoach; he was on his way to his cousin, William Cuthbert's, at Flat Rock. Now George Cuthbert is a type of the finest kind of Southern soldier. We can not make them any better than he is. Before the war I knew him; he traveled in Europe with my sister, Kate, and Mary Withers. At once I offered him a seat in the comfortable hack Nathan Davis had engaged for me.

---

[91] Flat Rock was the summer resort of many cultured families from the low countries of the South before the war. Many attractive houses had been built there. It lies in the region which has since become famous as the Asheville region, and in which stands Biltmore.

Molly sat opposite to me, and often when I was tired held my feet in her lap. Captain Cuthbert's man sat with the driver. We had ample room. We were a dilapidated company. I was so ill I could barely sit up, and Captain Cuthbert could not use his right hand or arm at all. I had to draw his match, light his cigar, etc. He was very quiet, grateful, gentle, and, I was going to say, docile. He is a fiery soldier, one of those whose whole face becomes transfigured in battle, so one of his men told me, describing his way with his company. He does not blow his own trumpet, but I made him tell me the story of his duel with the Mercury's reporter. He seemed awfully ashamed of wasting time in such a scrape.

That night we stopped at a country house half-way toward our journey's end. There we met Mr. Charles Lowndes. Rawlins Lowndes, his son, is with Wade Hampton.

First we drove, by mistake, into Judge King's yard, our hackman mistaking the place for the hotel. Then we made Farmer's Hotel (as the seafaring men say).

Burnet Rhett, with his steed, was at the door; horse and man were caparisoned with as much red and gold artillery uniform as they could bear. He held his horse. The stirrups were Mexican, I believe; they looked like little sidesaddles. Seeing his friend and crony, George Cuthbert, alight and leave a veiled lady in the carriage, this handsome and undismayed young artillerist walked round and round the carriage, talked with the driver, looked in at the doors, and at the front. Suddenly I bethought me to raise my veil and satisfy his curiosity. Our eyes met, and I smiled. It was impossible to resist the comic disappointment on his face when a woman old enough to be George Cuthbert's mother, with the ravages of a year of gastric fever, almost fainting with fatigue, greeted his vision. He instantly mounted his gallant steed and pranced away to his *fiancée*. He is to marry the greatest heiress in the State, Miss Aiken. Then Captain Cuthbert told me his name.

At Kate's, I found Sally Rutledge, and then for weeks life was a blank; I remember nothing. The illness which had been creeping on for so long a time took me by the throat. At Greenville I had met many friends. I witnessed the wooing of Barny Heyward, once the husband of the lovely Lucy Izard, now a widower and a *bon parti*. He was there nursing Joe, his brother. So was the beautiful Henrietta Magruder Heyward, now a widow, for poor Joe died. There is something magnetic in Tatty Clinch's large and lustrous black eyes. No man has ever resisted their influence. She says her virgin heart has never beat one throb the faster for any mortal here below—until now, when it surrenders to Barny. Well, as I said, Joseph Heyward died, and rapidly did the bereaved beauty shake the dust of this poor Confederacy from her feet and plume her wings for flight across the water.

[Let me insert here now, much later, all I know of that brave spirit,

George Cuthbert. While I was living in the winter of 1863 at the corner of Clay and Twelfth Streets in Richmond, he came to see me. Never did man enjoy life more. The Preston girls were staying at my house then, and it was very gay for the young soldiers who ran down from the army for a day or so. We had heard of him, as usual, gallantly facing odds at Sharpsburg.[92] And he asked if he should chance to be wounded would I have him brought to Clay Street.

He was shot at Chancellorsville,[93] leading his men. The surgeon did not think him mortally wounded. He sent me a message that "he was coming at once to our house." He knew he would soon get well there. Also that "I need not be alarmed; those Yankees could not kill me." He asked one of his friends to write a letter to his mother. Afterward he said he had another letter to write, but that he wished to sleep first, he felt so exhausted. At his request they then turned his face away from the light and left him. When they came again to look at him, they found him dead. He had been dead for a long time. It was bitter cold; wounded men lost much blood and were weakened in that way; they lacked warm blankets and all comforts. Many died who might have been saved by one good hot drink or a few mouthfuls of nourishing food.

One of the generals said to me: "Fire and reckless courage like Captain Cuthbert's are contagious; such men in an army are invaluable; losses like this weakened us, indeed." But I must not linger longer around the memory of the bravest of the brave—a true exemplar of our old *régime*, gallant, gay, unfortunate.—M. B. C.]

*   *   *   *   *

August 8th.—Mr. Daniel Blake drove down to my sister's in his heavy, substantial English phaeton, with stout and strong horses to match. I went back with him and spent two delightful days at his hospitable mansion. I met there, as a sort of chaplain, the Rev. Mr.—. He dealt unfairly by me. We had a long argument, and when we knelt down for evening prayers, he introduced an extemporaneous prayer and prayed *for me* most palpably. There was I down on my knees, red-hot with rage and fury. David W. said it was a clear case of hitting a fellow when he was down. Afterward the fun of it all struck me, and I found it difficult to keep from shaking with laughter. It was not an edifying

---

[92] The battle of Sharpsburg, or Antietam, one of the bloodiest of the war, was fought in western Maryland, a few miles north of Harper's Ferry, on September 16 and 17, 1862, the Federals being under McClellan, and the Confederates under Lee.

[93] The battle of Chancellorsville, where the losses on each side were more than ten thousand men, was fought about fifty miles northwest of Richmond on May 2, 3, and 4, 1863. The Confederates were under Lee and the Federals under Hooker. In this battle Stonewall Jackson was killed.

religious exercise, to say the least, as far as I was concerned.

Before Chancellorsville, was fatal Sharpsburg.[94] My friend, Colonel Means, killed on the battle-field; his only son, Stark, wounded and a prisoner. His wife had not recovered from the death of her other child, Emma, who had died of consumption early in the war. She was lying on a bed when they told her of her husband's death, and then they tried to keep Stark's condition from her. They think now that she misunderstood and believed him dead, too. She threw something over her face. She did not utter one word. She remained quiet so long, some one removed the light shawl which she had thrown over her head and found she was dead. Miss Mary Stark, her sister, said afterward, "No wonder! How was she to face life without her husband and children? That was all she had ever lived for." These are sad, unfortunate memories. Let us run away from them.

What has not my husband been doing this year, 1862, when all our South Carolina troops are in Virginia? Here we were without soldiers or arms. He raised an army, so to speak, and imported arms, through the Trenholm firm. He had arms to sell to the Confederacy. He laid the foundation of a niter-bed; and the Confederacy sent to Columbia to learn of Professor Le Conte how to begin theirs. He bought up all the old arms and had them altered and repaired. He built ships. He imported clothes and shoes for our soldiers, for which things they had long stood sorely in need. He imported cotton cards and set all idle hands carding and weaving. All the world was set to spinning cotton. He tried to stop the sale of whisky, and alas, he called for reserves—that is, men over age, and he committed the unforgivable offense of sending the sacred negro property to work on fortifications away from their owners' plantations.

CHAPTER XIII. PORTLAND, ALA.

July 8, 1863—July 30, 1863

Portland, Ala., *July 8, 1863.*—My mother ill at her home on the plantation near here—where I have come to see her. But to go back first to my trip home from Flat Rock to Camden. At the station, I saw men sitting on a row of coffins smoking, talking, and laughing, with their feet drawn up tailor-fashion to keep them out of the wet. Thus does war harden people's hearts.

Met James Chesnut at Wilmington. He only crossed the river with

[94] During the summer of 1862, after the battle of Malvern Hill and before Sharpsburg, or Antietam, the following important battles had taken place: Harrison's Landing, July 3d and 4th; Harrison's Landing again, July 31st; Cedar Mountain, August 9th; Bull Run (second battle), August 29th and 30th, and South Mountain, September 14th.

me and then went back to Richmond. He was violently opposed to sending our troops into Pennsylvania: wanted all we could spare sent West to make an end there of our enemies. He kept dark about Vallandigham.[95] I am sure we could not trust him to do us any good, or to do the Yankees any harm. The Coriolanus business is played out.

As we came to Camden, Molly sat by me in the cars. She touched me, and, with her nose in the air, said: "Look, Missis." There was the inevitable bride and groom—at least so I thought—and the irrepressible kissing and lolling against each other which I had seen so often before. I was rather astonished at Molly's prudery. but there was a touch in this scene which was new. The man required for his peace of mind that the girl should brush his cheek with those beautiful long eyelashes of hers. Molly became so outraged in her blue-black modesty that she kept her head out of the window not to see! When we were detained at a little wayside station, this woman made an awful row about her room. She seemed to know me and appealed to me; said her brother-in-law was adjutant to Colonel K—, etc.

Molly observed, "You had better go yonder, ma'am, where your husband is calling you." The woman drew herself up proudly, and, with a toss, exclaimed: "Husband, indeed! I'm a widow. That is my cousin. I loved my dear husband too well to marry again, ever, ever!" Absolutely tears came into her eyes. Molly, loaded as she was with shawls and bundles, stood motionless, and said: "After all that gwine-on in the kyars! O, Lord, I should a let it go 'twas my husband and me! nigger as I am."

Here I was at home, on a soft bed, with every physical comfort; but life is one long catechism there, due to the curiosity of stay-at-home people in a narrow world.

In Richmond, Molly and Lawrence quarreled. He declared he could not put up with her tantrums. Unfortunately I asked him, in the interests of peace and a quiet house, to bear with her temper; I did, said I, but she was so good and useful. He was shabby enough to tell her what I had said at their next quarrel. The awful reproaches she overwhelmed me with then! She said she "was mortified that I had humbled her before Lawrence."

But the day of her revenge came. At negro balls in Richmond, guests were required to carry "passes," and, in changing his coat Lawrence forgot his pass. Next day Lawrence was missing, and Molly came to me laughing to tears. "Come and look," said she. "Here is the fine gentleman tied between two black niggers and marched off to jail." She laughed and jeered so she could not stand without holding on to the

---

[95] Clement Baird Vallandigham was an Ohio Democrat who represented the extreme wing of Northern sympathizers with the South. He was arrested by United States troops in May, 1863, court-martialed and banished to the Confederacy. Not being well received in the South, he went to Canada, but after the war returned to Ohio.

window. Lawrence disregarded her and called to me at the top of his voice: "Please, ma'am, ask Mars Jeems to come take me out of this. I ain't done nothing.'"

As soon as Mr. Chesnut came home I told him of Lawrence's sad fall, and he went at once to his rescue. There had been a fight and a disturbance at the ball. The police had been called in, and when every negro was required to show his "pass," Lawrence had been taken up as having none. He was terribly chopfallen when he came home walking behind Mr. Chesnut. He is always so respectable and well-behaved and stands on his dignity.

I went over to Mrs. Preston's at Columbia. Camden had become simply intolerable to me. There the telegram found me, saying I must go to my mother, who was ill at her home here in Alabama. Colonel Goodwyn, his wife, and two daughters were going, and so I joined the party. I telegraphed Mr. Chesnut for Lawrence, and he replied, forbidding me to go at all; it was so hot, the cars so disagreeable, fever would be the inevitable result. Miss Kate Hampton, in her soft voice, said: "The only trouble in life is when one can't decide in which way duty leads. Once know your duty, then all is easy."

I do not know whether she thought it my duty to obey my husband. But I thought it my duty to go to my mother, as I risked nothing but myself.

We had two days of an exciting drama under our very noses, before our eyes. A party had come to Columbia who said they had run the blockade, had come in by flag of truce, etc. Colonel Goodwyn asked me to look around and see if I could pick out the suspected crew. It was easily done. We were all in a sadly molting condition. We had come to the end of our good clothes in three years, and now our only resource was to turn them upside down, or inside out, and in mending, darning, patching, etc.

Near me on the train to Alabama sat a young woman in a traveling dress of bright yellow; she wore a profusion of curls, had pink cheeks, was delightfully airy and easy in her manner, and was absorbed in a flirtation with a Confederate major, who, in spite of his nice, new gray uniform and two stars, had a very Yankee face, fresh, clean-cut, sharp, utterly unsunburned, florid, wholesome, handsome. What more in compliment can one say of one's enemies? Two other women faced this man and woman, and we knew them to be newcomers by their good clothes. One of these women was a German. She it was who had betrayed them. I found that out afterward.

The handsomest of the three women had a hard, Northern face, but all were in splendid array as to feathers, flowers, lace, and jewelry. If they were spies why were they so foolish as to brag of New York, and compare us unfavorably with the other side all the time, and in loud, shrill accents? Surely that was not the way to pass unnoticed in the

Confederacy.

A man came in, stood up, and read from a paper, "The surrender of Vicksburg."[96] I felt as if I had been struck a hard blow on the top of my head, and my heart took one of its queer turns. I was utterly unconscious: not long, I dare say. The first thing I heard was exclamations of joy and exultation from the overdressed party. My rage and humiliation were great. A man within earshot of this party had slept through everything. He had a greyhound face, eager and inquisitive when awake, but now he was as one of the seven sleepers.

Colonel Goodwyn wrote on a blank page of my book (one of De Quincey's—the note is there now), that the sleeper was a Richmond detective.

Finally, hot and tired out, we arrived at West Point, on the Chattahoochee River. The dusty cars were quite still, except for the giggling flirtation of the yellow gown and her major. Two Confederate officers walked in. I felt mischief in the air. One touched the smart major, who was whispering to Yellow Gown. The major turned quickly. Instantly, every drop of blood left his face; a spasm seized his throat; it was a piteous sight. And at once I was awfully sorry for him. He was marched out of the car. Poor Yellow Gown's color was fast, but the whites of her eyes were lurid. Of the three women spies we never heard again. They never do anything worse to women, the high-minded Confederates, than send them out of the country. But when we read soon afterward of the execution of a male spy, we thought of the "major."

At Montgomery the boat waited for us, and in my haste I tumbled out of the omnibus with Dr. Robert Johnson's assistance, but nearly broke my neck. The thermometer was high up in the nineties, and they gave me a stateroom over the boiler. I paid out my Confederate rags of money freely to the maid in order to get out of that oven. Surely, go where we may hereafter, an Alabama steamer in August lying under the bluff with the sun looking down, will give one a foretaste, almost an adequate idea, of what's to come, as far as heat goes. The planks of the floor burned one's feet under the bluff at Selma, where we stayed nearly all day—I do not know why.

Met James Boykin, who had lost 1,200 bales of cotton at Vicksburg, and charged it all to Jeff Davis in his wrath, which did not seem exactly reasonable to me. At Portland there was a horse for James Boykin, and he rode away, promising to have a carriage sent for me at once. But he had to go seven miles on horseback before he reached my

---

[96] Vicksburg surrendered on July 4, 1863. Since the close of 1862, it had again and again been assaulted by Grant and Sherman. It was commanded by Johnston and Pemberton, Pemberton being in command at the time of the surrender. John C. Pemberton was a native of Philadelphia, a graduate of West Point, and had served in the Mexican War.

sister Sally's, and then Sally was to send back. On that lonely riverside Molly and I remained with dismal swamps on every side, and immense plantations, the white people few or none. In my heart I knew my husband was right when he forbade me to undertake this journey. There was one living thing at this little riverside inn- a white man who had a store opposite, and oh, how drunk he was! Hot as it was, Molly kept up a fire of pine knots. There was neither lamp nor candle in that deserted house. The drunken man reeled over now and then, lantern in hand; he would stand with his idiotic, drunken glare, or go solemnly staggering round us, but always bowing in his politeness. He nearly fell over us, but I sprang out of his way as he asked, "Well, madam, what can I do for you?"

Shall I ever forget the headache of that night and the fright, My temples throbbed with dumb misery. I sat upon a chair, Molly on the floor, with her head resting against my chair. She was as near as she could get to me, and I kept my hand on her. "Missis," said she, "now I do believe you are scared, scared of that poor, drunken thing. If he was sober I could whip him in a fair fight, and drunk as he is I kin throw him over the banister, ef he so much as teches you. I don't value him a button!"

Taking heart from such brave words I laughed. It seemed an eternity, but the carriage came by ten o'clock, and then, with the coachman as our sole protector, we poor women drove eight miles or more over a carriage road, through long lanes, swamps of pitchy darkness, with plantations on every side.

The house, as we drew near, looked like a graveyard in a nightmare, so vague and phantom-like were its outlines.

I found my mother ill in bed, feeble still, but better than I hoped to see her. "I knew you would come," was her greeting, with outstretched hands. Then I went to bed in that silent house, a house of the dead it seemed. I supposed I was not to see my sister until the next day. But she came in some time after I had gone to bed. She kissed me quietly, without a tear. She was thin and pale, but her voice was calm and kind.

As she lifted the candle over her head, to show me something on the wall, I saw that her pretty brown hair was white. It was awfully hard not to burst out into violent weeping. She looked so sweet, and yet so utterly brokenhearted. But as she was without emotion, apparently, it would not become me to upset her by my tears.

Next day, at noon, Hetty, mother's old maid, brought my breakfast to my bedside. Such a breakfast it was! Delmonico could do no better. "It is ever so late, I know," to which Hetty replied: "Yes, we would not let Molly wake you." "What a splendid cook you have here." "My daughter, Tenah, is Miss Sally's cook. She's well enough as time- but when our Miss Mary comes to see us I does it myself," an courtesied down to the floor. "Bless your old soul," I cried, an rushed over and gave me a good hug.

She is my mother's factotum; has been her maid since she was six years old, when she was bought from a Virginia speculator along with her own mother and all her brothers and sisters. She has been pampered until she is a rare old tyrant at times. She can do everything better than any one else, and my mother leans on her heavily. Hetty is Dick's wife; Dick is the butler. They have over a dozen children and take life very easily.

Sally came in before I was out of bed, and began at once in the same stony way, pale and cold as ice, to tell me of the death of her children. It had happened not two weeks before. Her eyes were utterly without life; no expression whatever, and in a composed and sad sort of manner she told the tale as if it were something she had read and wanted me to hear:

"My eldest daughter, Mary, had grown up to be a lovely girl. She was between thirteen and fourteen, you know. Baby Kate had my sister's gray eyes; she was evidently to be the beauty of the family. Strange it is that here was one of my children who has lived and has gone and you have never seen her at all. She died first, and I would not go to the funeral. I thought it would kill me to see her put under the ground. I was lying down, stupid with grief when Aunt Charlotte came to me after the funeral with this news: 'Mary has that awful disease, too.' There was nothing to say. I got up and dressed instantly and went to Mary. I did not leave her side again in that long struggle between life and death. I did everything for her with my own hands. I even prepared my darling for the grave. I went to her funeral, and I came home and walked straight to my mother and I begged her to be comforted; I would bear it all without one word if God would only spare me the one child left me now."

Sally has never shed a tear, but has grown twenty years older, cold, hard, careworn. With the same rigidity of manner, she began to go over all the details of Mary's illness. "I had not given up hope, no, not at all. As I sat by her side, she said: 'Mamma, put your hand on my knees; they are so cold.' I put my hand on her knee; the cold struck to my heart. I knew it was the coldness of death." Sally put out her hand on me, and it seemed to recall the feeling. She fell forward in an agony of weeping that lasted for hours. The doctor said this reaction was a blessing; without it she must have died or gone mad.

While the mother was so bitterly weeping, the little girl, the last of them, a bright child of three or four, crawled into my bed. "Now, Auntie," she whispered, "I want to tell you all about Mamie and Katie, but they watch me so. They say I must never talk about them. Katie died because she ate blackberries, I know that, and then Aunt Charlotte read Mamie a letter and that made her die, too. Maum Hetty says they have gone to God, but I know the people saved a place between them in the ground for me."

Uncle William was in despair at the low ebb of patriotism out here. "West of the Savannah River," said he, "it is property first, life next, honor last." He gave me an excellent pair of shoes. What a gift! For more than a year I have had none but some dreadful things Armstead makes for me, and they hurt my feet so. These do not fit, but that is nothing; they are large enough and do not pinch anywhere. I have absolutely a respectable pair of shoes!!

Uncle William says the men who went into the war to save their negroes are abjectly wretched. Neither side now cares a fig for these beloved negroes, and would send them all to heaven in a hand-basket, as Custis Lee says, to win in the fight.

General Lee and Mr. Davis want the negroes put into the army. Mr. Chesnut and Major Venable discussed the subject one night, but would they fight on our side or desert to the enemy? They don't go to the enemy, because they are comfortable as they are, and expect to be free anyway.

When we were children our nurses used to give us tea out in the open air on little pine tables scrubbed as clean as milk-pails. Sometimes, as Dick would pass us, with his slow and consequential step, we would call out, "Do, Dick, come and wait on us." "No, little missies, I never wait on pine tables. Wait till you get big enough to put your legs under your pa's mahogany."

I taught him to read as soon as I could read myself, perched on his knife-board. He won't look at me now; but looks over my head, scenting freedom in the air. He was always very ambitious. I do not think he ever troubled himself much about books. But then, as my father said, Dick, standing in front of his sideboard, has heard all subjects in earth or heaven discussed, and by the best heads in our world. He is proud, too, in his way. Hetty, his wife, complained that the other men servants looked finer in their livery. "Nonsense, old woman, a butler never demeans himself to wear livery. He is always in plain clothes." Somewhere he had picked that up.

He is the first negro in whom I have felt a change. Others go about in their black masks, not a ripple or an emotion showing, and yet on all other subjects except the war they are the most excitable of all races. Now Dick might make a very respectable Egyptian Sphinx, so inscrutably silent is he. He did deign to inquire about General Richard Anderson. "He was my young master once," said he. "I always will like him better than anybody else."

When Dick married Hetty, the Anderson house was next door. The two families agreed to sell either Dick or Hetty, whichever consented to be sold. Hetty refused outright, and the Andersons sold Dick that he might be with his wife. This was magnanimous on the Andersons' part, for Hetty was only a lady's-maid and Dick was a trained butler, on whom Mrs. Anderson had spent no end of pains in his dining-room education, and, of course, if they had refused to sell Dick, Hetty would have had to go to them. Mrs. Anderson was very much disgusted with Dick's ingratitude when she found he was willing to leave them. As a butler he is a treasure; he is overwhelmed with dignity, but that does not interfere with his work at all.

My father had a body-servant, Simon, who could imitate his master's voice perfectly. He would sometimes call out from the yard after my father had mounted his horse: "Dick, bring me my overcoat. I see you there, sir, hurry up." When Dick hastened out, overcoat in hand, and only Simon was visible, after several obsequious "Yes, marster; just as marster pleases," my mother had always to step out and prevent a fight. Dick never forgave her laughing.

Once in Sumter, when my father was very busy preparing a law case, the mob in the street annoyed him, and he grumbled about it as Simon was making up his fire. Suddenly he heard, as it were, himself speaking, "the Hon. S. D. Miller—Lawyer Miller," as the colored gentleman announced himself in the dark—appeal to the gentlemen outside to go away and leave a lawyer in peace to prepare his case for the next day. My father said he could have sworn the sound was that of his own voice. The crowd dispersed, but some noisy negroes came along, and upon them Simon rushed with the sulky whip, slashing around in the dark, calling himself "Lawyer Miller," who was determined to have peace.

Simon returned, complaining that "them niggers run so he never got in a hundred yards of one of them."

At Portland, we met a man who said: "Is it not strange that in this poor, devoted land of ours, there are some men who are making money by blockade-running, cheating our embarrassed government, and skulking the fight?"

Montgomery, July 30th.—Coming on here from Portland there was no stateroom for me. My mother alone had one. My aunt and I sat nodding in armchairs, for the doors and sofas were covered with sleepers, too. On the floor that night, so hot that even a little covering of clothes could not be borne, lay a motley crew. Black, white, and yellow disported themselves in promiscuous array. Children and their nurses, bared to the view, were wrapped in the profoundest slumber. No caste prejudices were here. Neither Garrison, John Brown, nor Gerrit Smith ever dreamed of equality more untrammeled. A crow-black, enormously fat negro man waddled in every now and then to look after the lamps. The atmosphere of that cabin was stifling, and the sight of those figures on the floor did not make it more tolerable. So we soon escaped and sat out near the guards.

The next day was the very hottest I have ever known. One supreme consolation was the watermelons, the very finest, and the ice. A very handsome woman, whom I did not know, rehearsed all our disasters in the field. And then, as if she held me responsible, she faced me furiously, "And where are our big men?" "Whom do you mean?" "I mean our leaders, the men we have a right to look to to save us. They got us into this scrape. Let them get us out of it. Where are our big men?" I sympathized with her and understood her, but I answered lightly, "I do not know the exact size you want them."

Here in Montgomery, we have been so hospitably received. Ye gods! how those women talked! and all at the same time! They put me under the care of General Dick Taylor's brother-in-law, a Mr. Gordon, who married one of the Beranges. A very pleasant arrangement it was for me. He was kind and attentive and vastly agreeable with his New Orleans anecdotes. On the first of last January all his servants left him but four. To these faithful few he gave free papers at once, that they might lose naught by loyalty should the Confederates come into authority once more. He paid high wages and things worked smoothly for some weeks. One day his wife saw some Yankee officers' cards on a table, and said to her maid, "I did not know any of these people had called?"

"Oh, Missis!" the maid replied, "they come to see me, and I have been waiting to tell you. It is too hard! I can not do it! I can not dance with those nice gentlemen at night at our Union Balls and then come here and be your servant the next day. I can't!" "So," said Mr. Gordon, "freedom must be followed by fraternity and equality." One by one the faithful few slipped away and the family were left to their own devices. Why not?

When General Dick Taylor's place was sacked his negroes moved down to Algiers, a village near New Orleans. An old woman came to Mr. Gordon to say that these negroes wanted him to get word to "Mars Dick" that they were dying of disease and starvation; thirty had died that day. Dick Taylor's help being out of the question, Mr. Gordon applied to a Federal officer. He found this one not a philanthropist, but a cynic, who said: "All right; it is working out as I expected. Improve negroes and Indians off the continent. Their strong men we put in the army. The rest will disappear."

Joe Johnston can sulk. As he is sent West, he says, "They may give Lee the army Joe Johnston trained." Lee is reaping where he sowed, he thinks, but then he was backing straight through Richmond when they stopped his retreating.

CHAPTER XIV. RICHMOND, VA.

August 10, 1863—*September* 7, 1863

Richmond, Va., *August 10, 1863.*—To-day I had letter from my sister, who wrote to inquire about her old playmate, friend, and lover, Boykin McCaa. It is nearly twenty years since each was married; each now has children nearly grown. "To tell the truth," she writes "in these last dreadful years, with David in Florida, where I can not often hear from him, and everything dismal, anxious, and disquieting, I had almost forgotten Boykin's existence, but he came here last night; he stood by my bedside and spoke to me kindly and affectionately, as if we had just parted. I said, holding out my hand, 'Boykin, you are very pale' He answered, 'I have come to tell you good by,' and then seized both my hands. His own hands were as cold and hard as ice; they froze the marrow of my bones. I screamed again and again until my whole household came rushing in, and then came the negroes from the yard, all wakened by my piercing shrieks. This may have been a dream, but it haunts me.

"Some one sent me an old paper with an account of his wounds and his recovery, but I know he is dead." "Stop!" said my husband at this point, and then he read from that day's Examiner these words: "Captain Burwell Boykin McCaa found dead upon the battle-field leading a cavalry charge at the head of his company. He was shot through the head."

The famous colonel of the Fourth Texas, by name John Bell Hood,[97] is here—him we call Sam, because his classmates at West Point did so—for what cause is not known. John Darby asked if he might bring his hero to us; bragged of him extensively; said he had won his three stars, etc., under Stonewall's eye, and that he was promoted by Stonewall's request. When Hood came with his sad Quixote face, the face of an old Crusader, who believed in his cause, his cross, and his crown, we were not prepared for such a man as a beau-ideal of the wild Texans. He is tall, thin, and shy; has blue eyes and light hair; a tawny beard, and a vast amount of it, covering the lower part of his face, the whole appearance that of awkward strength. Some one said that his great reserve of manner he carried only into the society of ladies. Major Venable added that he had often heard of the light of battle shining in a man's eyes. He had seen it once—when he carried to Hood orders from Lee, and found in the hottest of the fight that the man was transfigured. The fierce light of Hood's eyes I can never forget.

---

[97] Hood was a native of Kentucky and a graduate of West Point.

Hood came to ask us to a picnic next day at Drury's Bluff.[98] The naval heroes were to receive us and then we were to drive out to the Texan camp. We accused John Darby of having instigated this unlooked-for festivity. We were to have bands of music and dances, with turkeys, chickens, and buffalo tongues to eat. Next morning, just as my foot was on the carriage-step, the girls standing behind ready to follow me with Johnny and the Infant Samuel (Captain Shannon by proper name), up rode John Darby in red-hot haste, threw his bridle to one of the men who was holding the horses, and came toward us rapidly, clanking his cavalry spurs with a despairing sound as he cried: "Stop! it's all up. We are ordered back to the Rappahannock. The brigade is marching through Richmond now." So we unpacked and unloaded, dismissed the hacks and sat down with a sigh.

"Suppose we go and see them pass the turnpike," some one said. The suggestion was hailed with delight, and off we marched. Johnny and the Infant were in citizens' clothes, and the Straggler—as Hood calls John Darby, since the Prestons have been in Richmond—was all plaided and plumed in his surgeon's array. He never bated an inch of bullion or a feather; he was courting and he stalked ahead with Mary Preston, Buck, and Johnny. The Infant and myself, both stout and scant of breath, lagged last. They called back to us, as the Infant came toddling along, "Hurry up or we will leave you."

At the turnpike we stood on the sidewalk and saw ten thousand men march by. We had seen nothing like this before. Hitherto we had seen only regiments marching spick and span in their fresh, smart clothes, just from home and on their way to the army. Such rags and tags as we saw now. Nothing was like anything else. Most garments and arms were such as had been taken from the enemy. Such shoes as they had on. "Oh, our brave boys!" moaned Buck. Such tin pans and pots as were tied to their waists, with bread or bacon stuck on the ends of their bayonets. Anything that could be spiked was bayoneted and held aloft.

They did not seem to mind their shabby condition; they laughed, shouted, and cheered as they marched by. Not a disrespectful or light word was spoken, but they went for the men who were huddled behind us, and who seemed to be trying to make themselves as small as possible in order to escape observation.

Hood and his staff finally came galloping up, dismounted, and joined us. Mary Preston gave him a bouquet. Thereupon he unwrapped a Bible, which he carried in his pocket. He said his mother had given it to him. He pressed a flower in it. Mary Preston suggested that he had not worn or used it at all, being fresh, new, and beautifully kept. Every

---

[98] Drury's Bluff lies eight miles south of Richmond on the James River. Here, on May 16, 1864, the Confederates under Beauregard repulsed the Federals under Butler.

word of this the Texans heard as they marched by, almost touching us. They laughed and joked and made their own rough comments.

September 7th.—Major Edward Johnston did not get into the Confederacy until after the first battle of Manassas. For some cause, before he could evade that potentate, Seward rang his little bell and sent him to a prison in the harbor of New York. I forget whether he was exchanged or escaped of his own motion. The next thing I heard of my antebellum friend he had defeated Milroy in Western Virginia. There were so many Johnstons that for this victory they named him Alleghany Johnston.

He had an odd habit of falling into a state of incessant winking as soon as he became the least startled or agitated. In such times he seemed persistently to be winking one eye at you. He meant nothing by it, and in point of fact did not know himself that he was doing it. In Mexico he had been wounded in the eye, and the nerve vibrates independently of his will. During the winter of 1862 and 1863 he was on crutches. After a while he hobbled down Franklin Street with us, we proud to accommodate our pace to that of the wounded general. His ankle continued stiff; so when he sat down another chair had to be put before him. On this he stretched out his stiff leg, straight as a ramrod. At that time he was our only wounded knight, and the girls waited on him and made life pleasant for him.

One night I listened to two love-tales at once, in a distracted state of mind between the two. William Porcher Miles, in a perfectly modulated voice, in cadenced accents and low tones, was narrating the happy end of his affair. He had been engaged to sweet little Bettie Bierne, and I gave him my congratulations with all my heart. It was a capital match, suitable in every way, good for her, and good for him. I was deeply interested in Mr. Miles's story, but there was din and discord on the other hand; old Edward, our pet general, sat diagonally across the room with one leg straight out like a poker, wrapped in red carpet leggings, as red as a turkey-cock in the face. His head is strangely shaped, like a cone or an old-fashioned beehive; or, as Buck said, there are three tiers of it; it is like a pope's tiara.

There he sat, with a loud voice and a thousand winks, making love to Mary P. I make no excuse for listening. It was impossible not to hear him. I tried not to lose a word of Mr. Miles's idyl as the despair of the veteran was thundered into my other ear. I lent an ear to each conversationalist. Mary can not altogether control her voice, and her shrill screams of negation, "No, no, never," etc., utterly failed to suppress her wounded lover's obstreperous asseverations of his undying affection for her.

Buck said afterward: "We heard every word of it on our side of the room, even when Mamie shrieked to him that he was talking too loud. Now, Mamie," said we afterward, "do you think it was kind to tell him he was forty if he was a day?"

Strange to say, the pet general, Edward, rehabilitated his love in a day; at least two days after he was heard to say that he was "paying attentions now to his cousin, John Preston's second daughter; her name, Sally, but they called her Buck—Sally Buchanan Campbell Preston, a lovely girl." And with her he now drove, rode, and hobbled on his crutches, sent her his photograph, and in due time cannonaded her, from the same spot where he had courted Mary, with proposals to marry him.

Buck was never so decided in her "Nos" as Mary. ("Not so loud, at least"—thus in amendment, says Buck, who always reads what I have written, and makes comments of assent or dissent.) So again he began to thunder in a woman's ears his tender passion. As they rode down Franklin Street, Buck says she knows the people on the sidewalk heard snatches of the conversation, though she rode as rapidly as she could, and she begged him not to talk so loud. Finally, they dashed up to our door as if they had been running a race. Unfortunate in love, but fortunate in war, our general is now winning new laurels with Ewell in the Valley or with the Army of the Potomac.

I think I have told how Miles, still "so gently o'er me leaning," told of his successful love while General Edward Johnston roared unto anguish and disappointment over his failures. Mr. Miles spoke of sweet little Bettie Bierne as if she had been a French girl, just from a convent, kept far from the haunts of men wholly for him. One would think to hear him that Bettie had never cast those innocent blue eyes of hers on a man until he came along.

Now, since I first knew Miss Bierne in 1857, when Pat Calhoun was to the fore, she has been followed by a tale of men as long as a Highland chief's. Every summer at the Springs, their father appeared in the ballroom a little before twelve and chased the three beautiful Biernes home before him in spite of all entreaties, and he was said to frown away their too numerous admirers at all hours of the day.

This new engagement was confided to me as a profound secret. Of course, I did not mention it, even to my own household. Next day little Alston, Morgan's adjutant, and George Deas called. As Colonel Deas removed his gloves, he said: "Oh! the Miles and Bierne sensation— have you heard of it," "No, what is the row about?" "They are engaged to be married; that's all." "Who told you?" "Miles himself, as we walked down Franklin Street, this afternoon." "And did he not beg you not to mention it, as Bettie did not wish it spoken of?" "God bless my soul, so he did. And I forgot that part entirely."

Colonel Alston begged the stout Carolinian not to take his inadvertent breach of faith too much to heart. Miss Bettie's engagement had caused him a dreadful night. A young man, who was his intimate friend, came to his room in the depths of despair and handed him a letter from Miss Bierne, which was the cause of all his woe. Not knowing that she was already betrothed to Miles, he had proposed to her in an eloquent letter. In her reply, she positively stated that she was engaged to Mr. Miles, and instead of thanking her for putting him at once out of his misery, he considered the reason she gave as trebly aggravating the agony of the love-letter and the refusal. "Too late!" he yelled, "by Jingo!" So much for a secret.

Miss Bierne and I became fast friends. Our friendship was based on a mutual admiration for the honorable member from South Carolina. Colonel and Mrs. Myers and Colonel and Mrs. Chesnut were the only friends of Mr. Miles who were invited to the wedding. At the church door the sexton demanded our credentials. No one but those whose names he held in his hand were allowed to enter. Not twenty people were present—a mere handful grouped about the altar in that large church.

We were among the first to arrive. Then came a faint flutter and Mrs. Parkman (the bride's sister, swathed in weeds for her young husband, who had been killed within a year of her marriage) came rapidly up the aisle alone. She dropped upon her knees in the front pew, and there remained, motionless, during the whole ceremony, a mass of black crepe, and a dead weight on my heart. She has had experience of war. A cannonade around Richmond interrupted her marriage service—a sinister omen—and in a year thereafter her bridegroom was stiff and stark—dead upon the field of battle.

While the wedding-march turned our thoughts from her and thrilled us with sympathy, the bride advanced in white satin and point d'Alençon. Mrs. Myers whispered that it was Mrs. Parkman's wedding-dress that the bride had on.

She remembered the exquisite lace, and she shuddered with superstitious forebodings.

All had been going on delightfully in-doors, but a sharp shower cleared the church porch of the curious; and, as the water splashed, we wondered how we were to assemble ourselves at Mrs. McFarland's. All the horses in Richmond had been impressed for some sudden cavalry necessity a few days before. I ran between Mr. McFarland and Senator Semmes with my pretty Paris rose-colored silk turned over my head to save it, and when we arrived at the hospitable mansion of the McFarlands, Mr. McFarland took me straight into the drawing-room, man-like, forgetting that my ruffled plumes needed a good smoothing and preening.

Mrs. Lee sent for me. She was staying at Mrs. Caskie's. I was taken directly to her room, where she was lying on the bed. She said, before I had taken my seat: "You know there is a fight going on now at

Brandy Station?"[99] "Yes, we are anxious. John Chesnut's company is there, too." She spoke sadly, but quietly. "My son, Roony, is wounded; his brother has gone for him. They will soon be here and we shall know all about it unless Roony's wife takes him to her grandfather. Poor lame mother, I am useless to my children." Mrs. Caskie said: "You need not be alarmed. The General said in his telegram that it was not a severe wound. You know even Yankees believe General Lee."

That day, Mrs. Lee gave me a likeness of the General in a photograph taken soon after the Mexican War. She likes it so much better than the later ones. He certainly was a handsome man then, handsomer even than now. I shall prize it for Mrs. Lee's sake, too. She said old Mrs. Chesnut and her aunt, Nellie Custis (Mrs. Lewis) were very intimate during Washington's Administration in Philadelphia. I told her Mrs. Chesnut, senior, was the historical member of our family; she had so much to tell of Revolutionary times. She was one of the "white-robed choir" of little maidens who scattered flowers before Washington at Trenton Bridge, which everybody who writes a life of Washington asks her to give an account of.

Mrs. Ould and Mrs. Davis came home with me. Lawrence had a basket of delicious cherries. "If there were only some ice," said I. Respectfully Lawrence answered, and also firmly: "Give me money and you shall have ice." By the underground telegraph he had heard of an ice-house over the river, though its fame was suppressed by certain Sybarites, as they wanted it all. In a wonderfully short time we had mint-juleps and sherry-cobblers.

Altogether it has been a pleasant day, and as I sat alone I was laughing lightly now and then at the memory of some funny story. Suddenly, a violent ring; and a regular sheaf of telegrams were handed me. I could not have drawn away in more consternation if the sheets had been a nest of rattlesnakes. First, Frank Hampton was killed at Brandy Station. Wade Hampton telegraphed Mr. Chesnut to see Robert Barnwell, and make the necessary arrangements to recover the body. Mr. Chesnut is still at Wilmington. I sent for Preston Johnston, and my neighbor, Colonel Patton, offered to see that everything proper was done. That afternoon I walked out alone. Willie Mountford had shown me where the body, all that was left of Frank Hampton, was to be laid in the Capitol. Mrs. Petticola joined me after a while, and then Mrs. Singleton.

Preston Hampton and Peter Trezevant, with myself and Mrs. Singleton, formed the sad procession which followed the coffin. There was a company of soldiers drawn up in front of the State House porch. Mrs. Singleton said we had better go in and look at him before the coffin was finally closed. How I wish I had not looked. I remember him

---

[99] The battle of Brandy Station, Va., occurred June 9, 1863.

so well in all the pride of his magnificent manhood. He died of a saber-cut across the face and head, and was utterly disfigured. Mrs. Singleton seemed convulsed with grief. In all my life I had never seen such bitter weeping. She had her own troubles, but I did not know of them. We sat for a long time on the great steps of the State House. Everybody had gone and we were alone.

We talked of it all—how we had gone to Charleston to see Rachel in Adrienne Lecouvreur, and how, as I stood waiting in the passage near the drawing-room, I had met Frank Hampton bringing his beautiful bride from the steamer. They had just landed. Afterward at Mrs. Singleton's place in the country we had all spent a delightful week together. And now, only a few years have passed, but nearly all that pleasant company are dead, and our world, the only world we cared for, literally kicked to pieces. And she cried, "We are two lone women, stranded here." Rev. Robert Barnwell was in a desperate condition, and Mary Barnwell, her daughter, was expecting her confinement every day.

Here now, later, let me add that it was not until I got back to Carolina that I heard of Robert Barnwell's death, with scarcely a day's interval between it and that of Mary and her new-born baby. Husband, wife, and child were buried at the same time in the same grave in Columbia. And now, Mrs. Singleton has three orphan grandchildren. What a woful year it has been to her.

Robert Barnwell had insisted upon being sent to the hospital at Staunton. On account of his wife's situation the doctor also had advised it. He was carried off on a mattress. His brave wife tried to prevent it, and said: "It is only fever." And she nursed him to the last. She tried to say good-by cheerfully, and called after him: "As soon as my trouble is over I will come to you at Staunton." At the hospital they said it was typhoid fever. He died the second day after he got there. Poor Mary fainted when she heard the ambulance drive away with him. Then she crept into a low trundle-bed kept for the children in her mother's room.

She never left that bed again. When the message came from Staunton that fever was the matter with Robert and nothing more, Mrs. Singleton says she will never forget the expression in Mary's eyes as she turned and looked at her. "Robert will get well," she said, "it is all right." Her face was radiant, blazing with light. That night the baby was born, and Mrs. Singleton got a telegram that Robert was dead. She did not tell Mary, standing, as she did, at the window while she read it. She was at the same time looking for Robert's body, which might come any moment. As for Mary's life being in danger, she had never thought of such a thing. She was thinking only of Robert. Then a servant touched her and said: "Look at Mrs. Barnwell." She ran to the bedside, and the doctor, who had come in, said, "It is all over; she is dead." Not in anger, not in wrath, came the angel of death that day. He came to set

Mary free from a world grown too hard to bear.

* * * * *

During Stoneman's raid[100] I burned some personal papers. Molly constantly said to me, "Missis, listen to de guns. Burn up everything. Mrs. Lyons says they are sure to come, and they'll put in their newspapers whatever you write here, every day." The guns did sound very near, and when Mrs. Davis rode up and told me that if Mr. Davis left Richmond I must go with her, I confess I lost my head. So I burned a part of my journal but rewrote it afterward from memory—my implacable enemy that lets me forget none of the things I would. I am weak with dates. I do not always worry to look at the calendar and write them down. Besides I have not always a calendar at hand.

CHAPTER XV. CAMDEN, S. C.

September 10, 1863—November 5, 1863

Camden, S. C., *September 10, 1863.*—It is a comfort to turn from small political jealousies to our grand battles—to Lee and Kirby Smith after Council and Convention squabbles. Lee has proved to be all that my husband prophesied of him when he was so unpopular and when Joe Johnston was the great god of war. The very sound of the word convention or council is wearisome. Not that I am quite ready for Richmond yet. We must look after home and plantation affairs, which we have sadly neglected. Heaven help my husband through the deep waters.

The wedding of Miss Aiken, daughter of Governor Aiken, the largest slave-owner in South Carolina; Julia Rutledge, one of the bridesmaids; the place Flat Rock. We could not for a while imagine what Julia would do for a dress. My sister Kate remembered some muslin she had in the house for curtains, bought before the war, and laid aside as not needed now. The stuff was white and thin, a little coarse, but then we covered it with no end of beautiful lace. It made a charming dress, and how altogether lovely Julia looked in it! The night of the wedding it stormed as if the world were coming to an end— wind, rain, thunder, and lightning in an unlimited supply around the mountain cottage.

The bride had a *duchesse* dressing-table, muslin and lace; not one of the shifts of honest, war-driven poverty, but a millionaire's attempt

---

[100] George S. Stoneman, a graduate of West Point, was now a Major-General, and Chief of Artillery in the Army of the Potomac. His raid toward Richmond in 1863 was a memorable incident of the war. After the war, he became Governor of California.

at appearing economical, in the idea that that style was in better taste as placing the family more on the same plane with their less comfortable compatriots. A candle was left too near this light drapery and it took fire. Outside was lightning enough to fire the world; inside, the bridal chamber was ablaze, and there was wind enough to blow the house down the mountainside.

The English maid behaved heroically, and, with the aid of Mrs. Aiken's and Mrs. Mat Singleton's servants, put the fire out without disturbing the marriage ceremony, then being performed below. Everything in the bridal chamber was burned up except the bed, and that was a mass of cinders, soot, and flakes of charred and blackened wood.

At Kingsville I caught a glimpse of our army. Longstreet's corps was going West. God bless the gallant fellows! Not one man was intoxicated; not one rude word did I hear. It was a strange sight—one part of it. There were miles, apparently, of platform cars, soldiers rolled in their blankets, lying in rows, heads all covered, fast asleep. In their gray blankets, packed in regular order, they looked like swathed mummies. One man near where I sat was writing on his knee. He used his cap for a desk and he was seated on a rail. I watched him, wondering to whom that letter was to go—home, no doubt. Sore hearts for him there.

A feeling of awful depression laid hold of me. All these fine fellows were going to kill or be killed. Why? And a phrase got to beating about my head like an old song, "The Unreturning Brave." When a knot of boyish, laughing, young creatures passed me, a queer thrill of sympathy shook me. Ah, I know how your home-folks feel, poor children! Once, last winter, persons came to us in Camden with such strange stories of Captain—, Morgan's man; stories of his father, too; turf tales and murder, or, at least, how he killed people. He had been a tremendous favorite with my husband, who brought him in once, leading him by the hand. Afterward he said to me, "With these girls in the house we must be more cautious." I agreed to be coldly polite to—. "After all," I said, "I barely know him."

When he called afterward in Richmond I was very glad to see him, utterly forgetting that he was under a ban. We had a long, confidential talk. He told me of his wife and children; of his army career, and told Morgan stories. He grew more and more cordial and so did I. He thanked me for the kind reception given him in that house; told me I was a true friend of his, and related to me a scrape he was in which, if divulged, would ruin him, although he was innocent; but time would clear all things. He begged me not to repeat anything he had told me of his affairs, not even to Colonel Chesnut; which I promised promptly, and then he went away. I sat poking the fire thinking what a curiously interesting creature he was, this famous Captain—, when the folding-doors slowly opened and Colonel Chesnut appeared. He had come home two hours ago from the War Office with a headache, and had been lying on the sofa behind that folding-door listening for mortal hours.

"So, this is your style of being 'coldly polite,'" he said. Fancy my feelings. "Indeed, I had forgotten all about what they had said of him. The lies they told of him never once crossed my mind. He is a great deal cleverer, and, I dare say, just as good as those who malign him."

Mattie Reedy (I knew her as a handsome girl in Washington several years ago) got tired of hearing Federals abusing John Morgan. One day they were worse than ever in their abuse and she grew restive. By way of putting a mark against the name of so rude a girl, the Yankee officer said, "What is your name?" "Write 'Mattie Reedy' now, but by the grace of God one day I hope to call myself the wife of John Morgan." She did not know Morgan, but Morgan eventually heard the story; a good joke it was said to be. But he made it a point to find her out; and, as she was as pretty as she was patriotic, by the grace of God, she is now Mrs. Morgan! These timid Southern women under the guns can be brave enough.

Aunt Charlotte has told a story of my dear mother. They were up at Shelby, Ala., a white man's country, where negroes are not wanted. The ladies had with them several negroes belonging to my uncle at whose house they were staying in the owner's absence. One negro man who had married and dwelt in a cabin was for some cause particularly obnoxious to the neighborhood. My aunt and my mother, old-fashioned ladies, shrinking from everything outside their own door, knew nothing of all this. They occupied rooms on opposite sides of an open passage-way. Underneath, the house was open and unfinished. Suddenly, one night, my aunt heard a terrible noise—apparently as of a man running for his life, pursued by men and dogs, shouting, hallowing, barking. She had only time to lock herself in. Utterly cut off from her sister, she sat down, dumb with terror, when there began loud knocking at the door, with men swearing, dogs tearing round, sniffing, racing in and out of the passage and barking underneath the house like mad. Aunt Charlotte was sure she heard the panting of a negro as he ran into the house a few minutes before. What could have become of him? Where could he have hidden? The men shook the doors and windows, loudly threatening vengeance. My aunt pitied her feeble sister, cut off in the room across the passage. This fright might kill her!

The cursing and shouting continued unabated. A man's voice, in harshest accents, made itself heard above all: "Leave my house, you rascals!" said the voice. "If you are not gone in two seconds, I'll shoot!" There was a dead silence except for the noise of the dogs. Quickly the men slipped away. Once out of gunshot, they began to call their dogs. After it was all over my aunt crept across the passage.

"Sister, what man was it scared them away?" My mother laughed aloud in her triumph. "I am the man," she said.

"But where is John?" Out crept John from a corner of the room, where my mother had thrown some rubbish over him. "Lawd bless you, Miss Mary opened de do' for me and dey was right behind runnin' me—" Aunt says mother was awfully proud of her prowess. And she showed some moral courage, too!

At the President's in Richmond once, General Lee was there, and Constance and Hetty Cary came in; also Miss Sanders and others. Constance Cary[101] was telling some war anecdotes, among them, one of an attempt to get up a supper the night before at some high and mighty F. F. V.'s house, and of how several gentlefolks went into the kitchen to prepare something to eat by the light of one forlorn candle. One of the men in the party, not being of a useful temperament, turned up a tub and sat down upon it. Custis Lee, wishing also to rest, found nothing upon which to sit but a gridiron.

One remembrance I kept of the evening at the President's: General Lee bowing over the beautiful Miss Cary's hands in the passage outside. Miss—rose to have her part in the picture, and asked Mr. Davis to walk with her into the adjoining drawing-room. He seemed surprised, but rose stiffly, and, with a scowling brow, was led off. As they passed where Mrs. Davis sat, Miss—, with all sail set, looked back and said: "Don't be jealous, Mrs. Davis; I have an important communication to make to the President." Mrs. Davis's amusement resulted in a significant "Now! Did you ever?"

During Stoneman's raid, on a Sunday I was in Mrs. Randolph's pew. The battle of Chancellorsville was also raging. The rattling of ammunition wagons, the tramp of soldiers, the everlasting slamming of those iron gates of the Capitol Square just opposite the church, made it hard to attend to the service.

Then began a scene calculated to make the stoutest heart quail. The sexton would walk quietly up the aisle to deliver messages to worshipers whose relatives had been brought in wounded, dying, or dead. Pale-faced people would then follow him out. Finally, the Rev. Mr. Minnegerode bent across the chancel-rail to the sexton for a few minutes, whispered with the sexton, and then disappeared. The assistant clergyman resumed the communion which Mr. Minnegerode had been administering. At the church door stood Mrs. Minnegerode, as tragically wretched and as wild-looking as ever Mrs. Siddons was. She managed to say to her husband, "Your son is at the station, dead!" When these agonized parents reached the station, however, it proved to be some one else's son who was dead—but a son all the same. Pale and

---

[101] Miss Constance Cary afterward married Burton Harrison and settled in New York where she became prominent socially and achieved reputation as a novelist.

wan came Mr. Minnegerode back to his place within the altar rails. After the sacred communion was over, some one asked him what it all meant, and he said: "Oh, it was not my son who was killed, but it came so near it aches me yet!"

At home I found L. Q. Washington, who stayed to dinner. I saw that he and my husband were intently preoccupied by some event which they did not see fit to communicate to me. Immediately after dinner my husband lent Mr. Washington one of his horses and they rode off together. I betook myself to my kind neighbors, the Pattons, for information. There I found Colonel Patton had gone, too. Mrs. Patton, however, knew all about the trouble. She said there was a raiding party within forty miles of us and no troops were in Richmond! They asked me to stay to tea—those kind ladies—and in some way we might learn what was going on. After tea we went out to the Capitol Square, Lawrence and three men-servants going along to protect us. They seemed to be mustering in citizens by the thousands. Company after company was being formed; then battalions, and then regiments. It was a wonderful sight to us, peering through the iron railing, watching them fall into ranks.

Then we went to the President's, finding the family at supper. We sat on the white marble steps, and General Elzey told me exactly how things stood and of our immediate danger. Pickets were coming in. Men were spurring to and from the door as fast as they could ride, bringing and carrying messages and orders. Calmly General Elzey discoursed upon our present weakness and our chances for aid. After a while Mrs. Davis came out and embraced me silently.

"It is dreadful," I said. "The enemy is within forty miles of us— only forty!" "Who told you that tale?" said she. "They are within three miles of Richmond!" I went down on my knees like a stone. "You had better be quiet," she said. "The President is ill. Women and children must not add to the trouble." She asked me to stay all night, which I was thankful to do.

We sat up. Officers were coming and going; and we gave them what refreshment we could from a side table, kept constantly replenished. Finally, in the excitement, the constant state of activity and change of persons, we forgot the danger. Officers told us jolly stories and seemed in fine spirits, so we gradually took heart. There was not a moment's rest for any one. Mrs. Davis said something more amusing than ever: "We look like frightened women and children, don't we?"

Early next morning the President came down. He was still feeble and pale from illness. Custis Lee and my husband loaded their pistols, and the President drove off in Dr. Garnett's carriage, my husband and Custis Lee on horseback alongside him. By eight o'clock the troops from Petersburg came in, and the danger was over. The authorities will never strip Richmond of troops again. We had a narrow squeeze for it, but we escaped. It was a terrible night, although we made the best of it.

I was walking on Franklin Street when I met my husband. "Come with me to the War Office for a few minutes," said he, "and then I will go home with you." What could I do but go? He took me up a dark stairway, and then down a long, dark corridor, and he left me sitting in a window, saying he "would not be gone a second"; he was obliged to go into the Secretary of War's room. There I sat mortal hours. Men came to light the gas. From the first I put down my veil so that nobody might know me. Numbers of persons passed that I knew, but I scarcely felt respectable seated up there in that odd way, so I said not a word but looked out of the window. Judge Campbell slowly walked up and down with his hands behind his back—the saddest face I ever saw. He had jumped down in his patriotism from Judge of the Supreme Court, U. S. A., to be under-secretary of something or other—I do not know what—C. S. A. No wonder he was out of spirits that night!

Finally Judge Ould came; him I called, and he joined me at once, in no little amazement to find me there, and stayed with me until James Chesnut appeared. In point of fact, I sent him to look up that stray member of my family.

When my husband came he said: "Oh, Mr. Seddon and I got into an argument, and time slipped away! The truth is, I utterly forgot you were here." When we were once more out in the street, he began: "Now, don't scold me, for there is bad news. Pemberton has been fighting the Yankees by brigades, and he has been beaten every time; and now Vicksburg must go!" I suppose that was his side of the argument with Seddon.

Once again I visited the War Office. I went with Mrs. Ould to see her husband at his office. We wanted to arrange a party on the river on the flag-of-truce boat, and to visit those beautiful places, Claremont and Brandon. My husband got into one of his "too careful" fits; said there was risk in it; and so he upset all our plans. Then I was to go up to John Rutherford's by the canal-boat. That, too, he vetoed "too risky," as if anybody was going to trouble us!

October 24th.—James Chesnut is at home on his way back to Richmond; had been sent by the President to make the rounds of the Western armies; says Polk is a splendid old fellow. They accuse him of having been asleep in his tent at seven o'clock when he was ordered to attack at daylight, but he has too good a conscience to sleep so soundly.

The battle did not begin until eleven at Chickamauga[102] when Bragg had ordered the advance at daylight. Bragg and his generals do not agree. I think a general worthless whose subalterns quarrel with

---

[102] The battle of Chickamauga was fought on the river of the same name, near Chattanooga, September 19 and 20, 1863. The Confederates were commanded by Bragg and the Federals by Rosecrans. It was one of the bloodiest battles of the war; the loss on each side, including killed, wounded, and prisoners, was over 15,000.

him. Something is wrong about the man. Good generals are adored by their soldiers. See Napoleon, Cæsar, Stonewall, Lee.

Old Sam (Hood) received his orders to hold a certain bridge against the enemy, and he had already driven the enemy several miles beyond it, when the slow generals were still asleep. Hood has won a victory, though he has only one leg to stand on.

Mr. Chesnut was with the President when he reviewed our army under the enemy's guns before Chattanooga. He told Mr. Davis that every honest man he saw out West thought well of Joe Johnston. He knows that the President detests Joe Johnston for all the trouble he has given him, and General Joe returns the compliment with compound interest. His hatred of Jeff Davis amounts to a religion With him it colors all things.

Joe Johnston advancing, or retreating, I may say with more truth, is magnetic. He does draw the good-will of those by whom he is surrounded. Being such a good hater, it is a pity he had not elected to hate somebody else than the President of our country. He hates not wisely but too well. Our friend Breckinridge[103] received Mr. Chesnut with open arms. There is nothing narrow, nothing self-seeking, about Breckinridge. He has not mounted a pair of green spectacles made of prejudices so that he sees no good except in his own red-hot partizans.

October 27th.—Young Wade Hampton has been here for a few days, a guest of our nearest neighbor and cousin, Phil Stockton. Wade, without being the beauty or the athlete that his brother Preston is, is such a nice boy. We lent him horses, and ended by giving him a small party. What was lacking in company was made up for by the excellence of old Colonel Chesnut's ancient Madeira and champagne. If everything in the Confederacy were only as truly good as the old Colonel's wine-cellars! Then we had a salad and a jelly cake.

General Joe Johnston is so careful of his aides that Wade has never yet seen a battle. Says he has always happened to be sent afar off when the fighting came. He does not seem too grateful for this, and means to be transferred to his father's command. He says, "No man exposes himself more recklessly to danger than General Johnston, and no one strives harder to keep others out of it." But the business of this war is to save the country, and a commander must risk his men's lives to do it. There is a French saying that you can't make an omelet unless you are willing to break eggs.

November 5th.—For a week we have had such a tranquil, happy time here. Both my husband and Johnny are here still. James Chesnut spent his time sauntering around with his father, or stretched on the rug

[103] John C. Breckinridge had been Vice-President of the United States under Buchanan and was the candidate of the Southern Democrats for President in 1860. He joined the Confederate Army in 1861.

before my fire reading Vanity Fair and Pendennis. By good luck he had
not read them before. We have kept Esmond for the last. He owns that
he is having a good time. Johnny is happy, too. He does not care for
books. He will read a novel now and then, if the girls continue to talk of
it before him. Nothing else whatever in the way of literature does he
touch. He comes pulling his long blond mustache irresolutely as if he
hoped to be advised not to read it—"Aunt Mary, shall I like this thing?"
I do not think he has an idea what we are fighting about, and he does
not want to know. He says, "My company," "My men," with a pride, a
faith, and an affection which are sublime. He came into his inheritance
at twenty-one (just as the war began), and it was a goodly one, fine old
houses and an estate to match.

Yesterday, Johnny went to his plantation for the first time since the
war began. John Witherspoon went with him, and reports in this way:
"How do you do, Marster! How you come on?"—thus from every side
rang the noisiest welcome from the darkies. Johnny was silently
shaking black hands right and left as he rode into the crowd.

As the noise subsided, to the overseer he said: "Send down more
corn and fodder for my horses." And to the driver, "Have you any
peas?" "Plenty, sir." "Send a wagon-load down for the cows at
Bloomsbury while I stay there. They have not milk and butter enough
there for me. Any eggs? Send down all you can collect. How about my
turkeys and ducks? Send them down two at a time. How about the
mutton? Fat? That's good; send down two a week."

As they rode home, John Witherspoon remarked, "I was surprised
that you did not go into the fields to see your crops." "What was the
use?" "And the negroes; you had so little talk with them."

"No use to talk to them before the overseer. They are coming down
to Bloomsbury, day and night, by platoons and they talk me dead.
Besides, William and Parish go up there every night, and God knows
they tell me enough plantation scandal—overseer feathering his nest;
negroes ditto at my expense. Between the two fires I mean to get
something to eat while I am here."

For him we got up a charming picnic at Mulberry. Everything was
propitious—the most perfect of days and the old place in great beauty.
Those large rooms were delightful for dancing; we had as good a
dinner as mortal appetite could crave; the best fish, fowl, and game;
wine from a cellar that can not be excelled. In spite of blockade
Mulberry does the honors nobly yet. Mrs. Edward Stockton drove
down with me. She helped me with her taste and tact in arranging
things. We had no trouble, however. All of the old servants who have
not been moved to Bloomsbury scented the prey from afar, and they
literally flocked in and made themselves useful.

CHAPTER XVI. RICHMOND, VA.

November 28, 1863—*April* 11, 1864

Richmond, Va., *November 28, 1863.*—Our pleasant home sojourn was soon broken up. Johnny had to go back to Company A, and my husband was ordered by the President to make a second visit to Bragg's Army.[104]

So we came on here where the Prestons had taken apartments for me. Molly was with me. Adam Team, the overseer, with Isaac McLaughlin's help, came with us to take charge of the eight huge boxes of provisions I brought from home. Isaac, Molly's husband, is a servant of ours, the only one my husband ever bought in his life. Isaac's wife belonged to Rev. Thomas Davis, and Isaac to somebody else. The owner of Isaac was about to go West, and Isaac was distracted. They asked one thousand dollars for him. He is a huge creature, really a magnificent specimen of a colored gentleman. His occupation had been that of a stage- driver. Now, he is a carpenter, or will be some day. He is awfully grateful to us for buying him; is really devoted to his wife and children, though he has a strange way of showing it, for he has a mistress, *en titre*, as the French say, which fact Molly never failed to grumble about as soon as his back was turned. "Great big good-for-nothing thing come a-whimpering to marster to buy him for his wife's sake, and all the time he an—" "Oh, Molly, stop that!" said I.

Mr. Davis visited Charleston and had an enthusiastic reception. He described it all to General Preston. Governor Aiken's perfect old Carolina style of living delighted him. Those old gray-haired darkies and their noiseless, automatic service, the result of finished training-one does miss that sort of thing when away from home, where your own servants think for you; they know your ways and your wants; they save you all responsibility even in matters of your own ease and well doing. The butler at Mulberry would be miserable and feel himself a ridiculous failure were I ever forced to ask him for anything.

November 30th.-I must describe an adventure I had in Kingsville. Of course, I know nothing of children: in point of fact, am awfully afraid of them.

Mrs. Edward Barnwell came with us from Camden. She had a magnificent boy two years old. Now don't expect me to reduce that adjective, for this little creature is a wonder of childlike beauty, health, and strength. Why not? If like produces like, and with such a handsome pair to claim as father and mother! The boy's eyes alone would make

---

[104] Braxton Bragg was a native of North Carolina and had won distinction in the war with Mexico.

any girl's fortune.

At first he made himself very agreeable, repeating nursery rhymes and singing. Then something went wrong. Suddenly he changed to a little fiend, fought and kicked and scratched like a tiger. He did everything that was naughty, and he did it with a will as if he liked it, while his lovely mamma, with flushed cheeks and streaming eyes, was imploring him to be a good boy.

When we stopped at Kingsville, I got out first, then Mrs. Barnwell's nurse, who put the little man down by me. "Look after him a moment, please, ma'am," she said. "I must help Mrs. Barnwell with the bundles," etc. She stepped hastily back and the cars moved off. They ran down a half mile to turn. I trembled in my shoes. This child! No man could ever frighten me so. If he should choose to be bad again! It seemed an eternity while I waited for that train to turn and come back again. My little charge took things quietly. For me he had a perfect contempt, no fear whatever. And I was his abject slave for the nonce.

He stretched himself out lazily at full length. Then he pointed downward. "Those are great legs," said he solemnly, looking at his own. I immediately joined him in admiring them enthusiastically. Near him he spied a bundle. "Pussy cat tied up in that bundle." He was up in a second and pounced upon it. If we were to be taken up as thieves, no matter, I dared not meddle with that child. I had seen what he could do. There were several cooked sweet potatoes tied up in an old handkerchief—belonging to some negro probably. He squared himself off comfortably, broke one in half and began to eat. Evidently he had found what he was fond of. In this posture Mrs. Barnwell discovered us. She came with comic dismay in every feature, not knowing what our relations might be, and whether or not we had undertaken to fight it out alone as best we might. The old nurse cried, "Lawsy me!" with both hands uplifted. Without a word I fled. In another moment the Wilmington train would have left me. She was going to Columbia.

We broke down only once between Kingsville and Wilmington, but between Wilmington and Weldon we contrived to do the thing so effectually as to have to remain twelve hours at that forlorn station.

The one room that I saw was crowded with soldiers. Adam Team succeeded in securing two chairs for me, upon one of which I sat and put my feet on the other. Molly sat flat on the floor, resting her head against my chair. I woke cold and cramped. An officer, who did not give his name, but said he was from Louisiana, came up and urged me to go near the fire. He gave me his seat by the fire, where I found an old lady and two young ones, with two men in the uniform of common soldiers.

We talked as easily to each other all night as if we had known one another all our lives. We discussed the war, the army, the news of the day. No questions were asked, no names given, no personal discourse whatever, and yet if these men and women were not gentry, and of the best sort, I do not know ladies and gentlemen when I see them.

Being a little surprised at the want of interest Mr. Team and Isaac showed in my well-doing, I walked out to see, and I found them working like beavers. They had been at it all night. In the break-down my boxes were smashed. They had first gathered up the contents and were trying to hammer up the boxes so as to make them once more available.

At Petersburg a smartly dressed woman came in, looked around in the crowd, then asked for the seat by me. Now Molly's seat was paid for the same as mine, but she got up at once, gave the lady her seat and stood behind me. I am sure Molly believes herself my body-guard as well as my servant.

The lady then having arranged herself comfortably in Molly's seat began in plaintive accents to tell her melancholy tale. She was a widow. She lost her husband in the battles around Richmond. Soon some one went out and a man offered her the vacant seat. Straight as an arrow she went in for a flirtation with the polite gentleman. Another person, a perfect stranger, said to me, "Well, look yonder. As soon as she began whining about her dead beau I knew she was after another one." "Beau, indeed!" cried another listener, "she said it was her husband." "Husband or lover, all the same. She won't lose any time. It won't be her fault if she doesn't have another one soon."

But the grand scene was the night before: the cars crowded with soldiers, of course; not a human being that I knew. An Irish woman, so announced by her brogue, came in. She marched up and down the car, loudly lamenting the want of gallantry in the men who would not make way for her. Two men got up and gave her their seats, saying it did not matter, they were going to get out at the next stopping-place.

She was gifted with the most pronounced brogue I ever heard, and she gave us a taste of it. She continued to say that the men ought all to get out of that; that car was "shuteable" only for ladies. She placed on the vacant seat next to her a large looking-glass. She continued to harangue until she fell asleep.

A tired soldier coming in, seeing what he supposed to be an empty seat, quietly slipped into it. Crash went the glass. The soldier groaned, the Irish woman shrieked. The man was badly cut by the broken glass. She was simply a mad woman. She shook her fist in his face; said she was a lone woman and he had got into that seat for no good purpose. How did he dare to?—etc. I do not think the man uttered a word. The conductor took him into another car to have the pieces of glass picked out of his clothes, and she continued to rave. Mr. Team shouted aloud, and laughed as if he were in the Hermitage Swamp. The woman's unreasonable wrath and absurd accusations were comic, no doubt.

Soon the car was silent and I fell into a comfortable doze. I felt

Molly give me a gentle shake. "Listen, Missis, how loud Mars Adam
Team is talking, and all about ole marster and our business, and to
strangers. It's a shame." "Is he saying any harm of us?" "No, ma'am,
not that. He is bragging for dear life 'bout how ole ole marster is and
how rich he is, an' all that. I gwine tell him stop." Up started Molly.
"Mars Adam, Missis say please don't talk so loud. When people travel
they don't do that a way."

Mr. Preston's man, Hal, was waiting at the depot with a carriage to
take me to my Richmond house. Mary Preston had rented these
apartments for me.

I found my dear girls there with a nice fire. Everything looked so
pleasant and inviting to the weary traveler. Mrs. Grundy, who occupies
the lower floor, sent me such a real Virginia tea, hot cakes, and rolls.
Think of living in the house with Mrs. Grundy, and having no fear of
"what Mrs. Grundy will say."

My husband has come; he likes the house, Grundy's, and
everything. Already he has bought Grundy's horses for sixteen hundred
Confederate dollars cash. He is nearer to being contented and happy
than I ever saw him. He has not established a grievance yet, but I am on
the lookout daily. He will soon find out whatever there is wrong about
Cary Street.

I gave a party; Mrs. Davis very witty; Preston girls very handsome;
Isabella's fun fast and furious. No party could have gone off more
successfully, but my husband decides we are to have no more
festivities. This is not the time or the place for such gaieties.

Maria Freeland is perfectly delightful on the subject of her
wedding. She is ready to the last piece of lace, but her hard-hearted
father says "No." She adores John Lewis. That goes without saying.
She does not pretend, however, to be as much in love as Mary Preston.
In point of fact, she never saw any one before who was. But she is as
much in love as she can be with a man who, though he is not very
handsome, is as eligible a match as a girl could make. He is all that
heart could wish, and he comes of such a handsome family. His mother,
Esther Maria Coxe, was the beauty of a century, and his father was a
nephew of General Washington. For all that, he is far better looking
than John Darby or Mr. Miles. She always intended to marry better
than Mary Preston or Bettie Bierne.

Lucy Haxall is positively engaged to Captain Coffey, an
Englishman. She is convinced that she will marry him. He is her first
fancy.

Mr. Venable, of Lee's staff, was at our party, so out of spirits. He
knows everything that is going on. His depression bodes us no good.
To-day, General Hampton sent James Chesnut a fine saddle that he had
captured from the Yankees in battle array.

Mrs. Scotch Allan (Edgar Allan Poe's patron's wife) sent me ice-cream and lady-cheek apples from her farm. John R. Thompson,[105] the sole literary fellow I know in Richmond, sent me Leisure Hours in Town, by A Country Parson.

My husband says he hopes I will be contented because he came here this winter to please me. If I could have been satisfied at home he would have resigned his aide-de-campship and gone into some service in South Carolina. I am a good excuse, if good for nothing else.

Old tempestuous Keitt breakfasted with us yesterday. I wish I could remember half the brilliant things he said. My husband has now gone with him to the War Office. Colonel Keitt thinks it is time he was promoted. He wants to be a brigadier.

Now, Charleston is bombarded night and day. It fairly makes me dizzy to think of that everlasting racket they are beating about people's ears down there. Bragg defeated, and separated from Longstreet. It is a long street that knows no turning, and Rosecrans is not taken after all.

November 30th.—Anxiety pervades. Lee is fighting Meade. Misery is everywhere. Bragg is falling back before Grant.[106] Longstreet, the soldiers call him Peter the Slow, is settling down before Knoxville.

General Lee requires us to answer every letter, said Mr. Venable, and to do our best to console the poor creatures whose husbands and sons are fighting the battles of the country.

December 2d.—Bragg begs to be relieved of his command. The army will be relieved to get rid of him. He has a winning way of earning everybody's detestation. Heavens, how they hate him! The rapid flight of his army terminated at Ringgold. Hardie declines even a temporary command of the Western army. Preston Johnston has been sent out post-haste at a moment's warning. He was not even allowed time to go home and tell his wife good-by or, as Browne, the Englishman, said, "to put a clean shirt into his traveling bag." Lee and Meade are facing each other gallantly.[107]

---

[105] John R. Thompson was a native of Richmond and in 1847 became editor of the Southern Literary Messenger. Under his direction, that periodical acquired commanding influence. Mr. Thompson's health failed afterward. During the war he spent a part of his time in Richmond and a part in Europe. He afterward settled in New York and became literary editor of the Evening Post.

[106] The siege of Chattanooga, which had been begun on September 21st, closed late in November, 1863, the final engagements beginning on November 23d, and ending on November 25th. Lookout Mountain and Missionary Ridge were the closing incidents of the siege. Grant, Sherman, and Hooker were conspicuous on the Federal side and Bragg and Longstreet on the Confederate.

[107] Following the battle of Gettysburg on July 1st, 2d, and 3d, of this year, there had occurred in Virginia between Lee and Made engagements at Bristoe's Station, Kelly's Ford, and Rappahannock Station, the latter engagement taking place on November 7th. The author doubtless refers here to the positions of Lee and Meade at Mine Run, December 1st. December 2d Meade abandoned his, because (as he is reported to have

The first of December we went with a party of Mrs. Ould's getting up, to see a French frigate which lay at anchor down the river. The French officers came on board our boat. The Lees were aboard. The French officers were not in the least attractive either in manners or appearance, but our ladies were most attentive and some showered bad French upon them with a lavish hand, always accompanied by queer grimaces to eke out the scanty supply of French words, the sentences ending usually in a nervous shriek. "Are they deaf?" asked Mrs. Randolph.

The French frigate was a dirty little thing. Doctor Garnett was so buoyed up with hope that the French were coming to our rescue, that he would not let me say "an English man-of-war is the cleanest thing known in the world." Captain—said to Mary Lee, with a foreign contortion of countenance, that went for a smile, "I's bashlor." Judge Ould said, as we went to dinner on our own steamer, "They will not drink our President's health. They do not acknowledge us to be a nation. Mind, none of you say 'Emperor,' not once." Doctor Garnett interpreted the laws of politeness otherwise, and stepped forward, his mouth fairly distended with so much French, and said: "*Vieff l'Emperor.*" Young Gibson seconded him quietly, "*À la santé de l'Empereur.*" But silence prevailed. Preston Hampton was the handsomest man on board—"the figure of Hercules, the face of Apollo," cried an enthusiastic girl. Preston was as lazy and as sleepy as ever. He said of the Frenchmen: "They can't help not being good-looking, but with all the world open to them, to wear such shabby clothes!"

The lieutenant's name was Rousseau. On the French frigate, lying on one of the tables was a volume of Jean Jacques Rousseau's works, side by side, strange to say, with a map of South Carolina. This lieutenant was courteously asked by Mary Lee to select some lady to whom she might introduce him. He answered: "I shuse you," with a bow that was a benediction and a prayer.

And now I am in a fine condition for Hetty Cary's starvation party, where they will give thirty dollars for the music and not a cent for a morsel to eat. Preston said contentedly, "I hate dancing, and I hate cold water; so I will eschew the festivity to-night."

Found John R. Thompson at our house when I got home so tired to-night. He brought me the last number of the Cornhill. He knew how much I was interested in Trollope's story, Framley Parsonage.

December 4th.—My husband bought yesterday at the Commissary's one barrel of flour, one bushel of potatoes, one peck of rice, five pounds of salt beef, and one peck of salt—all for sixty dollars.

---

said) it would have cost him 30,000 men to carry Lee's breastworks, and he shrank from ordering such slaughter.

In the street a barrel of flour sells for one hundred and fifteen dollars.

December 5th.—Wigfall was here last night. He began by wanting to hang Jeff Davis. My husband managed him beautifully. He soon ceased to talk virulent nonsense, and calmed down to his usual strong common sense. I knew it was as quite late, but I had no idea of the hour. My husband beckoned me out. "It is all your fault," said he. "What?" "Why will you persist in looking so interested in all Wigfall is saying? Don't let him catch your eye. Look into the fire. Did you not hear it strike two?"

This attack was so sudden, so violent, so unlooked for, I could only laugh hysterically. However, as an obedient wife, I went back, gravely took my seat and looked into the fire. I did not even dare raise my eyes to see what my husband was doing—if he, too, looked into the fire. Wigfall soon tired of so tame an audience and took his departure.

General Lawton was here. He was one of Stonewall's generals. So I listened with all my ears when he said: "Stonewall could not sleep. So, every two or three nights you were waked up by orders to have your brigade in marching order before daylight and report in person to the Commander. Then you were marched a few miles out and then a few miles in again. All this was to make us ready, ever on the alert. And the end of it was this: Jackson's men would go half a day's march before Peter Longstreet waked and breakfasted. I think there is a popular delusion about the amount of praying he did. He certainly preferred a fight on Sunday to a sermon. Failing to manage a fight, he loved best a long Presbyterian sermon, Calvinistic to the core.

"He had shown small sympathy with human infirmity. He was a one-idea-ed man. He looked upon broken-down men and stragglers as the same thing. He classed all who were weak and weary, who fainted by the wayside, as men wanting in patriotism. If a man's face was as white as cotton and his pulse so low you scarce could feel it, he looked upon him merely as an inefficient soldier and rode off impatiently. He was the true type of all great soldiers. Like the successful warriors of the world, he did not value human life where he had an object to accomplish. He could order men to their death as a matter of course. His soldiers obeyed him to the death. Faith they had in him stronger than death. Their respect he commanded. I doubt if he had so much of their love as is talked about while he was alive. Now, that they see a few more years of Stonewall would have freed them from the Yankees, they deify him. Any man is proud to have been one of the famous Stonewall brigade. But, be sure, it was bitter hard work to keep up with him as all know who ever served under him. He gave his orders rapidly and distinctly and rode away, never allowing answer or remonstrance. It was, 'Look there—see that place—take it!' When you failed you were apt to be put under arrest. When you reported the place taken, he only said, 'Good!'"

Spent seventy-five dollars to-day for a little tea and sugar, and have five hundred left. My husband's pay never has paid for the rent of our lodgings. He came in with dreadful news just now. I have wept so often for things that never happened, I will withhold my tears now for a certainty. To-day, a poor woman threw herself on her dead husband's coffin and kissed it. She was weeping bitterly. So did I in sympathy.

My husband, as I told him to-day, could see me and everything that he loved hanged, drawn, and quartered without moving a muscle, if a crowd were looking on; he could have the same gentle operation performed on himself and make no sign. To all of which violent insinuation he answered in unmoved tones: "So would any civilized man.

Savages, however—Indians, at least—are more dignified in that particular than we are. Noisy, fidgety grief never moves me at all; it annoys me. Self-control is what we all need. You are a miracle of sensibility; self-control is what you need." "So you are civilized!" I said. "Some day I mean to be."

December 9th.—"Come here, Mrs. Chesnut," said Mary Preston to-day, "they are lifting General Hood out of his carriage, here, at your door." Mrs. Grundy promptly had him borne into her drawing-room, which was on the first floor. Mary Preston and I ran down and greeted him as cheerfully and as cordially as if nothing had happened since we saw him standing before us a year ago. How he was waited upon! Some cut-up oranges were brought him. "How kind people are," said he. "Not once since I was wounded have I ever been left without fruit, hard as it is to get now." "The money value of friendship is easily counted now," said some one, "oranges are five dollars apiece."

December 10th.—Mrs. Davis and Mrs. Lyons came. We had luncheon brought in for them, and then a lucid explanation of the *chronique scandaleuse*, of which Beck J. is the heroine. We walked home with Mrs. Davis and met the President riding alone. Surely that is wrong. It must be unsafe for him when there are so many traitors, not to speak of bribed negroes. Burton Harrison[108] says Mr. Davis prefers to go alone, and there is none to gainsay him.

My husband laid the law down last night. I felt it to be the last drop in my full cup. "No more feasting in this house," said he. "This is no time for junketing and merrymaking." "And you said you brought me here to enjoy the winter before you took me home and turned my face to a dead wall." He is the master of the house; to hear is to obey.

December 14th.—Drove out with Mrs. Davis. She had a watch in her hand which some poor dead soldier wanted to have sent to his family. First, we went to her mantua-maker, then we drove to the Fair

---

[108] Burton Harrison, then secretary to Jefferson Davis, who married Miss Constance Cary and became well known as a New York lawyer. He died in Washington in 1904.

Grounds where the band was playing. Suddenly, she missed the watch. She remembered having it when we came out of the mantua-maker's. We drove beck instantly, and there the watch was lying near the steps of the little porch in front of the house. No one had passed in, apparently; in any case, no one had seen it.

Preston Hampton went with me to see Conny Cary. The talk was frantically literary, which Preston thought hard on him. I had just brought the St. Denis number of Les Miserables.

Sunday, Christopher Hampton walked to church with me. Coming out, General Lee was seen slowly making his way down the aisle, bowing royally to right and left. I pointed him out to Christopher Hampton when General Lee happened to look our way. He bowed low, giving me a charming smile of recognition. I was ashamed of being so pleased. I blushed like a schoolgirl.

We went to the White House. They gave us tea. The President said he had been on the way to our house, coming with all the Davis family, to see me, but the children became so troublesome they turned back. Just then, little Joe rushed in and insisted on saying his prayers at his father's knee, then and there. He was in his night-clothes.

December 19th.—A box has come from home for me. Taking advantage of this good fortune and a full larder, have asked Mrs. Davis to dine with me. Wade Hampton sent me a basket of game. We had Mrs. Davis and Mr. and Mrs. Preston. After dinner we walked to the church to see the Freeland-Lewis wedding. Mr. Preston had Mrs. Davis on his arm. My husband and Mrs. Preston, and Burton Harrison and myself brought up the rear. Willie Allan joined us, and we had the pleasure of waiting one good hour. Then the beautiful Maria, loveliest of brides, sailed in on her father's arm, and Major John Coxe Lewis followed with Mrs. Freeland. After the ceremony such a kissing was there up and down the aisle. The happy bridegroom kissed wildly, and several girls complained, but he said: "How am I to know Maria's kin whom I was to kiss? It is better to show too much affection for one's new relations than too little."

December 21st.—Joe Johnston has been made Commander-in-chief of the Army of the West. General Lee had this done, 'tis said. Miss Agnes Lee and "little Robert" (as they fondly call General Lee's youngest son in this hero-worshiping community) called. They told us the President, General Lee, and General Elzey had gone out to look at the fortifications around Richmond. My husband came home saying he had been with them, and lent General Lee his gray horse.

Mrs. Howell, Mrs. Davis's mother, says a year ago on the cars a man said, "We want a Dictator." She replied, "Jeff Davis will never consent to be a Dictator." The man turned sharply toward her "And, pray, who asks him? Joe Johnston will be made Dictator by the Army of the West." "Imperator" was suggested. Of late the Army of the West has not been in a condition to dictate to friend or foe. Certainly Jeff Davis did hate to put Joe Johnston at the head of what is left of it. Detached from General Lee, what a horrible failure is Longstreet! Oh, for a day of Albert Sidney Johnston out West! And Stonewall, could he come back to us here!

General Hood, the wounded knight, came for me to drive. I felt that I would soon find myself chaperoning some girls, but I asked no questions. He improved the time between Franklin and Cary Streets by saying, "I do like your husband so much." "So do I," I replied simply.

Buck was ill in bed, so William said at the door, but she recovered her health and came down for the drive in black velvet and ermine, looking queenly. And then, with the top of the landau thrown back, wrapped in furs and rugs, we had a long drive that bitter cold day.

One day as we were hieing us home from the Fair Grounds, Sam, the wounded knight, asked Brewster what are the symptoms of a man's being in love. Sam (Hood is called Sam entirely, but why I do not know) said for his part he did not know; at seventeen he had fancied himself in love, but that was "a long time ago." Brewster spoke on the symptoms of love: "When you see her, your breath is apt to come short. If it amounts to mild strangulation, you have got it bad. You are stupidly jealous, glowering with jealousy, and have a gloomy fixed conviction that she likes every fool you meet better than she does you, especially people that you know she has a thorough contempt for; that is, you knew it before you lost your head, I mean, before you fell in love. The last stages of unmitigated spooniness, I will spare you," said Brewster, with a giggle and a wave of the hand. "Well," said Sam, drawing a breath of relief, "I have felt none of these things so far, and yet they say I am engaged to four young ladies, a liberal allowance, you will admit, for a man who can not walk without help."

Another day (the Sabbath) we called on our way from church to see Mrs. Wigfall. She was ill, but Mr. Wigfall insisted upon taking me into the drawing-room to rest a while. He said Louly was there; so she was, and so was Sam Hood, the wounded knight, stretched at full length on a sofa and a rug thrown over him. Louis Wigfall said to me: "Do you know General Hood?" "Yes," said I, and the General laughed with his eyes as I looked at him; but he did not say a word. I felt it a curious commentary upon the reports he had spoken of the day before. Louly Wigfall is a very handsome girl.

December 24th.—As we walked, Brewster reported a row he had had with General Hood. Brewster had told those six young ladies at the Prestons' that "old Sam" was in the habit of saying he would not marry if he could any silly, sentimental girl, who would throw herself away upon a maimed creature such as he was. When Brewster went home he took pleasure in telling Sam how the ladies had complimented his good sense, whereupon the General rose in his wrath and threatened to break his crutch over Brewster's head. To think he could be such a fool—to go about repeating to everybody his whimperings.

I was taking my seat at the head of the table when the door opened and Brewster walked in unannounced. He took his stand in front of the open door, with his hands in his pockets and his small hat pushed back as far as it could get from his forehead. "What!" said he, "you are not ready yet? The generals are below. Did you get my note?" I begged my husband to excuse me and rushed off to put on my bonnet and furs. I met the girls coming up with a strange man. The flurry of two major-generals had been too much for me and I forgot to ask the new one's name. They went up to dine in my place with my husband, who sat eating his dinner, with Lawrence's undivided attention given to him, amid this whirling and eddying in and out of the world militant. Mary Preston and I then went to drive with the generals. The new one proved to be Bruckner,[109] who is also a Kentuckian. The two men told us they had slept together the night before Chickamauga. It is useless to try: legs can't any longer be kept out of the conversation. So General Buckner said: "Once before I slept with a man and he lost his leg next day." He had made a vow never to do so again. "When Sam and I parted that morning, we said: 'You or I may be killed, but the cause will be safe all the same.'"

After the drive everybody came in to tea, my husband in famous good humor, we had an unusually gay evening. It was very nice of my husband to take no notice of my conduct at dinner, which had been open to criticism. All the comfort of my life depends upon his being in good humor.

Christmas Day, 1863.—Yesterday dined with the Prestons. Wore one of my handsomest Paris dresses (from Paris before the war). Three magnificent Kentucky generals were present, with Senator Orr from South Carolina, and Mr. Miles. General Buckner repeated a speech of Hood's to him to show how friendly they were. "I prefer a ride with you to the company of any woman in the world," Buckner had answered. "I prefer your company to that of any man, certainly," was Hood's reply. This became the standing joke of the dinner; it flashed up in every form. Poor Sam got out of it so badly, if he got out of it at all. General Buckner said patronizingly, "Lame excuses, all. Hood never gets out of any scrape—that is, unless he can fight out." Others dropped in after dinner; some without arms, some without legs; von Borcke, who can not speak because of a wound in his throat. Isabella said: "We have all kinds now, but a blind one." Poor fellows, they laugh at wounds. "And they yet can show many a scar."

---

[109] Simon B. Buckner was a graduate of West Point and had served in the Mexican War. In 1887 he was elected Governor of Kentucky and, at the funeral of General Grant, acted as one of the pall-bearers.

We had for dinner oyster soup, besides roast mutton, ham, boned turkey, wild duck, partridge, plum pudding, sauterne, burgundy, sherry, and Madeira. There is life in the old land yet!

At my house to-day after dinner, and while Alex Haskell and my husband sat over the wine, Hood gave me an account of his discomfiture last night. He said he could not sleep after it; it was the hardest battle he had ever fought in his life, "and I was routed, as it were; she told me there was no hope; that ends it. You know at Petersburg on my way to the Western army she half-promised me to think of it. She would not say 'Yes,' but she did not say 'No'—that is, not exactly. At any rate, I went off saying, 'I am engaged to you,' and she said, 'I am not engaged to you.' After I was so fearfully wounded I gave it up. But, then, since I came," etc.

"Do you mean to say," said I, "that you had proposed to her before that conversation in the carriage, when you asked Brewster the symptoms of love? I like your audacity." "Oh, she understood, but it is all up now, for she says, 'No!'"

My husband says I am extravagant. "No, my friend, not that," said I. "I had fifteen hundred dollars and I have spent every cent of it in my housekeeping. Not one cent for myself, not one cent for dress nor any personal want whatever." He calls me "hospitality run mad."

January 1, 1864.—General Hood's an awful flatterer—I mean an awkward flatterer. I told him to praise my husband to some one else, not to me. He ought to praise me to somebody who would tell my husband, and then praise my husband to another person who would tell me. Man and wife are too much one person—to wave a compliment straight in the face of one about the other is not graceful.

One more year of Stonewall would have saved us. Chickamauga is the only battle we have gained since Stonewall died, and no results follow as usual. Stonewall was not so much as killed by a Yankee: he was shot by his own men; that is hard. General Lee can do no more than keep back Meade. "One of Meade's armies, you mean," said I, "for they have only to double on him when Lee whips one of them."

General Edward Johnston says he got Grant a place—*esprit de corps*, you know. He could not bear to see an old army man driving a wagon; that was when he found him out West, put out of the army for habitual drunkenness. He is their right man, a bull-headed Suwarrow. He don't care a snap if men fall like the leaves fall; he fights to win, that chap does. He is not distracted by a thousand side issues; he does not see them. He is narrow and sure—sees only in a straight line. Like Louis Napoleon, from a battle in the gutter, he goes straight up. Yes, as with Lincoln, they have ceased to carp at him as a rough clown, no gentleman, etc. You never hear now of Lincoln's nasty fun; only of his wisdom. Doesn't take much soap and water to wash the hands that the rod of empire sway. They talked of Lincoln's drunkenness, too. Now, since Vicksburg they have not a word to say against Grant's habits. He has the disagreeable habit of not retreating before irresistible veterans. General Lee and Albert Sidney Johnston show blood and breeding. They are of the Bayard and Philip Sidney order of soldiers. Listen: if General Lee had had Grant's resources he would have bagged the last Yankee, or have had them all safe back in Massachusetts. "You mean if he had not the weight of the negro question upon him?" "No, I mean if he had Grant's unlimited allowance of the powers of war—men, money, ammunition, arms."

Mrs. Ould says Mrs. Lincoln found the gardener of the White House so nice, she would make him a major-general. Lincoln remarked to the secretary: "Well, the little woman must have her way sometimes."

A word of the last night of the old year. "Gloria Mundi" sent me a cup of strong, good coffee. I drank two cups and so I did not sleep a wink. Like a fool I passed my whole life in review, and bitter memories maddened me quite. Then came a happy thought. I mapped out a story of the war. The plot came to hand, for it was true. Johnny is the hero, a light dragoon and heavy swell. I will call it F. F.'s, for it is the F. F.'s both of South Carolina and Virginia. It is to be a war story, and the filling out of the skeleton was the best way to put myself to sleep.

January 4th.—Mrs. Ives wants us to translate a French play. A genuine French captain came in from his ship on the James River and gave us good advice as to how to make the selection. General Hampton sent another basket of partridges, and all goes merry as a marriage bell.

My husband came in and nearly killed us. He brought this piece of news: "North Carolina wants to offer terms of peace!" We needed only a break of that kind to finish us. I really shivered nervously, as one does when the first handful of earth comes rattling down on the coffin in the grave of one we cared for more than all who are left.

January 5th.—At Mrs. Preston's, met the Light Brigade in battle array, ready to sally forth, conquering and to conquer. They would stand no nonsense from me about staying at home to translate a French play. Indeed, the plays that have been sent us are so indecent I scarcely know where a play is to be found that would do at all.

While at dinner the President's carriage drove up with only General Hood. He sent up to ask in Maggie Howell's name would I go with them? I tied up two partridges between plates with a serviette, for Buck, who is ill, and then went down. We picked up Mary Preston. It was Maggie's drive; as the soldiers say, I was only on "escort duty." At the Prestons', Major Venable met us at the door and took in the partridges to Buck. As we drove off Maggie said: "Major Venable is a Carolinian, I see." "No; Virginian to the core." "But, then, he was a professor in the South Carolina College before the war." Mary Preston said: "She is taking a fling at your weakness for all South Carolina."

Came home and found my husband in a bitter mood. It has all gone wrong with our world. The loss of our private fortune the smallest part. He intimates, "with so much human misery filling the air, we might stay at home and think." "And go mad?" said I. "Catch me at it! A yawning grave, with piles of red earth thrown on one side; that is the only future I ever see. You remember Emma Stockton? She and I were as blithe as birds that day at Mulberry. I came here the next day, and when I arrived a telegram said: 'Emma Stockton found dead in her bed.' It is awfully near, that thought. No, no. I will not stop and think of death always."

January 8th.—Snow of the deepest. Nobody can come to-day, I thought. But they did! My girls, first; then Constance Cary tripped in— the clever Conny. Hetty is the beauty, so called, though she is clever enough, too; but Constance is actually clever and has a classically perfect outline. Next came the four Kentuckians and Preston Hampton. He is as tall as the Kentuckians and ever so much better looking. Then we had egg-nog.

I was to take Miss Cary to the Semmes's. My husband inquired the price of a carriage. It was twenty-five dollars an hour! He cursed by all his gods at such extravagance. The play was not worth the candle, or carriage, in this instance. In Confederate money it sounds so much worse than it is. I did not dream of asking him to go with me after that lively overture. "I did intend to go with you," he said, "but you do not ask me." "And I have been asking you for twenty years to go with me, in vain. Think of that!" I said, tragically. We could not wait for him to dress, so I sent the twenty-five-dollar-an-hour carriage back for him. We were behind time, as it was. When he came, the beautiful Hetty Cary and her friend, Captain Tucker, were with him. Major von Borcke and Preston Hampton were at the Cary's, in the drawing-room when we called for Constance, who was dressing. I challenge the world to produce finer specimens of humanity than these three: the Prussian von Borcke, Preston Hampton, and Hetty Cary.

We spoke to the Prussian about the vote of thanks passed by Congress yesterday—"thanks of the country to Major von Borcke." The poor man was as modest as a girl—in spite of his huge proportions. "That is a compliment, indeed!" said Hetty. "Yes. I saw it. And the happiest, the proudest day of my life as I read it. It was at the hotel breakfast-table. I try to hide my face with the newspaper, I feel it grow so red. But my friend he has his newspaper, too, and he sees the same thing. So he looks my way—he says, pointing to me—'Why does he grow so red? He has got something there!' and he laughs. Then I try to read aloud the so kind compliments of the Congress—but—he—you— I can not—" He puts his hand to his throat. His broken English and the difficulty of his enunciation with that wound in his windpipe makes it all very touching—and very hard to understand.

The Semmes charade party was a perfect success. The play was charming. Sweet little Mrs. Lawson Clay had a seat for me banked up among women. The female part of the congregation, strictly segregated from the male, were placed all together in rows. They formed a gay parterre, edged by the men in their black coats and gray uniforms. Toward the back part of the room, the mass of black and gray was solid. Captain Tucker bewailed his fate. He was stranded out there with those forlorn men, but could see us laughing, and fancied what we were saying was worth a thousand charades. He preferred talking to a clever woman to any known way of passing a pleasant hour. "So do I," somebody said.

On a sofa of state in front of all sat the President and Mrs. Davis. Little Maggie Davis was one of the child actresses. Her parents had a right to be proud of her; with her flashing black eyes, she was a marked figure on the stage. She is a handsome creature and she acted her part admirably. The shrine was beautiful beyond words. The Semmes and Ives families are Roman Catholics, and understand getting up that sort of thing. First came the "Palmers Gray," then Mrs. Ives, a solitary figure, the loveliest of penitent women. The Eastern pilgrims were delightfully costumed; we could not understand how so much Christian piety could come clothed in such odalisque robes. Mrs. Ould, as a queen, was as handsome and regal as heart could wish for. She was accompanied by a very satisfactory king, whose name, if I ever knew, I have forgotten. There was a resplendent knight of St. John, and then an American Indian. After their orisons they all knelt and laid something on the altar as a votive gift.

Burton Harrison, the President's handsome young secretary, was gotten up as a big brave in a dress presented to Mr. Davis by Indians for some kindness he showed them years ago. It was a complete warrior's outfit, scant as that is. The feathers stuck in the back of Mr. Harrison's head had a charmingly comic effect. He had to shave himself as clean as a baby or he could not act the beardless chief, Spotted Tail, Billy Bowlegs, Big Thunder, or whatever his character was. So he folded up his loved and lost mustache, the Christianized red Indian, and laid it on the altar, the most sacred treasure of his life, the witness of his most heroic sacrifice, on the shrine.

Senator Hill, of Georgia, took me in to supper, where were ices, chicken salad, oysters, and champagne. The President came in alone, I suppose, for while we were talking after supper and your humble servant was standing between Mrs. Randolph and Mrs. Stanard, he approached, offered me his arm and we walked off, oblivious ``'`
Senator Hill. Remember this, ladies, and forgive me for recoi
but Mrs. Stanard and Mrs. Randolph are the handsomest wo
Richmond; I am no older than they are, or younger, either, sac
Now, the President walked with me slowly up and down t'

room, and our conversation was of the saddest. Nobody knows so well as he the difficulties which beset this hard-driven Confederacy. He has a voice which is perfectly modulated, a comfort in this loud and rough soldier world. I think there is a melancholy cadence in his voice at times, of which he is unconscious when he talks of things as they are now.

My husband was so intensely charmed with Hetty Cary that he declined at the first call to accompany his wife home in the twenty-five-dollar-an-hour carriage. He ordered it to return. When it came, his wife (a good manager) packed the Carys and him in with herself, leaving the other two men who came with the party, when it was divided into "trips," to make their way home in the cold. At our door, near daylight of that bitter cold morning, I had the pleasure to see my husband, like a man, stand and pay for that carriage! To-day he is pleased with himself, with me, and with all the world; says if there was no such word as "fascinating" you would have to invent one to describe Hetty Cary.

January 9th.—Met Mrs. Wigfall. She wants me to take Halsey to Mrs. Randolph's theatricals. I am to get him up as Sir Walter Raleigh. Now, General Breckinridge has come. I like him better than any of them. Morgan also is here.[110] These huge Kentuckians fill the town. Isabella says, "They hold Morgan accountable for the loss of Chattanooga." The follies of the wise, the weaknesses of the great! She shakes her head significantly when I beg in to tell why I like him so well. Last night General Buckner came for her to go with him and rehearse at the Carys' for Mrs. Randolph's charades.

The President's man, Jim, that he believed in as we all believe in our own servants, "our own people," as we call them, and Betsy, Mrs. Davis's maid, decamped last night. It is miraculous that they had the fortitude to resist the temptation so long. At Mrs. Davis's the hired servants all have been birds of passage. First they were seen with gold galore, and then they would fly to the Yankees, and I am sure they had nothing to tell. It is Yankee money wasted.

I do not think it had ever crossed Mrs. Davis's brain that these two could leave her. She knew, however, that Betsy had eighty dollars in gold and two thousand four hundred dollars in Confederate notes.

Everybody who comes in brings a little bad news—not much, in itself, but by cumulative process the effect is depressing, indeed.

January 12th.—To-night there will be a great gathering of Kentuckians. Morgan gives them a dinner. The city of Richmond entertains John Morgan. He is at free quarters. The girls dined here.

---

[110] John H. Morgan, a native of Alabama, entered the Confederate army in 1861 as a Captain and in 1862 was made a Major-General. He was captured by the Federals in 1863 and confined in an Ohio penitentiary, but he escaped and once more joined the Confederate army. In September, 1864, he was killed in battle near Greenville, Tenn.

Conny Cary came back for more white feathers. Isabella had appropriated two sets and obstinately refused Constance Cary a single feather from her pile. She said, sternly: "I have never been on the stage before, and I have a presentiment when my father hears of this, I will never go again. I am to appear before the footlights as an English dowager duchess, and I mean to rustle in every feather, to wear all the lace and diamonds these two houses can compass"—(mine and Mrs. Preston's). She was jolly but firm, and Constance departed without any additional plumage for her Lady Teazle.

January 14th.—Gave Mrs. White twenty-three dollars for a turkey. Came home wondering all the way why she did not ask twenty-five; two more dollars could not have made me balk at the bargain, and twenty-three sounds odd.

January 15th.—What a day the Kentuckians have had! Mrs. Webb gave them a breakfast; from there they proceeded en masse to General Lawton's dinner, and then came straight here, all of which seems equal to one of Stonewall's forced marches. General Lawton took me in to supper. In spite of his dinner he had misgivings. "My heart is heavy," said he, "even here. All seems too light, too careless, for such terrible times. It seems out of place here in battle-scarred Richmond." "I have heard something of that kind at home," I replied. "Hope and fear are both gone, and it is distraction or death with us. I do not see how sadness and despondency would help us. If it would do any good, we would be sad enough."

We laughed at General Hood. General Lawton thought him better fitted for gallantry on the battle-field than playing a lute in my lady's chamber. When Miss Giles was electrifying the audience as the Fair Penitent, some one said: "Oh, that is so pretty!" Hood cried out with stern reproachfulness: "That is not pretty; it is elegant."

Not only had my house been rifled for theatrical properties, but as the play went on they came for my black velvet cloak. When it was over, I thought I should never get away, my cloak was so hard to find. But it gave me an opportunity to witness many things behind the scenes—that cloak hunt did. Behind the scenes! I know a little what that means now.

General Jeb Stuart was at Mrs. Randolph's in his cavalry jacket and high boots. He was devoted to Hetty Cary. Constance Cary said to me, pointing to his stars, "Hetty likes them that way, you know—gilt-edged and with stars."

January 16th—A visit from the President's handsome and accomplished secretary, Burton Harrison. I lent him Country Clergyman in Town and Elective Affinities. He is to bring me Mrs. Norton's Lost and Saved.

At Mrs. Randolph's, my husband complimented one of the ladies, who had amply earned his praise by her splendid acting. She pointed to a young man, saying, "You see that wretch; he has not said one word to me!" My husband asked innocently, "Why should he? And why is he a wretch?" "Oh, you know!" Going home I explained this riddle to him; he is always a year behindhand in gossip. "They said those two were engaged last winter, and now there seems to be a screw loose; but that sort of thing always comes right." The Carys prefer James Chesnut to his wife. I don't mind. Indeed, I like it. I do, too.

Every Sunday Mr. Minnegerode cried aloud in anguish his litany, "from pestilence and famine, battle, murder, and sudden death," and we wailed on our knees, "Good Lord deliver us," and on Monday, and all the week long, we go on as before, hearing of nothing but battle, murder, and sudden death, which are daily events. Now I have a new book; that is the unlooked-for thing, a pleasing incident in this life of monotonous misery. We live in a huge barrack. We are shut in, guarded from light without.

At breakfast to-day came a card, and without an instant's interlude, perhaps the neatest, most fastidious man in South Carolina walked in. I was uncombed, unkempt, tattered, and torn, in my most comfortable, worst worn, wadded green silk dressing-gown, with a white woolen shawl over my head to keep off draughts. He has not been in the war yet, and now he wants to be captain of an engineer corps. I wish he may get it! He has always been my friend; so he shall lack no aid that I can give. If he can stand the shock of my appearance to-day, we may reasonably expect to continue friends until death. Of all men, the fastidious Barny Heywood to come in. He faced the situation gallantly.

January 18th.—Invited to Dr. Haxall's last night to meet the Lawtons. Mr. Benjamin[111] dropped in. He is a friend of the house. Mrs. Haxall is a Richmond leader of society, a *ci-devant* beauty and belle, a charming person still, and her hospitality is of the genuine Virginia type. Everything Mr. Benjamin said we listened to, bore in mind, and gave heed to it diligently. He is a Delphic oracle, of the innermost shrine, and is supposed to enjoy the honor of Mr. Davis's unreserved confidence.

Lamar was asked to dinner here yesterday; so he came to-day. We had our wild turkey cooked for him yesterday, and I dressed myself within an inch of my life with the best of my four-year-old finery. Two of us, my husband and I, did not damage the wild turkey seriously. So Lamar enjoyed the *réchauffé*, and commended the art with which Molly had hid the slight loss we had inflicted upon its mighty breast. She had piled fried oysters over the turkey so skilfully, that unless we had told

---

[111] Judah P. Benjamin, was born, of Jewish parentage, at St. Croix in the West Indies, and was elected in 1852 to represent Louisiana in the United States Senate, where he served until 1861. In the Confederate administration he served successively from 1861 to 1865 as Attorney-General, Secretary of War, and Secretary of State. At the close of the war he went to England where he achieved remarkable success at the bar.

about it, no one would ever have known that the huge bird was making his second appearance on the board.

Lamar was more absent-minded and distrait than ever. My husband behaved like a trump—a well-bred man, with all his wits about him; so things went off smoothly enough. Lamar had just read Romola. Across the water he said it was the rage. I am sure it is not as good as Adam Bede or Silas Marner. It is not worthy of the woman who was to "rival all but Shakespeare's name below." "What is the matter with Romola?" he asked. "Tito is so mean, and he is mean in such a very mean way, and the end is so repulsive. Petting the husband's illegitimate children and left-handed wives may be magnanimity, but human nature revolts at it." "Woman's nature, you mean!" "Yes, and now another test. Two weeks ago I read this thing with intense interest, and already her Savonarola has faded from my mind. I have forgotten her way of showing Savonarola as completely as I always do forget Bulwer's Rienzi."

"Oh, I understand you now! It is like Milton's devil—he has obliterated all other devils. You can't fix your mind upon any other. The devil always must be of Miltonic proportions or you do not believe in him; Goethe's Mephistopheles disputes the crown of the causeway with Lucifer. But soon you begin to feel that Mephistopheles to be a lesser devil, an emissary of the devil only. Is there any Cardinal Wolsey but Shakespeare's? any Mirabeau but Carlyle's Mirabeau? But the list is too long of those who have been stamped into your brain by genius. The saintly preacher, the woman who stands by Hetty and saves her soul; those heavenly minded sermons preached by the author of Adam Bede, bear them well in mind while I tell you how this writer, who so well imagines and depicts female purity and piety, was a governess, or something of that sort, and perhaps wrote for a living; at any rate, she had an elective affinity, which was responded to, by George Lewes, and so she lives with Lewes. I do not know that she caused the separation between Lewes and his legal wife. They are living in a villa on some Swiss lake, and Mrs. Lewes, of the hour, is a charitable, estimable, agreeable, sympathetic woman of genius."

Lamar seemed without prejudices on the subject; at least, he expressed neither surprise nor disapprobation. He said something of "genius being above law," but I was not very clear as to what he said on that point. As for me I said nothing for fear of saying too much. "You know that Lewes is a writer," said he. "Some people say the man she lives with is a noble man." "They say she is kind and good if—a fallen woman." Here the conversation ended.

January 20th.—And now comes a grand announcement made by the Yankee Congress. They vote one million of men to be sent down here to free the prisoners whom they will not take in exchange. I actually thought they left all these Yankees here on our hands as part of their plan to starve us out. All Congressmen under fifty years of age are to leave politics and report for military duty or be conscripted. What enthusiasm there is in their councils! Confusion, rather, it seems to me! Mrs. Ould says "the men who frequent her house are more despondent now than ever since this thing began."

Our Congress is so demoralized, so confused, so depressed. They have asked the President, whom they have so hated, so insulted, so crossed and opposed and thwarted in every way, to speak to them, and advise them what to do.

January 21st.—Both of us were too ill to attend Mrs. Davis's reception. It proved a very sensational one. First, a fire in the house, then a robbery—said to be an arranged plan of the usual bribed servants there and some escaped Yankee prisoners. To-day the Examiner is lost in wonder at the stupidity of the fire and arson contingent. If they had only waited a few hours until everybody was asleep; after a reception the household would be so tired and so sound asleep. Thanks to the editor's kind counsel maybe the arson contingent will wait and do better next time.

Letters from home carried Mr. Chesnut off to-day. Thackeray is dead. I stumbled upon Vanity Fair for myself. I had never heard of Thackeray before. I think it was in 1850. I know I had been ill at the New York Hotel,[112] and when left alone, I slipped down-stairs and into a bookstore that I had noticed under the hotel, for something to read. They gave me the first half of Pendennis. I can recall now the very kind of paper it was printed on, and the illustrations, as they took effect upon me. And yet when I raved over it, and was wild for the other half, there were people who said it was slow; that Thackeray was evidently a coarse, dull, sneering writer; that he stripped human nature bare, and made it repulsive, etc.

January 22d.—At Mrs. Lyons's met another beautiful woman, Mrs. Penn, the wife of Colonel Penn, who is making shoes in a Yankee prison. She had a little son with her, barely two years old, a mere infant. She said to him, *"Faites comme Butler."* The child crossed his eyes and made himself hideous, then laughed and rioted around as if he enjoyed the joke hugely.

Went to Mrs. Davis's. It was sad enough. Fancy having to be always ready to have your servants set your house on fire, being bribed to do it. Such constant robberies, such servants coming and going daily to the Yankees, carrying one's silver, one's other possessions, does not conduce to home happiness.

Saw Hood on his legs once more. He rode off on a fine horse, and

---

[112] The New York Hotel, covering a block front on Broadway at Waverley Place, was a favorite stopping place for Southerners for many years before the war and after it. In comparatively recent times it was torn down and supplanted by a business block.

managed it well, though he is disabled in one hand, too. After all, as the woman said, "He has body enough left to hold his soul." "How plucky of him to ride a gay horse like that." "Oh, a Kentuckian prides himself upon being half horse and half man!" "And the girl who rode beside him. Did you ever see a more brilliant beauty? Three cheers for South Carolina!!"

I imparted a plan of mine to Brewster. I would have a breakfast, a luncheon, a matinee, call it what you please, but I would try and return some of the hospitalities of this most hospitable people. Just think of the dinners, suppers, breakfasts we have been to. People have no variety in war times, but they make up for that lack in exquisite cooking.

"Variety?" said he. "You are hard to please, with terrapin stew, gumbo, fish, oysters in every shape, game, and wine—as good as wine ever is. I do not mention juleps, claret cup, apple toddy, whisky punches and all that. I tell you it is good enough for me. Variety would spoil it. Such hams as these Virginia people cure; such home-made bread—there is no such bread in the world. Call yours a 'cold collation.'" "Yes, I have eggs, butter, hams, game, everything from home; no stint just now; even fruit."

"You ought to do your best. They are so generous and hospitable and so unconscious of any merit, or exceptional credit, in the matter of hospitality." "They are no better than the Columbia people always were to us." So I fired up for my own country.

January 23d.—My luncheon was a female affair exclusively. Mrs. Davis came early and found Annie and Tudie making the chocolate. Lawrence had gone South with my husband; so we had only Molly for cook and parlor-maid. After the company assembled we waited and waited. Those girls were making the final arrangements. I made my way to the door, and as I leaned against it ready to turn the knob, Mrs. Stanard held me like Coleridge's Ancient Mariner, and told how she had been prevented by a violent attack of cramps from running the blockade, and how providential it all was. All this floated by my ear, for I heard Mary Preston's voice raised in high protest on the other side of the door. "Stop!" said she. "Do you mean to take away the whole dish?" "If you eat many more of those fried oysters they will be missed. Heavens! She is running away with a plug, a palpable plug, out of that jelly cake!"

Later in the afternoon, when it was over and I was safe, for all had gone well and Molly had not disgraced herself before the mistresses of those wonderful Virginia cooks, Mrs. Davis and I went out for a walk. Barny Heyward and Dr. Garnett joined us, the latter bringing the welcome news that "Muscoe Russell's wife had come."

January 25th.—The President walked home with me from church (I was to dine with Mrs. Davis). He walked so fast I had no breath to talk; so I was a good listener for once. The truth is I am too much afraid of him to say very much in his presence. We had such a nice dinner. After dinner Hood came for a ride with the President.

Mr. Hunter, of Virginia, walked home with me. He made himself utterly agreeable by dwelling on his friendship and admiration of my husband. He said it was high time Mr. Davis should promote him, and that he had told Mr. Davis his opinion on that subject to-day.

Tuesday, Barny Heyward went with me to the President's reception, and from there to a ball at the McFarlands'. Breckinridge alone of the generals went with us. The others went to a supper given by Mr. Clay, of Alabama.

I had a long talk with Mr. Ould, Mr. Benjamin, and Mr. Hunter. These men speak out their thoughts plainly enough. What they said means "We are rattling down hill, and nobody to put on the brakes." I wore my black velvet, diamonds, and point lace. They are borrowed for all "theatricals," but I wear them whenever they are at home.

February 1st.—Mrs. Davis gave her "Luncheon to Ladies Only" on Saturday. Many more persons there than at any of these luncheons which we have gone to before. Gumbo, ducks and olives, chickens in jelly, oysters, lettuce salad, chocolate cream, jelly cake, claret, champagne, etc., were the good things set before us.

To-day, for a pair of forlorn shoes I have paid $85. Colonel Ives drew my husband's pay for me. I sent Lawrence for it (Mr. Chesnut ordered him back to us; we needed a man servant here). Colonel Ives wrote that he was amazed I should be willing to trust a darky with that great bundle of money, but it came safely. Mr. Petigru says you take your money to market in the market basket, and bring home what you buy in your pocket-book.

February 5th.—When Lawrence handed me my husband's money (six hundred dollars it was) I said: "Now I am pretty sure you do not mean to go to the Yankees, for with that pile of money in your hands you must have known there was your chance." He grinned, but said nothing.

At the President's reception Hood had a perfect ovation. General Preston navigated him through the crowd, handling him as tenderly, on his crutches, as if he were the Princess of Wales's new-born baby that I read of to-day. It is bad for the head of an army to be so helpless. But old Blücher went to Waterloo in a carriage, wearing a bonnet on his head to shade his inflamed eyes—a heroic figure, truly; an old, red-eyed, bonneted woman, apparently, back in a landau. And yet, "Blücher to the rescue!"

Afterward at the Prestons', for we left the President's at an early hour. Major von Borcke was trying to teach them his way of pronouncing his own name, and reciting numerous travesties of it in this country, when Charles threw open the door, saying, "A gentleman has called for Major Bandbox." The Prussian major acknowledged this to be the worst he had heard yet.

Off to the Ives's theatricals. I walked with General Breckinridge. Mrs. Clay's Mrs. Malaprop was beyond our wildest hopes. And she was in such bitter earnest when she pinched Conny Cary's (Lydia Languish's) shoulder and called her "an antricate little huzzy," that Lydia showed she felt it, and next day the shoulder was black and blue. It was not that the actress had a grudge against Conny, but that she was intense.

Even the back of Mrs. Clay's head was eloquent as she walked away. "But," said General Breckinridge, "watch Hood; he has not seen the play before and Bob Acres amazes him." When he caught my eye, General Hood nodded to me and said, "I believe that fellow Acres is a coward." "That's better than the play," whispered Breckinridge, "but it is all good from Sir Anthony down to Fag."

Between the acts Mrs. Clay sent us word to applaud. She wanted encouragement; the audience was too cold. General Breckinridge responded like a man. After that she was fired by thunders of applause, following his lead. Those mighty Kentuckians turned claqueurs, were a host in themselves. Constance Cary not only acted well, but looked perfectly beautiful.

During the farce Mrs. Clay came in with all her feathers, diamonds, and fallals, and took her seat by me. Said General Breckinridge, "What a splendid head of hair you have." "And all my own," said she. Afterward she said, they could not get false hair enough, so they put a pair of black satin boots on top of her head and piled hair over them.

We adjourned from Mrs. Ives's to Mrs. Ould's, where we had the usual excellent Richmond supper. We did not get home until three. It was a clear moonlight night—almost as light as day. As we walked along I said to General Breckinridge, "You have spent a jolly evening." "I do not know," he answered. "I have asked myself more than once to-night, 'Are you the same man who stood gazing down on the faces of the dead on that awful battle-field, The soldiers lying there stare at you with their eyes wide open. Is this the same world? Here and there?'"

Last night, the great Kentucky contingent came in a body. Hood brought Buck in his carriage. She said she "did not like General Hood," and spoke with a wild excitement in those soft blue eyes of hers—or, are they gray or brown? She then gave her reasons in the lowest voice, but loud and distinct enough for him to hear: "Why? He spoke so harshly to Cy, his body-servant, as we got out of the carriage. I saw how he hurt Cy's feelings, and I tried to soothe Cy's mortification."

"You see, Cy nearly caused me to fall by his awkwardness, and I stormed at him," said the General, vastly amused. "I hate a man who speaks roughly to those who dare not resent it," said she. The General did own himself charmed with her sentiments, but seemed to think his wrong-doing all a good joke. He and Cy understand each other.

February 9th.—This party for Johnny was the very nicest I have ever had, and I mean it to be my last. I sent word to the Carys to bring their own men. They came alone, saying, "they did not care for men." "That means a raid on ours," growled Isabella. Mr. Lamar was devoted to Constance Cary. He is a free lance; so that created no heart-burning.

Afterward, when the whole thing was over, and a success, the lights put out, etc., here trooped in the four girls, who stayed all night with me. In dressing-gowns they stirred up a hot fire, relit the gas, and went in for their supper; *réchauffé* was the word, oysters, hot coffee, etc. They kept it up till daylight.

Of course, we slept very late. As they came in to breakfast, I remarked, "The church-bells have been going on like mad. I take it as a rebuke to our breaking the Sabbath. You know Sunday began at twelve o'clock last night." "It sounds to me like fire-bells," somebody said.

Soon the Infant dashed in, done up in soldier's clothes: "The Yankees are upon us!" said he. "Don't you hear the alarm-bells? They have been ringing day and night!" Alex Haskell came; he and Johnny went off to report to Custis Lee and to be enrolled among his "locals," who are always detailed for the defense of the city. But this time the attack on Richmond has proved a false alarm.

A new trouble at the President's house: their trusty man, Robert, broken out with the smallpox.

We went to the Webb ball, and such a pleasant time we had. After a while the P. M. G. (Pet Major-General) took his seat in the comfortable chair next to mine, and declared his determination to hold that position. Mr. Hunter and Mr. Benjamin essayed to dislodge him. Mrs. Stanard said: "Take him in the flirtation room; there he will soon be captured and led away," but I did not know where that room was situated. Besides, my bold Texan made a most unexpected sally: "I will not go, and I will prevent her from going with any of you." Supper was near at hand, and Mr. Mallory said: "Ask him if the varioloid is not at his house. I know it is." I started as if I were shot, and I took Mr. Clay's arm and went in to supper, leaving the P. M. G. to the girls. Venison and everything nice.

February 12th.—John Chesnut had a basket of champagne carried to my house, oysters, partridges, and other good things, for a supper after the reception. He is going back to the army to-morrow.

James Chesnut arrived on Wednesday. He has been giving Buck his opinion of one of her performances last night. She was here, and the General's carriage drove up, bringing some of our girls. They told her he could not come up and he begged she would go down there for a moment. She flew down, and stood ten minutes in that snow, Cy holding the carriage-door open. "But, Colonel Chesnut, there was no harm. I was not there ten minutes. I could not get in the carriage because I did not mean to stay one minute. He did not hold my hands—that is, not half the time—Oh, you saw!—well, he did kiss my hands. Where is the harm of that?" All men worship Buck. How can they help it, she is so lovely.

Lawrence has gone back ignominiously to South Carolina. At breakfast already in some inscrutable way he had become intoxicated; he was told to move a chair, and he raised it high over his head, smashing Mrs. Grundy's chandelier. My husband said : "Mary, do tell Lawrence to go home; I am too angry to speak to him." So Lawrence went without another word. He will soon be back, and when he comes will say, "Shoo!! I knew Mars Jeems could not do without me." And indeed he can not.

Buck, reading my journal, opened her beautiful eyes in amazement and said: "So little do people know themselves! See what you say of me!" I replied: "The girls heard him say to you, 'Oh, you are so childish and so sweet!' Now, Buck, you know you are not childish. You have an abundance of strong common sense. Don't let men adore you so—if you can help it. You are so unhappy about men who care for you, when they are killed."

Isabella says that war leads to love-making. She says these soldiers do more courting here in a day than they would do at home, without a war, in ten years.

In the pauses of conversation, we hear, "She is the noblest woman God ever made!" "Goodness!" exclaims Isabella. "Which one?" The amount of courting we hear in these small rooms. Men have to go to the front, and they say their say desperately. I am beginning to know all about it. The girls tell me. And I overhear—I can not help it. But this style is unique, is it not? "Since I saw you—last year—standing by the turnpike gate, you know-my battle-cry has been: 'God, my country, and you!'" So many are lame. Major Venable says: "It is not 'the devil on two sticks,' now; the farce is 'Cupid on Crutches.'"

General Breckinridge's voice broke in: "They are my cousins. So I determined to kiss them good-by. Good-by nowadays is the very devil, it means forever, in all probability, you know; all the odds against us. So I advanced to the charge soberly, discreetly, and in the fear of the Lord. The girls stood in a row—four of the very prettiest I ever saw." Sam, with his eyes glued to the floor, cried: "You were afraid—you backed out." "But I did nothing of the kind. I kissed every one of them honestly, heartily."

February 13th.—My husband is writing out some resolutions for the Congress. He is very busy, too, trying to get some poor fellows reprieved. He says they are good soldiers but got into a scrape. Buck came in. She had on her last winter's English hat, with the pheasant's wing. Just then Hood entered most unexpectedly. Said the blunt soldier to the girl: "You look mighty pretty in that hat; you wore it at the turnpike gate, where I surrendered at first sight." She nodded and smiled, and flew down the steps after Mr. Chesnut, looking back to say that she meant to walk with him as far as the Executive Office.

The General walked to the window and watched until the flutter of her garment was gone. He said: "The President was finding fault with some of his officers in command, and I said: 'Mr. President, why don't you come and lead us yourself; I would follow you to the death.'" "Actually, if you stay here in Richmond much longer you will grow to be a courtier. And you came a rough Texan."

Mrs. Davis and General McQueen came. He tells me Muscoe Garnett is dead. Then the best and the cleverest Virginian I know is gone. He was the most scholarly man they had, and his character was higher than his requirements.

To-day a terrible onslaught was made upon the President for nepotism. Burton Harrison's and John Taylor Wood's letters denying the charge that the President's cotton was unburned, or that he left it to be bought by the Yankees, have enraged the opposition. How much these people in the President's family have to bear! I have never felt so indignant.

February 16th.—Saw in Mrs. Howell's room the little negro Mrs. Davis rescued yesterday from his brutal negro guardian. The child is an orphan. He was dressed up in little Joe's clothes and happy as a lord. He was very anxious to show me his wounds and bruises, but I fled. There are some things in life too sickening, and cruelty is one of them.

Somebody said: "People who knew General Hood before the war said there was nothing in him. As for losing his property by the war, some say he never had any, and that West Point is a pauper's school, after all. He has only military glory, and that he has gained since the war began."

"Now," said Burton Harrison, "only military glory! I like that! The glory and the fame he has gained during the war—that is Hood. What was Napoleon before Toulon? Hood has the impassive dignity of an Indian chief. He has always a little court around him of devoted friends. Wigfall, himself, has said he could not get within Hood's lines."

February 17th.—Found everything in Main Street twenty per cent dearer. They say it is due to the new currency bill.

I asked my husband: "Is General Johnston ordered to reenforce Polk, They said he did not understand the order."

"After five days' delay," he replied. "They say Sherman is marching to Mobile.[113] When they once get inside of our armies what is

---

[113] General Polk, commanding about 24,000 men scattered throughout Mississippi and Alabama, found it impossible to check the advance of Sherman at the head of some 40,000, and moved from Meridian south to protect Mobile. February 16, 1864, Sherman took possession of Meridian.

to molest them, unless it be women with broomsticks?" General Johnston writes that "the Governor of Georgia refuses him provisions and the use of his roads." The Governor of Georgia writes: "The roads are open to him and in capital condition. I have furnished him abundantly with provisions from time to time, as he desired them." I suppose both of these letters are placed away side by side in our archives.

February 20th.—Mrs. Preston was offended by the story of Buck's performance at the Ive's. General Breckinridge told her "it was the most beautifully unconscious act he ever saw." The General was leaning against the wall, Buck standing guard by him "on her two feet." The crowd surged that way, and she held out her arm to protect him from the rush. After they had all passed she handed him his crutches, and they, too, moved slowly away. Mrs. Davis said: "Any woman in Richmond would have done the same joyfully, but few could do it so gracefully. Buck is made so conspicuous by her beauty, whatever she does can not fail to attract attention."

Johnny stayed at home only one day; then went to his plantation, got several thousand Confederate dollars, and in the afternoon drove out with Mrs. K—. At the Bee Store he spent a thousand of his money; bought us gloves and linen. Well, one can do without gloves, but linen is next to life itself.

Yesterday the President walked home from church with me. He said he was so glad to see my husband at church; had never seen him there before remarked on how well he looked, etc. I replied that he looked so well "because you have never before seen him in the part of 'the right man in the right place.'" My husband has no fancy for being planted in pews, but he is utterly Christian in his creed.

February 23d.—At the President's, where General Lee breakfasted, a man named Phelan told General Lee all he ought to do; planned a campaign for him. General Lee smiled blandly the while, though he did permit himself a mild sneer at the wise civilians in Congress who refrained from trying the battle-field in person, but from afar dictated the movements of armies. My husband said that, to his amazement, General Lee came into his room at the Executive Office to "pay his respects and have a talk." "Dear me! Goodness gracious!" said I. "That was a compliment from the head of the army, the very first man in the world, we Confederates think."

February 24th.—Friends came to make taffy and stayed the livelong day. They played cards. One man, a soldier, had only two teeth left in front and they lapped across each other. On account of the condition of his mouth, he had maintained a dignified sobriety of aspect, though he told some funny stories. Finally a story was too much for him, and he grinned from ear to ear. Maggie gazed, and then called out as the negro fiddlers call out dancing figures, "Forward two and cross over!" Fancy our faces. The hero of the two teeth, relapsing into a decorous arrangement of mouth, said: "Cavalry are the eyes of an army; they bring the news; the artillery are the boys to make a noise; but the infantry do the fighting, and a general or so gets all the glory."

February 26th.—We went to see Mrs. Breckinridge, who is here with her husband. Then we paid our respects to Mrs. Lee. Her room was like an industrial school: everybody so busy. Her daughters were all there plying their needles, with several other ladies. Mrs. Lee showed us a beautiful sword, recently sent to the General by some Marylanders, now in Paris. On the blade was engraved, "*Aide toi et Dieu t'aidera.*" When we came out someone said, "Did you see how the Lees spend their time? What a rebuke to the taffy parties!"

Another maimed hero is engaged to be married. Sally Hampton has accepted John Haskell. There is a story that he reported for duty after his arm was shot off; suppose in the fury of the battle he did not feel the pain.

General Breckinridge once asked, "What's the name of the fellow who has gone to Europe for Hood's leg?" "Dr. Darby." "Suppose it is shipwrecked?" "No matter; half a dozen are ordered." Mrs. Preston raised her hands: "No wonder the General says they talk of him as if he were a centipede; his leg is in everybody's mouth."

March 3d.—Hetty, the handsome, and Constance, the witty, came; the former too prudish to read Lost and Saved, by Mrs. Norton, after she had heard the plot. Conny was making a bonnet for me. Just as she was leaving the house, her friendly labors over, my husband entered, and quickly ordered his horse. "It is so near dinner," I began. "But I am going with the President. I am on duty. He goes to inspect the fortifications. The enemy, once more, are within a few miles of Richmond." Then we prepared a luncheon for him. Constance Cary remained with me.

After she left I sat down to Romola, and I was absorbed in it. How hardened we grow to war and war's alarms! The enemy's cannon or our own are thundering in my ears, and I was dreadfully afraid some infatuated and frightened friend would come in to cheer, to comfort, and interrupt me. Am I the same poor soul who fell on her knees and prayed, and wept, and fainted, as the first gun boomed from Fort Sumter? Once more we have repulsed the enemy. But it is humiliating, indeed, that he can come and threaten us at our very gates whenever he so pleases. If a forlorn negro had not led them astray (and they hanged him for it) on Tuesday night, unmolested, they would have walked into Richmond. Surely there is horrid neglect or mismanagement somewhere.

March 4th.—The enemy has been reenforced and is on us again. Met Wade Hampton, who told me my husband was to join him with some volunteer troops; so I hurried home. Such a cavalcade rode up to luncheon! Captain Smith Lee and Preston Hampton, the handsomest, the oldest and the youngest of the party. This was at the Prestons'. Smith Lee walked home with me; alarm-bells ringing; horsemen galloping; wagons rattling. Dr. H. stopped us to say "Beast" Butler was on us with sixteen thousand men. How scared the Doctor looked! And, after all, it was only a notice to the militia to turn out and drill.

March 5th.—Tom Fergurson walked home with me. He told me of Colonel Dahlgren's[114] death and the horrid memoranda found in his pocket. He came with secret orders to destroy this devoted city, hang the President and his Cabinet, and burn the town! Fitzhugh Lee was proud that the Ninth Virginia captured him.

Found Mrs. Semmes covering her lettuces and radishes as calmly as if Yankee raiders were a myth. While "Beast" Butler holds Fortress Monroe he will make things lively for us. On the alert must we be now.

March 7th.—Shopping, and paid $30 for a pair of gloves; $50 for a pair of slippers; $24 for six spools of thread; $32 for five miserable, shabby little pocket handkerchiefs. When I came home found Mrs. Webb. At her hospital there was a man who had been taken prisoner by Dahlgren's party. He saw the negro hanged who had misled them, unintentionally, in all probability. He saw Dahlgren give a part of his bridle to hang him. Details are melancholy, as Emerson says. This Dahlgren had also lost a leg.

Constance Cary, in words too fine for the occasion, described the homely scene at my house; how I prepared sandwiches for my husband; and broke, with trembling hand, the last bottle of anything to drink in the house, a bottle I destined to go with the sandwiches. She called it a Hector and Andromache performance.

March 8th.—Mrs. Preston's story. As we walked home, she told me she had just been to see a lady she had known more than twenty years before. She had met her in this wise: One of the chambermaids of the St. Charles Hotel (New Orleans) told Mrs. Preston's nurse it was when Mary Preston was a baby—that up among the servants in the garret there was a sick lady and her children. The maid was sure she was a lady, and thought she was hiding from somebody. Mrs. Preston went up, knew the lady, had her brought down into comfortable rooms, and nursed her until she recovered from her delirium and fever. She had run away, indeed, and was hiding herself and her children from a worthless husband. Now, she has one son in a Yankee prison, one mortally wounded, and the last of them dying there under her eyes of

---

[114] Colonel Ulric Dahlgren was a son of the noted Admiral, John H. Dahlgren, who, in July, 1863, had been placed in command of the South Atlantic Blockading Squadron and conducted the naval operations against Charleston, between July 10 and September 7, 1863. Colonel Dahlgren distinguished himself at Fredericksburg, Chancellorsville and Gettysburg. The raid in which he lost his life on March 4, 1864, was planned by himself and General Kilpatrick.

consumption. This last had married here in Richmond, not wisely, and too soon, for he was a mere boy; his pay as a private was eleven dollars a month, and his wife's family charged him three hundred dollars a month for her board; so he had to work double tides, do odd jobs by night and by day, and it killed him by exposure to cold in this bitter climate to which his constitution was unadapted.

They had been in Vicksburg during the siege, and during the bombardment sought refuge in a cave. The roar of the cannon ceasing, they came out gladly for a breath of fresh air. At the moment when they emerged, a bomb burst there, among them, so to speak, struck the son already wounded, and smashed off the arm of a beautiful little grandchild not three years old. There was this poor little girl with her touchingly lovely face, and her arm gone. This mutilated little martyr, Mrs. Preston said, was really to her the crowning touch of the woman's affliction. Mrs. Preston put up her hand, "Her baby face haunts me."

March 11th.—Letters from home, including one from my husband's father, now over ninety, written with his own hand, and certainly his own mind still. I quote: "Bad times; worse coming. Starvation stares me in the face. Neither John's nor James's overseer will sell me any corn." Now, what has the government to do with the fact that on all his plantations he made corn enough to last for the whole year, and by the end of January his negroes had stolen it all, Poor old man, he has fallen on evil days, after a long life of ease and prosperity.

To-day, I read The Blithedale Romance. Blithedale leaves such an unpleasant impression. I like pleasant, kindly stories, now that we are so harrowed by real life. Tragedy is for our hours of ease.

March 12th.—An active campaign has begun everywhere. Kilpatrick still threatens us. Bragg has organized his fifteen hundred of cavalry to protect Richmond. Why can't my husband be made colonel of that? It is a new regiment. No; he must be made a general!

"Now," says Mary Preston, "Doctor Darby is at the mercy of both Yankees and the rolling sea, and I am anxious enough; but, instead of taking my bed and worrying mamma, I am taking stock of our worldly goods and trying to arrange the wedding paraphernalia for two girls."

There is love-making and love-making in this world. What a time the sweethearts of that wretch, young Shakespeare, must have had. What experiences of life's delights must have been his before he evolved the Romeo and Juliet business from his own internal consciousness; also that delicious Beatrice and Rosalind. The poor creature that he left his second best bedstead to came in second best all the time, no doubt; and she hardly deserved more. Fancy people wondering that Shakespeare and his kind leave no progeny like themselves! Shakespeare's children would have been half his only; the other half only the second best bedstead's. What would you expect of that commingling of materials? Goethe used his lady-loves as school-books are used: he studied them from cover to cover, got all that could be got of self-culture and knowledge of human nature from the study of them, and then threw them aside as if of no further account in his life.

Byron never could forget Lord Byron, poet and peer, and *mauvais sujet*, and he must have been a trying lover; like talking to a man looking in the glass at himself. Lady Byron was just as much taken up with herself. So, they struck each other, and bounded apart.

[Since I wrote this, Mrs. Stowe has taken Byron in hand. But I know a story which might have annoyed my lord more than her and Lady Byron's imagination of wickedness—for he posed a fiend, but was tender and kind. A clerk in a country store asked my sister to lend him a book, he "wanted something to read; the days were so long." "What style of book would you prefer?" she said. "Poetry." "Any particular poet?" "*Brown*. I hear him much spoken of." "Brown*ing*?" "No; Brown—short—that is what they call him." "Byron, you mean." "No, I mean the poet, Brown."]

"Oh, you wish you had lived in the time of the Shakespeare creature!" He knew all the forms and phases of true love. Straight to one's heart he goes in tragedy or comedy. He never misses fire. He has been there, in slang phrase. No doubt the man's bare presence gave pleasure to the female world; he saw women at their best, and he effaced himself. He told no tales of his own life. Compare with him old, sad, solemn, sublime, sneering, snarling, fault-finding Milton, a man whose family doubtless found "*les absences délicieuses*." That phrase describes a type of man at a touch; it took a Frenchwoman to do it.

"But there is an Italian picture of Milton, taken in his youth, and he was as beautiful as an angel." "No doubt. But love flies before everlasting posing and preaching—the deadly requirement of a man always to be looked up to-a domestic tyrant, grim, formal, and awfully learned. Milton was only a mere man, for he could not do without women. When he tired out the first poor thing, who did not fall down, worship, and obey him, and see God in him, and she ran away, he immediately arranged his creed so that he could take another wife; for wife he must have, a la Mohammedan creed. The deer-stealer never once thought of justifying theft simply because he loved venison and could not come by it lawfully. Shakespeare was a better man, or, may I say, a purer soul, than self-upholding, Calvinistic, Puritanic, king-killing Milton. There is no muddling of right and wrong in Shakespeare, and no pharisaical stuff of any sort."

Then George Deas joined us, fresh from Mobile, where he left peace and plenty. He went to sixteen weddings and twenty-seven tea-parties. For breakfast he had everything nice. Lily told of what she had seen the day before at the Spottswood.. She was in the small parlor, waiting for someone, and in the large drawing-room sat Hood, solitary, sad, with crutches by his chair. He could not see them. Mrs. Buckner came in and her little girl who, when she spied Hood, bounded into the next room, and sprang into his lap. Hood smoothed her little dress down and held her close to him. She clung around his neck for a while, and then, seizing him by the beard, kissed him to an illimitable extent. "Prettiest picture I ever saw," said Lily. "The soldier and the child."

John R. Thompson sent me a New York Herald only three days old. It is down on Kilpatrick for his miserable failure before Richmond. Also it acknowledges a defeat before Charleston and a victory for us in Florida.

General Grant is charmed with Sherman's successful movements; says he has destroyed millions upon millions of our property in Mississippi. I hope that may not be true, and that Sherman may fail as Kilpatrick did. Now, if we still had Stonewall or Albert Sidney Johnston where Joe Johnston and Polk are, I would not give a fig for Sherman's chances. The Yankees say that at last they have scared up a man who succeeds, and they expect him to remedy all that has gone wrong. So they have made their brutal Suwarrow, Grant, lieutenant-general.

Doctor—at the Prestons' proposed to show me a man who was not an F. F. V. Until we came here, we had never heard of our social position. We do not know how to be rude to people who call. To talk of social position seems vulgar. Down our way, that sort of thing was settled one way or another beyond a peradventure, like the earth and the sky. We never gave it a thought. We talked to whom, we pleased, and if they were not *comme il faut*, we were ever so much more polite to the poor things. No reflection on Virginia. Everybody comes to Richmond.

Somebody counted fourteen generals in church to-day, and suggested that less piety and more drilling of commands would suit the times better. There were Lee, Longstreet, Morgan, Hoke, Clingman, Whiting, Pegram, Elzey, Gordon, and Bragg. Now, since Dahlgren failed to carry out his orders, the Yankees disown them, disavowing all. He was not sent here to murder us all, to hang the President, and burn the town. There is the note-book, however, at the Executive Office, with orders to hang and burn.

March 15th.—Old Mrs. Chesnut is dead. A saint is gone and James Chesnut is broken-hearted. He adored his mother. I gave $375 for my mourning, which consists of a black alpaca dress and a crepe veil. With bonnet, gloves, and all it came to $500. Before the blockade such things as I have would not have been thought fit for a chamber-maid.

Everybody is in trouble. Mrs. Davis says paper money has depreciated so much in value that they can not live within their income; so they are going to dispense with their carriage and horses.

March 18th.—Went out to sell some of my colored dresses. What a scene it was—such piles of rubbish, and mixed up with it, such splendid Parisian silks and satins. A mulatto woman kept the shop under a roof in an out-of- the-way old house. The *ci-devant* rich white women sell to, and the negroes buy of, this woman.

After some whispering among us Buck said: "Sally is going to marry a man who has lost an arm, and she is proud of it. The cause glorifies such wounds." Annie said meekly, "I fear it will be my fate to marry one who has lost his head." "Tudy has her eyes on one who has lost an eye. What a glorious assortment of noble martyrs and heroes!" "The bitterness of this kind of talk is appalling."

General Lee had tears in his eyes when he spoke of his daughter-in-law just dead—that lovely little Charlotte Wickham, Mrs. Roony Lee. Roony Lee says "Beast" Butler was very kind to him while he was a prisoner. The "Beast" has sent him back his war-horse. The Lees are men enough to speak the truth of friend or enemy, fearing not the consequences.

March 19th.—A new experience: Molly and Lawrence have both gone home, and I am to be left for the first time in my life wholly at the mercy of hired servants. Mr. Chesnut, being in such deep mourning for his mother, we see no company. I have a maid of all work.

Tudy came with an account of yesterday's trip to Petersburg. Constance Cary raved of the golden ripples in Tudy's hair. Tudy vanished in a halo of glory, and Constance Cary gave me an account of a wedding, as it was given to her by Major von Borcke. The bridesmaids were dressed in black, the bride in Confederate gray, homespun. She had worn the dress all winter, but it had been washed and turned for the wedding. The female critics pronounced it "flabby-dabby." They also said her collar was only "net," and she wore a cameo breastpin. Her bonnet was self-made.

March 24th.—Yesterday, we went to the Capitol grounds to see our returned prisoners. We walked slowly up and down until Jeff Davis was called upon to speak. There I stood, almost touching the bayonets when he left me. I looked straight into the prisoners' faces, poor fellows. They cheered with all their might, and I wept for sympathy, and enthusiasm. I was very deeply moved. These men were so forlorn, so dried up, and shrunken, with such a strange look in some of their eyes; others so restless and wild-looking; others again placidly vacant, as if they had been dead to the world for years. A poor woman was too much for me. She was searching for her son. He had been expected back. She said he was taken prisoner at Gettysburg. She kept going in and out among them with a basket of provisions she had brought for him to eat. It was too pitiful. She was utterly unconscious of the crowd. The anxious dread, expectation, hurry, and hope which led her on showed in her face.

A sister of Mrs. Lincoln is here. She brings the freshest scandals from Yankeeland. She says she rode with Lovejoy. A friend of hers commands a black regiment. Two Southern horrors—a black regiment and Lovejoy.

March 31st.—Met Preston Hampton. Constance Cary was with me. She showed her regard for him by taking his overcoat and leaving him in a drenching rain. What boyish nonsense he talked; said he was in love with Miss Dabney now, that his love was so hot within him that he was waterproof, the rain sizzed and smoked off. It did not so much as dampen his ardor or his clothes.

April 1st.—Mrs. Davis is utterly depressed. She said the fall of Richmond must come; she would send her children to me and Mrs. Preston. We begged her to come to us also. My husband is as depressed as I ever knew him to be. He has felt the death of that angel mother of his keenly, and now he takes his country's woes to heart.

April 11th.—Drove with Mrs. Davis and all her infant family; wonderfully clever and precocious children, with unbroken wills. At one time there was a sudden uprising of the nursery contingent. They laughed, fought, and screamed. Bedlam broke loose. Mrs. Davis scolded, laughed, and cried. She asked me if my husband would speak to the President about the plan in South Carolina, which everybody said suited him. "No, Mrs. Davis," said I. "That is what I told Mr. Davis," said she. "Colonel Chesnut rides so high a horse. Now Browne is so much more practical. He goes forth to be general of conscripts in Georgia. His wife will stay at the Cobbs's."

Mrs. Ould gave me a luncheon on Saturday. I felt that this was my last sad farewell to Richmond and the people there I love so well. Mrs. Davis sent her carriage for me, and we went to the Oulds' together. Such good things were served—oranges, guava jelly, etc. The Examiner says Mr. Ould, when he goes to Fortress Monroe, replenishes his larder; why not? The Examiner has taken another fling at the President, as, "haughty and austere with his friends, affable, kind, subservient to his enemies." I wonder if the Yankees would indorse that certificate. Both sides abuse him. He can not please anybody, it seems. No doubt he is right.

My husband is now brigadier-general and is sent to South Carolina to organize and take command of the reserve troops. C. C. Clay and L. Q. C. Lamar are both spoken of to fill the vacancy made among Mr. Davis's aides by this promotion.

To-day, Captain Smith Lee spent the morning here and gave a review of past Washington gossip. I am having such a busy, happy life, with so many friends, and my friends are so clever, so charming. But the change to that weary, dreary Camden! Mary Preston said: "I do think Mrs. Chesnut deserves to be canonized; she agrees to go back to Camden." The Prestons gave me a farewell dinner; my twenty-fourth wedding day, and the very pleasantest day I have spent in Richmond.

Maria Lewis was sitting with us on Mrs. Huger's steps, and Smith Lee was lauding Virginia people as usual. As Lee would say, there "hove in sight" Frank Parker, riding one of the finest of General Bragg's horses; by his side Buck on Fairfax, the most beautiful horse in Richmond, his brown coat looking like satin, his proud neck arched, moving slowly, gracefully, calmly, no fidgets, aristocratic in his bearing to the tips of his bridle-reins. There sat Buck tall and fair, managing her horse with infinite ease, her English riding-habit showing plainly the exquisite proportions of her figure. "Supremely lovely," said Smith Lee. "Look at them both," said I proudly; "can you match those two in Virginia?" "Three cheers for South Carolina!" was the answer of Lee, the gallant Virginia sailor.

CHAPTER XVII. CAMDEN, S. C.

May 8, 1864—*June* 1, 1864

Camden, S. C., *May 8, 1864.*—My friends crowded around me so in those last days in Richmond, I forgot the affairs of this nation utterly; though I did show faith in my Confederate country by buying poor Bones's (my English maid's) Confederate bonds. I gave her gold thimbles, bracelets; whatever was gold and would sell in New York or London, I gave.

My friends in Richmond grieved that I had to leave them—not half so much, however, as I did that I must come away. Those last weeks were so pleasant. No battle, no murder, no sudden death, all went merry as a marriage bell. Clever, cordial, kind, brave friends rallied around me.

Maggie Howell and I went down the river to see an exchange of prisoners. Our party were the Lees, Mallorys, Mrs. Buck Allan, Mrs. Ould. We picked up Judge Ould and Buck Allan at Curl's Neck. I had seen no genuine Yankees before; prisoners, well or wounded, had been German, Scotch, or Irish. Among our men coming ashore was an officer, who had charge of some letters for a friend of mine whose *fiancé* had died; I gave him her address. One other man showed me some wonderfully ingenious things he had made while a prisoner. One said they gave him rations for a week; he always devoured them in three days, he could not help it; and then he had to bear the inevitable agony of those four remaining days! Many were wounded, some were maimed for life. They were very cheerful. We had supper—or some nondescript meal—with ice-cream on board. The band played Home, Sweet Home.

One man tapped another on the shoulder: "Well, how do you feel, old fellow?" "Never was so near crying in my life—for very comfort."

Governor Cummings, a Georgian, late Governor of Utah, was

among the returned prisoners. He had been in prison two years. His wife was with him. He was a striking-looking person, huge in size, and with snow-white hair, fat as a prize ox, with no sign of Yankee barbarity or starvation about him.

That evening, as we walked up to Mrs. Davis's carriage, which was waiting for us at the landing, Dr. Garnett with Maggie Howell, Major Hall with me, suddenly I heard her scream, and some one stepped back in the dark and said in a whisper. "Little Joe! he has killed himself!" I felt reeling, faint, bewildered. A chattering woman clutched my arm: "Mrs. Davis's son? Impossible. Whom did you say? Was he an interesting child? How old was he?" The shock was terrible, and unnerved as I was I cried, "For God's sake take her away!"

Then Maggie and I drove two long miles in silence except for Maggie's hysterical sobs. She was wild with terror. The news was broken to her in that abrupt way at the carriage door so that at first she thought it had all happened there, and that poor little Joe was in the carriage.

Mr. Burton Harrison met us at the door of the Executive Mansion. Mrs. Semmes and Mrs. Barksdale were there, too. Every window and door of the house seemed wide open, and the wind was blowing the curtains. It was lighted, even in the third story. As I sat in the drawing-room, I could hear the tramp of Mr. Davis's step as he walked up and down the room above. Not another sound. The whole house as silent as death. It was then twelve o'clock; so I went home and waked General Chesnut, who had gone to bed. We went immediately back to the President's, found Mrs. Semmes still there, but saw no one but her. We thought some friends of the family ought to be in the house.

Mrs. Semmes said when she got there that little Jeff was kneeling down by his brother, and he called out to her in great distress: "Mrs. Semmes, I have said all the prayers I know how, but God will not wake Joe."

Poor little Joe, the good child of the family, was so gentle and affectionate. He used to run in to say his prayers at his father's knee. Now he was laid out somewhere above us, crushed and killed. Mrs. Semmes, describing the accident, said he fell from the high north piazza upon a brick pavement. Before I left the house I saw him lying there, white and beautiful as an angel, covered with flowers; Catherine, his nurse, flat on the floor by his side, was weeping and wailing as only an Irishwoman can.

Immense crowds came to the funeral, everybody sympathetic, but some shoving and pushing rudely. There were thousands of children, and each child had a green bough or a bunch of flowers to throw on little Joe's grave, which was already a mass of white flowers, crosses, and evergreens. The morning I came away from Mrs. Davis's, early as it was, I met a little child with a handful of snow drops. "Put these on little Joe," she said; "I knew him so well," and then she turned and fled without another word. I did not know who she was then or now.

As I walked home I met Mr. Reagan, then Wade Hampton. But I could see nothing but little Joe and his brokenhearted mother. And Mr. Davis's step still sounded in my ears as he walked that floor the livelong night.

General Lee was to have a grand review the very day we left Richmond. Great numbers of people were to go up by rail to see it. Miss Turner McFarland writes: "They did go, but they came back faster than they went. They found the army drawn up in battle array." Many of the brave and gay spirits that we saw so lately have taken flight, the only flight they know, and their bodies are left dead upon the battlefield. Poor old Edward Johnston is wounded again, and a prisoner. Jones's brigade broke first; he was wounded the day before.

At Wilmington we met General Whiting. He sent us to the station in his carriage, and bestowed upon us a bottle of brandy, which had run the blockade. They say Beauregard has taken his sword from Whiting. Never! I will not believe it. At the capture of Fort Sumter they said Whiting was the brains, Beauregard only the hand. Lucifer, son of the morning! How art thou fallen! That they should even say such a thing!

My husband and Mr. Covey got out at Florence to procure for Mrs. Miles a cup of coffee. They were slow about it and they got left. I did not mind this so very much, for I remembered that we were to remain all day at Kingsville, and that my husband could overtake me there by the next train. My maid belonged to the Prestons. She was only traveling home with me, and would go straight on to Columbia. So without fear I stepped off at Kingsville. My old Confederate silk, like most Confederate dresses, had seen better days, and I noticed that, like Oliver Wendell Holmes's famous "one-hoss stray," it had gone to pieces suddenly, and all over. It was literally in strips. I became painfully aware of my forlorn aspect when I asked the telegraph man the way to the hotel, and he was by no means respectful to me. I was, indeed, alone—an old and not too respectable-looking woman. It was my first appearance in the character, and I laughed aloud.

A very haughty and highly painted dame greeted me at the hotel. "No room," said she. "Who are you?" I gave my name. "Try something else," said she. "Mrs. Chesnut don't travel round by herself with no servants and no nothing." I looked down. There I was, dirty, tired, tattered, and torn. "Where do you come from?" said she.

"My home is in Camden." "Come, now, I know everybody in Camden." I sat down meekly on a bench in the piazza, that was free to all wayfarers.

"Which Mrs. Chesnut?" said she (sharply). "I know both." "I am now the only one. And now what is the matter with you? Do you take me for a spy? I know you perfectly well. I went to school with you at

Miss Henrietta de Leon's, and my name was Mary Miller." "The Lord sakes alive! and to think you are her! Now I see. Dear! dear me! Heaven sakes, woman, but you are broke!" "And tore," I added, holding up my dress. "But I had had no idea it was so difficult to effect an entry into a railroad wayside hotel." I picked up a long strip of my old black dress, torn off by a man's spur as I passed him getting off the train.

It is sad enough at Mulberry without old Mrs. Chesnut, who was the good genius of the place. It is so lovely here in spring. The giants of the forest—the primeval oaks, water-oaks, live-oaks, willow-oaks, such as I have not seen since I left here-with opopanax, violets, roses, and yellow jessamine, the air is laden with perfume. Araby the Blest was never sweeter.

Inside, are creature comforts of all kinds—green peas, strawberries, asparagus, spring lamb, spring chicken, fresh eggs, rich, yellow butter, clean white linen for one's beds, dazzling white damask for one's table. It is such a contrast to Richmond, where I wish I were.

Fighting is going on. Hampton is frantic, for his laggard new regiments fall in slowly; no fault of the soldiers; they are as disgusted as he is. Bragg, Bragg, the head of the War Office, can not organize in time.

John Boykin has died in a Yankee prison. He had on a heavy flannel shirt when lying in an open platform car on the way to a cold prison on the lakes. A Federal soldier wanted John's shirt. Prisoners have no rights; so John had to strip off and hand his shirt to him. That caused his death. In two days he was dead of pneumonia—may be frozen to death. One man said: "They are taking us there to freeze." But then their men will find our hot sun in August and July as deadly as our men find their cold Decembers. Their snow and ice finish our prisoners at a rapid rate, they say. Napoleon's soldiers found out all that in the Russian campaign.

Have brought my houseless, homeless friends, refugees here, to luxuriate in Mulberry's plenty. I can but remember the lavish kindness of the Virginia people when I was there and in a similar condition. The Virginia people do the rarest acts of hospitality and never seem to know it is not in the ordinary course of events.

The President's man, Stephen, bringing his master's Arabian to Mulberry for safe-keeping, said: "Why, Missis, your niggers down here are well off. I call this Mulberry place heaven, with plenty to eat, little to do, warm house to sleep in, a good church."

John L. Miller, my cousin, has been killed at the head of his regiment. The blows now fall so fast on our heads they are bewildering. The Secretary of War authorizes General Chesnut to reorganize the men who have been hitherto detailed for special duty, and also those who have been exempt. He says General Chesnut originated the plan and organized the corps of clerks which saved Richmond in the Dahlgren raid.

May 27th.—In all this beautiful sunshine, in the stillness and shade of these long hours on this piazza, all comes back to me about little Joe; it haunts me—that scene in Richmond where all seemed confusion, madness, a bad dream! Here I see that funeral procession as it wound among those tall white monuments, up that hillside, the James River tumbling about below over rocks and around islands; the dominant figure, that poor, old, gray-haired man, standing bareheaded, straight as an arrow, clear against the sky by the open grave of his son. She, the bereft mother, stood back, in her heavy black wrappings, and her tall figure drooped. The flowers, the children, the procession as it moved, comes and goes, but those two dark, sorrow-stricken figures stand; they are before me now!

That night, with no sound but the heavy tramp of his feet overhead, the curtains flapping in the wind, the gas flaring, I was numb, stupid, half-dead with grief and terror. Then came Catherine's Irish howl. Cheap, was that. Where was she when it all happened? Her place was to have been with the child. Who saw him fall? Whom will they kill next of that devoted household?

Read to-day the list of killed and wounded.[115] One long column was not enough for South Carolina's dead. I see Mr. Federal Secretary Stanton says he can reenforce Suwarrow Grant at his leisure whenever he calls for more. He has just sent him 25,000 veterans. Old Lincoln says, in his quaint backwoods way, "Keep a-peggin'." Now we can only peg out. What have we left of men, etc., to meet these "reenforcements as often as reenforcements are called for?" Our fighting men have all gone to the front; only old men and little boys are at home now.

It is impossible to sleep here, because it is so solemn and still. The moonlight shines in my window sad and white, and the soft south wind, literally comes over a bank of violets, lilacs, roses, with orange-blossoms and magnolia flowers.

Mrs. Chesnut was only a year younger than her husband. He is ninety-two or three. She was deaf; but he retains his senses wonderfully for his great age. I have always been an early riser. Formerly I often saw him sauntering slowly down the broad passage from his room to hers, in a flowing flannel dressing-gown when it was winter In the spring he was apt to be in shirt-sleeves, with suspenders hanging down his back. He had always a large hair-brush in his hand.

He would take his stand on the rug before the fire in her room,

---

[115] During the month of May, 1864, important battles had been fought in Virginia, including that of the Wilderness on May 6th-7th, and the series later in that month around Spottsylvania Court House.

brushing scant locks which were fleecy white. Her maid would be doing hers, which were dead-leaf brown, not a white hair in her head. He had the voice of a stentor, and there he stood roaring his morning compliments. The people who occupied the room above said he fairly shook the window glasses. This pleasant morning greeting ceremony was never omitted.

Her voice was "soft and low" (the oft-quoted). Philadelphia seems to have lost the art of sending forth such voices now. Mrs. Binney, old Mrs. Chesnut's sister, came among us with the same softly modulated, womanly, musical voice. Her clever and beautiful daughters were *criard.* Judge Han said: "Philadelphia women scream like macaws." This morning as I passed Mrs. Chesnut's room, the door stood wide open, and I heard a pitiful sound. The old man was kneeling by her empty bedside sobbing bitterly. I fled down the middle walk, anywhere out of reach of what was never meant for me to hear.

June 1st.—We have been to Bloomsbury again and hear that William Kirkland has been wounded. A scene occurred then, Mary weeping bitterly and Aunt B. frantic as to Tanny's danger. I proposed to make arrangements for Mary to go on at once. The Judge took me aside, frowning angrily. "You are unwise to talk in that way. She can neither take her infant nor leave it. The cars are closed by order of the government to all but soldiers."

I told him of the woman who, when the conductor said she could not go, cried at the top of her voice, "Soldiers, I want to go to Richmond to nurse my wounded husband." In a moment twenty men made themselves her body-guard, and she went on unmolested. The Judge said I talked nonsense. I said I would go on in my carriage if need be. Besides, there would be no difficulty in getting Mary a "permit."

He answered hotly that in no case would he let her go, and that I had better *not* go back into the house. We were on the piazza and my carriage at the door. I took it and crossed over to see Mary Boykin. She was weeping, too, so washed away with tears one would hardly know her. "So many killed. My son and my husband—I do not hear a word from them."

Gave to-day for two pounds of tea, forty pounds of coffee, and sixty pounds of sugar, $800.

Beauregard is a gentleman and was a genius as long as Whiting did his engineering for him. Our Creole general is not quite so clever as he thinks himself.

Mary Ford writes for school-books for her boys. She is in great distress on the subject. When Longstreet's corps passed through Greenville there was great enthusiasm; handkerchiefs were waved, bouquets and flowers were thrown the troops; her boys, having nothing else to throw, threw their school-books.

CHAPTER XVIII. COLUMBIA, S. C.

July 6, 1864—January 17, 1865

Columbia, S. C., July 6, 1864.—At the Prestons' Mary was laughing at Mrs. Lyons's complaint—the person from whom we rented rooms in Richmond. She spoke of Molly and Lawrence's deceitfulness. They went about the house quiet as mice while we were at home; or Lawrence sat at the door and sprang to his feet whenever we passed. But when we were out, they sang, laughed, shouted, and danced. If any of the Lyons family passed him. Lawrence kept his seat, with his hat on, too. Mrs. Chesnut had said: "Oh!" so meekly to the whole tirade, and added, "I will see about it."

Colonel Urquhart and Edmund Rhett dined here; charming men both—no brag, no detraction. Talk is never pleasant where there is either. Our noble Georgian dined here. He says Hampton was the hero of the Yankee rout at Stony Creek.[116] He claims that citizens, militia, and lame soldiers kept the bridge at Staunton and gallantly repulsed Wilson's raiders.

At Mrs. S.'s last night. She came up, saying, "In New Orleans four people never met together without dancing." Edmund Rhett turned to me: "You shall be pressed into service." "No, I belong to the reserve corps—too old to volunteer or to be drafted as a conscript." But I had to go.

My partner in the dance showed his English descent; he took his pleasure sadly. "Oh, Mr. Rhett, at his pleasure, can be a most agreeable companion!" said someone. "I never happened to meet him," said I, "when he pleased to be otherwise." With a hot, draggled, old alpaca dress, and those clod-hopping shoes, to tumble slowly and gracefully through the mazes of a July dance was too much for me. "What depresses you so?" he anxiously inquired. "Our carnival of death." What a blunder to bring us all together here!-a reunion of consumptives to dance and sing until one can almost hear the death-rattle!

July 25th.—Now we are in a cottage rented from Doctor Chisolm. Hood is a full general. Johnston[117] has been removed and superseded. Early is threatening Washington City. Semmes, of whom we have been so proud, risked the Alabama in a sort of duel of ships. He has lowered

---

[116] The battle of Stony Creek in Virginia was fought on June 28-29, 1864.

[117] General Johnston in 1863 had been appointed to command the Army of the Tennessee, with headquarters at Dalton, Georgia. He was to oppose the advance of Sherman's army toward Atlanta. In May, 1864, he fought unsuccessful battles at Resaca and elsewhere, and in July was compelled to retreat across the Chattahoochee River. Fault was found with him because of his continual retreating. There were tremendous odds against him. On July 17th he was superseded by Hood.

the flag of the famous Alabama to the Kearsarge.[118] Forgive who may! I can not. We moved into this house on the 20th of July. My husband was telegraphed to go to Charleston. General Jones sent for him. A part of his command is on the coast.

The girls were at my house. Everything was in the utmost confusion. We were lying on a pile of mattresses in one of the front rooms while the servants were reducing things to order in the rear. All the papers are down on the President for this change of commanders except the Georgia papers. Indeed, Governor Brown's constant complaints, I dare say, caused it—these and the rage of the Georgia people as Johnston backed down on them.

Isabella soon came. She said she saw the Preston sisters pass her house, and as they turned the corner there was a loud and bitter cry. It seemed to come from the Hampton house. Both girls began to run at full speed. "What is the master?" asked Mrs. Martin. "Mother, listen; that sounded like the cry of a broken heart," said Isabella; "something has gone terribly wrong at the Prestons.'"

Mrs. Martin is deaf, however, so she heard nothing and thought Isabella fanciful. Isabella hurried over there, and learned that they had come to tell Mrs. Preston that Willie was killed—Willie! his mother's darling. No country ever had a braver soldier, a truer gentleman, to lay down his life in her cause.

July 26th.—Isabella went with me to the bulletin-board. Mrs. D. (with the white linen as usual pasted on her chin) asked me to read aloud what was there written. As I slowly read on, I heard a suppressed giggle from Isabella. I know her way of laughing at everything, and tried to enunciate more distinctly—to read more slowly, and louder, with more precision. As I finished and turned round, I found myself closely packed in by a crowd of Confederate soldiers eager to hear the news. They took off their caps, thanked me for reading all that was on the boards, and made way for me, cap in hand, as I hastily returned to the carriage, which was waiting for us. Isabella proposed, "Call out to them to give three cheers for Jeff Davis and his generals." "You forget, my child, that we are on our way to a funeral."

Found my new house already open hospitably to all comers. My husband had arrived. He was seated at a pine table, on which someone had put a coarse, red table-cover, and by the light of one tallow candle

---

[118] Raphael Semmes was a native of Maryland and had served in the Mexican War. The Alabama was built for the Confederate States at Birkenhead, England, and with an English crew and English equipment was commanded by Semmes. In 1863 and 1864 the Alabama destroyed much Federal shipping. On June 19, 1864, she was sunk by the Federal ship Kearsarge in a battle off Cherbourg. Claims against England for damages were made by the United States, and as a result the Geneva Arbitration Court was created. Claims amounting to $15,500,000 were finally awarded. This case has much importance in the history of international law.

was affably entertaining Edward Barnwell, Isaac Hayne, and Uncle Hamilton. He had given them no tea, however. After I had remedied that oversight, we adjourned to the moonlighted piazza. By tallow-candle-light and the light of the moon, we made out that wonderful smile of Teddy's, which identifies him as Gerald Grey.

We have laughed so at broken hearts—the broken hearts of the foolish love stories. But Buck, now, is breaking her heart for her brother Willie. Hearts do break in silence, without a word or a sigh. Mrs. Means and Mary Barnwell made no moan—simply turned their faces to the wall and died. How many more that we know nothing of!

When I remember all the true-hearted, the light-hearted the gay and gallant boys who have come laughing, singing and dancing in my way in the three years now past; how I have looked into their brave young eyes and helped then as I could in every way and then saw them no more forever how they lie stark and cold, dead upon the battle-field, or moldering away in hospitals or prisons, which is worse-I think if I consider the long array of those bright youth and loyal men who have gone to their death almost before my very eyes, my heart might break, too. Is anything worth it—this fearful sacrifice, this awful penalty we pay for war?

Allen G. says Johnston was a failure. Now he will wait and see what Hood can do before he pronounces judgment on him. He liked his address to his army. It was grand and inspiring, but every one knows a general has not time to write these things himself. Mr. Kelly, from New Orleans, says Dick Taylor and Kirby Smith have quarreled. One would think we had a big enough quarrel on hand for one while already. The Yankees are enough and to spare. General Lovell says, "Joe Brown, with his Georgians at his back, who importuned our government to remove Joe Johnston, they are scared now, and wish they had not."

In our democratic Republic, if one rises to be its head, whomever he displeases takes a Turkish revenge and defiles the tombs of his father and mother; hints that his father was a horse-thief and his mother no better than she should be; his sisters barmaids and worse, his brothers Yankee turncoats and traitors. All this is hurled at Lincoln or Jeff Davis indiscriminately.

August 2d.—Sherman again. Artillery parked and a line of battle formed before Atlanta. When we asked Brewster what Sam meant to do at Atlanta he answered, "Oh—oh, like the man who went, he says he means to stay there!" Hope he may, that's all.

Spent to-day with Mrs. McCord at her hospital. She is dedicating her grief for her son, sanctifying it, one might say, by giving up her soul and body, her days and nights, to the wounded soldiers at her hospital. Every moment of her time is surrendered to their needs.

To-day General Taliaferro dined with us. He served with Hood at the second battle of Manassas and at Fredericksburg, where Hood won his major-general's spurs. On the battle-field, Hood, he said, "has military inspiration." We were thankful for that word. All now depends on that army at Atlanta. If that fails us, the game is up.

August 3d.—Yesterday was such a lucky day for my housekeeping in our hired house. Oh, ye kind Columbia folk! Mrs. Alex Taylor, *née* Hayne, sent me a huge bowl of yellow butter and a basket to match of every vegetable in season. Mrs. Preston's man came with mushrooms freshly cut and Mrs. Tom Taylor's with fine melons.

Sent Smith and Johnson (my house servant and a carpenter from home, respectively) to the Commissary's with our wagon for supplies. They made a mistake, so they said, and went to the depot instead, and stayed there all day. I needed a servant sadly in many ways all day long, but I hope Smith and Johnson had a good time. I did not lose patience until Harriet came in an omnibus because I had neither servants nor horse to send to the station for her.

Stephen Elliott is wounded, and his wife and father have gone to him. Six hundred of his men were destroyed in a mine; and part of his brigade taken prisoners: Stoneman and his raiders have been captured. This last fact gives a slightly different hue to our horizon of unmitigated misery.

General L—told us of an unpleasant scene at the President's last winter. He called there to see Mrs. McLean. Mrs. Davis was in the room and he did not speak to her. He did not intend to be rude; it was merely an oversight. And so he called again and tried to apologize, to remedy his blunder, but the President was inexorable, and would not receive his overtures of peace and good-will. General L—is a New York man. Talk of the savagery of slavery, heavens! How perfect are our men's manners down here, how suave, how polished are they. Fancy one of them forgetting to speak to Mrs. Davis in her own drawing-room.

August 6th.—Archer came, a classmate of my husband's at Princeton; they called him Sally Archer then, he was so girlish and pretty. No trace of feminine beauty about this grim soldier now. He has a hard face, black-bearded and sallow, with the saddest black eyes. His hands are small, white, and well-shaped; his manners quiet. He is abstracted and weary-looking, his mind and body having been deadened by long imprisonment. He seemed glad to be here, and James Chesnut was charmed. "Dear Sally Archer," he calls him cheerily, and the other responds in a far-off, faded kind of way.

Hood and Archer were given the two Texas regiments at the beginning of the war. They were colonels and Wigfall was their general. Archer's comments on Hood are: "He does not compare intellectually with General Johnston, who is decidedly a man of culture and literary attainments, with much experience in military matters. Hood, however, has youth and energy to help counterbalance all this.

He has a simple-minded directness of purpose always. He is awfully shy, and he has suffered terribly, but then he has had consolations— such a rapid rise in his profession, and then his luck to be engaged to the beautiful Miss—."

They tried Archer again and again on the heated controversy of the day, but he stuck to his text. Joe Johnston is a fine military critic, a capital writer, an accomplished soldier, as brave as Cæsar in his own person, but cautious to a fault in manipulating an army. Hood has all the dash end fire of a reckless young soldier, and his Texans would follow him to the death. Too much caution might be followed easily by too much headlong rush. That is where the swing-back of the pendulum might ruin us.

August 10th.—To-day General Chesnut and his staff departed. His troops are ordered to look after the mountain passes beyond Greenville on the North Carolina and Tennessee quarter.

Misery upon misery. Mobile[119] is going as New Orleans went. Those Western men have not held their towns as we held and hold Charleston, or as the Virginians hold Richmond. And they call us a "frill-shirt, silk-stocking chivalry," or "a set of dandy Miss Nancys." They fight desperately in their bloody street brawls, but we bear privation and discipline best.

August 14th.—We have conflicting testimony. Young Wade Hampton, of Joe Johnston's staff, says Hood lost 12,000 men in the battles of the 22d[120] and 24th, but Brewster, of Hood's staff, says not three thousand at the utmost. Now here are two people strictly truthful, who tell things so differently. In this war people see the same things so oddly one does not know what to believe.

Brewster says when he was in Richmond Mr. Davis said Johnston would have to be removed and Sherman blocked. He could not make Hardee full general because, when he had command of an army he was always importuning the War Department for a general-in-chief to be sent there over him. Polk would not do, brave soldier and patriot as he was. He was a good soldier, and would do his best for his country, and do his duty under whomever was put over him by those in authority. Mr. Davis did not once intimate to him who it was that he intended to promote to the head of the Western Army.

Brewster said to-day that this "blow at Joe Johnston, cutting off his head, ruins the schemes of the enemies of the government. Wigfall asked me to go at once, and get Hood to decline to take this command, for it will destroy him if he accepts it. He will have to fight under Jeff Davis's orders; no one can do that now and not lose caste in the

---

[119] The battle of Mobile Bay, won under Farragut, was fought on August 5, 1864.

[120] On July 22d, Hood made a sortie from Atlanta, but after a battle was obliged to return.

Western Army. Joe Johnston does not exactly say that Jeff Davis betrays his plans to the enemy, but he says he dares not let the President know his plans, as there is a spy in the War Office who invariably warns the Yankees in time. Consulting the government on military movements is played out. That's Wigfall's way of talking. Now," added Brewster, "I blame the President for keeping a man at the head of his armies who treats the government with open scorn and contumely, no matter how the people at large rate this disrespectful general."

August 19th.—Began my regular attendance on the Wayside Hospital. To-day we gave wounded men, as they stopped for an hour at the station, their breakfast. Those who are able to come to the table do so. The badly wounded remain in wards prepared for them, where their wounds are dressed by nurses and surgeons, and we take bread and butter, beef, ham, and hot coffee to them.

One man had hair as long as a woman's, the result of a vow, he said. He had pledged himself not to cut his hair until peace was declared and our Southern country free. Four made this vow together. All were dead but himself. One was killed in Missouri, one in Virginia, and he left one at Kennesaw Mountain. This poor creature had had one arm taken off at the socket. When I remarked that he was utterly disabled and ought not to remain in the army, he answered quietly, "I am of the First Texas. If old Hood can go with one foot, I can go with one arm, eh?"

How they quarreled and wrangled among themselves- Alabama and Mississippi, all were loud for Joe Johnston, save and except the long-haired, one-armed hero, who cried at the top of his voice: "Oh! you all want to be kept in trenches and to go on retreating, eh?" "Oh, if we had had a leader, such as Stonewall, this war would have been over long ago! What we want is a leader!" shouted a cripple.

They were awfully smashed-up, objects of misery, wounded, maimed, diseased. I was really upset, and came home ill. This kind of thing unnerves me quite.

Letters from the army. Grant's dogged stay about Richmond is very disgusting, and depressing to the spirits. Wade Hampton has been put in command of the Southern cavalry.

A Wayside incident. A pine box, covered with flowers, was carefully put upon the train by some gentlemen. Isabella asked whose remains were in the box. Dr. Gibbes replied: "In that box lies the body of a young man whose family antedates the Bourbons of France. He was the last Count de Choiseul, and he has died for the South." Let his memory be held in perpetual remembrance by all who love the South!

August 22d.—Hope I may never know a raid except from hearsay. Mrs. Huger describes the one at Athens. The proudest and most timid of women were running madly in the streets, corsets in one hand, stockings in the other- *déshabillé* as far as it will go, Mobile is half taken. The railroad between us and Richmond has been tapped. Notes from a letter written by a young lady who is riding a high horse. Her *fiancé*, a maimed hero, has been abused. "You say to me with a sneer, 'So you love that man.' Yes, I do, and I thank God that I love better than all the world the man who is to be my husband. 'Proud of him, are you?' Yes, I am, in exact proportion to my love. You say, 'I am selfish.' Yes, I am selfish. He is my second self, so utterly absorbed am I in him. There is not a moment, day or night, that I do not think of him. In point of fact, I do not think of anything else." No reply was deemed necessary by the astounded recipient of this outburst of indignation, who showed me the letter and continued to observe: "Did you ever? She seems so shy, so timid, so cold."

Sunday Isabella took us to a chapel, Methodist, of course; her father had a hand in building it. It was not clean, but it was crowded, hot, and stuffy. An eloquent man preached with a delightful voice and wonderful fluency; nearly eloquent, and at times nearly ridiculous. He described a scene during one of his sermons when "beautiful young faces were turned up to me, radiant faces though bathed in tears, moral rainbows of emotion playing over them," etc.

He then described his own conversion, and stripped himself naked morally. All that is very revolting to one's innate sense of decency. He tackled the patriarchs. Adam, Noah, and so on down to Joseph, who was "a man whose modesty and purity were so transcendent they enabled him to resist the greatest temptation to which fallen man is exposed." "Fiddlesticks! that is played out!" my neighbor whispered. "Everybody gives up now that old Mrs. Pharaoh was forty." "Mrs. Potiphar, you goose, and she was fifty!" "That solves the riddle." "Sh-sh!!" from the devout Isabella.

At home met General Preston on the piazza. He was vastly entertaining. Gave us Darwin, Herodotus, and Livy. We understood him and were delighted, but we did not know enough to be sure when it was his own wisdom or when wise saws and cheering words came from the authors of whom he spoke.

August 23d.—All in a muddle, and yet the news, confused as it is, seems good from all quarters. There is a row in New Orleans. Memphis[121] has been retaken; 2,000 prisoners have been captured at Petersburg, and a Yankee raid on Macon has come to grief.

At Mrs. Izard's met a clever Mrs. Calhoun. Mrs. Calhoun is a violent partizan of Dick Taylor; says Taylor does the work and Kirby Smith gets the credit for it. Mrs. Calhoun described the behavior of some acquaintance of theirs at Shreveport, one of that kind whose faith removes mountains. Her love for and confidence in the Confederate

---

[121] General Forrest made his raid on Memphis in August of this year.

army were supreme. Why not! She knew so many of the men who composed that dauntless band. When her husband told her New Orleans had surrendered to a foe whom she despised, she did not believe a word of it. He told her to "pack up his traps, as it was time for him to leave Shreveport." She then determined to run down to the levee and see for herself, only to find the Yankee gunboats having it all their own way. She made a painful exhibition of herself. First. she fell on her knees and prayed; then she got up and danced with rage; then she raved and dashed herself on the ground in a fit. There was patriotism run mad for you! As I did not know the poor soul, Mrs. Calhoun's fine acting was somewhat lost on me, but the others enjoyed it.

Old Edward Johnston has been sent to Atlanta against his will, and Archer has been made major-general and, contrary to his earnest request, ordered not to his beloved Texans but to the Army of the Potomac.

Mr. C. F. Hampton deplores the untimely end of McPherson.[122] He was so kind to Mr. Hampton at Vicksburg last winter, and drank General Hampton's health then and there. Mr. Hampton has asked Brewster, if the report of his death prove a mistake, and General McPherson is a prisoner, that every kindness and attention be shown to him. General McPherson said at his own table at Vicksburg that General Hampton was the ablest general on our side.

Grant can hold his own as well as Sherman. Lee has a heavy handful in the new Suwarrow. He has worse odds than any one else, for when Grant has ten thousand slain, he has only to order another ten thousand, and they are there, ready to step out to the front. They are like the leaves of Vallambrosa.

August 29th.—I take my hospital duty in the morning. Most persons prefer afternoon, but I dislike to give up my pleasant evenings. So I get up at five o'clock and go down in my carriage all laden with provisions. Mrs. Fisher and old Mr. Bryan generally go with me. Provisions are commonly sent by people to Mrs. Fisher's. I am so glad to be a hospital nurse once more. I had excuses enough, but at heart I felt a coward and a skulker. I think I know how men feel who hire a substitute and shirk the fight. There must be no dodging of duty. It will not do now to send provisions and pay for nurses. Something inside of me kept calling out, "Go, you shabby creature; you can't bear to see what those fine fellows have to bear."

Mrs. Izard was staying with me last night, and as I slipped away I begged Molly to keep everything dead still and not let Mrs. Izard be disturbed until I got home. About ten I drove up and there was a row to

---

[122] General McPherson was killed before Atlanta during the sortie made by Hood on July 22d. He was a native of Ohio, a graduate of West Point, and under Sherman commanded the Army of the Tennessee.

wake the dead. Molly's eldest daughter, who nurses her baby sister, let the baby fall, and, regardless of Mrs. Izard, as I was away, Molly was giving the nurse a switching in the yard, accompanied by howls and yells worthy of a Comanche! The small nurse welcomed my advent, no doubt, for in two seconds peace was restored. Mrs. Izard said she sympathized with the baby's mother; so I forgave the uproar.

I have excellent servants; no matter for their short comings behind my back. They save me all thought as to household matters, and they are so kind, attentive, and quiet. They must know what is at hand if Sherman is not hindered from coming here—"Freedom! my masters!" But these sphinxes give no sign, unless it be increased diligence and absolute silence, as certain in their action and as noiseless as a law of nature, at any rate when we are in the house.

That fearful hospital haunts me all day long, and is worse at night. So much suffering, such loathsome wounds, such distortion, with stumps of limbs not half cured, exhibited to all. Then, when I was so tired yesterday, Molly was looking more like an enraged lioness than anything else, roaring that her baby's neck was broken, and howling cries of vengeance. The poor little careless nurse's dark face had an ashen tinge of gray terror. She was crouching near the ground like an animal trying to hide, and her mother striking at her as she rolled away. All this was my welcome as I entered the gate. It takes these half-Africans but a moment to go back to their naked savage animal nature.

Mrs. Izard is a charming person. She tried so to make me forget it all and rest.

September 2d.—The battle has been raging at Atlanta,[123] and our fate hanging in the balance. Atlanta, indeed, is gone. Well, that agony is over. Like David, when the child was dead, I will get up from my knees, will wash my face and comb my hair. No hope; we will try to have no fear.

At the Prestons' I found them drawn up in line of battle every moment looking for the Doctor on his way to Richmond. Now, to drown thought, for our day is done, read Dumas's *Maîtres d'Armes*. Russia ought to sympathize with us. We are not as barbarous as this, even if Mrs. Stowe's word be taken. Brutal men with unlimited power are the same all over the world. See Russell's India—Bull Run Russell's. They say General Morgan has been killed. We are hard as stones; we sit unmoved and hear any bad news chance may bring. Are we stupefied?

September 19th.—My pink silk dress I have sold for $600, to be paid for in instalments, two hundred a month for three months. And I sell my eggs and butter from home for two hundred dollars a month.

---

[123] After the battle, Atlanta was taken possession of and partly burned by the Federals.

Does it not sound well -four hundred dollars a month regularly. But in what? In Confederate money. *Hélas!*

September 21st.—Went with Mrs. Rhett to hear Dr. Palmer. I did not know before how utterly hopeless was our situation. This man is so eloquent, it was hard to listen and not give way. Despair was his word, and martyrdom. He offered us nothing more in this world than the martyr's crown. He is not for slavery, he says; he is for freedom, and the freedom to govern our own country as we see fit. He is against foreign interference in our State matters. That is what Mr. Palmer went to war for, it appears. Every day shows that slavery is doomed the world over; for that he thanked God. He spoke of our agony, and then came the cry, "Help us, O God! Vain is the help of man." And so we came away shaken to the depths.

The end has come. No doubt of the fact. Our army has so moved as to uncover Macon and Augusta. We are going to be wiped off the face of the earth. What is there to prevent Sherman taking General Lee in the rear? We have but two armies, and Sherman is between them now.[124]

September 24th.-These stories of our defeats in the valley fall like blows upon a dead body. Since Atlanta fell I have felt as if all were dead within me forever. Captain Ogden, of General Chesnut's staff, dined here to-day. Had ever brigadier, with little or no brigade, so magnificent a staff? The reserves, as somebody said, have been secured only by robbing the cradle and the grave-the men too old, the boys too young. Isaac Hayne, Edward Barnwell, Bacon, Ogden, Richardson, Miles are the picked men of the agreeable world.

October 1st.-Mary Cantey Preston's wedding day has come and gone and Mary is Mrs. John Darby now. Maggie Howell dressed the bride's hair beautifully, they said, but it was all covered by her veil, which was of blond-lace, and the dress tulle and blond-lace, with diamonds and pearls. The bride walked up the aisle on her father's arm, Mrs. Preston on Dr. Darby's. I think it was the handsomest wedding party I ever saw. John Darby[125] had brought his wedding uniform home with him from England, and it did all honor to his perfect figure. I forget the name of his London tailor—the best, of course! "Well," said Isabella, "it would be hard for any man to live up to those clothes."

---

[124] During the summer and autumn of 1864 several important battles had occurred In addition to the engagements by Sherman's army farther south, there had occurred in Virginia the battle of Cold Harbor in the early part of June; those before Petersburg in the latter part of June and during July and August; the battle of Winchester on September 19th, during Sheridan's Shenandoah campaign, and the battle of Cedar Creek on October 19th. [125] After the war, Dr. Darby became professor of Surgery in the University of the City of New York; he had served as Medical Director in the Army of the Confederate States and as Professor of Anatomy and Surgery in the University of South Carolina; had also served with distinction in European wars.

And now, to the amazement of us all, Captain Chesnut (Johnny) who knows everything, has rushed into a flirtation with Buck such as never was. He drives her every day, and those wild, runaway, sorrel colts terrify my soul as they go tearing, pitching, and darting from side to side of the street. And my lady enjoys it. When he leaves her, he kisses her hand, bowing so low to do it unseen that we see it all.

Saturday.—The President will be with us here in Columbia next Tuesday, so Colonel McLean brings us word. I have begun at once to prepare to receive him in my small house. His apartments have been decorated as well as Confederate stringency would permit. The possibilities were not great, but I did what I could for our honored chief; besides I like the man—he has been so kind to me, and his wife is one of the few to whom I can never be grateful enough for her generous appreciation and attention.

I went out to the gate to greet the President, who met me most cordially; kissed me, in fact. Custis Lee and Governor Lubbock were at his back.

Immediately after breakfast (the Presidential party arrived a little before daylight) General Chesnut drove off with the President's aides, and Mr. Davis sat out on our piazza. There was nobody with him but myself. Some little boys strolling by called out, "Come here and look; there is a man on Mrs. Chesnut's porch who looks just like Jeff Davis on postage-stamps." People began to gather at once on the street. Mr. Davis then went in.

Mrs. McCord sent a magnificent bouquet—I thought, of course, for the President; but she gave me such a scolding afterward. She did not know he was there; I, in my mistake about the bouquet, thought she knew, and so did not send her word.

The President was watching me prepare a mint julep for Custis Lee when Colonel McLean came to inform us that a great crowd had gathered and that they were coming to ask the President to speak to them at one o'clock. An immense crowd it was—men, women, and children. The crowd overflowed the house, the President's hand was nearly shaken off. I went to the rear, my head intent on the dinner to be prepared for him, with only a Confederate commissariat.. But the patriotic public had come to the rescue. I had been gathering what I could of eatables for a month, and now I found that nearly everybody in Columbia was sending me whatever they had that they thought nice enough for the President's dinner. We had the sixty-year-old Madeira from Mulberry, and the beautiful old china, etc. Mrs. Preston sent a boned turkey stuffed with truffles, stuffed tomatoes, and stuffed peppers. Each made a dish as pretty as it was appetizing.

A mob of small boys only came to pay their respects to the President. He seemed to know how to meet that odd delegation.

Then the President's party had to go, and we bade them an

affectionate farewell. Custis Lee and I had spent much time gossiping on the back porch. While I was concocting dainties for the dessert, he sat on the banister with a cigar in his mouth. He spoke very candidly, telling me many a hard truth for the Confederacy, and about the bad time which was at hand.

October 18th.—Ten pleasant days I owe to my sister. Kate has descended upon me unexpectedly from the mountains of Flat Rock. We are true sisters; she understands me without words, and she is the cleverest, sweetest woman I know, so graceful and gracious in manner, so good and unselfish in character, but, best of all, she is so agreeable. Any time or place would be charming with Kate for a companion. General Chesnut was in Camden; but I could not wait. I gave the beautiful bride, Mrs. Darby, a dinner, which was simply perfection. I was satisfied for once in my life with my own table, and I know pleasanter guests were never seated around any table whatsoever.

My house is always crowded. After all, what a number of pleasant people we have been thrown in with by war's catastrophes. I call such society glorious. It is the windup, but the old life as it begins to die will die royally. General Chesnut came back disheartened. He complains that such a life as I lead gives him no time to think.

October 28th.-Burton Harrison writes to General Preston that supreme anxiety reigns in Richmond.

Oh, for one single port! If the Alabama had had in the whole wide world a port to take her prizes to and where she could be refitted, I believe she would have borne us through. Oh, for one single port by which we could get at the outside world and refit our whole Confederacy! If we could have hired regiments from Europe, or even have imported ammunition and food for our soldiers!

"Some days must be dark and dreary." At the mantua-maker's, however, I saw an instance of faith in our future: a bride's paraphernalia, and the radiant bride herself, the bridegroom expectant and elect now within twenty miles of Chattanooga and outward bound to face the foe.

Saw at the Laurens's not only Lizzie Hamilton, a perfect little beauty, but the very table the first Declaration of Independence was written upon. These Laurenses are grandchildren of Henry Laurens, of the first Revolution. Alas! we have yet to make good our second declaration of independence-Southern independence-from Yankee meddling and Yankee rule. Hood has written to ask them to send General Chesnut out to command one of his brigades. In whose place?

If Albert Sidney Johnston had lived! Poor old General Lee has no backing. Stonewall would have saved us from Antietam. Sherman will now catch General Lee by the rear, while Grant holds him by the head, and while Hood and Thomas are performing an Indian war-dance on the frontier. Hood means to cut his way to Lee; see if he doesn't The

"Yanks" have had a struggle for it. More than once we seemed to have been too much for them. We have been so near to success it aches one to think of it. So runs the table-talk.

Next to our house, which Isabella calls "Tillytudlem," since Mr. Davis's visit, is a common of green grass and very level, beyond which comes a belt of pine-trees. On this open space, within forty paces of us, a regiment of foreign deserters has camped. They have taken the oath of allegiance to our government, and are now being drilled and disciplined into form before being sent to our army. They are mostly Germans, with some Irish, however. Their close proximity keeps me miserable. Traitors once, traitors forever.

Jordan has always been held responsible for all the foolish proclamations, and, indeed, for whatever Beauregard reported or proclaimed. Now he has left that mighty chief, and, lo, here comes from Beauregard the silliest and most boastful of his military bulletins. He brags of Shiloh; that was not the way the story was told to us.

A letter from Mrs. Davis, who says: "Thank you, a thousand times, my dear friend, for your more than maternal kindness to my dear child." That is what she calls her sister, Maggie Howell. "As to Mr. Davis, he thinks the best ham, the best Madeira, the best coffee, the best hostess in the world, rendered Columbia delightful to him when he passed through. We are in a sad and anxious state here just now. The dead come in; but the living do not go out so fast. However, we hope all things and trust in God as the only one able to resolve the opposite state of feeling into a triumphant, happy whole. I had a surprise of an unusually gratifying nature a few days since. I found I could not keep my horses, so I sold them. The next day they were returned to me with a handsome anonymous note to the effect that they had been bought by a few friends for me. But I fear I can not feed them. Strictly between us, things look very anxious here."

November 6th.-Sally Hampton went to Richmond with the Rev. Mr. Martin. She arrived there on Wednesday. On Thursday her father, Wade Hampton, fought a great battle, but just did not win it-a victory narrowly missed. Darkness supervened and impenetrable woods prevented that longed-for consummation. Preston Hampton rode recklessly into the hottest fire. His father sent his brother, Wade, to bring him back. Wade saw him reel in the saddle and galloped up to him, General Hampton following. As young Wade reached him, Preston fell from his horse, and the one brother, stooping to raise the other, was himself shot down. Preston recognized his father, but died without speaking a word. Young Wade, though wounded, held his brother's head up. Tom Taylor and others hurried up. The General took his dead son in his arms, kissed him, and handed his body to Tom Taylor and his friends, bade them take care of Wade, and then rode back to his post. At the head of his troops in the thickest of the fray he directed the fight for the rest of the day. Until night he did not know young Wade's fate; that boy might be dead, too! Now, he says, no son of his must be in his command. When Wade recovers, he must join some other division. The agony of such a day, and the anxiety and the duties of the battle-field-it is all more than a mere man can bear.

Another letter from Mrs. Davis. She says: "I was dreadfully shocked at Preston Hampton's fate-his untimely fate. I know nothing more touching in history than General Hampton's situation at the supremest moment of his misery, when he sent one son to save the other and saw both fall; and could not know for some moments whether both were not killed."

A thousand dollars have slipped through my fingers already this week. At the Commissary's I spent five hundred to-day for candles, sugar, and a lamp, etc. Tallow candles are bad enough, but of them there seems to be an end, too. Now we are restricted to smoky, terrabine lamps- terrabine is a preparation of turpentine. When the chimney of the lamp cracks, as crack it will, we plaster up the place with paper, thick old letter-paper, preferring the highly glazed kind. In the hunt for paper queer old letters come to light.

Sherman, in Atlanta, has left Thomas to take care of Hood. Hood has thirty thousand men, Thomas forty thousand, and as many more to be had as he wants; he has only to ring the bell and call for them. Grant can get all that he wants, both for himself and for Thomas. All the world is open to them, while we are shut up in a bastile.. We are at sea, and our boat has sprung a leak.

November 17th.—Although Sherman[126]1 took Atlanta, he does not mean to stay there, be it heaven or hell. Fire and the sword are for us here; that is the word. And now I must begin my Columbia life anew and alone. It will be a short shrift.

Captain Ogden came to dinner on Sunday and in the afternoon asked me to go with him to the Presbyterian Church and hear Mr. Palmer. We went, and I felt very youthful, as the country people say; like a girl and her beau. Ogden took me into a pew and my husband sat afar off. What a sermon! The preacher stirred my blood. My very flesh crept and tingled. A red-hot glow of patriotism passed through me. Such a sermon must strengthen the hearts and the hands of many people. There was more exhortation to fight and die, *à la* Joshua, than meek Christianity.

---

[126] General Sherman had started from Chattanooga for his march across Georgia on May 6, 1864. He had won the battles of Dalton, Resaca, and New Hope Church in May, the battle of Kennesaw Mountain in June, the battles of Peach Tree Creek and Atlanta in July, and had formally occupied Atlanta on September 2d. On November 16th, he started on his march from Atlanta to the sea and entered Savannah on December 23d. Early in 1865 he moved his army northward through the Carolinas, and on April 26th received the surrender of General Joseph E. Johnston.

November 25th.—Sherman is thundering at Augusta's very doors. My General was on the wing, somber, and full of care. The girls are merry enough; the staff, who fairly live here, no better. Cassandra, with a black shawl over her head, is chased by the gay crew from sofa to sofa, for she avoids them, being full of miserable anxiety. There is nothing but distraction and confusion. All things tend to the preparation for the departure of the troops. It rains all the time, such rains as I never saw before; incessant torrents. These men come in and out in the red mud and slush of Columbia streets. Things seem dismal and wretched to me to the last degree, but the staff, the girls, and the youngsters do not see it.

Mrs. S. (born in Connecticut) came, and she was radiant. She did not come to see me, but my nieces. She says exultingly that "Sherman will open a way out at last, and I will go at once to Europe or go North to my relatives there." How she derided our misery and "mocked when our fear cometh." I dare say she takes me for a fool. I sat there dumb, although she was in my own house. I have heard of a woman so enraged that she struck some one over the head with a shovel. To-day, for the first time in my life, I know how that mad woman felt. I could have given Mrs. S. the benefit of shovel and tongs both.

That splendid fellow, Preston Hampton; "home they brought their warrior, dead," and wrapped in that very Legion flag he had borne so often in battle with his own hands.

A letter from Mrs. Davis to-day, under date of Richmond, Va., November 20, 1864. She says: "Affairs West are looking so critical now that, before you receive this, you and I will be in the depths or else triumphant. I confess I do not sniff success in every passing breeze, but I am so tired, hoping, fearing, and being disappointed, that I have made up my mind not to be disconsolate, even though thieves break through and steal. Some people expect another attack upon Richmond shortly, but I think the avalanche will not slide until the spring breaks up its winter quarters. I have a blind kind of prognostics of victory for us, but somehow I am not cheered. The temper of Congress is less vicious, but more concerted in its hostile action." Mrs. Davis is a woman that my heart aches for in the troubles ahead.

My journal, a quire of Confederate paper, lies wide open on my desk in the corner of my drawing-room. Everybody reads it who chooses. Buck comes regularly to see what I have written last, and makes faces when it does not suit her. Isabella still calls me Cassandra, and puts her hands to her ears when I begin to wail. Well, Cassandra only records what she hears; she does not vouch for it. For really, one nowadays never feels certain of anything.

November 28th.—We dined at Mrs. McCord's. She is as strong a cordial for broken spirits and failing heart as one could wish. How her strength contrasts with our weakness. Like Doctor Palmer, she strings one up to bear bravely the worst. She has the intellect of a man and the perseverance and endurance of a woman.

We have lost nearly all of our men, and we have no money, and it looks as if we had taught the Yankees how to fight since Manassas. Our best and bravest are under the sod; we shall have to wait till another generation grows up. Here we stand, despair in our hearts ("Oh, Cassandra, don't!" shouts Isabella), with our houses burning or about to be, over our heads.

The North have just got things ship-shape; a splendid army, perfectly disciplined, with new levies coming in day and night. Their gentry do not go into the ranks. They hardly know there is a war up there.

December 1st.—At Coosawhatchie Yankees are landing in great force. Our troops down there are raw militia, old men and boys never under fire before; some college cadets, in all a mere handful. The cradle and the grave have been robbed by us, they say. Sherman goes to Savannah and not to Augusta.

December 2d.—Isabella and I put on bonnets and shawls and went deliberately out for news. We determined to seek until we found. Met a man who was so ugly, I could not forget him or his sobriquet; he was awfully in love with me once. He did not know me, but blushed hotly when Isabella told him who I was. He had forgotten me, I hope, or else I am changed by age and care past all recognition. He gave us the encouraging information that Grahamville had been burned to the ground.

When the call for horses was made, Mrs. McCord sent in her fine bays. She comes now with a pair of mules, and looks too long and significantly at my ponies. If I were not so much afraid of her, I would hint that those mules would be of far more use in camp than my ponies. But they will seize the ponies, no doubt.

In all my life before, the stables were far off from the house and I had nothing to do with them. Now my ponies are kept under an open shed next to the back piazza. Here I sit with my work, or my desk, or my book, basking in our Southern sun, and I watch Nat feed, curry, and rub down the horses, and then he cleans their stables as thoroughly as Smith does my drawing-room. I see their beds of straw comfortably laid. Nat says, "Ow, Missis, ain't lady's business to look so much in de stables." I care nothing for his grumbling, and I have never had horses in better condition. Poor ponies, you deserve every attention, and enough to eat. Grass does not grow under your feet. By night and day you are on the trot.

To-day General Chesnut was in Charleston on his way from Augusta to Savannah by rail. The telegraph is still working between Charleston and Savannah. Grahamville certainly is burned. There was fighting down there to-day. I came home with enough to think about,

Heaven knows! And then all day long we compounded a pound cake in honor of Mrs. Cuthbert, who has things so nice at home. The cake was a success, but was it worth all that trouble?

As my party were driving off to the concert, an omnibus rattled up. Enter Captain Leland, of General Chesnut's staff, of as imposing a presence as a field-marshal, handsome and gray-haired. He was here on some military errand and brought me a letter. He said the Yankees had been repulsed, and that down in those swamps we could give a good account of ourselves if our government would send men enough. With a sufficient army to meet them down there, they could be annihilated. "Where are the men to come from?" asked Mamie, wildly. "General Hood has gone off to Tennessee. Even if he does defeat Thomas there, what difference would that make here?"

December 3d.—We drank tea at Mrs. McCord's; she had her troubles, too. The night before a country cousin claimed her hospitality, one who fain would take the train at five this morning. A little after midnight Mrs. McCord was startled out of her first sleep by loud ringing of bells; an alarm at night may mean so much just now. In an instant she was on her feet. She found her guest, who thought it was daylight, and wanted to go. Mrs. McCord forcibly demonstrated how foolish it was to get up five hours too soon. Mrs. McCord, once more in her own warm bed, had fallen happily to sleep. She was waked by feeling two ice-cold hands pass cautiously over her face and person. It was pitch dark. Even Mrs. McCord gave a scream in her fright. She found it was only the irrepressible guest up and at her again. So, though it was only three o'clock, in order to quiet this perturbed spirit she rose and at five drove her to the station, where she had to wait some hours. But Mrs. McCord said, "anything for peace at home." The restless people who will not let others rest!

December 5th.—Miss Olivia Middleton and Mr. Frederick Blake are to be married. We Confederates have invented the sit-up-all-night for the wedding night; Isabella calls it the wake, not the wedding, of the parties married. The ceremony will be performed early in the evening; the whole company will then sit up until five o'clock, at which hour the bridal couple take the train for Combahee. Hope Sherman will not be so inconsiderate as to cut short the honeymoon.

In tripped Brewster, with his hat on his head, both hands extended, and his greeting, "Well, here we are!" He was travel-stained, disheveled, grimy with dirt. The prophet would have to send him many times to bathe in Jordan before he could be pronounced clean.

Hood will not turn and pursue Sherman. Thomas is at his heels with forty thousand men, and can have as many more as he wants for the asking. Between Thomas and Sherman Hood would be crushed. So he was pushing—I do not remember where or what. I know there was no comfort in anything he said.

Serena's account of money spent: Paper and envelopes, $12.00; tickets to concert, $10.00; tooth-brush, $10.00; total, $32.00.

December 14th.—And now the young ones are in bed and I am wide awake. It is an odd thing; in all my life how many persons have I seen in love? Not a half-dozen. And I am a tolerably close observer, a faithful watcher have I been from my youth upward of men and manners. Society has been for me only an enlarged field for character study.

Flirtation is the business of society; that is, playing at love-making. It begins in vanity, it ends in vanity. It is spurred on by idleness and a want of any other excitement. Flattery, battledore and shuttlecock, how in this game flattery is dashed backward and forward. It is so soothing to self-conceit. If it begins and ends in vanity, vexation of spirit supervenes sometimes. They do occasionally burn their fingers awfully, playing with fire, but there are no hearts broken. Each party in a flirtation has secured a sympathetic listener, to whom he or she can talk of himself or herself—somebody who, for the time, admires one exclusively, and, as the French say, *excessivement.* It is a pleasant, but very foolish game, and so to bed.

Hood and Thomas have had a fearful fight, with carnage and loss of generals excessive in proportion to numbers. That means they were leading and urging their men up to the enemy. I know how Bartow and Barnard Bee were killed bringing up their men. One of Mr. Chesnut's sins thrown in his teeth by the Legislature of South Carolina was that he procured the promotion of Gist, "State Rights" Gist, by his influence in Richmond. What have these comfortable, stay-at-home patriots to say of General Gist now? "And how could man die better than facing fearful odds," etc.

So Fort McAlister has fallen! Good-by, Savannah! Our Governor announces himself a follower of Joe Brown, of Georgia. Another famous Joe.

December 19th.—The deep waters are closing over us and we are in this house, like the outsiders at the time of the flood. We care for none of these things. We eat, drink, laugh, dance, in lightness of heart.

Doctor Trezevant came to tell me the dismal news. How he piled on the agony! Desolation, mismanagement, despair. General Young, with the flower of Hampton's cavalry, is in Columbia. Horses can not be found to mount them. Neither the Governor of Georgia nor the Governor of South Carolina is moving hand or foot. They have given up. The Yankees claim another victory for Thomas.[127] Hope it may prove like most of their victories, brag and bluster. Can't say why, maybe I am benumbed, but I do not feel so intensely miserable.

---

[127] Reference is here made to the battle between Hood and Thomas at Nashville, the result of which was the breaking up of Hood's army as a fighting force.

December 27th.—Oh, why did we go to Camden? The very dismalest Christmas overtook us there. Miss Rhett went with us—a brilliant woman and very agreeable. "The world, you know, is composed," said she, "of men, women, and Rhetts" (see Lady Montagu). Now, we feel that if we are to lose our negroes, we would as soon see Sherman free them as the Confederate Government; freeing negroes is the last Confederate Government craze. We are a little too slow about it; that is all.

Sold fifteen bales of cotton and took a sad farewell look at Mulberry. It is a magnificent old country-seat, with old oaks, green lawns and all. So I took that last farewell of Mulberry, once so hated, now so beloved.

January 7th.—Sherman is at Hardieville and Hood in Tennessee, the last of his men not gone, as Louis Wigfall so cheerfully prophesied.

Serena went for a half-hour to-day to the dentist. Her teeth are of the whitest and most regular, simply perfection. She fancied it was better to have a dentist look in her mouth before returning to the mountains. For that look she paid three hundred and fifty dollars in Confederate money. "Why, has this money any value at all?" she asked. Little enough in all truth, sad to say.

Brewster was here and stayed till midnight. Said he must see General Chesnut. He had business with him. His "me and General Hood" is no longer comic. He described Sherman's march of destruction and desolation. "Sherman leaves a track fifty miles wide, upon which there is no living thing to be seen," said Brewster before he departed.

January 10th.—You do the Anabasis business when you want to get out of the enemy's country, and the Thermopylae business when they want to get into your country. But we retreated in our own country and we gave up our mountain passes without a blow. But never mind the Greeks; if we had only our own Game Cock, Sumter, our own Swamp Fox, Marion. Marion's men or Sumter's, or the equivalent of them, now lie under the sod, in Virginia or Tennessee.

January 14th.—Yesterday I broke down—gave way to abject terror under the news of Sherman's advance with no news of my husband. To-day, while wrapped up on the sofa, too dismal even for moaning, there was a loud knock. Shawls on and all, just as I was, I rushed to the door to find a telegram from my husband: "All well; be at home Tuesday." It was dated from Adam's Run. I felt as lighthearted as if the war were over. Then I looked at the date and the place—Adam's Run. It ends as it began—in a run -Bull's Run, from which their first sprightly running astounded the world, and now Adam's Run. But if we must run, who are left to run? From Bull Run they ran full-handed. But we have fought until maimed soldiers, women, and children are all that remain to run.

To-day Kershaw's brigade, or what is left of it, passed through. What shouts greeted it and what bold shouts of thanks it returned! It was all a very encouraging noise, absolutely comforting. Some true men are left, after all.

January 16th.—My husband is at home once more—for how long, I do not know. His aides fill the house, and a group of hopelessly wounded haunt the place. The drilling and the marching go on outside. It rains a flood, with freshet after freshet. The forces of nature are befriending us, for our enemies have to make their way through swamps.

A month ago my husband wrote me a letter which I promptly suppressed after showing it to Mrs. McCord. He warned us to make ready, for the end had come. Our resources were exhausted, and the means of resistance could not be found. We could not bring ourselves to believe it, and now, he thinks, with the railroad all blown up, the swamps made impassable by the freshets, which have no time to subside, so constant is the rain, and the negroes utterly apathetic (would they be so if they saw us triumphant?), if we had but an army to seize the opportunity we might do something; but there are no troops; that is the real trouble.

To-day Mrs. McCord exchanged $16,000 in Confederate bills for $300 in gold—sixteen thousand for three hundred.

January 17th.—The Bazaar for the benefit of the hospitals opens now. Sherman marches constantly. All the railroads are smashed, and if I laugh at any mortal thing it is that I may not weep. Generals are as plenty as blackberries, but none are in command.

The Peace Commissioner, Blair, came. They say he gave Mr. Davis the kiss of peace. And we send Stephens, Campbell, all who have believed in this thing, to negotiate for peace. No hope, no good. Who dares hope?

Repressed excitement in church. A great railroad character was called out. He soon returned and whispered something to Joe Johnston and they went out together. Somehow the whisper moved around to us that Sherman was at Branchville. "Grant us patience, good Lord," was prayed aloud. "Not Ulysses Grant, good Lord," murmured Teddy, profanely. Hood came yesterday. He is staying at the Prestons' with Jack. They sent for us. What a heartfelt greeting he gave us. He can stand well enough without his crutch, but he does very slow walking. How plainly he spoke out dreadful words about "my defeat and discomfiture; my army destroyed, my losses," etc., etc. He said he had nobody to blame but himself. A telegram from Beauregard to-day to my husband. He does not know whether Sherman intends to advance on Branchville, Charleston, or Columbia.

Isabella said: "Maybe you attempted the impossible," and began one of her merriest stories. Jack Preston touched me on the arm and we slipped out. "He did not hear a word she was saying. He has forgotten us all. Did you notice how he stared in the fire? And the lurid spots which came out in his face and the drops of perspiration that stood on his forehead?" "Yes. He is going over some bitter scene; he sees Willie Preston with his heart shot away. He sees the panic at Nashville and the dead on the battlefield at Franklin." "That agony on his face comes again and again," said tender-hearted Jack. "I can't keep him out of those absent fits."

Governor McGrath and General Winder talk of preparations for a defense of Columbia. If Beauregard can't stop Sherman down there, what have we got here to do it with? Can we cheek or impede his march? Can any one?

Last night General Hampton came in. I am sure he would do something to save us if he were put in supreme command here. Hampton says Joe Johnston is equal, if not superior, to Lee as a commanding officer.

My silver is in a box and has been delivered for safe keeping to Isaac McLaughlin, who is really my beau-ideal of a grateful negro. I mean to trust him. My husband cares for none of these things now, and lets me do as I please.

Tom Archer died almost as soon as he got to Richmond. Prison takes the life out of men. He was only half-alive when here. He had a strange, pallid look and such a vacant stare until you roused him. Poor pretty Sally Archer: that is the end of you.[128]

CHAPTER XIX. LINCOLNTON, N. C.

February 16, 1865—*March* 15, 1865

Lincolnton, N.C., *February 16, 1865.*—A change has come o'er the spirit of my dream. Dear old quire of yellow, coarse, Confederate home-made paper, here you are again. An age of anxiety and suffering has passed over my head since last I wrote and wept over your forlorn pages.

My ideas of those last days are confused. The Martins left Columbia the Friday before I did, and Mammy, the negro woman, who had nursed them, refused to go with them. That daunted me. Then Mrs. McCord, who was to send her girls with me, changed her mind. She sent them up-stairs in her house and actually took away the staircase; that was her plan.

Then I met Mr. Christopher Hampton, arranging to take off his

---

[128] Under last date entry, January 17th, the author chronicles events of later occurrence; it was her not infrequent custom to jot down happenings in dateless lines or paragraphs. Mr. Blair visited President Davis January 12th; Stephens, Hunter and Campbell were appointed Peace Commissioners, January 28th.

sisters. They were flitting, but were to go only as far as Yorkville. He said it was time to move on. Sherman was at Orangeburg, barely a day's journey from Columbia, and had left a track as bare and blackened as a fire leaves on the prairies.

So my time had come, too. My husband urged me to go home. He said Camden would be safe enough. They had no spite against that old town, as they have against Charleston and Columbia. Molly, weeping and wailing, came in while we were at table. Wiping her red-hot face with the cook's grimy apron, she said I ought to go among our own black people on the plantation; they would take care of me better than any one else. So I agreed to go to Mulberry or the Hermitage plantation, and sent Lawrence down with a wagon-load of my valuables.

Then a Miss Patterson called—a refugee from Tennessee. She had been in a country overrun by Yankee invaders, and she described so graphically all the horrors to be endured by those subjected to fire and sword, rapine and plunder, that I was fairly scared, and determined to come here. This is a thoroughly out-of-all-routes place. And yet I can go to Charlotte, am half-way to Kate at Flat Rock, and there is no Federal army between me and Richmond.

As soon as my mind was finally made up, we telegraphed to Lawrence, who had barely got to Camden in the wagon when the telegram was handed to him; so he took the train and came back. Mr. Chesnut sent him with us to take care of the party.

We thought that if the negroes were ever so loyal to us, they could not protect me from an army bent upon sweeping us from the face of the earth, and if they tried to do so so much the worse would it be for the poor things with their Yankee friends. I then left them to shift for themselves, as they are accustomed to do, and I took the same liberty. My husband does not care a fig for the property question, and never did. Perhaps, if he had ever known poverty, it would be different. He talked beautifully about it, as he always does about everything. I have told him often that, if at heaven's gate St. Peter would listen to him a while, and let him tell his own story, he would get in, and the angels might give him a crown extra.

Now he says he has only one care—that I should be safe, and not so harassed with dread; and then there is his blind old father. "A man," said he, "can always die like a patriot and a gentleman, with no fuss, and take it coolly. It is hard not to envy those who are out of all this, their difficulties ended—those who have met death gloriously on the battle-field, their doubts all solved. One can but do his best and leave the result to a higher power."

After New Orleans, those vain, passionate, impatient little Creoles were forever committing suicide, driven to it by despair and "Beast" Butler. As we read these things, Mrs. Davis said: "If they want to die, why not first kill 'Beast' Butler, rid the world of their foe and be saved the trouble of murdering themselves?" That practical way of removing their intolerable burden did not occur to them. I repeated this suggestive anecdote to our corps of generals without troops, here in this house, as they spread out their maps on my table where lay this quire of paper from which I write. Every man Jack of them had a safe plan to stop Sherman, if -

Even Beauregard and Lee were expected, but Grant had double-teamed on Lee. Lee could not save his own—how could he come to save us? Read the list of the dead in those last battles around Richmond and Petersburg[129] if you want to break your heart.

I took French leave of Columbia—slipped away without a word to anybody. Isaac Hayne and Mr. Chesnut came down to the Charlotte depot with me. Ellen, my maid, left her husband and only child, but she was willing to come, and, indeed, was very cheerful in her way of looking at it.

"I wan' travel 'roun' wid Missis some time—stid uh Molly goin' all de time."

A woman, fifty years old at least, and uglier than she was old, sharply rebuked my husband for standing at the car window for a last few words with me. She said rudely: "Stand aside, sir! I want air!" With his hat off, and his grand air, my husband bowed politely, and said: "In one moment, madam; I have something important to say to my wife."

She talked aloud and introduced herself to every man, claiming his protection. She had never traveled alone before in all her life. Old age and ugliness are protective in some cases. She was ardently patriotic for a while. Then she was joined by her friend, a man as crazy as herself to get out of this. From their talk I gleaned she had been for years in the Treasury Department. They were about to cross the lines. The whole idea was to get away from the trouble to come down here. They were Yankees, but were they not spies?

Here I am broken-hearted and an exile. And in such a place! We have bare floors, and for a feather-bed, pine table, and two chairs I pay $30 a day. Such sheets! But fortunately I have some of my own. At the door, before I was well out of the hack, the woman of the house packed Lawrence back, neck and heels: she would not have him at any price. She treated him as Mr. F.'s aunt did Clenman in Little Dorrit. She said his clothes were too fine for a nigger. "His airs, indeed." Poor Lawrence was humble and silent. He said at last, "Miss Mary, send me back to Mars Jeems." I began to look for a pencil to write a note to my husband, but in the flurry could not find one. "Here is one," said

---

[129] Battles at Hatchen's Run, in Virginia, had been fought on February 5, 6, and 7, 1865.

Lawrence, producing one with a gold case. "Go away," she shouted, "I want no niggers here with gold pencils and airs." So Lawrence fled before the storm, but not before he had begged me to go back. He said, "if Mars Jeems knew how you was treated he'd never be willing for you to stay here."

The Martins had seen my, to them, well-known traveling case as the hack trotted up Main Street, and they arrived at this juncture out of breath. We embraced and wept. I kept my room.

The Fants are refugees here, too; they are Virginians, and have been in exile since the second battle of Manassas. Poor things; they seem to have been everywhere, and seen and suffered everything. They even tried to go back to their own house, but found one chimney only standing alone; even that had been taken possession of by a Yankee who had written his name upon it.

The day I left home I had packed a box of flour, sugar rice, and coffee, but my husband would not let me bring it. He said I was coming to a land of plenty—unexplored North Carolina, where the foot of the Yankee marauder was unknown, and in Columbia they would need food. Now I have written for that box and many other things to be sent me by Lawrence, or I shall starve.

The Middletons have come. How joyously I sprang to my feet to greet them. Mrs. Ben Rutledge described the hubbub in Columbia. Everybody was flying in every direction like a flock of swallows. She heard the enemy's guns booming in the distance. The train no longer run, from Charlotte to Columbia. Miss Middleton possesses her soul in peace. She is as cool, clever, rational, and entertaining as ever, and we talked for hours. Mrs. Reed was in a state of despair. I can well understand that sinking of mind and body during the first days as the abject misery of it all closes in upon you. I remember my suicidal tendencies when I first came here.

February 18th.—Here I am, thank God, settled at the McLean's, in a clean, comfortable room, airy and cozy. With a grateful heart I stir up my own bright wood fire My bill for four days at this splendid hotel here was $240 with $25 additional for fire. But once more my lines have fallen in pleasant places.

As we came up on the train from Charlotte a soldier took out of his pocket a filthy rag. If it had lain in the gutter for months it could not have looked worse. He unwrapped the thing carefully and took out two biscuits of the species known as "hard tack." Then he gallantly handed me one and with an ingratiating smile asked me "to take some." Then he explained, saying, "Please take these two; swap with me; give me something softer that I can eat; I am very weak still." Immediately, for his benefit, my basket of luncheon was emptied, but as for his biscuit, I would not choose any. Isabella asked, "But what did you say to him when he poked them under your nose?" and I replied, "I held up both hands, saying, 'I would not take from you anything that is yours—far from it! I would not touch them for worlds.'"

A tremendous day's work and I helped with a will; our window glass was all to be washed. Then the brass andirons were to be polished. After we rubbed them bright how pretty they were. Presently Ellen would have none of me. She was scrubbing the floor. "You go—dat's a good missis—an' stay to Miss Isabella's till de flo' dry." I am very docile now, and I obeyed orders.

February 19th.—The Fants say all the trouble at the hotel came from our servants' bragging. They represented us as millionaires, and the Middleton men servants smoked cigars. Mrs. Reed's averred that he had never done anything in his life but stand behind his master at table with a silver waiter in his hand. We were charged accordingly, but perhaps the landlady did not get the best of us after all, for we paid her in Confederate money. Now that they won't take Confederate money in the shops here how are we to live? Miss Middleton says quartermasters' families are all clad in good gray cloth, but the soldiers go naked. Well, we are like the families of whom the novels always say they are poor but honest. Poor? Well-nigh beggars are we, for I do not know where my next meal is to come from.

Called on Mrs. Ben Rutledge to-day. She is lovely, exquisitely refined. Her mother, Mrs. Middleton, came in. "You are not looking well, dear? Anything the matter?" "No—but, mamma, I have not eaten a mouthful to-day. The children can eat mush; I can't. I drank my tea, however." She does not understand taking favors, and, blushing violently, refused to let me have Ellen make her some biscuit. I went home and sent her some biscuit all the same.

February 22d.—Isabella has been reading my diaries. How we laugh because my sage divinations all come to naught. My famous "insight into character" is utter folly. The diaries were lying on the hearth ready to be burned, but she told me to hold on to them; think of them a while and don't be rash. Afterward when Isabella and I were taking a walk, General Joseph E. Johnston joined us. He explained to us all of Lee's and Stonewall Jackson's mistakes. We had nothing to say—how could we say anything? He said he was very angry when he was ordered to take command again. He might well have been in a genuine rage. This on and off procedure would be enough to bewilder the coolest head. Mrs. Johnston knows how to be a partizan of Joe Johnston and still not make his enemies uncomfortable. She can be pleasant and agreeable, as she was to my face.

A letter from my husband who is at Charlotte. He came near being taken a prisoner in Columbia, for he was asleep the morning of the 17th, when the Yankees blew up the railroad depot. That woke him, of course, and he found everybody had left Columbia, and the town was surrendered by the mayor, Colonel Goodwyn. Hampton and his command had been gone several hours. Isaac Hayne came away with General Chesnut. There was no fire in the town when they left. They overtook Hampton's command at Meek's Mill. That night, from the hills where they encamped, they saw the fire, and knew the Yankees were burning the town, as we had every reason to expect they would. Molly was left in charge of everything of mine, including Mrs. Preston's cow, which I was keeping, and Sally Goodwyn's furniture.

Charleston and Wilmington have surrendered. I have no further use for a newspaper. I never want to see another one as long as I live. Wade Hampton has been made a lieutenant-general, too late. If he had been made one and given command in South Carolina six months ago I believe he would have saved us. Shame, disgrace, beggary, all have come at once, and are hard to bear—the grand smash! Rain, rain, outside, and naught but drowning floods of tears inside. I could not bear it; so I rushed down in that rainstorm to the Martins'. Rev. Mr. Martin met me at the door. "Madam," said he, "Columbia is burned to the ground." I bowed my head and sobbed aloud. "Stop that!" he said, trying to speak cheerfully. "Come here, wife," said he to Mrs. Martin. "This woman cries with her whole heart, just as she laughs." But in spite of his words, his voice broke down, and he was hardly calmer than myself.

February 23d.—I want to get to Kate, I am so utterly heart-broken. I hope John Chesnut and General Chesnut may at least get into the same army. We seem scattered over the face of the earth. Isabella sits there calmly reading. I have quieted down after the day's rampage. May our heavenly Father look down on us and have pity.

They say I was the last refugee from Columbia who was allowed to enter by the door of the cars. The government took possession then and women could only be smuggled in by the windows. Stout ones stuck and had to be pushed, pulled, and hauled in by main force. Dear Mrs. Izard, with all her dignity, was subjected to this rough treatment. She was found almost too much for the size of the car windows.

February 25th.—The Pfeifers, who live opposite us here, are descendants of those Pfeifers who came South with Mr. Chesnut's ancestors after the Fort Duquesne disaster. They have now, therefore, been driven out of their Eden, the valley of Virginia, a second time. The present Pfeifer is the great man, the rich man *par excellence* of Lincolnton. They say that with something very near to tears in his eyes he heard of our latest defeats. "It is only a question of time with us now," he said. "The raiders will come, you know."

In Washington, before I knew any of them. except by sight, Mrs. Davis, Mrs. Emory, and Mrs. Johnston were always together, inseparable friends, and the trio were pointed out to me as the cleverest women in the United States. Now that I do know them all well, I think the world was right in its estimate of them.

Met a Mr. Ancrum of serenely cheerful aspect, happy and hopeful. "All right now," said he. "Sherman sure to be thrashed. Joe Johnston is in command." Dr. Darby says, when the oft-mentioned Joseph, the malcontent, gave up his command to Hood, he remarked with a smile, "I hope you will be able to stop Sherman; it was more than I could do." General Johnston is not of Mr. Ancrum's way of thinking as to his own powers, for he stayed here several days after he was ordered to the front. He must have known he could do no good, and I am of his opinion.

When the wagon, in which I was to travel to Flat Rock, drove up to the door, covered with a tent-like white cloth, in my embarrassment for an opening in the conversation I asked the driver's name. He showed great hesitation in giving it, but at last said: "My name is Sherman," adding, "and now I see by your face that you won't go with me. My name is against me these times." Here he grinned and remarked: "But you would leave Lincolnton."

That name was the last drop in my cup, but I gave him Mrs. Glover's reason for staying here. General Johnston had told her this "might be the safest place after all." He thinks the Yankees are making straight for Richmond and General Lee's rear, and will go by Camden and Lancaster, leaving Lincolnton on their west flank.

The McLeans are kind people. They ask no rent for for their rooms—only $20 a week for firewood. Twenty dollars! and such dollars—mere waste paper.

Mrs. Munroe took up my photograph book, in which I have a picture of all the Yankee generals. "I want to see the men who are to be our masters," said she. "Not mine" I answered, "thank God, come what may. This was a free fight. We had as much right to fight to get out as they had to fight to keep us in. If they try to play the masters, anywhere upon the habitable globe will I go, never to see a Yankee, and if I die on the way so much the better." Then I sat down and wrote to my husband in language much worse than anything I can put in this book. As I wrote I was blinded by tears of rage. Indeed, I nearly wept myself away.

February 26th.—Mrs. Munroe offered me religious books, which I declined, being already provided with the Lamentations of Jeremiah, the Psalms of David, the denunciations of Hosea, and, above all, the patient wail of Job. Job is my comforter now. I should be so thankful to know life never would be any worse with me. My husband is well, and has been ordered to join the great Retreater. I am bodily comfortable, if somewhat dingily lodged, and I daily part with my raiment for food. We find no one who will exchange eatables for Confederate money; so we are devouring our clothes.

Opportunities for social enjoyment are not wanting. Miss Middleton and Isabella often drink a cup of tea with me. One might search the whole world and not find two cleverer or more agreeable women. Miss Middleton is brilliant and accomplished. She must have been a hard student all her life. She knows everybody worth knowing, and she has been everywhere. Then she is so high-bred, high-hearted, pure, and true. She is so clean-minded; she could not harbor a wrong thought. She is utterly unselfish, a devoted daughter and sister. She is one among the many large-brained women a kind Providence has thrown in my way, such as Mrs. McCord, daughter of Judge Cheves; Mary Preston Darby, Mrs. Emory, granddaughter of old Franklin, the American wise man, and Mrs. Jefferson Davis. How I love to praise my friends!

As a ray of artificial sunshine, Mrs. Munroe sent me an Examiner. Daniel thinks we are at the last gasp, and now England and France are bound to step in. England must know if the United States of America are triumphant they will tackle her next, and France must wonder if she will not have to give up Mexico. My faith fails me. It is all too late; no help for us now from God or man.

Thomas, Daniel says, was now to ravage Georgia, but Sherman, from all accounts, has done that work once for all. There will be no aftermath. They say no living thing is found in Sherman's track, only chimneys, like telegraph poles, to carry the news of Sherman's army backward.

In all that tropical down-pour, Mrs. Munroe sent me overshoes and an umbrella, with the message, "Come over" I went, for it would be as well to drown in the streets as to hang myself at home to my own bedpost. At Mrs. Munroe's I met a Miss McDaniel. Her father, for seven years, was the Methodist preacher at our negro church. The negro church is in a grove just opposite Mulberry house. She says her father has so often described that fine old establishment and its beautiful lawn, live-oaks, etc. Now, I dare say there stand at Mulberry only Sherman's sentinels -stacks of chimneys. We have made up our minds for the worst. Mulberry house is no doubt razed to the ground.

Miss McDaniel was inclined to praise us. She said: "As a general rule the Episcopal minister went to the family mansion, and the Methodist missionary preached to the negroes and dined with the overseer at his house, but at Mulberry her father always stayed at the 'House,' and the family were so kind and attentive to him." It was rather pleasant to hear one's family so spoken of among strangers.

So, well equipped to brave the weather, armed cap-a-pie, so to speak, I continued my prowl farther afield and brought up at the Middletons'. I may have surprised them for "at such an inclement season" they hardly expected a visitor. Never, however, did lonely old woman receive such a warm and hearty welcome. Now we know the worst. Are we growing hardened? We avoid all allusion to Columbia; we never speak of home, and we begin to deride the certain poverty that lies ahead.

How it pours! Could I live many days in solitary confinement? Things are beginning to be unbearable, but I must sit down and be satisfied. My husband is safe so far. Let me be thankful it is no worse with me. But there is the gnawing pain all the same. What is the good of being here at all, Our world has simply gone to destruction. And across the way the fair Lydia languishes. She has not even my resources against ennui. She has no Isabella, no Miss Middleton, two as brilliant women as any in Christendom. Oh, how does she stand it! I mean to go to church if it rains cats and dogs. My feet are wet two or three times a day. We never take cold; our hearts are too hot within us for that.

A carriage was driven up to the door as I was writing. I began to tie on my bonnet, and said to myself in the glass, "Oh, you lucky woman!" I was all in a tremble, so great was my haste to be out of this. Mrs. Glover had the carriage. She came for me to go and hear Mr. Martin preach. He lifts our spirits from this dull earth; he takes us up to heaven. That I will not deny. Still he can not hold my attention; my heart wanders and my mind strays back to South Carolina. Oh, vandal Sherman! what are you at there, hard-hearted wretch that you are! A letter from General Chesnut, who writes from camp near Charlotte under date of February 28th:

"I thank you a thousand, thousand times for your kind letters. They are now my only earthly comfort, except the hope that all is not yet lost. We have been driven like a wild herd from our country. And it is not from a want of spirit in the people or soldiers, nor from want of energy and competency in our commanders. The restoration of Joe Johnston, it is hoped, will redound to the advantage of our cause and the reestablishment of our fortunes! I am still in not very agreeable circumstances. For the last four days completely water-bound.

"I am informed that a detachment of Yankees were sent from Liberty Hill to Camden with a view to destroying all the houses, mills, and provisions about that place. No particulars have reached me. You know I expected the worst that could be done, and am fully prepared for any report which may be made.

"It would be a happiness beyond expression to see you even for an hour. I have heard nothing from my poor old father. I fear I shall never see him again. Such is the fate of war. I do not complain. I have deliberately chosen my lot, and am prepared for any fate that awaits me. My care is for you, and I trust still in the good cause of my country and the justice and mercy of God."

It was a lively, rushing, young set that South Carolina put to the fore. They knew it was a time of imminent danger, and that the fight would be ten to one. They expected to win by activity, energy, and enthusiasm. Then came the wet blanket, the croakers; now, these are posing, wrapping Cæsar's mantle about their heads to fall with dignity. Those gallant youths who dashed so gaily to the front lie mostly in bloody graves. Well for them, maybe. There are worse things than honorable graves. Wearisome thoughts. Late in life we are to begin anew and have laborious, difficult days ahead.

We have contradictory testimony. Governor Aiken has passed through, saying Sherman left Columbia as he found it, and was last heard from at Cheraw. Dr. Chisolm walked home with me. He says that is the last version of the story; Now my husband wrote that he himself saw the fires which burned up Columbia. The first night his camp was near enough to the town for that.

They say Sherman has burned Lancaster—that Sherman nightmare, that ghoul, that hyena! But I do not believe it. He takes his time. There are none to molest him.

He does things leisurely and deliberately. Why stop to do so needless a thing as burn Lancaster court-house, the jail, and the tavern? As I remember it, that description covers Lancaster. A raiding party they say did for Camden.

No train from Charlotte yesterday. Rumor says Sherman is in Charlotte.

February 29th.—Trying to brave it out. They have plenty, yet let our men freeze and starve in their prisons. Would you be willing to be as wicked as they are? A thousand times, no! But we must feed our army first—if we can do so much as that. Our captives need not starve if Lincoln would consent to exchange prisoners; but men are nothing to the United States—things to throw away. If they send our men back they strengthen our army, and so again their policy is to keep everybody and everything here in order to help starve us out. That, too, is what Sherman's destruction means—to starve us out.

Young Brevard asked me to play accompaniments for him. The guitar is my instrument, or was; so I sang and played, to my own great delight. It was a distraction. Then I made egg-nog for the soldier boys below and came home. Have spent a very pleasant evening. Begone, dull care; you and I never agree.

Ellen and I are shut up here. It is rain, rain, everlasting rain. As our money is worthless, are we not to starve? Heavens! how grateful I was to-day when Mrs. McLean sent me a piece of chicken. I think the emptiness of my larder has leaked out. To-day Mrs. Munroe sent me hot cakes and eggs for my breakfast.

March 5th.—Is the sea drying up? Is it going up into mist and coming down on us in a water-spout? The rain, it raineth every day. The weather typifies our tearful despair, on a large scale. It is also Lent now—a quite convenient custom, for we, in truth, have nothing to eat. So we fast and pray, and go dragging to church like drowned rats to be preached at.

My letter from my husband was so—well, what in a woman you would call heart-broken, that I began to get ready for a run up to Charlotte. My hat was on my head, my traveling-bag in my hand, and Ellen was saying "Which umbrella, ma'am?" "Stop, Ellen," said I, "someone is speaking out there." A tap came at the door, and Miss McLean threw the door wide open as she said in a triumphant voice: "Permit me to announce General Chesnut." As she went off she sang out, "Oh, does not a meeting like this make amends?"

We went after luncheon to see Mrs. Munroe. My husband wanted to thank her for all her kindness to me. I was awfully proud of him. I used to think that everybody had the air and manners of a gentleman. I know now that these accomplishments are things to thank God for. Father O'Connell came in, fresh from Columbia, and with news at last. Sherman's men had burned the convent. Mrs. Munroe had pinned her faith to Sherman because he was a Roman Catholic, but Father O'Connell was there and saw it. The nuns and girls marched to the old Hampton house (Mrs. Preston's now), and so saved it. They walked between files of soldiers. Men were rolling tar barrels and lighting torches to fling on the house when the nuns came. Columbia is but dust and ashes, burned to the ground. Men, women, and children have been left there homeless, houseless, and without one particle of food—reduced to picking up corn that was left by Sherman's horses on picket grounds and parching it to stay their hunger.

How kind my friends were on this, my fête day! Mrs. Rutledge sent me a plate of biscuit; Mrs. Munroe, nearly enough food supplies for an entire dinner; Miss McLean a cake for dessert. Ellen cooked and served up the material happily at hand very nicely, indeed. There never was a more successful dinner. My heart was too full to eat, but I was quiet and calm; at least I spared my husband the trial of a broken voice and tears. As he stood at the window, with his back to the room, he said: "Where are they now- my old blind father and my sister? Day and night I see her leading him out from under his own rooftree. That picture pursues me persistently. But come, let us talk of pleasanter things." To which I answered, "Where will you find them?"

He took off his heavy cavalry boots and Ellen carried them away to wash the mud off and dry them. She brought them back just as Miss Middleton walked in. In his agony, while struggling with those huge boots and trying to get them on, he spoke to her volubly in French. She turned away from him instantly, as she saw his shoeless plight, and said to me, "I had not heard of your happiness. I did not know the General was here." Not until next day did we have time to remember and laugh at that outbreak of French. Miss Middleton answered him in the same language. He told her how charmed he was with my surroundings, and that he would go away with a much lighter heart since he had seen the kind people with whom he would leave me.

I asked my husband what that correspondence between Sherman and Hampton meant—this while I was preparing something for our dinner. His back was still turned as he gazed out of the window. He spoke in the low and steady monotone that characterized our conversation the whole day, and yet there was something in his voice that thrilled me as he said: "The second day after our march from Columbia we passed the M.'s. He was a bonded man and not at home. His wife said at first that she could not find forage for our horses, but afterward she succeeded in procuring some. I noticed a very handsome girl who stood beside her as she spoke, and I suggested to her mother the propriety of sending her out of the track of both armies. Things were no longer as heretofore; there was so much straggling, so many camp followers, with no discipline, on the outskirts of the army. The girl answered quickly, 'I wish to stay with my mother.' That very night a party of Wheeler's men came to our camp, and such a tale they told of what had been done at the place of horror and destruction, the mother left raving. The outrage had been committed before her very face, she having been secured first . After this crime the fiends moved on. There were only seven of them. They had been gone but a short time when Wheeler's men went in pursuit at full speed and overtook them, cut their throats and wrote upon their breasts: 'These were the seven!'"

"But the girl?"

"Oh, she was dead!"

"Are his critics as violent as ever against the President?" asked I when recovered from pity and horror. "Sometimes I think I am the only friend he has in the world. At these dinners, which they give us everywhere, I spoil the sport, for I will not sit still and hear Jeff Davis abused for things he is no more responsible for than any man at that table. Once I lost my temper and told them it sounded like arrant nonsense to me, and that Jeff Davis was a gentleman and a patriot, with more brains than the assembled company." "You lost your temper truly," said I. "And I did not know it. I thought I was as cool as I am now. In Washington when we left, Jeff Davis ranked second to none, in intellect, and may be first, from the South, and Mrs. Davis was the friend of Mrs. Emory, Mrs. Joe Johnston, and Mrs. Montgomery Blair, and others of that circle. Now they rave that he is nobody, and never was." "And she?" I asked. "Oh, you would think to hear them that he found her yesterday in a Mississippi swamp!" "Well, in the French Revolution it was worse. When a man failed he was guillotined. Mirabeau did not die a day too soon, even Mirabeau."

He is gone. With despair in my heart I left that railroad station. an Green walked home with me. I met his wife and his four ragged ' boys a day or so ago. She is the neatest, the primmest, the softest men. Her voice is like the gentle cooing of a dove. That lowering black future hangs there all the same. The end of the war brings no hope of peace or of security to us. Ellen said I had a little piece of bread and a little molasses in store for my dinner to-day.

March 6th.—To-day came a godsend. Even a small piece of bread and the molasses had become things of the past. My larder was empty, when a tall mulatto woman brought a tray covered by a huge white serviette. Ellen ushered her in with a flourish, saying, "Mrs. McDaniel's maid." The maid set down the tray upon my bare table, and uncovered it with conscious pride. There were fowls ready for roasting, sausages, butter, bread, eggs, and preserves. I was dumb with delight. After silent thanks to heaven my powers of speech returned, and I exhausted myself in messages of gratitude to Mrs. McDaniel.

"Missis, you oughtn't to let her see how glad you was," said Ellen. "It was a lettin' of yo'sef down."

Mrs. Glover gave me some yarn, and I bought five dozen eggs with it from a wagon—eggs for Lent. To show that I have faith yet in humanity, I paid in advance in yarn for something to eat, which they promised to bring to-morrow. Had they rated their eggs at $100 a dozen in "Confederick" money, I would have paid it as readily as $10. But I haggle in yarn for the millionth part of a thread.

Two weeks have passed and the rumors from Columbia are still of the vaguest. No letter has come from there, no direct message, or messenger. "My God!" cried Dr. Frank Miles, "but it is strange. Can it be anything so dreadful they dare not tell us?" Dr. St. Julien Ravenel has grown pale and haggard with care. His wife and children were left there.

Dr. Brumby has at last been coaxed into selling me enough leather for the making of a pair of shoes, else I should have had to give up walking. He knew my father well. He intimated that in some way my father helped him through college. His own money had not sufficed, and so William C. Preston and my father advanced funds sufficient to let him be graduated. Then my uncle, Charles Miller, married his aunt. I listened in rapture, for all this tended to leniency in the leather business, and I bore off the leather gladly. When asked for Confederate money in trade I never stop to bargain. I give them $20 or $50 cheerfully for anything—either sum.

March 8th.—Colonel Childs came with a letter from my husband and a newspaper containing a full account of Sherman's cold-blooded brutality in Columbia. Then we walked three miles to return the call of my benefactress, Mrs. McDaniel. They were kind and hospitable at her house, but my heart was like lead; my head ached, and my legs were worse than my head, and then I had a nervous chill. So I came home; went to bed and stayed there until the Fants brought me a letter saying my husband would be here today. Then I got up and made ready to give him a cheerful reception. Soon a man called, Troy by name, the same who kept the little corner shop so near my house in Columbia, and of whom we bought things so often. We had fraternized. He now shook hands with me and looked in my face pitifully. We seemed to have been friends all our lives. He says they stopped the fire at the Methodist College, perhaps to save old Mr. McCartha's house. Mr. Sheriff Dent, being burned out, took refuge in our house. He contrived to find favor in Yankee eyes. Troy relates that a Yankee officer snatched a watch from Mrs. McCord's bosom. The soldiers tore the bundles of clothes that the poor wretches tried to save from their burning homes, and dashed them back into the flames. They meant to make a clean sweep. They were howling round the fires like demons, these Yankees in their joy and triumph at our destruction. Well, we have given them a big scare and kept them miserable for four years—the little handful of us.

A woman we met on the street stopped to tell us a painful coincidence. A general was married but he could not stay at home very long after the wedding. When his baby was born they telegraphed him, and he sent back a rejoicing answer with an inquiry, "Is it a boy or a girl?" He was killed before he got the reply. Was it not sad? His poor young wife says, "He did not live to hear that his son lived." The kind woman added, sorrowfully, "Died and did not know the sect of his child." "Let us hope it will be a Methodist," said Isabella, the irrepressible.

At the venison feast Isabella heard a good word for me and one for General Chesnut's air of distinction, a thing people can not give themselves, try as ever they may. Lord Byron says, Everybody knows a gentleman when he sees one, and nobody can tell what it is that makes a gentleman. He knows the thing, but he can't describe it. Now there are some French words that can not be translated, and we all know the thing they mean—*gracieuse* and *svelte*, for instance, as applied to a woman. Not that anything was said of me like that—far from it. I am fair, fat, forty, and jolly, and in my unbroken jollity, as far as they know, they found my charm. "You see, she doesn't howl; she doesn't cry; she never, never tells anybody about what she was used to at home and what she has lost." High praise, and I intend to try and deserve it ever after.

March 10th.—Went to church crying to Ellen, "It is Lent, we must fast and pray." When I came home my good fairy, Colonel Childs, had been here bringing rice and potatoes, and promising flour. He is a trump. He pulled out his pocket-book and offered to be my banker. He stood there on the street, Miss Middleton and Isabella witnessing the generous action, and straight out offered me money. "No, put up that," said I. "I am not a beggar, and I never will be; to die is so much easier."

Alas, after that flourish of trumpets, when he came with a sack of flour, I accepted it gratefully. I receive things I can not pay for, but money is different. There I draw a line, imaginary perhaps. Once before the same thing happened. Our letters of credit came slowly in 1845, when we went unexpectedly to Europe and our letters were to follow us. I was a poor little, inoffensive bride, and a British officer, who guessed our embarrassment, for we did not tell him (he came over with us on the ship), asked my husband to draw on his banker until the letters of credit should arrive. It was a nice thing for a stranger to do.

We have never lost what we never had. We have never had any money—only unlimited credit, for my husband's richest kind of a father insured us all manner of credit. It was all a mirage only at last, and it has gone just as we drew nigh to it.

Colonel Childs says eight of our Senators are for reconstruction, and that a ray of light has penetrated inward from Lincoln, who told Judge Campbell that Southern land would not be confiscated.

March 12th.—Better to-day. A long, long weary day in grief has passed away. I suppose General Chesnut is somewhere—but where? that is the question. Only once has he visited this sad spot, which holds, he says, all that he cares for on earth. Unless he comes or writes soon I will cease, or try to cease, this wearisome looking, looking, looking for him.

March 13th.—My husband at last did come for a visit of two hours. Brought Lawrence, who had been to Camden, and was there, indeed, during the raid. My husband has been ordered to Chester, S. C. We are surprised to see by the papers that we behaved heroically in leaving everything we had to be destroyed, without one thought of surrender. We had not thought of ourselves from the heroic point of view. Isaac McLaughlin hid and saved everything we trusted him with. A grateful negro is Isaac.

March 15th.—Lawrence says Miss Chesnut is very proud of the presence of mind and cool self-possession she showed in the face of the enemy. She lost, after all, only two bottles of champagne, two of her brother's gold-headed canes, and her brother's horses, including Claudia, the brood mare, that he valued beyond price, and her own carriage, and a fly-brush boy called Battis, whose occupation in life was to stand behind the table with his peacock feathers and brush the flies away. He was the sole member of his dusky race at Mulberry who deserted "Ole Marster" to follow the Yankees.

Now for our losses at the Hermitage. Added to the gold-headed canes and Claudia, we lost every mule and horse, and President Davis's beautiful Arabian was captured. John's were there, too. My light dragoon, Johnny, and heavy swell, is stripped light enough for the fight now. Jonathan, whom we trusted, betrayed us; and the plantation and mills, Mulberry house, etc., were saved by Claiborne, that black rascal, who was suspected by all the world. Claiborne boldly affirmed that Mr. Chesnut would not be hurt by destroying his place; the invaders would hurt only the negroes. "Mars Jeems," said he, "hardly ever come here and he takes only a little sompen nur to eat when he do come."

Fever continuing, I sent for St. Julien Ravenel. We had a wrangle over the slavery question. Then, he fell foul of everybody who had not conducted this war according to his ideas. Ellen had something nice to offer him (thanks to the ever-bountiful Childs!), but he was too angry, too anxious, too miserable to eat. He pitched into Ellen after he had disposed of me. Ellen stood glaring at him from the fireplace, her blue eye nearly white, her other eye blazing as a comet. Last Sunday, he gave her some Dover's powders for me; directions were written on the paper in which the medicine was wrapped, and he told her to show these to me, then to put what I should give her into a wine-glass and let me drink it. Ellen put it all into the wine-glass and let me drink it at one dose. "It was enough to last you your lifetime," he said. "It was murder." Turning to I Ellen: "What did you do with the directions?" "I nuvver see no d'rections. You nuvver gimme none." "I told you to show that paper to your mistress." "Well, I flung dat ole brown paper in de fire. What you makin' all dis fuss for? Soon as I give Missis de physic, she stop frettin' an' flingin' 'bout, she go to sleep sweet as a suckling baby, an' she slep two days an' nights, an' now she heap better." And Ellen withdrew from the controversy.

"Well, all is well that ends well, Mrs. Chesnut. You took opium enough to kill several persons. You were worried out and needed rest. You came near getting it—thoroughly. You were in no danger from your disease. But your doctor and your nurse combined were deadly." Maybe I was saved by the adulteration, the feebleness, of Confederate medicine.

*   *   *   *   *

A letter from my husband, written at Chester Court House on March 15th, says: "In the morning I send Lieut. Ogden with Lawrence to Lincolnton to bring you down. I have three vacant rooms; one with bedsteads, chairs, washstands, basins, and pitchers; the two others bare. You can have half of a kitchen for your cooking. I have also at Dr. Da Vega's, a room, furnished, to which you are invited (board, also). You can take your choice. If you can get your friends in Lincolnton to assume charge of your valuables, only bring such as you may need here. Perhaps it will be better to bring bed and bedding and the other indispensables."

CHAPTER XX. CHESTER, S. C.

March 21, 1865—*May* 1, 1865

Chester, S. C., *March 21, 1865.*—Another flitting has occurred. Captain Ogden came for me; the splendid Childs was true as steel to the last. Surely he is the kindest of men. Captain Ogden was slightly incredulous when I depicted the wonders of Colonel Childs's generosity. So I skilfully led out the good gentleman for inspection, and he walked to the train with us. He offered me Confederate money, silver, and gold; and finally offered to buy our cotton and pay us now in gold. Of course, I laughed at his overflowing bounty, and accepted nothing; but I begged him to come down to Chester or Camden and buy our cotton of General Chesnut there.

On the train after leaving Lincolnton, as Captain Ogden is a refugee, has had no means of communicating with his home since New Orleans fell, and was sure to know how refugees contrive to live, I beguiled the time acquiring information from him. "When people are without a cent, how do they live?" I asked. "I am about to enter the noble band of homeless, houseless refugees, and Confederate pay does not buy one's shoe-strings." To which he replied, "Sponge, sponge. Why did you not let Colonel Childs pay your bills?" "I have no bills," said I. "We have never made bills anywhere, not even at home, where they would trust us, and nobody would trust me in Lincolnton." "Why did you not borrow his money? General Chesnut could pay him at his leisure?" "I am by no means sure General Chesnut will ever again have any money," said I.

As the train rattled and banged along, and I waved my handkerchief in farewell to Miss Middleton, Isabella, and other devoted friends, I could only wonder if fate would ever throw me again with such kind, clever, agreeable, congenial companions, The McLeans refused to be paid for their rooms. No plummet can sound the depths of the hospitality and kindness of the North Carolina people.

Misfortune dogged us from the outset. Everything went wrong with the train. We broke down within two miles of Charlotte, and had to walk that distance; which was pretty rough on an invalid barely out of a fever. My spirit was further broken by losing an invaluable lace veil, which was worn because I was too poor to buy a cheaper one— that is, if there were any veils at all for sale in our region.

My husband had ordered me to a house in Charlotte kept by some great friends of his. They established me in the drawing-room, a really handsome apartment; they made up a bed there and put in a washstand and plenty of water, with everything refreshingly clean and nice. But it continued to be a public drawing-room, open to all, so that I was half dead at night and wanted to go to bed. The piano was there and the company played it.

The landlady announced, proudly, that for supper there were nine kinds of custard. Custard sounded nice and light, so I sent for some, but found it heavy potato pie. I said: "Ellen, this may kill me, though Dover's powder did not." "Don't you believe dat, Missis; try." We barricaded ourselves in the drawing-room that night and left the next day at dawn. Arrived at the station, we had another disappointment; the train was behind time. There we sat on our boxes nine long hours; for the cars might come at any moment, and we dared not move an inch from the spot.

Finally the train rolled in overloaded with paroled prisoners, but heaven helped us: a kind mail agent invited us, with two other forlorn women, into his comfortable and clean mail-car. Ogden, true to his theory, did not stay at the boarding-house as we did. Some Christian acquaintances took him in for the night. This he explained with a grin.

My husband was at the Chester station with a carriage. We drove at once to Mrs. Da Vega's.

March 24th.-I have been ill, but what could you expect? My lines, however, have again fallen in pleasant places. Mrs. Da Vega is young, handsome, and agreeable, a kind and perfect hostess; and as to the house, my room is all that I could ask and leaves nothing to be desired; so very fresh, clean, warm, and comfortable is it. It is the drawing-room suddenly made into a bedroom for me. But it is my very own. We are among the civilized of the earth once more.

March 27th.—I have moved again, and now I am looking from a window high, with something more to see than the sky. We have the third story of Dr. Da Vega's house, which opens on the straight street that leads to the railroad about a mile off.

Mrs. Bedon is the loveliest of young widows. Yesterday at church Isaac Hayne nestled so close to her cap-strings that I had to touch him and say, "Sit up!" Josiah Bedon was killed in that famous fight of the Charleston Light Dragoons. The dragoons stood still to be shot down in their; tracks, having no orders to retire. They had been forgotten, doubtless, and they scorned to take care of themselves.

In this high and airy retreat, as in Richmond, then in Columbia, and then in Lincolnton, my cry is still: If they would only leave me here in peace and if I were sure things never could be worse with me. Again am I surrounded by old friends. People seem to vie with each other to show how good they can be to me.

To-day Smith opened the trenches and appeared laden with a tray covered with a snow-white napkin. Here was my first help toward housekeeping again. Mrs. Pride has sent a boiled ham, a loaf of bread, a huge pancake; another neighbor coffee already parched and ground; a loaf of sugar already cracked; candles, pickles, and all the other things one must trust to love for now. Such money as we have avails us nothing, even if there were anything left in the shops to buy.

We had a jolly luncheon. James Lowndes called, the best of good company. He said of Buck, "She is a queen, and ought to reign in a palace. No Prince Charming yet; no man has yet approached her that I think half good enough for her."

Then Mrs. Prioleau Hamilton, *née* Levy, came with the story of family progress, not a royal one, from Columbia here: "Before we left home," said she, "Major Hamilton spread a map of the United States on the table, and showed me with his finger where Sherman was likely to go. Womanlike, I demurred. 'But, suppose he does not choose to go that way?' 'Pooh, pooh! what do you know of war?' So we set out, my husband, myself, and two children, all in one small buggy. The 14th of February we took up our line of march, and straight before Sherman's men for five weeks we fled together. By incessant hurrying and scurrying from pillar to post, we succeeded in acting as a sort of *avant-courier* of the Yankee army. Without rest and with much haste, we got here last Wednesday, and here we mean to stay and defy Sherman and his legions. Much the worse for wear were we."

The first night their beauty sleep was rudely broken into at Alston with a cry, "Move on, the Yanks are upon us!" So they hurried on, half-awake, to Winnsboro, but with no better luck. There they had to lighten the ship, leave trunks, etc., and put on all sail, for this time the Yankees were only five miles behind. "Whip and spur, ride for your life!" was the cry. "Sherman's objective point seemed to be our buggy," said she; "for you know that when we got to Lancaster Sherman was expected there, and he keeps his appointments; that is, he kept that one. Two small children were in our chariot, and I began to think of the Red Sea expedition. But we lost no time, and soon we were in Cheraw, clearly out of the track. We thanked God for all his mercies and hugged to our bosoms fond hopes of a bed and bath so much needed by all, especially for the children.

"At twelve o'clock General Hardee himself knocked us up with word to 'March! march!' for 'all the blue bonnets are over the border.' In mad haste we made for Fayetteville, when they said: 'God bless your soul! This is the seat of war now; the battle-ground where Sherman and Johnston are to try conclusions.' So we harked back, as the hunters say, and cut across country, aiming for this place. Clean clothes, my dear? Never a one except as we took off garment by garment and washed it and dried it by our camp fire, with our loins girded and in haste." I was snug and comfortable all that time in Lincolnton.

*   *   *   *   *

To-day Stephen D. Lee's corps marched through—only to surrender. The camp songs of these men were a heartbreak; so sad, yet so stirring. They would have warmed the blood of an Icelander. The leading voice was powerful, mellow, clear, distinct, pathetic, sweet. So, I sat down, as women have done before, when they hung up their harps by strange streams, and I wept the bitterness of such weeping. Music? Away, away! Thou speakest to me of things which in all my long life I have not found, and I shall not find. There they go, the gay and gallant few, doomed; the last gathering of the flower of Southern pride, to be killed, or worse, to a prison. They continue to prance by, light and jaunty. They march with as airy a tread as if they still believed the world was all on their side, and that there were no Yankee bullets for the unwary. What will Joe Johnston do with them now?

The Hood melodrama is over, though the curtain has not fallen on the last scene. Cassandra croaks and makes many mistakes, but to-day she believes that Hood stock is going down. When that style of enthusiasm is on the wane, the rapidity of its extinction is miraculous. It is like the snuffing out of a candle; "one moment white, then gone forever." No, that is not right; it is the snow-flake on the river that is referred to. I am getting things as much mixed as do the fine ladies of society.

Lee and Johnston have each fought a drawn battle; only a few more dead bodies lie stiff and stark on an unknown battle-field. For we do not so much as know where these drawn battles took place.

Teddy Barnwell, after sharing with me my first luncheon, failed me cruelly. He was to come for me to go down to the train and see Isabella pass by. One word with Isabella worth a thousand ordinary ones! So, she has gone by and I've not seen her.

Old Colonel Chesnut refuses to say grace; but as he leaves the table audibly declares, "I thank God for a good dinner." When asked why he did this odd thing he said: "My way is to be sure of a thing before I return thanks for it." Mayor Goodwyn thanked Sherman for promised protection to Columbia; soon after, the burning began.

I received the wife of a post-office robber. The poor thing had done no wrong, and I felt so sorry for her. Who would be a woman? Who that fool, a weeping, pining, faithful woman? She hath hard measures still when she hopes kindest. And all her beauty only makes ingrates!

March 29th.—I was awakened with a bunch of violets from Mrs. Pride. Violets always remind me of Kate and of the sweet South wind that blew in the garden of paradise part of my life. Then, it all came back: the dread unspeakable that lies behind every thought now.

Thursday.—I find I have not spoken of the box-car which held the Preston party that day on their way to York from Richmond. In the party were Mr. and Mrs. Lawson Clay, General and Mrs. Preston and their three daughters, Captain Rodgers, and Mr. Portman, whose father is an English earl, and connected financially and happily with Portman Square. In my American ignorance I may not state Mr. Portman's case plainly. Mr. Portman is, of course, a younger son. Then there was Cellie and her baby and wet-nurse, with no end of servants, male and female. In this ark they slept, ate, and drank, such being the fortune of war. We were there but a short time, but Mr. Portman, during that brief visit of ours, was said to have eaten three luncheons, and the number of his drinks, toddies, so called, were counted, too. Mr. Portman's contribution to the larder had been three small pigs. They were, however, run over by the train, and made sausage meat of unduly and before their time.

General Lee says to the men who shirk duty, "This is the people's war; when they tire, I stop." Wigfall says, "It is all over; the game is up." He is on his way to Texas, and when the hanging begins he can step over into Mexico.

I am plucking up heart, such troops do I see go by every day. They must turn the tide, and surely they are going for something more than surrender. It is very late, and the wind flaps my curtain, which seems to moan, "Too late." All this will end by making me a nervous lunatic.

Yesterday while I was driving with Mrs. Pride, Colonel McCaw passed us! He called out, "I do hope you are in comfortable quarters." "Very comfortable," I replied. "Oh, Mrs. Chesnut!" said Mrs. Pride, "how can you say that?" "Perfectly comfortable, and hope it may never be worse with me," said I. "I have a clean little parlor, 16 by 18, with its bare floor well scrubbed, a dinner-table, six chairs, and—well, that is all; but I have a charming lookout from my window high. My world is now thus divided into two parts—where Yankees are and where Yankees are not."

As I sat disconsolate, looking out, ready for any new tramp of men and arms, the magnificent figure of General Preston hove in sight. He was mounted on a mighty steed, worthy of its rider, followed by his trusty squire, William Walker, who bore before him the General's portmanteau. When I had time to realize the situation, I perceived at General Preston's right hand Mr. Christopher Hampton and Mr. Portman, who passed by. Soon Mrs. Pride, in some occult way, divined or heard that they were coming here, and she sent me at once no end of good things for my tea-table. General Preston entered very soon after, and with him Clement Clay, of Alabama, the latter in pursuit of his wife's trunk. I left it with the Rev. Mr. Martin, and have no doubt it is perfectly safe, but where? We have written to Mr. Martin to inquire. Then Wilmot de Saussure appeared. "I am here," he said, "to consult with General Chesnut. He and I always think alike." He added, emphatically: "Slavery is stronger than ever." "If you think so," said I, "you will find that for once you and General Chesnut do not think alike. He has held that slavery was a thing of the past, this many a year."

I said to General Preston: "I pass my days and nights partly at this window. I am sure our army is silently dispersing. Men are moving the wrong way, all the time. They slip by with no songs and no shouts now. They have given the thing up. See for yourself. Look there." For a while the streets were thronged with soldiers and then they were empty again. But the marching now is without tap of drum.

March 31st.—Mr. Prioleau Hamilton told us of a great adventure. Mrs. Preston was put under his care on the train. He soon found the only other women along were "strictly unfortunate females," as Carlyle calls them, beautiful and aggressive. He had to communicate the unpleasant fact to Mrs. Preston, on account of their propinquity, and was lost in admiration of her silent dignity, her quiet self-possession, her calmness, her deafness and blindness, her thoroughbred ignoring of all that she did not care to see. Some women, no matter how ladylike, would have made a fuss or would have fidgeted, but Mrs. Preston dominated the situation and possessed her soul in innocence and peace.

Met Robert Johnston from Camden. He has been a prisoner, having been taken at Camden. The Yankees robbed Zack Cantey of his forks and spoons. When Zack did not seem to like it, they laughed at him. When he said he did not see any fun in it, they pretended to weep and wiped their eyes with their coat-tails. All this maddening derision Zack said was as hard to bear as it was to see them ride off with his horse, Albine. They stole all of Mrs. Zack's jewelry and silver. When the Yankee general heard of it he wrote her a very polite note, saying how sorry he was that she had been annoyed, and returned a bundle of Zack's love-letters, written to her before she was married. Robert Johnston said Miss Chesnut was a brave and determined spirit. One Yankee officer came in while they were at breakfast and sat down to warm himself at the fire. "Rebels have no rights," Miss Chesnut said to him politely. "I suppose you have come to rob us. Please do so and go. Your presence agitates my blind old father." The man jumped up in a rage, and said, "What do you take me for—a robber?" "No, indeed," said she, and for very shame he marched out empty-handed.

April 3d.—Saw General Preston ride off. He came to tell me good-by. I told him he looked like a Crusader on his great white horse, with William, his squire, at his heels. Our men are all consummate riders, and have their servants well mounted behind them, carrying cloaks and traps—how different from the same men packed like sardines in dirty railroad cars, usually floating inch deep in liquid tobacco juice.

For the kitchen and Ellen's comfort I wanted a pine table and a kitchen chair. A woman sold me one to-day for three thousand Confederate dollars.

Mrs. Hamilton has been disappointed again. Prioleau Hamilton says the person into whose house they expected to move to-day came to say she could not take boarders for three reasons: First, "that they had smallpox in the house." "And the two others?" "Oh, I did not ask for the two others!"

April 5th.—Miss Middleton's letter came in answer to mine, telling her how generous my friends here were to me. "We long," she says, "for our own small sufficiency of wood, corn, and vegetables. Here is a struggle unto death, although the neighbors continue to feed us, as you would say, 'with a spoon.' We have fallen upon a new device. We keep a cookery book on the mantelpiece, and when the dinner is deficient we just read off a pudding or a creme. It does not entirely satisfy the appetite, this dessert in imagination, but perhaps it is as good for the digestion."

As I was ready to go, though still up-stairs, some one came to say General Hood had called. Mrs. Hamilton cried out, "Send word you are not at home." "Never!" said I. "Why make him climb all these stairs when you must go in five minutes?" "If he had come here dragging Sherman as a captive at his chariot wheels I might say 'not at home,' but not now." And I ran down and greeted him on the sidewalk in the face of all, and walked slowly beside him as he toiled up the weary three stories, limping gallantly. He was so well dressed and so cordial; not depressed in the slightest. He was so glad to see me. He calls his report self-defense; says Joe Johnston attacked him and he was obliged to state things from his point of view. And now follow statements, where one may read between the lines what one chooses. He had been offered a command in Western Virginia, but as General Lee was concerned because he and Joe Johnston were not on cordial terms, and as the fatigue of the mountain campaign would be too great for him, he would like the chance of going across the Mississippi. Texas was true to him, and would be his home, as it had voted him a ranch somewhere out there. They say General Lee is utterly despondent, and has no plan if Richmond goes, as go it must.

April 7th.—Richmond has fallen and I have no heart to write about it. Grant broke through our lines and Sherman cut through them. Stoneman is this side of Danville. They are too many for us. Everything is lost in Richmond, even our archives. Blue black is our horizon. Hood says we shall all be obliged to go West—to Texas, I mean, for our own part of the country will be overrun.

Yes, a solitude and a wild waste it may become, but, as to that, we can rough it in the bush at home.

De Fontaine, in his newspaper, continues the old cry. "Now Richmond is given up," he says, "it was too heavy a load to carry, and we are stronger than ever." "Stronger than ever?" Nine-tenths of our army are under ground and where is another army to come from? Will they wait until we grow one?

April 15th.—What a week it has been—madness, sadness, anxiety, turmoil, ceaseless excitement. The Wigfalls passed through on their way to Texas. We did not see them. Louly told Hood they were bound for the Rio Grande, and intended to shake hands with Maximilian, Emperor of Mexico. Yankees were expected here every minute. Mrs. Davis came. We went down to the cars at daylight to receive her. She dined with me. Lovely Winnie, the baby, came, too. Buck and Hood were here, and that queen of women, Mary Darby. Clay behaved like a trump. He was as devoted to Mrs. Davis in her adversity as if they had never quarreled in her prosperity. People sent me things for Mrs. Davis, as they did in Columbia for Mr. Davis. It was a luncheon or breakfast only she stayed for here. Mrs. Brown prepared a dinner for her at the station.

I went down with her. She left here at five o'clock. My heart was like lead, but we did not give way. She was as calm and smiling as ever. It was but a brief glimpse of my dear Mrs. Davis, and under altered skies.

April 17th.—A letter from Mrs. Davis, who writes: "Do come to me, and see how we get on. I shall have a spare room by the time you arrive, indifferently furnished, but, oh, so affectionately placed at your service. You will receive such a loving welcome. One perfect bliss have I. The baby, who grows fat and is smiling always, is christened, and not old enough to develop the world's vices or to be snubbed by it. The name so long delayed is Varina Anne. My name is a heritage of woe.

"Are you delighted with your husband? I am delighted with him as well as with my own. It is well to lose an Arabian horse if one elicits such a tender and at the same time knightly letter as General Chesnut wrote to my poor old Prometheus. I do not think that for a time he felt the vultures after the reception of the General's letter.

"I hear horrid reports about Richmond. It is said that all below Ninth Street to the Rocketts has been burned by the rabble, who mobbed the town. The Yankee performances have not been chronicled. May God take our cause into His own hands."

April 19th.—Just now, when Mr. Clay dashed up-stairs, pale as a sheet, saying, "General Lee has capitulated," I saw it reflected in Mary Darby's face before I heard him speak. She staggered to the table, sat down, and wept aloud. Mr. Clay's eyes were not dry. Quite beside herself Mary shrieked, "Now we belong to negroes and Yankees!" Buck said, "I do not believe it."

How different from ours of them is their estimate of us. How contradictory is their attitude toward us. To keep the despised and iniquitous South within their borders, as part of their country, they are willing to enlist millions of men at home and abroad, and to spend billions, and we know they do not love fighting *per se*, nor spending money. They are perfectly willing to have three killed for our one. We hear they have all grown rich, through "shoddy," whatever that is. Genuine Yankees can make a fortune trading jack-knives. "Somehow it is borne in on me that we will have to pay the piper," was remarked to-day. "No; blood can not be squeezed from a turnip. You can not pour anything out of an empty cup. We have no money even for taxes or to be confiscated."

While the Preston girls are here, my dining-room is given up to them, and we camp on the landing, with our one table and six chairs. Beds are made on the dining-room floor. Otherwise there is no furniture, except buckets of water and bath-tubs in their improvised chamber. Night and day this landing and these steps are crowded with the *élite* of the Confederacy, going and coming, and when night comes, or rather, bedtime, more beds are made on the floor of the landing-place for the war-worn soldiers to rest upon. The whole house is a bivouac. As Pickens said of South Carolina in 1861, we are "an armed camp."

My husband is rarely at home. I sleep with the girls, and my room is given up to soldiers. General Lee's few, but undismayed, his remnant of an army, or the part from the South and West, sad and crestfallen, pass through Chester. Many discomfited heroes find their way up these stairs. They say Johnston will not be caught as Lee was. He can retreat; that is his trade. If he would not fight Sherman in the hill country of Georgia, what will he do but retreat in the plains of North Carolina with Grant, Sherman, and Thomas all to the fore?

We are to stay here. Running is useless now; so we mean to bide a Yankee raid, which they say is imminent. Why fly? They are everywhere, these Yankees, like red ants, like the locusts and frogs which were the plagues of Egypt.

The plucky way in which our men keep up is beyond praise. There is no howling, and our poverty is made a matter of laughing. We deride our own penury. Of the country we try not to speak at all.

April 22d.—This yellow Confederate quire of paper, my journal, blotted by entries, has been buried three days with the silver sugar-dish, teapot, milk-jug, and a few spoons and forks that follow my fortunes as I wander. With these valuables was Hood's silver cup, which was partly crushed when he was wounded at Chickamauga.

It has been a wild three days, with aides galloping around with messages, Yankees hanging over us like a sword of Damocles. We have been in queer straits. We sat up at Mrs. Bedon's dressed, without once going to bed for forty-eight hours, and we were aweary.

Colonel Cadwallader Jones came with a despatch, a sealed secret despatch. It was for General Chesnut. I opened it. Lincoln, old Abe Lincoln, has been killed, murdered, and Seward wounded! Why? By whom? It is simply maddening, all this.

I sent off messenger after messenger for General Chesnut. I have not the faintest idea where he is, but I know this foul murder will bring upon us worse miseries. Mary Darby says, "But they murdered him themselves. No Confederates are in Washington." "But if they see fit to accuse us of instigating it?" "Who murdered him? Who knows?" "See if they don't take vengeance on us, now that we are ruined and can not repel them any longer."

The death of Lincoln I call a warning to tyrants. He will not be the last President put to death in the capital, though he is the first.

Buck never submits to be bored. The bores came to tea at Mrs. Bedon's, and then sat and talked, so prosy, so wearisome was the discourse, so endless it seemed, that we envied Buck, who was mooning on the piazza. She rarely speaks now.

A NEWSPAPER EXTRA.

HIGHLY IMPORTANT NEWS!
AN ARMISTICE AGREED
UPON!!!

Lincoln Assassinated and Seward Mortally Wounded in Washington!!

GREENSBORO, April 19, 1865.
GENERAL ORDER NO. 14.

It is announced to the Army that a suspension of arms has been agreed upon pending negotiations between the two Governments.

During its continuance the two armies are to occupy their present position.

By command of General Johnston:
[SIGNED,] ARCHER ANDERSON,
Lieut. Col. and A. A. G.

Official Copy: ISAAC HAYNE.

WASHINGTON, April 12, 1865
TO MAJOR-GENERAL SHERMAN:

President Lincoln was murdered, about ten o'clock last night, in his private box at Ford's Theatre, in this city, by an assassin, who shot him in the head with a pistol ball. At the same hour Mr. Seward's house was entered by another assassin, who *stabbed the Secretary in several places.* It is thought he may possibly recover, but his son Fred may possibly die of the wounds he received.

The assassin of the President leaped from the private box, brandishing his dagger and exclaiming: *"Sic Semper Tyrannis—*

VIRGINIA IS REVENGED!" Mr. Lincoln fell senseless from his seat, and continued in that condition until 22 minutes past 10 o'clock this morning, at which time he breathed his last.

Vice President Johnson now becomes President, and will take the oath of office and assume the duties to-day.

[SIGNED,] E. M. STANTON

TO THE CITIZENS OF CHESTER.

CHESTER, S.C., April 22, 1865

FLOUR and MEAL given out to the citizens by order of Major MITCHELL, Chief Commissary of South Carolina, to be returned when called for, is *badly wanted to ration General Johnston's army.* Please return the same at once.

E. M. GRAHAM, Agent Subsistence Dep't.

HEADQUARTERS RESERVE FORCES S. C.

CHESTERVILLE, APRIL 20, 1865

The Brigadier-General Commanding has been informed that, in view of the approach of the enemy, a large quantity of supplies of various kinds were given out by the various Government officers at this post to the citizens of the place. He now calls upon, and earnestly requests all citizens, who may have such stores in their possession, to return them to the several Departments to which they belong. The stores are much needed at this time for the use of soldiers, passing through the place, and for the sick at the Hospital.

By command of Brig. Gen. Chesnut:

M. R. CLARK, Major and A. A. General.

A NEWSPAPER EXTRA.

April 23d.—My silver wedding-day, and I am sure the unhappiest day of my life. Mr. Portman came with Christopher Hampton. Portman told of Miss Kate Hampton, who is perhaps the most thoroughly ladylike person in the world. When he told her that Lee had surrendered she started up from her seat and said, "That is a lie." "Well, Miss Hampton, I tell the tale as it was told me. I can do no more."

No wonder John Chesnut is bitter. They say Mulberry has been destroyed by a corps commanded by General Logan. Some one asked coolly, "Will General Chesnut be shot as a soldier, or hung as a senator?" "I am not of sufficient consequence," answered he. "They will stop short of brigadiers. I resigned my seat in the United States Senate weeks before there was any secession. So I can not be hung as a senator. But after all it is only a choice between drumhead court martial, short shrift, and a lingering death at home from starvation."

These negroes are unchanged. The shining black mask they wear does not show a ripple of change; they are sphinxes. Ellen has had my diamonds to keep for a week or so. When the danger was over she handed them back to me with as little apparent interest in the matter as if they had been garden peas.

Mrs. Huger was in church in Richmond when the news of the surrender came. Worshipers were in the midst of the communion service. Mr. McFarland was called out to send away the gold from his bank. Mr. Minnegerode's English grew confused. Then the President was summoned, and distress of mind showed itself in every face. The night before one of General Lee's aides, Walter Taylor, was married, and was off to the wars immediately after the ceremony.

One year ago we left Richmond. The Confederacy has double-quicked down hill since then. One year since I stood in that beautiful Hollywood by little Joe Davis's grave. Now we have burned towns, deserted plantations, sacked villages. "You seem resolute to look the worst in the face," said General Chesnut, wearily. "Yes, poverty, with no future and no hope." "But no slaves, thank God!" cried Buck. "We would be the scorn of the world if the world thought of us at all. You see, we are exiles and paupers." "Pile on the agony." "How does our famous captain, the great Lee, bear the Yankees' galling chain?" I asked. "He knows how to possess his soul in patience," answered my husband. "If there were no such word as subjugation, no debts, no poverty, no negro mobs backed by Yankees; if all things were well, you would shiver and feel benumbed," he went on, pointing at me in an oratorical attitude. "Your sentence is pronounced—Camden for life."

May 1st.—In Chester still. I climb these steep steps alone. They have all gone, all passed by. Buck went with Mr. C. Hampton to York. Mary, Mrs. Huger, and Pinckney took flight together. One day just before they began to dissolve in air, Captain Gay was seated at the table, halfway between me on the top step and John in the window, with his legs outside. Said some one to-day, "She showed me her engagement ring, and I put it back on her hand. She is engaged, but not to me." "By the heaven that is above us all, I saw you kiss her hand." "That I deny." Captain Gay glared in angry surprise, and insisted that he had seen it. "Sit down, Gay," said the cool captain in his most mournful way. "You see, my father died when I was a baby, and my grandfather took me in hand. To him I owe this moral maxim. He is ninety years old, a wise old man. Now, remember my grandfather's teaching forevermore—'A gentleman must not kiss and tell.'"

General Preston came to say good-by. He will take his family abroad at once. Burnside, in New Orleans, owes him some money and will pay it. "There will be no more confiscation, my dear madam," said he; "they must see that we have been punished enough." "They do not think so, my dear general. This very day a party of Federals passed in hot pursuit of our President."

A terrible fire-eater, one of the few men left in the world who believe we have a right divine, being white, to hold Africans, who are black, in bonds forever; he is six feet two; an athlete; a splendid specimen of the animal man; but he has never been under fire; his place in the service was a bomb-proof office, so-called. With a face red-hot with rage he denounced Jeff Davis and Hood. "Come, now," said Edward, the handsome, "men who could fight and did not, they are the men who ruined us. We wanted soldiers. If the men who are cursing Jeff Davis now had fought with Hood, and fought as Hood fought, we'd be all right now."

And then he told of my trouble one day while Hood was here. "Just such a fellow as you came up on this little platform, and before Mrs. Chesnut could warn him, began to heap insults on Jeff Davis and his satrap, Hood. Mrs. Chesnut held up her hands. 'Stop, not another ward. You shall not abuse my friends here! Not Jeff Davis behind his back, not Hood to his face, for he is in that room and hears you.'" Fancy how dumfounded this creature was.

Mrs. Huger told a story of Joe Johnston in his callow days before he was famous. After an illness Johnston's hair all fell out; not a hair was left on his head, which shone like a fiery cannon-ball. One of the gentlemen from Africa who waited at table sniggered so at dinner that he was ordered out by the grave and decorous black butler. General Huger, feeling for the agonies of young Africa, as he strove to stifle his mirth, suggested that Joe Johnston should cover his head with his handkerchief. A red silk one was produced, and turban-shaped, placed on his head. That completely finished the gravity of the butler, who fled in helplessness. His guffaw on the outside of the door became plainly audible. General Huger then suggested, as they must have the waiter back, or the dinner could not go on, that Joe should eat with his hat on, which he did.

CHAPTER XXI. CAMDEN, S. C.

May 2, 1865—August 2, 1865

Camden, S. C., *May 2, 1865.*—Since we left Chester nothing but solitude, nothing but tall blackened chimneys, to show that any man has ever trod this road before. This is Sherman's track. It is hard not to curse him. I wept incessantly at first. The roses of the gardens are already hiding the ruins. My husband said Nature is a wonderful renovator. He tried to say something else and then I shut my eyes and made a vow that if we were a crushed people, crushed by weight, I would never be a whimpering, pining slave.

We heard loud explosions of gunpowder in the direction of

Camden. Destroyers were at it there. Met William Walker, whom Mr. Preston left in charge of a car-load of his valuables. General Preston was hardly out of sight before poor helpless William had to stand by and see the car plundered. "My dear Missis! they have cleaned me out, nothing left," moaned William the faithful. We have nine armed couriers with us. Can they protect us?

Bade adieu to the staff at Chester. No general ever had so remarkable a staff, so accomplished, so agreeable, so well bred, and, I must say, so handsome, and can add so brave and efficient.

May 4th.—Home again at Bloomsbury. From Chester to Winnsboro we did not see one living thing, man, woman, or animal, except poor William trudging home after his sad disaster. The blooming of the gardens had a funereal effect.

Nature is so luxuriant here, she soon covers the ravages of savages. No frost has occurred since the seventh of March, which accounts for the wonderful advance in vegetation. This seems providential to these starving people. In this climate so much that is edible can be grown in two months.

At Winnsboro we stayed at Mr. Robertson's. There we left the wagon train. Only Mr. Brisbane, one of the general's couriers, came with us on escort duty. The Robertsons were very kind and hospitable, brimful of Yankee anecdotes. To my amazement the young people of Winnsboro had a May-day celebration amid the smoking ruins. Irrepressible is youth.

The fidelity of the negroes is the principal topic. There seems to be not a single case of a negro who betrayed his master, and yet they showed a natural and exultant joy at being free. After we left Winnsboro negroes were seen in the fields plowing and hoeing corn, just as in antebellum times. The fields in that respect looked quite cheerful. We did not pass in the line of Sherman's savages, and so saw some houses standing.

Mary Kirkland has had experience with the Yankees. She has been pronounced the most beautiful woman on this side of the Atlantic, and has been spoiled accordingly in all society. When the Yankees came, Monroe, their negro manservant, told her to stand up and hold two of her children in her arms, with the other two pressed as close against her knees as they could get. Mammy Selina and Lizzie then stood grimly on each side of their young missis and her children. For four mortal hours the soldiers surged through the rooms of the house. Sometimes Mary and her children were roughly jostled against the wall, but Mammy and Lizzie were stanch supporters. The Yankee soldiers taunted the negro women for their foolishness in standing by their cruel slave-owners, and taunted Mary with being glad of the protection of her poor ill-used slaves. Monroe meanwhile had one leg bandaged and pretended to be lame, so that he might not be enlisted as a soldier, and kept making pathetic appeals to Mary.

"Don't answer them back, Miss Mary," said he. "Let 'em say what dey want to; don't answer 'em back. Don't give 'em any chance to say you are impudent to 'em."

One man said to her: "Why do you shrink from us and avoid us so? We did not come here to fight for negroes; we hate them. At Port Royal I saw a beautiful white woman driving in a wagon with a coal-black negro man. If she had been anything to me I would have shot her through the heart." "Oh, oh!" said Lizzie, "that's the way you talk in here. I'll remember that when you begin outside to beg me to run away with you."

Finally poor Aunt Betsy, Mary's mother, fainted from pure fright and exhaustion. Mary put down her baby and sprang to her mother, who was lying limp in a chair, and fiercely called out, "Leave this room, you wretches! Do you mean to kill my mother? She is ill; I must put her to bed." Without a word they all slunk out ashamed. "If I had only tried that hours ago," she now said. Outside they remarked that she was "an insolent rebel huzzy, who thinks herself too good to speak to a soldier of the United States," and one of them said: "Let us go in and break her mouth." But the better ones held the more outrageous back. Monroe slipped in again and said: "Missy, for God's sake, when dey come in be sociable with 'em. Dey will kill you."

"Then let me die."

The negro soldiers were far worse than the white ones.

Mrs. Bartow drove with me to Mulberry. On one side of the house we found every window had been broken, every bell torn down, every piece of furniture destroyed, and every door smashed in. But the other side was intact. Maria Whitaker and her mother, who had been left in charge, explained this odd state of things. The Yankees were busy as beavers, working like regular carpenters, destroying everything when their general came in and stopped them. He told them it was a sin to destroy a fine old house like that, whose owner was over ninety years old. He would not have had it done for the world. It was wanton mischief. He explained to Maria that soldiers at such times were excited, wild, and unruly. They carried off sacks full of our books, since unfortunately they found a pile of empty sacks in the garret. Our books, our letters, our papers were afterward strewn along the Charleston road. Somebody found things of ours as far away as Vance's Ferry.

This was Potter's raid.[130] Sherman took only our horses. Potter's raid came after Johnston's surrender, and ruined us finally, burning our

---

[130] The reference appears to be to General Edward E. Potter, a native of New York City, who died in 1889. General Potter entered the Federal service early in the war. He recruited a regiment of North Carolina troops and engaged in operations in North and South Carolina and Eastern Tennessee.

mills and gins and a hundred bales of cotton. Indeed, nothing is left to us now but the bare land, and the debts contracted for the support of hundreds of negroes during the war.

J. H. Boykin was at home at the time to look after his own interests, and he, with John de Saussure, has saved the cotton on their estates, with the mules and farming utensils and plenty of cotton as capital to begin on again. The negroes would be a good riddance. A hired man would be a good deal cheaper than a man whose father and mother, wife and twelve children have to be fed, clothed, housed, and nursed, their taxes paid, and their doctor's bills, all for his half-done, slovenly, lazy work. For years we have thought negroes a nuisance that did not pay. They pretend exuberant loyalty to us now. Only one man of Mr. Chesnut's left the plantation with the Yankees.

When the Yankees found the Western troops were not at Camden, but down below Swift Creek, like sensible folk they came up the other way, and while we waited at Chester for marching orders we were quickly ruined after the surrender. With our cotton saved, and cotton at a dollar a pound, we might be in comparatively easy circumstances. But now it is the devil to pay, and no pitch hot. Well, all this was to be.

Godard Bailey, editor, whose prejudices are all against us, described the raids to me in this wise: They were regularly organized. First came squads who demanded arms and whisky. Then came the rascals who hunted for silver, ransacked the ladies' wardrobes and scared women and children into fits—at least those who could be scared. Some of these women could not be scared. Then came some smiling, suave, well-dressed officers, who "regretted it all so much." Outside the gate officers, men, and bummers divided even, share and share alike, the piles of plunder.

When we crossed the river coming home, the ferry man at Chesnut's Ferry asked for his fee. Among us all we could not muster the small silver coin he demanded. There was poverty for you. Nor did a stiver appear among us until Molly was hauled home from Columbia, where she was waging war with Sheriff Dent's family. As soon as her foot touched her native heath, she sent to hunt up the cattle. Many of our cows were found in the swamp; like Marion's men they had escaped the enemy. Molly sells butter for us now on shares.

Old Cuffey, head gardener at Mulberry, and Yellow Abram, his assistant, have gone on in the even tenor of their way. Men may come and men may go, but they dig on forever. And they say they mean to "as long as old master is alive." We have green peas, asparagus, lettuce, spinach, new potatoes, and strawberries in abundance—enough for ourselves and plenty to give away to refugees. It is early in May and yet two months since frost. Surely the wind was tempered to the shorn lamb in our case.

Johnny went over to see Hampton. His cavalry are ordered to

reassemble on the 20th—a little farce to let themselves down easily; they know it is all over. Johnny, smiling serenely, said, "The thing is up and forever."

Godard Bailey has presence of mind. Anne Sabb left a gold card-case, which was a terrible oversight, among the cards on the drawing-room table. When the Yankee raiders saw it their eyes glistened. Godard whispered to her: "Let them have that gilt thing and slip away and hide the silver." "No!" shouted a Yank, "you don't fool me that way; here's your old brass thing; don't you stir; fork over that silver." And so they deposited the gold card-case in Godard's hands, and stole plated spoons and forks, which had been left out because they were plated. Mrs. Beach says two officers slept at her house. Each had a pillow-case crammed with silver and jewelry—"spoils of war," they called it.

Floride Cantey heard an old negro say to his master: "When you all had de power you was good to me, and I'll protect you now. No niggers nor Yankees shall tech you. If you want anything call for Sambo. I mean, call for Mr. Samuel; dat my name now."

May 10th.—A letter from a Pharisee who thanks the Lord she is not as other women are; she need not pray, as the Scotch parson did, for a good conceit of herself. She writes, "I feel that I will not be ruined. Come what may, God will provide for me." But her husband had strengthened the Lord's hands, and for the glory of God, doubtless, invested some thousands of dollars in New York, where Confederate moth did not corrupt nor Yankee bummers break through and steal. She went on to tell us: "I have had the good things of this world, and I have enjoyed them in their season. But I only held them as steward for God. My bread has been cast upon the waters and will return to me."

E. M. Boykin said to-day: "We had a right to strike for our independence, and we did strike a bitter blow.

They must be proud to have overcome such a foe. I dare look any man in the face. There is no humiliation in our position after such a struggle as we made for freedom from the Yankees." He is sanguine. His main idea is joy that he has no negroes to support, and need hire only those he really wants.

Stephen Elliott told us that Sherman said to Joe Johnston, "Look out for yourself. This agreement only binds the military, not the civil, authorities." Is our destruction to begin anew? For a few weeks we have had peace.

Sally Reynolds told a short story of a negro pet of Mrs. Kershaw's. The little negro clung to Mrs. Kershaw and begged her to save him. The negro mother, stronger than Mrs. Kershaw, tore him away from her. Mrs. Kershaw wept bitterly. Sally said she saw the mother chasing the child before her as she ran after the Yankees, whipping him at every step. The child yelled like mad, a small rebel blackamoor.

May 16th.—We are scattered and stunned, the remnant of heart left alive within us filled with brotherly hate. We sit and wait until the drunken tailor who rules the United States of America issues a proclamation, and defines our anomalous position.

Such a hue and cry, but whose fault? Everybody is blamed by somebody else. The dead heroes left stiff and stark on the battle-field escape, blame every man who stayed at home and did not fight. I will not stop to hear excuses. There is not one word against those who stood out until the bitter end, and stacked muskets at Appomattox.

May 18th.—A feeling of sadness hovers over me now, day and night, which no words of mine can express. There is a chance for plenty of character study in. this Mulberry house, if one only had the heart for it. Colonel Chesnut, now ninety-three, blind and deaf, is apparently as strong as ever, and certainly as resolute of will. Partly patriarch, partly grand seigneur, this old man is of a species that we shall see no more— the last of a race of lordly planters who ruled this Southern world, but now a splendid wreck. His manners are unequaled still, but underneath this smooth exterior lies the grip of a tyrant whose will has never been crossed. I will not attempt what Lord Byron says he could not do, but must quote again: "Everybody knows a gentleman when he sees him. I have never met a man who could describe one." We have had three very distinct specimens of the genus in this house—three generations of gentlemen, each utterly different from the other—father, son, and grandson.

African Scipio walks at Colonel Chesnut's side. He is six feet two, a black Hercules, and as gentle as a dove in all his dealings with the blind old master, who boldly strides forward, striking with his stick to feel where he is going. The Yankees left Scipio unmolested. He told them he was absolutely essential to his old master, and they said, "If you want to stay so bad, he must have been good to you always." Scip says he was silent, for it "made them mad if you praised your master."

Sometimes this old man will stop himself, just as he is going off in a fury, because they try to prevent his attempting some feat impossible in his condition of lost faculties. He will ask gently, "I hope that I never say or do anything unseemly! Sometimes I think I am subject to mental aberrations." At every footfall he calls out, "Who goes there?" If a lady's name is given he uncovers and stands, with hat off, until she passes. He still has the old-world art of bowing low and gracefully.

Colonel Chesnut came of a race that would brook no interference with their own sweet will by man, woman, or devil. But then such manners has he, they would clear any man's character, if it needed it. Mrs. Chesnut, his wife, used to tell us that when she met him at Princeton, in the nineties of the eighteenth century, they called him "the

Young Prince." He and Mr. John Taylor,[131] of Columbia, were the up-country youths whose parents were wealthy enough to send them off to college.

When a college was established in South Carolina, Colonel John Chesnut, the father of the aforesaid Young Prince, was on the first board of trustees. Indeed, I may say that, since the Revolution of 1776, there has been no convocation of the notables of South Carolina, in times of peace anti prosperity, or of war and adversity, in which a representative man of this family has not appeared. The estate has been kept together until now. Mrs. Chesnut said she drove down from Philadelphia on her bridal trip, in a chariot and four—a cream-colored chariot with outriders.

They have a saying here-on account of the large families with which people are usually blessed, and the subdivision of property consequent upon that fact, besides the tendency of one generation to make and to save, and the next to idle and to squander, that there are rarely more than three generations between shirt-sleeves and shirt-sleeves. But these Chesnuts have secured four, from the John Chesnut who was driven out from his father's farm in Virginia by the French and Indians, when that father had been killed at Fort Duquesne,[132] to the John Chesnut who saunters along here now, the very perfection of a lazy gentleman, who cares not to move unless it be for a fight, a dance, or a fox-hunt.

The first comer of that name to this State was a lad when he arrived after leaving his land in Virginia; and being without fortune otherwise, he went into Joseph Kershaw's grocery shop as a clerk, and the Kershaws, I think, so remember that fact that they have it on their coat-of-arms. Our Johnny, as he was driving me down to Mulberry yesterday, declared himself delighted with the fact that the present Joseph Kershaw had so distinguished himself in our war, that they might let the shop of a hundred years ago rest for a while. "Upon my soul," cried the cool captain, "I have a desire to go in there and look at the Kershaw tombstones. I am sure they have put it on their marble

---

[131] John Taylor was graduated from Princeton in 1790 and became a planter in South Carolina. He served in Congress from 1806 to 1810, and in the latter year was chosen to fill a vacancy in the United States Senate, caused by the resignation of Thomas Sumter. In 1826 he was chosen Governor of South Carolina. He died in 1832.

[132] Fort Duquesne stood at the junction of the Monongahela and Alleghany Rivers. Captain Trent, acting for the Ohio Company, with some Virginia militiamen, began to build this fort in February, 1754. On April 17th of the same year, 700 Canadians and French forced him to abandon the work. The French then completed the fortress and named it Fort Duquesne. The unfortunate expedition of General Braddock, in the summer of 1755, was an attempt to retake the fort, Braddock's defeat occurring eight miles east of it. In 1758 General Forbes marched westward from Philadelphia and secured possession of the place, after the French, alarmed at his approach, had burned it. Forbes gave it the name of Pittsburg.

tablets that we had an ancestor one day a hundred years ago who was a clerk in their shop." This clerk became a captain in the Revolution.

In the second generation the shop had so far sunk that the John Chesnut of that day refused to let his daughter marry a handsome, dissipated Kershaw, and she, a spoiled beauty, who could not endure to obey orders when they were disagreeable to her, went up to her room and therein remained, never once coming out of it for forty years. Her father let her have her own way in that; he provided servants to wait upon her and every conceivable luxury that she desired, but neither party would give in.

I am, too, thankful that I am an old woman, forty-two my last birthday. There is so little life left in me now to be embittered by this agony. "Nonsense! I am a pauper," says my husband, "and I am as smiling and as comfortable as ever you saw me." "When you have to give up your horses? How then?"

May 21st.—They say Governor Magrath has absconded, and that the Yankees have said, "If you have no visible governor, we will send you one." If we had one and they found him, they would clap him in prison instanter.

The negroes have flocked to the Yankee squad which has recently come, but they were snubbed, the rampant freedmen. "Stay where you are," say the Yanks. "We have nothing for you." And they sadly "peruse" their way. Now that they have picked up that word "peruse," they use it in season and out. When we met Mrs. Preston's William we asked, "Where are you going?" "Perusing my way to Columbia," he answered.

When the Yanks said they had no rations for idle negroes, John Walker answered mildly, "This is not at all what we expected." The colored women, dressed in their gaudiest array, carried bouquets to the Yankees, making the day a jubilee. But in this house there is not the slightest change. Every negro has known for months that he or she was free, but I do not see one particle of change in their manner. They are, perhaps, more circumspect, polite, and quiet, but that is all. Otherwise all goes on in antebellum *statu quo.* Every day I expect to miss some familiar face, but so far have been disappointed.

Mrs. Huger we found at the hotel here, and we brought her to Bloomsbury. She told us that Jeff Davis was traveling leisurely with his wife twelve miles a day, utterly careless whether he were taken prisoner or not, and that General Hampton had been paroled.

Fighting Dick Anderson and Stephen Elliott, of Fort Sumter memory, are quite ready to pray for Andy Johnson, and to submit to the powers that be. Not so our belligerent clergy. "Pray for people when I wish they were dead," cries Rev. Mr. Trapier. "No, never! I will pray for President Davis till I die. I will do it to my last gasp. My chief is a prisoner, but I am proud of him still. He is a spectacle to gods and men.

He will bear himself as a soldier, a patriot, a statesman, a Christian gentleman. He is the martyr of our cause." And I replied with my tears. "Look here: taken in woman's clothes?" asked Mr. Trapier. "Rubbish, stuff, and nonsense. If Jeff Davis has not the pluck of a true man, then there is no courage left on this earth. If he does not die game, I give it up. Something, you see, was due to Lincoln and the Scotch cap that he hid his ugly face with, in that express car, when he rushed through Baltimore in the night. It is that escapade of their man Lincoln that set them on making up the woman's clothes story about Jeff Davis."

Mrs. W. drove up. She, too, is off for New York, to sell four hundred bales of cotton and a square, or something, which pays tremendously in the Central Park region, and to capture and bring home her *belle fille*, who remained North during the war. She knocked at my door. The day was barely dawning. I was in bed, and as I sprang up, discovered that my old Confederate night-gown had to be managed, it was so full of rents. I am afraid I gave undue attention to the sad condition of my gown, but could nowhere see a shawl to drape my figure.

She was very kind. In case my husband was arrested and needed funds, she offered me some "British securities" and bonds. We were very grateful, but we did not accept the loan of money, which would have been almost the same as a gift, so slim was our chance of repaying it. But it was a generous thought on her part; I own that.

Went to our plantation, the Hermitage, yesterday. Saw no change; not a soul was absent from his or her post. I said, "Good colored folks, when are you going to kick off the traces and be free?" In their furious, emotional way, they swore devotion to us all to their dying day. Just the same, the minute they see an opening to better themselves they will move on. William, my husband's foster-brother, came up. "Well, William, what do you want?" asked my husband. "Only to look at you, marster; it does me good."

June 1st.—The New York Herald quotes General Sherman as saying, "Columbia was burned by Hampton's sheer stupidity." But then who burned everything on the way in Sherman's march to Columbia, and in the line of march Sherman took after leaving Columbia? We came, for three days of travel, over a road that had been laid bare by Sherman's torches. Nothing but smoking ruins was left in Sherman's track. That I saw with my own eyes. No living thing was left, no house for man or beast. They who burned the countryside for a belt of forty miles, did they not also burn the town? To charge that to "Hampton's stupidity" is merely an afterthought. This Herald announces that Jeff Davis will be hanged at once, not so much for treason as for his assassination of Lincoln. "Stanton," the Herald says, "has all the papers in his hands to convict him."

The Yankees here say, "The black man must go as the red man has gone; this is a white man's country." The negroes want to run with the hare, but hunt with the hounds. They are charming in their professions to us, but declare that they are to be paid by these blessed Yankees in lands and mules for having been slaves. They were so faithful to us during the war, why should the Yankees reward them, to which the only reply is that it would be by way of punishing rebels.

Mrs. Adger[133] saw a Yankee soldier strike a woman, and she prayed God to take him in hand according to his deed.

The soldier laughed in her face, swaggered off, stumbled down the steps, and then his revolver went off by the concussion and shot him dead.

The black ball is in motion. Mrs. de Saussure's cook shook the dust off her feet and departed from her kitchen to-day-free, she said. The washerwoman is packing to go.

Scipio Africanus, the Colonel's body-servant, is a soldierly looking black creature, fit to have delighted the eyes of old Frederick William of Prussia, who liked giants. We asked him how the Yankees came to leave him. "Oh, I told them marster couldn't do without me nohow; and then I carried them some nice hams that they never could have found, they were hid so good."

Eben dressed himself in his best and went at a run to meet his Yankee deliverers—so he said. At the gate he met a squad coming in. He had adorned himself with his watch and chain, like the cordage of a ship, with a handful of gaudy seals. He knew the Yankees came to rob white people, but he thought they came to save niggers. "Hand over that watch!" they said. Minus his fine watch and chain, Eben returned a sadder and a wiser man. He was soon in his shirt-sleeves, whistling at his knife-board. "Why? You here? Why did you come back so soon?" he was asked. "Well, I thought may be I better stay with ole marster that give me the watch, and not go with them that stole it." The watch was the pride of his life. The iron had entered his soul.

Went up to my old house, "Kamschatka." The Trapiers live there now. In those drawing-rooms where the children played Puss in Boots, where we have so often danced and sung, but never prayed before, Mr. Trapier held his prayer-meeting. I do not think I ever did as much weeping or as bitter in the same space of time. I let myself go; it did me good. I cried with a will. He prayed that we might have strength to stand up and bear our bitter disappointment, to look on our ruined

---

[133] Elizabeth K. Adger, wife of the Rev. John B. Adger, D. D., of Charleston, a distinguished Presbyterian divine, at one time a missionary to Smyrna where he translated the Bible into the Armenian tongue. He was afterward and before the war a professor in the Theological Seminary at Columbia. His wife was a woman of unusual judgment and intelligence, sharing her husband's many hardships and notable experiences in the East.

homes and our desolated country and be strong. And he prayed for the man "we elected to be our ruler and guide." We knew that they had put him in a dungeon and in chains.[134] Men watch him day and night. By orders of Andy, the bloody-minded tailor, nobody above the rank of colonel can take the benefit of the amnesty oath, nobody who owns over twenty thousand dollars, or who has assisted the Confederates. And now, ye rich men, howl, for your misery has come upon you. You are beyond the outlaw, camping outside. Howell Cobb and R. M. T. Hunter have been arrested. Our turn will come next, maybe. A Damocles sword hanging over a house does not conduce to a pleasant life.

June 12th.—Andy, made lord of all by the madman, Booth, says, "Destruction only to the wealthy classes." Better teach the negroes to stand alone before you break up all they leaned on, O Yankees! After all, the number who possess over $20,000 are very few.

Andy has shattered some fond hopes. He denounces Northern men who came South to espouse our cause. They may not take the life-giving oath. My husband will remain quietly at home. He has done nothing that he had not a right to do, nor anything that he is ashamed of. He will not fly from his country, nor hide anywhere in it. These are his words. He has a huge volume of Macaulay, which seems to absorb him. Slily I slipped Silvio Pellico in his way. He looked at the title and moved it aside. "Oh," said I, "I only wanted you to refresh your memory as to a prisoner's life and what a despotism can do to make its captives happy!"

Two weddings—in Camden, Ellen Douglas Ancrum to Mr. Lee, engineer and architect, a clever man, which is the best investment now. In Columbia, Sally Hampton and John Cheves Haskell, the bridegroom, a brave, one-armed soldier.

A wedding to be. Lou McCord's. And Mrs. McCord is going about frantically, looking for eggs "to mix and make into wedding-cake," and finding none. She now drives the funniest little one-mule vehicle.

*   *   *   *   *

I have been ill since I last wrote in this journal. Serena's letter came. She says they have been visited by bushwhackers, the roughs that always follow in the wake of an army. My sister Kate they forced back against the wall. She had Katie, the baby, in her arms, and Miller, the brave boy, clung to his mother, though he could do no more. They

---

[134] Mr. Davis, while encamped near Irwinsville, Gal, had been captured on May 10th by a body of Federal cavalry under Lieutenant-Colonel Pritchard. He was taken to Fortress Monroe and confined there for two years, his release being effected on May 13, 1867, when he was admitted to bail in the sum of $100,000, the first name on his bail-bond being that of Horace Greeley.

tried to pour brandy down her throat. They knocked Mary down with the butt end of a pistol, and Serena they struck with an open hand, leaving the mark on her cheek for weeks.

Mr. Christopher Hampton says in New York people have been simply intoxicated with the fumes of their own glory. Military prowess is a new wrinkle of delight to them. They are mad with pride that, ten to one, they could, after five years' hard fighting, prevail over us, handicapped, as we were, with a majority of aliens, quasi foes, and negro slaves whom they tried to seduce, shut up with us. They pay us the kind of respectful fear the British meted out to Napoleon when they sent him off with Sir Hudson Lowe to St. Helena, the lone rock by the sea, to eat his heart out where he could not alarm them more.

Of course, the Yankees know and say they were too many for us, and yet they would all the same prefer not to try us again. Would Wellington be willing to take the chances of Waterloo once more with Grouchy, Blücher, and all that left to haphazard? Wigfall said to old Cameron[135] in 1861, "Then you will a sutler be, and profit shall accrue." Christopher Hampton says that in some inscrutable way in the world North, everybody "has contrived to amass fabulous wealth by this war."

There are two classes of vociferous sufferers in this community: 1. Those who say, "If people would only pay me what they owe me!" 2. Those who say, "If people would only let me alone. I can not pay them. I could stand it if I had anything with which to pay debts."

Now we belong to both classes. Heavens! the sums people owe us and will not, or can not, pay, would settle all our debts ten times over and leave us in easy circumstances for life. But they will not pay. How can they?

We are shut in here, turned with our faces to a dead wall. No mails. A letter is sometimes brought by a man on horseback, traveling through the wilderness made by Sherman. All railroads have been destroyed and the bridges are gone. We are cut off from the world, here to eat out our hearts. Yet from my window I look out on many a gallant youth and maiden fair. The street is crowded and it is a gay sight. Camden is thronged with refugees from the low country, and here they disport themselves. They call the walk in front of Bloomsbury "the Boulevard."

H. Lang tells us that poor Sandhill Milly Trimlin is dead, and that as a witch she had been denied Christian burial. Three times she was buried in consecrated ground in different churchyards, and three times she was dug up by a superstitious horde, who put her out of their holy ground. Where her poor, old, ill-used bones are lying now I do not

---

[135] Simon Cameron became Secretary of War in Lincoln's Administration, on March 4, 1861. On January 11, 1862, he resigned and was made Minister to Russia.

know. I hope her soul is faring better than her body. She was a good, kind creature. Why supposed to be a witch? That H. Lang could not elucidate.

Everybody in our walk of life gave Milly a helping hand. She was a perfect specimen of the Sandhill "tackey" race, sometimes called "country crackers." Her skin was yellow and leathery, even the whites of her eyes were bilious in color. She was stumpy, strong, and lean, hard-featured, horny-fisted. Never were people so aided in every way as these Sandhillers. Why do they remain Sandhillers from generation to generation? Why should Milly never have bettered her condition?

My grandmother lent a helping hand to her grandmother. My mother did her best for her mother, and I am sure the so-called witch could never complain of me. As long as I can remember, gangs of these Sandhill women traipsed in with baskets to be filled by charity, ready to carry away anything they could get. All are made on the same pattern, more or less alike. They were treated as friends and neighbors, not as beggars. They were asked in to take seats by the fire, and there they sat for hours, stony-eyed, silent, wearing out human endurance and politeness. But their husbands and sons, whom we never saw, were citizens and voters! When patience was at its last ebb, they would open their mouths and loudly demand whatever they had come to seek.

One called Judy Bradly, a one-eyed virago, who played the fiddle at all the Sandhill dances and fandangoes, made a deep impression on my youthful mind. Her list of requests was always rather long, and once my grandmother grew restive and actually hesitated. "Woman, do you mean to let me starve?" she cried furiously. My grandmother then attempted a meek lecture as to the duty of earning one's bread. Judy squared her arms akimbo and answered, "And pray, who made you a judge of the world? Lord, Lord, if I had 'er knowed I had ter stand all this jaw, I wouldn't a took your ole things," but she did take them and came afterward again and again.

June 27th.—An awful story from Sumter. An old gentleman, who thought his son dead or in a Yankee prison, heard some one try the front door. It was about midnight, and these are squally times. He called out, "What is that?" There came no answer. After a while he heard some one trying to open a window and he fired. The house was shaken by a fall. Then, after a long time of dead silence, he went round the house to see if his shot had done any harm, and found his only son bathed in his own blood on his father's door-step. The son was just back from a Yankee prison—one of his companions said—and had been made deaf by cold and exposure. He did not hear his father hail him. He had tried to get into the house in the same old way he used to employ when a boy.

My sister-in-law in tears of rage and despair, her servants all gone to "a big meeting at Mulberry," though she had made every appeal against their going. "Send them adrift," some one said, "they do not obey you, or serve you; they only live on you." It would break her heart to part with one of them. But that sort of thing will soon right itself. They will go off *to better themselves*—we have only to cease paying wages—and that is easy, for we have no money.

July 4th.—Saturday I was in bed with one of my worst headaches. Occasionally there would come a sob and I thought of my sister insulted and my little sweet Williams. Another of my beautiful Columbia quartette had rough experiences. A raider asked the plucky little girl, Lizzie Hamilton, for a ring which she wore. "You shall not have it," she said. The man put a pistol to her head, saying, "Take it off, hand it to me, or I will blow your brains out." "Blow away," said she. The man laughed and put down his pistol, remarking, "You knew I would not hurt you." "Of course, I knew you dared not shoot me. Even Sherman would not stand that."

There was talk of the negroes where the Yankees had been—negroes who flocked to them and showed them where silver and valuables had been hid by the white people. Ladies'-maids dressed themselves in their mistresses' gowns before the owners' faces and walked off. Now, before this every one had told me how kind, faithful, and considerate the negroes had proven. I am sure, after hearing these tales, the fidelity of my own servants shines out brilliantly. I had taken their conduct too much as a matter of course. In the afternoon I had some business on our place, the Hermitage. John drove me down. Our people were all at home, quiet, orderly, respectful, and at their usual work. In point of fact things looked unchanged. There was nothing to show that any one of them had even seen the Yankees, or knew that there was one in existence.

July 26th.—I do not write often now, not for want of something to say, but from a loathing of all I see and hear, and why dwell upon those things?

Colonel Chesnut, poor old man, is worse—grows more restless. He seems to be wild with "homesickness." He wants to be at Mulberry. When there he can not see the mighty giants of the forest, the huge, old, wide-spreading oaks, but he says he feels that he is there so soon as he hears the carriage rattling across the bridge at the Beaver Dam.

I am reading French with Johnny—anything to keep him quiet. We gave a dinner to his company, the small remnant of them, at Mulberry house. About twenty idle negroes, trained servants, came without leave or license and assisted. So there was no expense. They gave their time and labor for a good day's feeding. I think they love to be at the old place.

Then I went up to nurse Kate Withers. That lovely girl, barely eighteen, died of typhoid fever. Tanny wanted his sweet little sister to have a dress for Mary Boykin's wedding, where she was to be one of the bridesmaids. So Tanny took his horses, rode one, and led the other thirty miles in the broiling sun to Columbia, where he sold the led horse and came back with a roll of Swiss muslin. As he entered the door, he saw Kate lying there dying. She died praying that she might die. She was weary of earth and wanted to be at peace. I saw her die and saw her put in her coffin. No words of mine can tell how unhappy I am. Six young soldiers, her friends, were her pall-bearers. As they marched out with that burden sad were their faces.

Princess Bright Eyes writes: "Our soldier boys returned, want us to continue our weekly dances." Another maiden fair indites: "Here we have a Yankee garrison. We are told the officers find this the dullest place they were ever in. They want the ladies to get up some amusement for them. They also want to get into society."

From Isabella in Columbia: "General Hampton is home again. He looks crushed. How can he be otherwise? His beautiful home is in ruins, and ever present with him must be the memory of the death tragedy which closed forever the eyes of his glorious boy, Preston! Now! there strikes up a serenade to General Ames, the Yankee commander, by a military band, of course. . . . Your last letters have been of the meagerest. What is the matter?"

* * * * *

August 2d.—Dr. Boykin and John Witherspoon were talking of a nation in mourning, of blood poured out like rain on the battle-fields-for what? "Never let me hear that the blood of the brave has been shed in vain! No; it sends a cry down through all time."

THE END

CPSIA information can be obtained
at www.ICGtesting.com
Printed in the USA
LVHW091029020220
645569LV00001B/153

9 781420 965575